Green Spirituality

GREEN SPIRITUALITY

One answer to
global environmental problems
and world poverty

Chris Philpott

authorHOUSE®

AuthorHouse™ UK Ltd.
500 Avebury Boulevard
Central Milton Keynes, MK9 2BE
www.authorhouse.co.uk
Phone: 08001974150

First published by AuthorHouse 1/19/2011.

ISBN: 978-1-4520-8290-5 (sc)

ACKNOWLEDGEMENTS

This book has been a long journey of over 13 years and my gratitude is to the people who helped me make it happen. I thank my partner Felicity Rock for putting up with the long hours I have spent with books or on the computer. My debt to my editor Hugh Fraser is greater than I can express in words. Meeting Hugh in a field near the E.On owned Kingsnorth coal fired power station at the Third UK Climate Camp in Kent in 2008 was one to the greatest pieces of good .fortune in my life. He understands what I am about being a green activist himself and has skilfully and with great dedication spent nearly two years editing the book, even adding content and greatly enhancing the last chapter by suggesting I look at Ecovillages as an example of the resolution of environmental problems and world poverty highlighted in the book. I thank my friends Tom Hellberg, John-Francis Phipps, Ruth Wallsgrove, James Ashenford, Kate Gilloway and Sue Minton who helped with the manuscript. I thank the late Daphne Rock for suggesting a practical section at the end of each chapter. I would like to thank Katherine Thompson, Glynn Thomas, Dave Hastings and Jeremy Foster for helping me with the photographs. Diana Korchien has been invaluable as a source of advice on producing a stunning front cover which has only been realized with the exceptional skills of graphic artist George Sander-Jackson. My friend Ryan Compton generously gave of his time and skills in developing my website, my gratitude to him. I have been blessed by the support and encouragement from established writers, particularly Mark Lynas, George Marshall, Dr. Fazlun Khalid, Rianne ten Veen, Satish Kumar, John-Francis Phipps, Christopher Titmus, Vandana Shiva, Richard Douthwaite, Sir Nicholas Stern and William Bloom. I would like to salute the people of India and particularly their spiritual leaders for providing me with great insight into the relationship between spirituality and environmental problems. My indebtedness to the international Green movement for their inspiration to write this book knows no bounds.

One of the great difficulties of the book has been authenticating and checking the content of the spiritual tradition chapters. The Christian chapter was the most difficult to get right and I am indebted to Dr. Sue Minton, Mark Dowd, Jonathon Essex, Jo Rathbone, Jo Winn-Smith, Rev. Brian Nash , Rev. M.A. Sweet and Rev. Tony Dumper, for their help and advice. I thank Rabbi Margaret Jacobi and Professor Normon Solomon for their help with the Judaism chapter. I was particularly worried about the content of the chapter on Islam and thank Dawud Muhammed for checking this for me and the advice of Malise Ruthven. The Hinduism chapter was difficult to write and I thank Dermot Killingsley for checking it and Suresh Pala for advice. The Buddhism chapter was close to my heart but thank the Rev. Saido and Christopher Titmus for their support and advice with its content. Having seen Jainism first hand in India I knew it was complex, so I am greatly indebted to internationally renowned Jain scholar, Dr. Natubhai Shah, for his help and advice. The Sikhism chapter was greatly enhanced by the input and advice of Dr. Gurnam Singh. Shamanism has a vast array of forms and I appreciate the help of shamanism writers John Grim and Michael Samuels for their help and advice in improving the chapter. I am blessed that some of my friends are pagans and would like to credit Jeannie Johnathon, Tiziana Stupia and Geoff Blenkinsop for their help and advice. For the Spiritualism chapter I appreciate the advice of Viv Little from Leamington Spiritualist church. Lastly my gratitude goes to Paddy and Anne Vickers of the local Bahá'í group for checking the Bahá'í chapter.

For the actual production of the book I would like to thank Liam Brandon and Erin Watson of Authorhouse for their help and encouragement.

Chris Philpott
Leamington Spa, Warwickshire, UK, June 2010

CONTENTS

INTRODUCTION

Wise spirits caution us; the Planet issues warnings

Contained within the covers of this book are two of the most important messages for mankind in many centuries: read of the green credentials of the spiritual traditions in Part 1 and you will gain a rich, three dimensional sense of their wisdom. They all recognise how the livelihoods of all their peoples depend ultimately on Nature's bounty and on man's undertaking to respect it, cherish it and treat it as sacred.

Move on to Nature's bounty and its state of health in Part 2 and you will see just how dire the strains we are exerting have become. Then in Part 3 you will find real-world examples of self-supporting communities all around the world populated by individuals who have chosen to reshape their lives around the constraints imposed on us all by Nature, forces for good that they honour and celebrate.

Researching and writing this book has completed my changed sense of place on the Planet. The notion "I have a right to all the things I can afford" once lead to "with money I can address any dissatisfaction"—with an exotic holiday, a new kitchen or moving house. Only a connection with the richness of our own inner life, our spirit, can cure us of such illusions, it is now abundantly clear.

We lose sight of the sacredness of our Home Planet at our peril. The spiritual traditions all warn us of this. Current feedback from the Planet is stark: "Your livelihoods here on Earth are totally dependent on a million million other organisms, all of you warmed by and protected from the rays of the sun. The destruction of their livelihoods is the destruction of *your* livelihoods, a process you are bringing to an ever quickening conclusion."

The good news: our destructive ways are parts of the illusion. The bad news: to cease our destructiveness we have to recognise our illusion and end it. If we don't, Nature will. But if we humans do chose to end our destructiveness we have this wealth of wisdom to guide us.

Consider this an invitation to join the growing numbers discovering this for themselves.

In my research I have made every effort to check that the spiritual writings are quoted accurately, and the information is correct. If you can illuminate further on any of them please leave a comment on my website, www.greenspirituality.org. Thank you.

FOREWORD

by Dr Vandana Shiva

Spirituality and ecology

Ecological sustainability is based on recognizing and seeing the delicate and fragile interconnectedness of life. Spirituality is the heightened and deep awareness of our place in creation.

Industrialism and capitalism have led to the separation of economy from ecology and a separation of our material existence from our spiritual being.

Now this separation is threatening our very survival. An economic system divorced from the real economies of nature and society is showing signs of collapse. The Planet's climate regulation systems have been impacted by our fossil fuel based civilization. This materialism, devoid of ecology and spirituality, is failing not just ecologically and spiritually, it is also failing materially.

Mahatma Gandhi had anticipated the ecological destructiveness inherent in industrialization which he called "modern civilization" which, Gandhi stated,

> ...seeks to increase bodily comforts, and it fails miserably even in doing so. This civilization is such that one has only to be patient and it will be self destroyed. ... there is no end to the victims destroyed in the fire of (this) civilization. Its deadly effect is that people come under its scorching flames believing it to be all good.
>
> It is a charge against India that her people are so uncivilized, ignorant and stolid that it is not possible to induce them to adopt any changes. It is a charge really against our strength. What we have tested and found true on the anvil of experience, we dare not change. Many thrust their advice upon India, but

she remains steady. This is her beauty; it is the sheet anchor of our hope.

The old duality between materialism and spiritualism is out-moded, no longer working. Our material survival needs an ecological and spiritual anchor.

With this book, *Green Spirituality*, Chris Philpott helps us rediscover the ecological and spiritual sheet anchor that we so desperately need at this most difficult of times.

Dr Vandana Shiva is an author, physicist, ecologist and international environmental activist well known in the field of environmental awareness.

Part 1

The Great Spiritual Traditions And Their Green Aspects

CHAPTER 1: CHRISTIANITY.

Introduction

Christians follow the teachings of Jesus of Nazareth who lived around 2,000 years ago. Christianity might have remained the minor faith group it had become within the Roman Empire were it not for the conversion to the faith of Emperor Constantine around 300 years later. Today, Christianity is followed by approximately 2 billion people spread through the five continents, around one quarter of humanity.

Jesus's twelve disciples were his original followers, four of them recording his teachings in their gospels. Christianity today exists in three main groupings, the Roman Catholic, Eastern Orthodox and the reformed Protestant Churches. The break-away Protestant churches arose out of the Reformation in the 16th century and include the Anglican, Methodist, Presbyterian, Baptist, Pentecostal and Quaker churches. Overall membership of Christian churches has been in decline in the developed world for some decades. Meanwhile, however, it has been expanding in the developing world, especially in sub-Saharan Africa, Latin America and parts of Asia, where it has been estimated a quarter of a billion people practise Charismatic Christianity, which focuses on gifts of the Holy Spirit such as speaking in tongues, performing miracles and prophecy.

History

Jesus of Nazareth, around whose life story Christianity is centred, was a Jew who lived in Judea from about 7 BCE to 30 CE. According to the accounts of his disciples, Jesus was born of the virgin Mary, an event foretold to his mother by the Angel Gabriel. Mary married Joseph, a carpenter who gained knowledge of the same event in a dream sent to him by God. Days after the birth of Jesus, the family were visited by three wise men from afar bearing gifts as offerings to the newborn child. Biblical texts refer to the visit being made in the expectation of a 'messiah' or 'chosen' one, soon to enter the world. The Jewish faith speaks of a messiah's coming and the presence of the scholars. The wise three knew of the prophesy, which meant this baby, Jesus, would grow up to hold 'high office'.

Brief though the account of his childhood is, we know Jesus was born into the Jewish faith. His knowledge about God, the religious law and the prophets was remarkable. His adult ministry started after meeting John the Baptist, a mystic and prophet -recognised also by Islam and Bahá'aí - who we are told came from an ascetic religious community similar to the Essenes.

According to recently uncovered ancient texts compiled by biblical scholars of the time, John's baptism of Jesus, a significant event witnessed by his followers on the banks of the river Jordon, transformed the humble Jesus into Christ the Messiah.

During the three short years of his ministry, Jesus was 'on the road' preaching and healing. He pulled good crowds and would call on people to repent their sins and to follow his own ways and beliefs. He had a reputation for doing good works among the ordinary and the poor, healing, exorcising evil spirits and preaching of the imminent coming of the Kingdom of God. Helping his reputation were the miracles he seemed able to perform witnessed by the crowds he drew. The scriptures describe seventeen in all.

Although Jesus grew up as a conventional Jew, his message of universal salvation stood against the Jewish tradition which saw only the ritually purified as eligible. Jesus said that even those who were ritually impure and who did not atone for their sins in the accepted Jewish manner could enter God's new kingdom, if they were prepared to repent.

Throughout his ministry, Jesus actively associated with uneducated, humble and downcast members of society. Jesus clearly valued and viewed all people as equals, practising what he preached by standing up for those on the margins of society.

Jesus used parables (moral tales) to illustrate his teachings and to convey the message of how those who followed his way of life would 'enter the Kingdom of God'.

The teachings Christians follow are the accounts of how Jesus went about his life as much as his preachings. The two are inseparable. Through the parables, Jesus illustrated by example how his approach to life contrasted with the conventions of the times. His central messages include forgiveness and its importance in overcoming sin through faith in God alone.

Relevant to us here with our focus on Green spirituality is how Jesus would preach wherever he found himself, which was almost invariably out in the open air and in natural settings—perhaps they were safer. He used examples from the natural world, such as water and light (John 4: 13 and 14) and (John 8: 12) to illustrate his sermons. "I am come a light into the world that whosoever believeth on me should not abide in darkness." (John 12: 46)

From the start, what Jesus said often put him in conflict with the Jewish authorities who considered him a threat to their leadership. This was because he was popular, his preaching drew large crowds, at least some of whom believed he might free them from their Roman oppressors - political anathema to the Jewish overlords. His frequent association with sinners further irritated the Jewish leadership who considered them ritually impure. He also broke the law of the Sabbath by engaging in healing work on the day of rest when no work of any form was permitted.

In the Gospels we read how Jesus drew in men from diverse livelihoods and beliefs to hear and reflect on his teachings, some to follow him. His most loyal followers known as the twelve disciples chose to share the same simple life, suffering hardship together and passing on Jesus's teachings. It was on these trusty few that the entire Christian message would depend after his crucifixion. They took to delivering his teachings all around Galilee. It was this that eventually led to the establishing of the early Christian church.

Sensing his time on Earth was near its end, Jesus brought his disciples together for the Jewish festival of Passover in Jerusalem. That evening he shared with them what came to be known as the Last Supper. Symbolically he broke the bread and gave it to them saying,

"This is my body which is given for you: this do in remembrance of me."
(Luke 22:19) He also gave them wine and said "This cup is the new
testament in my blood, which is shed for you." (Luke 22:20) It was at
this meal Jesus told the twelve that his betrayer was at the table.

The fateful betrayal came within hours when Judas Iscariot, one of
the twelve, identified him to the chief priests and temple authorities
for a payment of 30 pieces of silver. Characteristically, Jesus forgave
him. On interrogation by the high priests, Jesus was judged as being
blasphemous against God: he 'claimed to be the Son of God' ("Ye say
that I am," was his response by Luke's account) They then took him
to Pontius Pilate, the Roman governor, for sentencing. Pilate was very
reluctant to condemn Jesus to death as demanded by the high priests of
Judaism. Only later, on the insistence of a large noisy mob, did Pilate
concede to the death penalty. Jesus suffered terribly: his execution was
by the brutal and slow death of crucifixion, nailed by wrists and ankles
to a tall, raised cross. He was crucified with common criminals yet in
a display of extraordinary compassion he uttered of his executioners,
"forgive them for they know not what they do."

Jesus's body was taken down from the cross and placed in a guarded
tomb. Yet, three days later, the stone protecting the tomb was found to
be rolled away and the body gone. Miraculously, Jesus appeared to his
disciples, an occurrence referred to as the Resurrection.

Jesus's re-appearance, witnessed by his mother and five hundred
others, came to be seen as the sign of his divinity: that he, Jesus, had
overcome mortality.

Jesus might have been just another prophet in the Jewish tradition
had he not been publicly executed and had he not come back from
the dead three days after. And yet as subsequent years and decades
would prove, those receptive to his teachings of forgiveness and of
unconditional love would not be found among the Jewish people but
among the Greek diaspora and peoples of the Levant and Asia Minor
(Turkey, today) and even Romans.

His crucifixion and protracted death on the cross was the focal point
of the four Gospels and what became the New Testament. The Acts
of the Apostles chronicles how the apostles set about replacing Judas
and gives accounts of their itinerant teaching tours around Galilee and
beyond.

We might never have heard of Christianity had it not been for
these efforts of Jesus's close-knit disciples in spreading the word. A

major figure in this endeavour was a late joiner, Paul. A less likely candidate would have been hard to find: for a start, he was not a Jew but a tax collector for the Romans. Then, he had he never met Jesus. Not only that, but he had initially *persecuted* Jesus's followers. Paul had an overwhelmingly powerful vision on the road to Damascus, a mystical experience. It led to his conversion. The later New Testament books record Paul's campaign to spread Christianity beyond the borders of Judea, building up many groups of followers, some as far as Greece. Paul was a practical man, advising and supporting congregations through his preaching and writing inspiring letters, many of which are also included in the New Testament.

Paul's revolutionary contribution to Christianity was his redefining the faith as one for non-Jews to join, emphasising that Christ had died for the sins of all mankind. And it is Paul's writings that make first mention of the Trinity, the unity encompassing three different aspects of the one God: the Father, the Son and the Holy Ghost.

The drive and inspiration of the original apostles helped greatly by Paul did not wither with their passing, but continued, in part because, due to the persecution of Christians, the faith continued as an underground movement. Despite the risks, groups, now calling themselves churches, spread through parts of the Roman Empire. A few influential personages seem to have joined, though in secret. Then in the 4th century CE came the breakthrough, when the Roman Emperor himself converted to the faith. First, Constantine had forbidden continued persecution of Christians. Then, ahead of a crucial battle, he was moved to invoke the aid of the Christian God. Victory ensued and in celebration of this he converted formally. These developments allowed Christianity to spread throughout the vast Roman Empire, an expansion hitherto unimaginable for what had been a small, fragmented, much persecuted sect. Unsurprisingly, with expansion came change.

Much of what ensued in the 1,200 years that followed has less to do with Jesus's teachings than the power struggles of successive rulers: the Roman Empire had succumbed to civil wars, splits and rejoinings, but all along, the power of the Church as an organisation was waxing. Then it suffered a split of its own. In the 8th century the churches of the Eastern Empire decided to break from Rome and became the Eastern Orthodox Church centred on Constantinople (later Istanbul), as it still is today.

In due course the Western popes and their Vatican state assumed greater and greater power until they wielded more power throughout Europe than any monarch. The papacy became politicised - and corrupt. Trouble was not long coming. From 1521 on, the Western, Roman church found itself facing off challenges in what became the Reformation. A variety of entirely new church movements no longer under the authority of the Pope sprang up. In the West, this gave the impetus to a new Bible-focused Christianity whose leaders maintained that the Bible was a greater authority than the church and was a guide to living the way of life of Jesus himself.

With the energy of reformers such as Martin Luther, these non-conformist or Protestant Christian churches grew to be numerous. From Germany and Switzerland the spark spread to the Netherlands and via King Henry VIII to England and Wales and in yet another form to Scotland. It was in pursuit of religious freedom that the Quakers and Plymouth Brethren migrated to and settled in North America. Meanwhile, both the Western, Roman Church and the Eastern, Orthodox Church continued with few, if any reforms. Today the Eastern Orthodox Church still holds sway in Russia, parts of the Balkans, including Greece and in tiny pockets throughout the Caucasus and the Middle East, vestigial Greek and Roman colonies.

The Scriptures

In putting together the New Testament there were many writings to choose from. Scholars agreed on the final collection of the New Testament in 325CE. The gospels of Matthew, Mark, Luke and John in the New Testament present accounts of the ministry of Jesus and founding of the Christian community. Of the four, the Gospel of Luke has come to be accepted as the most reliable.

Doctrine

Christian doctrine is based on the New Testament and the Old Testament which was part of the scriptures of Judaism, the exact origins of which are lost in pre-history. Its book of Genesis describes God making the world in six days and resting on the seventh day. It says He created male and female in his own image and placed Man at the top of the hierarchy of all living things. Different strains of Christianity view these and other biblical accounts very differently—some interpret them literally, others see them as allegory. On one verse, however, most are agreed.

The Nicene Creed says that there is "…One God, the Father Almighty, maker of all things visible and invisible."

With few exceptions, Christians see God as having three aspects or forms, 'God the Father, God the Son and God the Holy Spirit'. God manifests as a caring, overviewing parent (the Father), as a compassionate, forgiving Jesus (the Son) or in the form of the Holy Spirit, which inspired Jesus. This Holy Spirit of God is said to make its presence felt within all Christians once they accept Jesus Christ as their saviour.

All the mainstream strands of Christianity place similar importance on the teachings of the Old and New Testaments. Jesus summarised the Old Testament's ten commandments into two things that God requires of his people: to love God and to love other people. "You shall love the Lord your God with all your heart, with all your soul, and with all your mind. This is the first and greatest commandment. And the second is like it: You shall love your neighbour as you love yourself. On these two commandments hang all the law and the prophets." (Matthew 22:37-40)

Christian faith leads some followers to believe that those who ignore the Church's teachings therefore lead an evil life and will end up in the realm of the Devil and suffer eternal torment in a region they call Hell. Literal interpretations like these governed the lives of many millions over many centuries but they have fallen away in all but Roman Catholic, Eastern Orthodox and certain of the most traditional strains of Protestantism. Thus the world as once depicted by numerous writers and other artists inspired by biblical writings was one in which the opposing forces of good and evil were engaged in an endless battle.

Another theme central to certain Christian doctrines is redemption. Thus Christ is seen as having come into the world to save sinners, which takes in everyone ready to hear. By declaring a belief in Christ and in his message sinners will be saved from their sins and will reside with Christ in Heaven when they die. Thus a belief in an afterlife plays a central part in Christian faith.

Ceremonies and Festivals

Christian churches of all strands have a ceremony of induction or initiation into membership of the church known as baptism or Christening. This rite performed by the clergyman may exceptionally involve people joining as adults but it is ordinarily combined with the naming ceremony for a newborn child. The families of both new parents participate as witnesses. The water which the clergyman splashes over the head of the infant is symbolic of the total immersion baptism of Jesus's day, still practised in certain Protestant forms known as Baptist churches.

In weekly and daily worship, in its ceremonies and festivals, the Christian calendar follows the birth of Jesus and the life of Christ, the most important service for Protestant churchgoers being taking Holy Communion and for Catholic and Orthodox, the Mass. These celebrate the Last Supper which Jesus shared with his disciples before his betrayal and crucifixion and at which Jesus broke bread, gave it to the disciples and poured wine for them. The bread was symbolic of his body and the wine of his blood which would be sacrificed for them and all who followed

In the Roman Catholic Church and certain Protestant ones the belief is that the bread and wine actually transform into the body and blood of Christ. Communion is however, not open to all. In order to partake in the communion, a baptised person first has to undergo a period of training and be 'confirmed' as a full member of the church.

Most Christian services of worship include readings from the Bible that follow the Christian calendar and the clergyman may address the congregation on a topical or a moral issue. Special services are performed at festival times such as the celebration of the birth of Christ at Christmas on 25th December. Easter, which falls in the northern Spring, is the time when Christians celebrate the crucifixion and the resurrection of Christ.

The Christian funeral service is intended as a celebration of the deceased person's life and the expression of good will, so that they might join Christ in heaven. It concludes with a burial where a tombstone will mark the grave, or a similar ceremony (cremation) concluding with the scattering of the ashes.

The Christian church views marriage as the natural state of bonding for men and women to live together. In the marriage ceremony, a minister joins the man and woman together in the sight of God, witnessed by friends and members of their families. The priest blesses the couple and encourages them to bring their children up as Christians – only Roman Catholicism insists that the children of a mixed marriage should be raised in its tradition.

Green Christianity

Christianity has a long if limited historical tradition of reflection on Nature and human responsibility, though it seems many of this faith have overlooked it. If God is to be found in every person and in all of creation, then any kind of despoiling of creation would be against the law of God, some have argued.

On the Bible's opening page we are told (Genesis 1: 26) "and God said, Let us make man in our image and let them have dominion over the fish of the sea, and over the fowl of the air, and over the cattle and over all the earth, and over every creeping thing that creepeth upon the earth." The word 'dominion' derives from *Dominus* the Latin for 'Lord'. Some have interpreted this text as 'practising lordship over Creation' or exercising 'stewardship' over nature. This is a crucial issue and one we explore further in the chapter on food production.

There is also a recurring theme of the preservation of species in the Bible with such stories as that of Noah and the Ark (Genesis 9:8-10) and a prohibition to cut down trees unnecessarily (Deut 20:19). This we explore in the chapter on bio-diversity.

We now know that Jesus was essentially very 'Green' because he followed the two basic principles of Green thinking: care and concern for the environment and the pursuit of social justice. In his ministry, Jesus maintained a Green lifestyle by living like others in a simple way and owning few possessions. He lived in tune with the natural world spending significant time in natural settings praying, contemplating and preaching. The Jesus we meet in the Gospels was genuinely at one with Nature as shown by his frequent use of examples from Nature to illustrate his parables and spiritual teachings.

Later in Christian history, St Francis of Assisi in Italy epitomised the good relationship between Christians and the natural world, leading him to found an order of friars who took vows of poverty, chastity and obedience. They wandered the land preaching the Gospel. St Francis worked on the basis that the natural world was an expression of God and developed a wonderful relationship with animals, emphasising compassion and mercy towards nature.

Christianity's message of peace and love is Green. Christ taught "love your enemies, bless them that curse you, do good to them that hate you." (Matt 5:44) It is clear from this that Jesus's message stands against any form of war. We know that war not only kills people and destroys homes but it also destroys Nature's creatures, landscapes and the environment generally. Christianity is about people loving and caring for one another in an unselfish way. Acted on with integrity, this means people need to take care of the environment as well and restricting war to last resort only would arguably be a prerequisite to this.

Jesus's message aligns well with the Green outlook of today: amassing wealth and material possessions benefits neither the individual nor the environment. The experience of truly valuing and recognising the gift of life comes to people who care for each other, for Nature and for their environment.

Jesus's life was a shining example of the pursuit of another Green principle: social justice. Throughout his ministry Jesus associated with the poor, the destitute and the downtrodden. The sick who benefited from Jesus's healing had no means of paying for their treatment. Jesus stood up against corruption, as when he humiliated the moneylenders in the temple. He was also against all forms of racism and prejudice of the sort meted out in Judea to Samaritans. In one of Jesus's stories (Luke 10: 29 - 35), the person modelling true compassion for the robbed and injured traveller who has been passed up by a Jewish priest and then by a temple assistant is the 'Good Samaritan'. He tends to the fallen man's wounds, puts him on his own donkey and takes him to the nearest inn. The story was Jesus's response to a hostile question from a temple lawyer.

Christian communities, of which there are many throughout the world, often exemplify the Green way of life. In my travels in south India, I looked for examples of simple Christian communities living in an ecological way. I found in monastic life a fine example of simple existence that impacts minimally on the environment. At the Asirvanam Monastery, a community near Bangalore in Karnataka state, resident monks follow the rule of St Benedict requiring them to take a vow of poverty. However, they contribute to the support of the monastic community by the manual work they carry out.

The community of around a dozen monks work on a 120 ha (300 acre) organic farm helping to create employment for some 300 local people, the proceeds of which help to run a free medical clinic and school for all who need them. This is a truly a mixed farm with pigs and cattle, bananas, fruit and vegetables, all raised to organic standards, reducing the farm's impact on the environment to a minimum.

With such balanced and measured use of resources the brothers and fathers of this monastery personally have little adverse effect on the environment. Beyond creating wealth for others while using minimal resources, their life of prayer, meditation and manual labour only reinforces a benefit for the local ecology as well as for the community. I was truly inspired.

Kurisumala ashram is a Christian community set in the mountains of Kerala, one of India's most southerly states. In the last thirty years, this community has converted a bare mountaintop into a productive dairy farm through the manual labour of monks following the Cistercian tradition. The monks again work the land and provide a moderate level of employment for the local people by having a dairy to process milk produced from surrounding areas as well as at the farm.

Additionally, their dairy herds produce pedigree breeding cattle for other parts of India. The fathers have little if any material wealth and what wealth they generate through their community they give away to the poor and the needy. They fill their day with prayer, meditation, worship and strict adherence to manual labour.

Because the monks follow mostly benign agricultural systems (though livestock rearing has now been identified as a major source of methane, a powerful greenhouse gas and of local water pollution from runoff) and because they are not consumers of material goods, the impacts on their local environment is relatively small.

Ecological sins and the confessional

There are many examples around the world of Christians pursuing Green agendas. In Africa, the Association of African Earth Keeping (AEK) Churches base their Christian way of life on Earth-healing ministries with some amazing results: they plant forests, carry out water conservation projects and create game sanctuaries. Members maintain a high level of dedication. AEK Churches expect the people of the community to confess their ecological 'sins', such as cutting down trees. They see the church as protector of the Earth from destruction.

In Europe, Green Christians are represented by the European Christian Environmental Network (ECEN), which aims to link church worship and prayers with awareness of Earth's creation and the rising threats to it

It suggests actions to counter unsustainable consumption. ECEN worked hard to realise a meaningful awareness initiative ahead of the 15th UN Climate Summit in Copenhagen in December 2009. Despite

COP15's failure, ECEN's is a declaration that stands as an indicator of the urgency recognised in our situation:

A crucial time in history
In December (7 - 18 December 2009) Denmark will host the 15th UN Climate Summit. The liturgical material compiled here in Copenhagen focuses on this major event when the nations of the world meet to negotiate a replacement of the Kyoto Protocol that runs out in 2012. This is a crucial time in history. It is no exaggeration to say that the future of creation and its inhabitants is at stake. The challenges of the climate crisis and the vast task we all face—as inhabitants of God's creation—to reduce our carbon footprint, to change our environmental behaviour, in short to *turn*, so that we and future generations may *live*—is immense and overwhelming.

In the United Kingdom, Christian Ecology Link has organised climate change conferences and encouraged churches to recycle waste and use Green energy. Its Operation Noah, founded in 2003—"Faith motivated, Science-informed, Hope-driven" - was the first Christian campaign to focus exclusively on the issue of climate change. In this it has been joined by the Environmental Issues Network of Churches Together in Britain and Ireland. Its mission is to encourage Britain and Ireland's churches and governments to lead a radical transformation in both our culture and economic systems; a transformation towards simpler, liveable and supportable lifestyles that will increase happiness and well-being, while safeguarding the whole of God's creation for future generations.

In the UK the John Ray Initiative formed in 1997 recognizes as urgent the need to respond to the global environmental crisis and the challenges of sustainable development and environmental stewardship. It promotes responsible environmental stewardship in accordance with Christian principles and aims to stimulate action in pursuit of environmental protection and sustainable development - including action by decision makers and leaders.

It helps local churches to understand environmental issues in the context of the Christian faith and take practical action such as encouraging churches to use Green sources of energy. In 1999 the Eco-Congregation project launched. It now has over 500 churches as members.

In America, the Episcopal Power and Light Organisation (instituted by the the Rev Steve McAusland and the Rev Sally Bingham in California) promotes the use of 'Green' energy by churches. There is also the 'White Violet Centre' for Eco Justice in the state of Indiana, run by Catholic volunteers who promote organic agriculture, wetland conservation and the preservation of endangered species. The National Council of Churches of Christ's Eco-Justice Programs include campaigns covering 15 different areas from bio-diversity to water conservation. And in 2006 the following news item turned heads in the US:

Presbyterian Church USA asks its 2.3 million members each to become carbon neutral
Coming from one of the more conservative of the mainstream US Protestant denominations, this announcement from the Presbyterian Church USA, (PCUSA) caused some shock. It asked its 2.3 million members each to make a bold witness by aspiring to carbon neutral lives.

Going carbon neutral relies on the appealing but unproven notion of carbon offsets. First having made all the (unaudited) cuts we can in our personal lives and in the selection of goods and services we consume, we invest in hopefully well audited carbon-saving projects in order to compensate for the residual emissions we are unable to eliminate. Offsets have been likened to medieval Christian indulgences bought to compensate for sins committed and confessed.

Christianity's roots as the faith of a simple rural people gave it an essential Green foundation in which the cycles of the seasons and Nature's bounty were valued and given respect in the form of gratitude and a promise to sustain the good Earth. These aspects paled into insignificance, however, as the faith became codified within a Church lead by power-hungry political operators in the Middle Ages. Christianity has never seen as central any obligation to the Creator to take care of, or responsibility for, the Planet if doing so would jeopardise the pursuit of wealth or livelihood of its members. In a majority of its numerous sects and denominations, the church today remains a deeply conservative institution. It has been slow to address the gathering global crises, and signs of response have been at best selective. That said, there exists a deep-rooted wisdom in the Green Spirituality of the Christian tradition. With one in four of today's humans following this faith, a change in all its leaders over to a Green orientation would indeed put humanity in a much improved position to control itself and to end the destructive relationship with the Earth that we will be reviewing in Part 2.

Christian websites

www.christianitytoday.com
www.christianity.org.uk
www.christianity.com
www.christianityonline.com
www.rationalchristianity.net
www.christianityexplored.com
www.clarifyingchristianity.com
www.christianityfreebies.com
www.godandscience.org
www.christian-ecology.org.uk
www.arocha.org www.jri.org
http://nccecojustice.org/index.php
www.climate.org/topics/national-action/presbyterians-climate-neutral.html
http://www.ecen.org/cms/uploads/creationliturgy09.pdf
www.quakergreenaction.org
www.ecocongregation.org
www.conservation.catholic.org
www.webofcreation.org
www.leaderu.com

CHAPTER 2: JUDAISM

Introduction

The Jewish people has a history dating back some 4,000 years to its origins in the Middle East. Today there are an estimated 15.5 to 16.5 million Jews, 5.7 million in the USA, 362,000 in Canada, 5.35 million Jews in Israel, the remaining 4 to 5 million mainly in Europe. The number that actively practise Judaism is open to debate. Yet despite small numbers in relation to other global religions, Judaism has had a disproportionate influence on world history.

History

Judaism springs directly from the early history and customs of the Jewish people. It still features both in worship and in daily life. That history begins with Abraham who lived in Canaan - modern Syria, Palestine and Israel - and his second son, Isaac. It tells of how, driven perhaps by famine, the Israelites, as the descendents of Isaac called themselves, migrated from Canaan to Egypt. There they took to working for the Egyptian pharaohs as slaves for several generations. Then under the leadership of Moses they left for the 'Promised Land'. It took an eventful

40 years of wandering in the desert before Joshua finally led them to Canaan, where as twelve tribes they settled for almost 200 years.

During this time of independence, the Jews were ruled by a series of kings: Saul, David and Solomon. Solomon built the first temple in Jerusalem. After his reign, the united kingdom split into two: *Israel*, ten tribes in the north and *Judah*, two tribes in the south. The *Israel* kingdom was in the eighth century BCE conquered by the Assyrian empire and no clear records remain of the fate of these Jewish people. Two centuries later, in 586 BCE *Judah* was conquered by Babylon's army and the Judaist elite exiled to Babylon. This exile ended when Babylon was itself conquered–by the Persians, who allowed Jews to return to Judea and subsequently permitted the construction of a temple there to replace one destroyed by the Babylonians.

During the following several centuries, the Jewish people thrived, with adequate autonomy under Persian, then Hellenic rule. The Sadducees and the Pharisees emerged during this stable period as moral and spiritual leaders with great power and influence. Things were less peaceful from 312 – 63 BCE when Judah fell under the bellicose Seleucid empire. In 165 BCE a Jewish revolt resulted in the Hasmonean Kingdom of Israel being formed. It lost its true independence after only 25 years and was finally ended 103 years later in 63 BCE with the capture of Jerusalem by the Romans. In 37 BCE they appointed Herod as king over Judea. Friction continued under Roman rule which followed.

The Jewish-Roman wars of the 1st and 2nd centuries CE resulted in the death or exile of a majority of the Jewish people. Judaism was now found mainly in the diaspora, but even this declined further after the Roman emperor Constantine converted to Christianity in 313 CE. By the fifth century CE there was discrimination against surviving Jews even in the Levant.

In 1096 Pope Urban II in Rome ordered the Crusades against the Muslim empire. At the same time he denounced the Jews as a demonic race. Jews who had escaped to Europe and formed communities came to experience increasing levels of unpopularity. They were expelled from England in 1290 and from France in 1306. Although Jewish culture had flourished in Spain thanks to the tolerance exercised by the Moors, its Muslim rulers, expulsions began there in 1492 as the Moorish grip on Spain began loosening.

During the Inquisition, which lasted almost seven hundred years in all, the treatment and abuse handed out to heretics, especially Jews, was appalling beyond belief. Many of those that did not perish were forced to convert to Christianity. Communities were highly fragmented and often survived in secrecy, with few records.

By the 1890's Jews had settled throughout Europe though most concentrated in Poland and western Russia ('The Pale') and also in Germany and the United Kingdom. Life was difficult for Jews in many countries. Russia's oppressive restrictions of Jewish settlement began in the 1750s. Between 1880 and 1928 two million Jews left Russia, mostly for the US, over 150,000 to the UK and over 100,000 to Palestine. The Zionist movement was founded in 1897 with the aim of creating a Jewish state, location as yet undetermined. Lands in Uganda and South Africa were weighed before the focus moved to the Palestinian territories. However, by 1917 90,000 Jews had settled in Palestine and the British, under the Balfour Declaration, indicated support for Jews to settle. However, the Declaration used the word "home" rather than "state", and specified that its establishment must not "prejudice the civil and religious rights of existing non-Jewish communities in Palestine."

In the 1939 - 1945 World War, Hitler pursued a policy of genocide of Jews throughout Europe. His henchman Himmler, as the 'Commissioner for Strengthening German Nationhood', implemented this. Between October and December 1941, 200,000 German and East European Jews were shot. Between 1941- 42 two million Russian Jews were killed. After this, Hitler instigated the "final solution" and so the holocaust unfolded when the SS set up special extermination camps to gas Jews in even larger numbers. By the end of the war 90% of the Jewish populations of Poland, Germany, Austria, Latvia, Lithuania and Estonia had been murdered by the Nazis. Some 70 per cent of all the Jews in other parts of Europe had also been killed. The final death toll of Jews from the Nazi extermination policy was estimated at some 6 million men, women and children.

In 1948, in a unilateral move, the State of Israel was declared following a concerted and murderous guerrilla campaign. Thousands more Jews immigrated to Palestine in the years post-1948.

The state of Israel is still fighting for recognition and the right to exist. Indeed the attacks pursued against it by a succession of Arab alliances, in 1954, 1967, 1973, 2006 and in 2008, demonstrated refusal by Israel's opponents to accept its right to exist over the rights of the inhabitants of Palestine whom Israel displaced. All were successfully beaten off only with major US support. However, as a succession of peace initiatives took hold, a growing list or Arab states have signed up as agreeing to Israel's right to statehood, including even the moderate Palestinian group, Fatah under Mahmood Abaas.

The recurrent theme throughout the history of the Jewish people is their belief that they are the chosen people of God. They claim a special covenant with God, and that this special relationship has been vindicated by their survival as a race and as a religion through endless years of persecution.

Doctrine

Judaic doctrine is found in the Hebrew Bible and in the Talmud. God, thought of as neither male or female, is omnipresent, omnipotent, omniscient, eternal and holy and perfect. Some Jews believe in the creation story of Genesis as the literal word of God and for others it is seen as a mythical account. God rested on the seventh day of his creation and all Jews observe this day as the Sabbath. Traditionally no work or domestic tasks are carried out on this day. Human beings are seen as the pinnacle of God's creation with a duty to obey God's laws and use the environment in a responsible manner.

Prophets were special individuals considered to be the messengers of God. They characterize the history of the Jewish people. They each developed a special relationship with God. Abraham was the first to make a covenant, or *b'rit* with God. This concept of covenant is fundamental to traditional Judaism: it involves rights and obligations of both Jews and God. Abraham had a son called Isaac who in turn had a son called Jacob. Abraham, Isaac and Jacob were the ancestors of the twelve tribes of Israel. They are known as the Patriarchs and are both the physical and spiritual ancestors of Judaism and their descendants are the Jewish people. Of the prophets, Moses was the greatest. He climbed Mount Sinai where God presented him with the ten commandments on a tablet of stone. These commandments were guidelines given by God to the Jews on how they should lead their lives. The commandments are:

1. There is only one Eternal God.
2. You shall have no other gods besides Me. Idol worship is forbidden.
3. You shall not swear falsely by the name of the Eternal One your God.

4. You shall observe the Sabbath day and keep it holy. Six days shall you labour and do all your work, but the seventh day is the Sabbath of the Eternal One your God.
5. Honour your father and mother, as the Eternal One your God has commanded you.
6. You shall not murder.
7. You shall not commit adultery.
8. You shall not steal.
9. You shall not bear false witness against your neighbour.
10. You shall not covet your neighbour's wife or possessions.

God said to Moses that those that followed these rules would be given longevity, fecundity, prosperity and a share of the promised land of Israel. Those that did not obey the law were sinners. Through the course of time Rabbis became the authoritative interpreters of the scriptures. This eventually led to the Halakhah or the law which all Jews must follow in order to obey God.

A person can be born a Jew or convert to Judaism; some consider that a Jew should only marry another Jew. At death the Jewish doctrine states that there is the continuation of the soul but unlike some other religions there is a heavy emphasis on concentrating on what is done in this life rather than reflecting on the afterlife.

From what we have read so far there might be an impression that Judaism is simply a religion of restrictive rules and practices with a lack of individual opportunities to explore spirituality, but there is a mystical dimension. The Essenes of Qumran were a Jewish mystical sect who lived a Spartan life in the deserts of Palestine practising prayer and purification found in an austere manual of discipline. They believed they were the true interpreters of the scriptures.

In France and Spain, in the Middle Ages, the Kabbalah movement emerged as another mystical branch of Judaism. The movement centred on understanding En Sof or the infinite and the Sefrot or ten powers of the godheads, which emanated from it. Kabbalists earnestly sought the presence of God through pursuing moral and esoteric discipline. They thought that the realisation of God could be achieved through meditation and curbing sensual and worldly desire. They saw that the many realms of spiritual reality were only accessible through spiritual practices.

In the eighteenth century Hasidism developed in Europe. In this form of Judaism, the Hasidic Masters became the spiritual leaders and not the rabbis. These masters followed a more mystical approach to Judaism and, like the Kabbalists, actively sought the presence of God.

Judaism is far from uniform in doctrinal practice and belief. Initially, modernizers led on local issues. Non-Orthodox Judaism arose first in Germany in the early nineteenth century when Israel Jacobson attempted to reconcile the basic principles of Judaism with the Enlightenment values of rational thought and scientific evidence. In the UK the Reform movement began around 1860 and 1880 in the US. Ritual piety, dress and dietary laws were rejected in the belief that individuals should have free choice in which traditions to follow. The Torah was no longer seen as a document literally handed down to Moses by God but rather as their ancestors' record of their encounter with God. Many Reformist Jews dropped the idea of a future Messiah, the resurrection of the dead and future reward and punishment. By the late 19th century the movement had spread throughout Europe and under the leadership of Rabbi Isaac Mayer Wise in North America where it now has more than 900 congregations and 1.5 million members, the largest Jewish following in the US. Today, Reform Jews are committed to the absolute equality of women in all areas of Jewish life and were the first movement to ordain women rabbis. They are also committed to the full participation of gays and lesbians in synagogue life as well as society at large. Interestingly, however, there are very few Jews affiliated to the Reform Movement living in Israel.

Scriptures

The Scriptures of Judaism are based on the Hebrew Bible. The Five books of Moses, Genesis, Exodus, Leviticus, Numbers and Deuteronomy are called the Torah, seen by traditionalist Orthodox Jews as written by Moses and the literal word of God.

The fundamental text of rabbinic Judaism is the Talmud, which is composed of the Mishnah and the Gemara sections. The Mishnah is short and describes the early days of rabbinic Judaism. In the Gemara, dating from the 5th and 6th centuries CE, rabbis debate biblical law and reflect the daily life of the Jewish people of the time. As following the law is synonymous with being a good Jew, the Talmud provides the essential reference on how to live according to God's rules.

As Judaism grew, Covenantal law developed which was basically a binding promise between two parties in the form of a document called a covenant. This led to laws to prevent murder, robbery, incest and adultery. Other laws required respect for parents.

Those with most influence on how Jewish law was interpreted and implemented were the Pharisees. They were laymen, moral leaders who emphasised purity as being of paramount importance. They may well have expected their suffering to be rewarded in the after life. The Sadducees, on the other hand, were the hereditary priesthood class.

The laws developed under Judaism were concerned with how the individual behaved in the society. Orthodox Judaism remains a religion requiring conformity.

Customs and Ceremonies

Many Jewish customs express requirements of the Judaic law laid down in biblical texts, among them dietary laws. Pork alone among meats is forbidden. Slaughter of permitted livestock has to be by a qualified person and only certain parts of the animal may be eaten.

The Sabbath or Shabath or day of rest is observed on Saturdays. It starts on the Friday night with the ritual lighting of candles and with a special meal. Non-essential work cannot be carried out on the Holy Day. Orthodox Jews cook their meals in advance.

Ritual purity is important to most Jews. By one custom, women are considered impure for one week after menstruation. In this period women have to abstain from sexual relations and perform ritual washing.

Worship in Judaism centres on attending synagogue where there are three services a day. The marriage service has two parts: a betrothal where the bridegroom presents the bride with a ring in the presence of witnesses; then the marriage proper, under a special bridal canopy when the couple are blessed and express their union in sharing a cup of wine.

The ritual when a person dies is the Taharah, the washing of the body. The funeral service is followed by a burial for Orthodox Jews, perhaps a cremation for Progressive Jews. This is followed by seven days of intensive mourning and a further period of thirty days mourning. Every year the person is remembered at a Jahrzeit ('year-time') ceremony, which celebrates the person's life.

Circumcision of males was recommended in the Bible (Genesis17:10-14). At the ceremony of Brit Milah a boy has to be circumcised on the eighth day by an official called a Mohel. This reinacts the covenant Abraham had with God. For girls there is a blessing ceremony in the synagogue.

In Judaism there is a rite of passage for boys at 13 called the Barmitzvah. The ceremony symbolises the individual's ablity to meet the obligations required of him by the Jewish law. The ceremony consists of reading passages from the Torah and the saying of special prayers. In both Progressive and Orthodox Judaism girls have a similar ceremony at the age of 12.

Festivals

Some Jewish festivals are very Green in nature as they focus on the agrarian year showing that early Jews had a strong connection with the land. *Pesach* or Passover commemorates the exodus of the Israelites from Egypt and celebrates spring growth. *Shavuot* is another spring festival and commemorates the giving of the Ten Commandments to Moses and celebrates the wheat harvest and the first fruits. At this time all Jews renew their pledge of allegiance to God.

Tabernacles is an autumn festival held to remember the protection by God of the Israelites in the desert and celebrate the final harvest of the year. *Sukkot* is a harvest holiday, comparable in some ways to the American Thanksgiving. This is followed by *Yom Kippur* or 'Day of Atonement'. Jews have traditionally observed this holiday with a 25-hour period of fasting and intensive prayer. It is believed to be the last chance to change God's judgment of one's deeds in the previous year and His decisions on one's fate in the coming year.

At Passover, it also being a cleansing festival, no leavened foods are eaten; houses are cleaned thoroughly, symbolising the cleansing of the soul.

Green Judaism

The desert Wilderness of Sinai provided the backdrop for the formative part of the story by which people of the Jewish faith have defined themselves: those 41 years produced Moses, his Mount Sinai experience and the Ten Commandments.

Genesis had placed man at the centre of creation, and was given the responsibility by God to respect and conserve his creation (Gen.1-2). The beginning of Genesis tells that humanity was created in God's image and we are therefore expected to be respectful and follow God's example in dealings with the rest of His creation. There is an imperative that man must look after God's creation in the statement "take heed that you do not corrupt and destroy my universe. For if you spoil it there is no one to repair it after you."(Eccl.7: 13 Rabbah Midrash) Some Jews have said that placing man at the top of the hierarchy of creation with "dominion over" nature has led to the over-exploitation of the natural world and to just the ecological destruction cited in the Bible. Other Jews have argued that ultimately God owns all creation and man's responsibility is to use God's creation wisely using natural systems along the lines of "speak to the Earth and it will tell you what you need to know" (Job12: 7-9). God in fact made a covenant to protect the whole of creation which he made with Noah after the Great Flood (Genesis 9). Each view has its supporters, but the 'use God's creation wisely' view appears to be gaining the upper hand as more Jews become Green.

Judaism has much to say about how agriculture should be practised in a natural way. There were many Jewish laws to ensure the land was kept in good condition for future generations, ideas to which we will return in the chapter on food.

Judaism was one of the first religions to be concerned about water and air pollution in urban areas. There were definite laws passed to prevent people suffering from the grave effects of pollution and even laws banning the indiscriminate dumping of waste.

Greens have always valued trees and the Jews were no different. The Bible forbids harvesting from new fruit trees for three years. On the fourth year the crop was to be a holy offering to the Lord and only on the fifth year could they eat the fruit (Lev 19: 23-25). This shows respect for the developing tree (Lev.19: 23-25). Conservation of trees was seen as important as they should not be destroyed by "taking an axe to them" (Deut 20:19). In the US, the Coalition on the Environment and Jewish Life in California put this teaching into practice in efforts to protect the redwood forests. Rabbi Lester Scharnberg campaigned against the Maxam Corporation (by 2008 in bankruptcy proceedings) cutting down redwood forests and even led Jews onto its land to plant redwood seedlings. Eventually the group persuaded the Maxam Corporation to preserve part of the redwood forests.

In the UK Jews are trying to educate their own about environmental problems. The Noah non-profit organisation staffed entirely by volunteers has been set up to raise awareness of environmental issues through educational and practical projects. Partners in Creation develops environmental action programmes for the home, synagogue and workplace. Its interactive software on environmental issues is to be used in Jewish primary schools.

In the US, the Coalition on the Environment and Jewish Life (COEJL) trains leaders in environmental education and provides educational materials. Its campaigns on the environment take in the Inter-faith Global Climate Change Campaign in 21 US states.

With shared historical roots, Judaism has some parallels with Christianity and both have a rich tradition of Green thinking. Judaism provides an example of the belief that following God's laws leads you to Godliness and in this state we better protect and sustain his environment.

Judaism websites

www.jewfaq.org
www.religioustolerance.org
www.coejl.org
www.judaism.about.com
www.jewishanswers.org
www.jewishvirtuallibrary.org
www.reformjudaism.org.uk/
www.religionfacts.com
www.ou.org
www.noahproject.org.uk
www.jewishclimatecampaign.org

CHAPTER 3: ISLAM

Introduction

To become Muslim, one must declare *shahaadah* (the bearing of witness) that there is no god but Allah and that Prophet Muhammad is the last Messenger of Allah. The word Islam means 'submission' that is to say, submission to the will of Allah. The word Muslim on the other hand, means 'one who submits himself entirely to the will of Allah'. There are today around one billion Muslims in the world in 83 countries.

In a gross and tragic error of Western media, Islam has come to be portrayed by some as a religion of violence. This is one of the impacts of the misdeeds of some Muslim fundamentalists. However, the truth is far removed from this, as Islam is in fact a faith promoting peace and harmony.

Violence is foreign to Islam because Allah has said in the Holy Qur'an, "do not let your hatred for a people cause you to be unjust." In relation to how Muslims approach people of other beliefs this quote from the Qur'an is clear: "Invite (them) to the way of your Lord with wisdom and good speech and debate them with that which is best. Surely your Lord is the One Who knows who is astray and knows those who are rightly guided" (16:125).

Islam touches all aspects of society and the clergy can become entwined with the political process as has been seen in the case of Iran, Iraq, Lebanon, Afghanistan and elsewhere. The seamless connection of Islam with the apparatus of state can and does give rise to authoritarian regimes. It can also lead to a clash of ideologies between an Islamic state based on Islamic law (sharia) and a secular state. These outcomes are not the result of Islamic faith itself but are perhaps the result of using the high offices that come to clergy as vehicles with which to gain and enlarge political influence.

Islam: a brief history

The Prophet Muhammad was born in the year 570 CE in Arabia. He lost both of his parents by the age of six and as a result was reared by his uncle Abu Taalib who was a respected member of the Quraysh, the ruling tribe in the Mecca region. Muhammad was a quiet and thoughtful boy who worked as a herdsman. At the age 25, he married a wealthy business woman named Khadijah who employed him as a trader. Because of his truthfulness and honesty as well as his sound business practises, Prophet Muhammad became known as al-Amin (the Trustworthy).

Being quiet and reflective, Muhammad would spend time by himself in a nearby cave called 'al-Hira'. He found the culture in which he was raised decadent and idolatrous. At the age of 40, he had a vision of the Angel Jibril (Gabriel) from whom he received his first revelation sent by Allah. The revelations continued over a period of 23 years and are known as 'al-Qur'an' (That Which is Recited or Read). The Qur'an in Muslim belief is God's final revelation to mankind. When he began to publicly preach to his people about these revelations, Prophet Muhammad and his small number of followers were boycotted and severely persecuted by the other people of his town, Mecca. However, during this time Muhammad's spiritual life prospered. In one experience, the Prophet is said to have journeyed to Jerusalem on a white horse named Buraaq. Once there, he ascended to the seven heavens where he met and greeted the other prophets and then stood before the throne of Allah where he received direct instructions and orders for mankind.

The religion of the Arab world before the advent of Islam was an animistic polytheism. As soon as Muhammad began to recite the Qur'an and to preach about the truth which God had revealed to him, he and his small group of followers began suffering persecution. The persecution escalated. By the year 622 it became so fierce that he (now aged 52) and his followers were forced to emigrate for their safety to Medina, a city approximately 415 km (260 miles) north of Mecca. There his message found more supporters whom he later called 'al-Ansaars' (the Helpers). Meanwhile, his conflict with Mecca came to armed strife. After several years of battles and skirmishes with the Quraysh, Prophet Muhammad was able to return to Mecca which he entered after its surrender, peacefully and without bloodshed or revenge. By the time of his death at age 63, most of the Arabia peninsula had been brought under the banner of Islam.

After the death of the Prophet, the leadership was assumed in turn by four of his most outstanding followers, Abu Bakr, Umar, Uthmaan and Ali. Thereafter, political strife arose amongst the Muslims. A division arose between those who called themselves Sunni Muslims and those who called themselves `Shi'ah. The word `shi'ah in the Arabic language means follower, supporter, partisan. Thus, the `Shi'ahs of Islam are those who believe Ali bin `Abi Taleb, Prophet Muhammad's cousin and son-in-law who was unjustly deprived of the political leadership directly following the death of the Prophet. They see themselves as supporters of Ali's right to be the first leader or 'Khalifatu Muhammad' (Heir to Prophet Muhammad's Leadership).

Sunni means 'one who adheres closely to the Sunnah of Muhammad'. 'Sunnah' means 'customary practice' which includes what one does, says and sees done without comment of approval or disapproval. The Sunnah of Muhammad includes the accounts of what he said, what he did and what was said and done in his presence without him making comments of approval or disapproval about it. The Sunni Muslims, however, do not believe that the leadership of the Muslims is dynastic. The leader should be chosen based on his qualifications. Therefore, the Sunni say, the choice of Abu Bakr as leader of the Muslims after the death of the Prophet was a divinely guided decision, in that the people were guided to choose him as a leader based on his qualifications.

Muhammad and the Scriptures

Muslims see Muhammad as the final messenger of God. Muhammad was a religious person. He had long detested the decadence and idolatry of the society in which he grew up. Muhammad the man is central to Islam. He is seen as displaying the qualities of the perfect man, qualities anyone could admire.

He displayed kindness to the poor, downtrodden and orphans - even to his enemies. He epitomised mercy and forgiveness, as after the war with the Quraysh when he forgave them even though he nearly died in the battle of Uhud. He exhibited generosity throughout his life, always giving away his money to the poor, and always inviting them back to his house to feed them even if his own family went hungry. Despite the possibility of access to enormous wealth he chose to live a simple life. He ate simple food, wore coarse clothing and slept on a mat on the floor. In his lifetime he remained humble, denying any titles which were bestowed on him and even eating with slaves. He was always sincere and truthful in his dealings with other people, and showed equal justice for all.

For believers, Muhammad is seen as the Messenger of God, bringing God's laws to the world and warning of the dire consequences if they are not followed. The Holy Qur'an is considered the revealed word of Allah rather than the main reference source for 'the life and sayings' of Prophet Muhammad.

The main source for the life of the Prophet is called *Seerah* (the Biography of the Prophet). The main source of the sayings and actions of the Prophet is the *Hadith* literature. These are descriptions of the prophet's pronouncements and actions, of which six are said to be the most authentic.

Muslims also recognise the Bible and the Judaic *Torah* as part of the revelation of God. Actually both the Christians and the Jews are mentioned in the Holy Qur'an as Ahlu-l-Kitaab (People of the Book) and the Bible and the *Torah* are mentioned in the Holy Qur'an as *Ingeel* (Bible) and *Tauraat* (Torah).

Muslims say that Muhammad came for specific reasons. He came to explain God's commandments and impart the wisdom of the Qur'an. He came to bring out the good qualities in human beings, by showing them how to follow God's laws. Muslims see him as an example of how people can worship and serve Allah.

Doctrine and worship

Islam, Christianity and Judaism are called the Abrahamic faiths as they all share stories involving Abraham, Adam, Noah, Ishmael, Moses, and Jesus. All are recognised in Islam as prophets. Adam is the first Prophet of Islam. Prophet Ibrahim (Abraham) built the first house of worship with his son Ismaa'il (Ishmael) in Mecca. Muslims do not believe that

Jesus is the 'Son of God' as Christians do. Islam departs from these other faiths by holding that Muhammad is the *final* messenger of God. People therefore have no longer any need to follow a path other than Islam.

Muslims describe God as Allah and he is "Eternal and absolute. None is born of Him, nor is He born. There is none like Him." (Sura 112). In other words God is All Knowing, and All Merciful, the Supreme, the Sovereign. Our place is to worship and serve him by doing his will. The Qur'an states that God is the creator of everything. "God is the one who created you and then provides for you."(Qur'an 30,40) and " Don't you see that everything in heaven and Earth bows to God in worship, sun, moon, stars, hills, trees, animals, and many people." (Qur'an 22,18). God can also dissolve creation at the appropriate time according to his will.

Like Christians, Muslims believe that the present life is only a trial preparation for the next realm of existence. Muslims believe in the existence of Satan as a source of evil in this world. They believe that God has a fixed term for everything and at the end of this world there will be a Last Day of Judgement. On this day it is believed that all the dead will be raised from their graves and everyone will be justly rewarded or punished according to whether they have followed God's laws.

The decision of whether a person goes to heaven or hell is based on the deeds of the person while on Earth, which are recorded by angels. The Qur'an states "those who believe and do good deeds, they are dwellers of Paradise, they dwell therein forever." (Qur'an,2:82). Those that fail the judgement go to hell.

Islam's five pillars

Central to Muslim doctrine are the five pillars of Islam, the five fundamentals of faith. These are:

1. The testimony of faith or Shahada is saying with conviction, *"La ilaha illa Allah, Muhammadur rasoolu Allah."* This saying means "There is no true god (deity) but God (Allah), and Muhammad is the Messenger (Prophet) of God." The first part, "There is no true god but God," means that none has the right to be worshipped but God alone as the sole Creator of all, and the Supreme Authority over everything and everyone in the universe.

2. Prayer: The practise of Salah or prayer five times a day is obligatory. These five times are dawn (Fajr), immediately after noon (Dhuhr), mid-afternoon ('Asr), sunset (Maghrib), and early night (Isha'). Ritual cleanliness and ablution are required before prayer, as are clean clothes and location, and the removal of shoes.

Worship is particularly important on Friday where it is obligatory for Muslims to attend the mosque for the noon prayer, called Jumuu'ah, which is accompanied by a sermon (Khutbah). There is no hierarchical clerical authority in Islam, no priests or ministers. Any learned person who knows the Qur'an and is chosen by the congregation leads prayers. Prayer consists of verses from the Qur'an and other prayers, spoken in Arabic, accompanied by various postures - standing, bowing, prostrating and sitting. Personal supplications (Du'ah) can be offered in one's own language.

3. Pilgrimage: Each male must, if they are able to do so, make at least one pilgrimage to Mecca in their lifetime, which is called the *Hajj*. Women may also attend if accompanied by a male. Regardless of the season, pilgrims wear special clothes (Ihram) - two, very simple, unsown white garments - which strips away all distinctions of wealth, status, class and culture; all stand together and equal before Allah (God).

4. Support for Community: Giving *Zakat* (Support of the Needy). The word *Zakat* means purification and growth and it is an act of purification through sharing what one has with others. The rationale behind this is that Muslims believe that everything belongs to God, and man holds wealth only in trust. This trust must be discharged, moreover, as instructed by God, as that portion of our wealth legally belongs to other people and must be given to them. This is an alms tax, payable on various categories of property, notably savings and investments, produce, inventory of goods, saleable crops and cattle and precious metals. Tax proceeds are to be used for the various categories of distribution specified by Islamic law. Setting aside a portion for those in need therefore purifies possessions. For most purposes this involves the payment each year of 2.5% of one's capital, provided that this capital reaches a certain minimum amount that is not

consumed by its owner. A generous person can pay more than this amount, though it is treated and rewarded as voluntary charity (Sadaqah). This amount of `money is provided to bridge the gap between the rich and the poor, and can be used in many useful projects for the welfare of the community.

5. Fasting: The practise of *Sawm* or fasting. Allah prescribes daily fasting for all able, adult Muslims during the whole of the month of *Ramadan*, the ninth month of the lunar calendar, beginning with the sighting of the new moon. On the physical side, fasting is from first light of dawn until sundown, abstaining from food, drink, and sexual relations. On the moral, behavioural side, one must abstain from lying, malicious gossip, and quarrelling and trivial nonsense. Exempted from the fast are the very old and the insane. Those who are sick, elderly, or on a journey, and women who are menstruating, pregnant, or nursing are permitted to break the fast, but must make up an equal number of days later in the year. If physically unable to do so, they must feed a needy person for each day missed. Children begin to fast (and to observe the prayers) from puberty, although many start earlier. Fasting is seen principally as a method of self-purification. By cutting oneself off from worldly pleasures and comforts, even for a short time, the fasting person gains true sympathy for those who go hungry regularly. He will achieve growth in his spiritual life, learning discipline, self-restraint, patience and flexibility.

Ceremonies and festivals

Set to fixed dates in the lunar Muslim Calendar, dates of each of the festivals move from one year to the next within the Gregorian calendar used in the West.

Festivals in Islam are called *Id* and share the intention of bringing the community together for celebration. A feature of *Id* (or *Eid*) is that celebration is extended to all; the poor are taken into people's houses and fed, the sick are visited and any differences settled.

The *Idu-l-Fitr* Festival is observed at the end of *Ramadan* (see above) Muslims express their joy and relief by offering a congregational prayer of gratitude to Allah for giving them their strength to fast for the whole month of *Ramadan*. The day is a religious holiday in Muslim countries. It is customary to visit friends and relatives, to give presents to children and to prepare special foods. Muslims generally wear their best or new clothes. The occasion is known as the time of *zakat-al-fitr*, the time for the payment of *zakat* (support for the needy).

The *Idu-l-Ad-haa* festival takes place during the *Hajj* pilgrimage. It commemorates the prophet Abraham's readiness to sacrifice his son Ishmail on Allah's command. Allah accepted Abraham's devotion and obedience and because of this, asked him to sacrifice a lamb instead. People attending a special service at the mosque observe this occasion. Following prayers, those Muslims who can afford to will sacrifice an animal (sheep, cows or camels) and share the sacrificial meat among relatives, neighbours and the poor.

Al Hijrah or the New Year festival takes place on the first day of the Muslim New Year and commemorates the anniversary of the migration of Muhammad from Mecca to a place of safety in Medina, and the establishment of the first Muslim community. Generally, it is a time for family meals, services at the mosque and celebration. For *Shi'ah* Muslims, it also marks the sad event of the martyrdom of Hussain, the grandson of Muhammad. *Shi'ah* Muslims differ from the majority at this time, as they 'eat the food of sorrow' by spending time in prayer, wearing black and telling stories about Hussain's death. Passion plays enacting the event are often put on in local communities.

The *Milaad an-Nabi* Festival takes place on the 12th day of the 3rd month and celebrates the Birthday of the Prophet Muhammad. Considering the Islamic way of life has been going over 1,400 years, this festival is quite a recent addition to the calendar. People gather at their local mosque to hear readings from the Qur'an and stories about Muhammad's life.

The *Lailat al-Baraat* Festival or Night of Forgiveness takes place 15 days before *Ramadan* begins and is a period of quiet reflection and prayer. Muslims believe that on this night, Allah determines the fate of humankind for the coming year. Grievances are settled, sins are confessed and the poor, sick, elderly and lonely are cared for. Many Muslims will visit their dead in the cemetery to pay their respects. The night often culminates with a firework display.

Islam's customs

Prophet Muhammad said: "The most perfect in faith amongst believers is he who is best in manners and kindest to his wife." Muhammad had eleven wives and he treated them all the exactly the same. He said throughout his life that women should be treated with respect. In Islam a woman is to be treated as God has endowed her, with rights, such as to be treated as an individual, with the right to own and dispose of her own property and earnings. She has the right to be educated and to work outside the home if she so chooses. She has the right to inherit from her father, mother and husband. A woman can lead a group of women in prayer according to certain schools of law, but she is not referred to as and cannot act as an imam.

Marriage in Islam is usually arranged between two families and a contract is drawn up and takes place in the mosque. The permission for marriage to four wives was revealed in the holy Qur'an. There is no ruling that a woman must be a virgin when she is married. In Islam, pre-marital sex is unlawful. A woman who is born a Muslim is expected to be a virgin, she has no excuse not to be a virgin, unless she has been married and divorced. A woman convert to Islam need not be a virgin.

There are certain stipulations on preparing and serving food. All meat has to be from animals killed in a certain way - called *Halal*. The animal is first calmed and then slaughtered by the cutting its jugular vein without showing the cutting blade. The Prophet was once asked, "Messenger of Allah! Are we rewarded for kindness to animals?" He said, "There is a reward for kindness to every living animal or human." The eating of pork is forbidden as it is considered to be unclean. Alcohol and drugs are banned.

The Qur'an clearly states that an Islamic state must protect life and property. The Qur'an teaches that this ideal state is meant to create a society of goodness, justice, and mercy. Underpinning the state is religious law and custom built on the principles that in a society there are obligations to God, as stated in the Qur'an: "he who obeys the messenger, obeys God" so that God is seen as the supreme authority in the implementation of the law and custom of the state.

What is revolutionary even today is the stance of Islam on trade terms. The practice of usury by the Jews, of charging interest on money loaned, was banned in the early Islamic state. So Islam recommends that commerce should ideally be practised without the gains from interest on loans.

Green Islam

From what we know of his ways, Muhammad could be said to have lived a Green lifestyle. His was a simple life: with few material possessions, his impact on the environment was minimal. With the emphasis in his own life on goodness, justice, mercy and obligations to God, He was in the eyes of Muslims the perfect man and his life a great example of living in harmony with all God's creations.

The state created by Muhammad in Arabia could be said to have been the first to be based on ecological principles. This is a not unreasonable claim: there are over 2,630 references to the environment in the Qur'an. It follows that Allah is taken as seeing it as an important issue.

The first principle of Green Islam is that God not man owns the Earth. Muhammad stated "The world is beautiful and verdant, and verily God, be He exalted, has made you His stewards in it, and He sees how you acquit yourselves." Therefore, in addition to being part of the Earth and part of the universe, man is also the executor of God's injunctions and commands and as such he is only a manager of the Earth and not a proprietor. Heaven and Earth and all that they contain belong to God alone. So the conservation of the environment is a religious duty demanded by God. God has said, "Do good, even as God has done you good, and do not pursue corruption in the earth. Verily, God does not love corrupters."

The second principle is that the Earth, although owned by God must be shared by others. The Qur'an is clear that God has created all of the resources upon which life depends. God created Nature for the sustenance of all people *and* living beings. The right to benefit from the essential environmental elements and resources, such as water, range land, fire and other sources of energy, forests, fish and wildlife, arable soil, air, and sunlight, is, in Islam, a right held in common by all members of society. Each individual is entitled to benefit from a common resource to the extent of his need, so long as he does not violate, infringe, or delay the equal rights of other members.

Here, within this ancient book we find the modern ideal of the "global commons" where ecological resources must by rights be shared and, more importantly, preserved by ecologically sound management so that each generation uses and makes the best use of Nature, according to its need, without disrupting or adversely affecting the interests of future generations. The following verse sums up how man must approach the environment: " Conduct your life as though you are living forever." The message of sustainability is clear.

Destruction of environment under capitalistic pursuit of maximum profit as we have seen throughout the world is less likely to occur under Islam because, "Allah has allowed trade but forbidden interest." The implication is repeated: that all wealth really belongs to God. The Qur'an tells that making 'windfall' profits is not what we are here for when it states "that which you lay out for increase through the property of (other) people will have no increase with God." Islamic banking operates on equity ownership, not interest earned.

Islam's third green principle is its emphasis on social justice and equality. Women have equal property rights. (More on this in our chapter on Poverty.)

Muslims today are becoming increasingly engaged with environmental issues. In the UK the Islamic Foundation for Ecology and Environmental Sciences (IFEES) provides training materials on environmental issues for Muslims. IFEES is also planning an environmental handbook for use by Imams. Other plans include an Islamic Environmental College, and centres for organic farming and alternative technology.

In 2009, at a meeting of religious leaders to combat climate change held in the UK, Egypt's Mufti Ali Gomaa proposed that Medina be transformed into a "green city" with mosques supplied with green energy. The Medina initiative is part of a seven-year climate change action plan adopted by Muslim leaders in Istanbul in 2009. One of the measures adopted was the creation of a Muslim 'eco-label' for goods and services ranging from printings of the Qur'an to the *hajj*. It was proposed for instance that the 15 million Qur'ans published each year would be printed on environmentally friendly paper.

Though events of recent years have given non-believer Westerners some insights into certain aspects of the Islamic world, Islam the faith and life today remains shrouded in mystery. People remain confused about what Islam stands for, why in extreme cases members of certain sects are driven to kill another's members. Along with this ignorance rides much prejudice. But, as we have seen in this chapter, there is no justification for this. Islam is a faith setting out the highest standards of morality and a morality that extends to guidance on ecological right livelihood. Those who label it a religion of terrorists and destroyers of the environment tell us more about themselves and their outlook than about true Islam, the Way of Peace.

Islamic web sites

www.islam.com
www.islamworld.net
www.islam-guide.com
www.islamreligion.com
www.islamonline.com
www.ifees.org.uk
www.islamicity.com
www.islamchannel.tv
www.beliefnet.com
www.bbc.co.uk/religion/religions/islam/subdivisions/sunnishia_1.shtml

CHAPTER 4 : HINDUISM

Introduction

Hinduism, arguably the oldest of the main world faiths, has 850 million to 1 billion followers worldwide. These are mainly in India but also in Nepal, Sri Lanka, other neighbouring countries and in South-East Asia and the Diaspora in the Caribbean, North America and Europe. The word Hindu was used first by the Persians to describe the way of life of the people of India. Unlike other faiths, Hinduism had no single founder, no defined era of origin, no central set of doctrines, no unifying creed, nor do adherents subscribe to a common canon of scriptures. Thus, it has been described as a collection of religions with a shared tradition. Many Hindus describe themselves as following the Sanātana Dharma or an eternal spiritual tradition.

Scriptures

The scriptural texts are very ancient and were themselves the written records of even earlier beliefs and practices characterised as Nature worship. The Vedas are the oldest texts with the Rig Veda being the oldest religious text still in use in the world. The Vedas are the work of a priestly class called Brahmins who composed them between 2000 to

1000 BCE. The Rig Veda consists of 1,028 Sanskrit hymns addressed to various Gods. The Yajur Veda is a collection of sacred formulas; the Sama Veda is a collection of Vedic chants; the Artharva Veda is a collection of Vedic charms. The theme of all the Vedas is immortality and how to attain it with the guidance of the priestly class.

The Upanishads (800-200 BCE) symbolise a rebellion against ritual. They contain commentaries on the Vedas and focus on the more mystical elements of Hinduism. They favour a more individual rather than institutional approach to finding God.

Another important text is the Mahabharata, the longest poem in the world with some 100,000 verses. Composed between 500 BCE and 100 BCE, the Mahabharata is an account of the wars of the house of Bharata. Krishna, who is regarded as an incarnation of the Hindu God Vishnu, plays a central role in the story about the dispute between the Kaurava and the Pandava families. The Bhagavad Gita is part of the work and regarded by some as the most important of all the Hindu scriptures.

The Ramyana is another literary work of ancient India. It tells the story of Prince Rama who was sent into exile in the forest with his wife, Sita and his brother, Lakshamana. Sita was abducted by the evil demon Ravana but ultimately rescued by Prince Rama with the help of the Monkey God, Hanuman. Rama then returns home a hero to regain his kingdom. Hanuman, the monkey God features in the story as a symbol of strength and is worshipped as a deity.

The Puranas are a series of writings written by Brahmins, which stem from the 4th to 6th centuries CE and later. These texts contain information about Hindu cosmology, stories of gods, summaries of sacred texts and guides to forms of worship, pilgrimage sites and cures.

Doctrine

A belief in the unity of everything and that all beings are part of God is the very foundation of Hindu doctrine. The purpose of life is to realize that we are part of God and by doing so we can leave this plane of existence and find union with God. Hinduism encompasses many different approaches to God. From the Bhagavad Gita, the most universally accepted of many venerated texts, we learn that Brahma created the world. The Mahabharata proclaims "the father of all creatures, God, made the sky, from the sky he made the water, from water he made fire and air, from fire and air, Earth came into existence." Mountains are said to be his bones, earth his flesh, sea his blood and sky his abdomen. Air is his breath and rivers are his nerves.

Brahma the creator is shown with four heads from which emanate the material elements. According to Hindu scripture, matter possesses three qualities or *Gunas*. *Tamas* is the quality of darkness and inertia. *Rajas* posses the quality of energy, passion and activity and *Sattva* is the quality of Goodness and Peace. All matter, which includes humans, is then a mixture of these three qualities.

Five elements are described: Sky is the father of all created things with qualities of motion, limitlessness and fathomlessness. Water is seen as an element vital to life. Air is seen as symbolic of God, the giver of life and health. Air also has the vibrant quality of *prana* (breath) in it, which prevails throughout Nature. Fire, the element that has been created by Brahma, is worshipped as the God Agni. The last element described in the scriptures is Earth or *Prthvi*. All Hindus see this as the Mother.

The Cosmology of Hinduism is one of the most detailed and precise of all the faiths. Time is divided into four *yugas* or ages that combine to make up a *kalpa* or aeon. One thousand *kalpas* is one day in the life of Brahma and his life lasts 311,140 billion years.

In the Satya (or Krita) *yuga*, the veil between the mundane and the transcendent is removed and perfection is achieved as the deities are worshipped in their actual form. This is a golden age when people are deeply religious and the cow of the *dharma* (moral law) is resting on four legs. In the second age of *Tetra yuga*, spirituality begins to decline as humans lose control of their passions. The cow of the *dharma* is now described as resting on three legs. In the third age of *Dvaapara yuga,* the veil between the spiritual and physical worlds starts to darken. Deities are now worshipped in their physical form. The cow of the *dharma* is now described as resting on two legs. The last age is that of *Kali yuga*. This is our present age. Now sex becomes the only source of pleasure and wealth is seen as the only mark of virtue. The worship of images is rife and religion becomes ritualistic. Now the cow of the *dharma* is described as resting on one leg. Although there is a single main God in Hinduism, he comes in many guises. God is seen as having three main aspects: Brahma, the creator, Vishnu, the saviour and protector of humankind and Shiva the destroyer of evil, the creator of new life and sustainer of life. Each God has a consort or female partner. Brahma has Saraswati as consort, who is

Goddess of wisdom and the arts. Vishnu has Lakshmi as his consort and she is considered the Goddess of Good Fortune. Shiva has Parvati, Durga or Shakti as his consort and she represents the female principle of Creation and mother of the world. She produces the food crops. This union gives rise to two sons, Karttikeya the destroyer of evil and Ganesha the bringer of good luck and remover of obstacles.

Vishnu is important as a peacemaker. He often comes to Earth as an avatar or representative of God on Earth. There have been nine previous incarnations of Vishnu including those of Rama, Krishna and the Buddha and one to come in the future, Kalki, who will bring the evil *Kali yuga* to an end and inaugurate a new *Krita yuga*. Krishna is quoted in the Bhagavad Gita as saying "I come into existence time after time to protect the good, to destroy the wicked and re-establish the holy Dharma."

Hinduism can be confusing because of the vast variety of deities - each village has its own local deity apart from the universal ones mentioned. Often Hindu temples will be dedicated to certain deities. Shrines are often found in homes, which are for the worship of a favourite deity or deities.

Hindus believe that the soul passes through a cycle of successive lives. Its next incarnation is dependent on how the previous lives were lived. All creatures go through a cycle of rebirth, which can only be broken by the attainment of *moksha* or God Realization. This level of consciousness resides in our *Atman* or the true self. The whole process is governed by Karma, as the law by which right actions give beneficial results and wrong actions give unwished for results. If bad Karma is accumulated a person can descend to animal form in the next reincarnation. There are three sorts of Karma: *Prabdha* begins to mature in the lifetime of the individual but there is little that can be done about it; *Kriyamana* is karma playing out in present time, which we can do something about; *Samcita* is Karma already accumulated but yet to have its effect.

According to the theory of the transmigration of souls, a soul coming down to Earth arrives at a place appropriate to its past karma or actions - as a human being, as an animal or as a plant. It is this that gives rise to the tradition of caste.

Among humans there are hundreds of castes, which are hereditary groups with different ways of life. Castes are classified in four groups called *Varnas*. Brahmins are the top of the hierarchy of *Varnas* as they are considered to be the earthly Devas (gods). They have the responsibility of reciting, practising and teaching the Vedas. The second *Varna* is that of the *Kshatriya* or warriors. They maintain conditions in which people practise the dharma or truth by ensuring that justice is visited on perpetrators of untruths or wrong actions, by force of arms when necessary. The third *Varna*, the *Vaisyas* are those of the propertied or the merchant class. Their role is to lay and maintain society's economic foundation so the *dharma* can prosper. The fourth is the *Sudra Varna*, whose role is to serve the needs of the other classes. The *Sudra Varna* may neither utter nor study the Vedas. Then there are also those in no *Varna* at all, who are called *Dalits* or Untouchables, of whom there are 15 million in India. Gandhi campaigned for Dalits to be given spiritual equality and respect. His campaign continues today.

In Hinduism it is essential to be guided on the spiritual path by a *guru* or spiritual guide. The guru is a person who has had experience on the spiritual path and shares this knowledge and experience with his *chela* or disciple. The guru will guide the student to commit to the traditional five observances of practising contentment, cleanliness, studiousness, self-control and contemplating the divine.

The guru may advocate yoga techniques. The yoga we know best in the West is *hatha* yoga or yoga postures, which are but aspects of a comprehensive system of ethical, mental and physical development, which became the eight limbs of yoga. Its creation in ancient times is credited to an incarnated being known only as Pantanjali. The first limb is abstention from violence, lying, theft, greed and sexual relations. The second limb requires observances of equanimity, self-discipline, simple living and seeing God in everything. The third limb is the requirement to practise *asana* or physical postures. The fourth limb is the practice of *pranayama* or breath control. The fifth limb is the practice of concentration. The sixth limb is the withdrawing of the senses from the world. The seventh limb is the regular practice of meditation. The final and eighth limb is the practice of contemplation, which leads to *Kaivalya* or a state of ecstasy. There are in fact many different *yogas* in the Hindu tradition. They all owe their origins to Pantanjali's inspiration.

Mantra yoga is explained in the Mandukya Upanishad, as the yoga of divine sound, such as that of the 'OM' mantra. This is the yoga that the Transcendental Meditation movement, founded by the late Maharishi Mahesh Yogi, teaches. With their personal mantra, a student can achieve an inner harmony by allowing its sound to sooth away distractions of the thinking mind.

Bhakti yoga is the yoga of devotion. The Bhakti yogi tries to identify closely with the object of devotion so that he no longer exists as a separate form. As Krishna said in the Bhagavad Gita "those who commune with me in love's devotion abide in me and I in them." I personally experienced this type of approach to God when attending the Iskcon ashram in Vrindavan where there was constant chanting for Krishna.

Dhyana Yoga is the yoga of pure meditation intent on liberating the individual ego from attachments. The Bhagavad Gita says, "with his senses, mind and reason controlled, who is intent on *moksa* (liberation), who has cast out desire, fear, anger, he is liberated forever" (5, 28).

Jnana Yoga is the yoga of knowledge and the coming to this knowledge through intuitive wisdom. This gives the aspirant discrimination between what is real and what is unreal through the development of tolerance, faith, balance, mind and body control and the cultivation of a longing for liberation.

Ahimsa, non-violence, is an ancient concept from Jainism adapted by Mahatma Gandhi during his campaign of protest and civil disobedience, for independence from the British Empire. Gandhi is perhaps the Hindu leader best known in the West because of many decades of negotiations and visits to the UK and elsewhere. On my visit to Gandhi's ashram in Ahmedabad in 2002, I was struck by the purity of Gandhi's message conveyed by the devotees through the simplicity of the lives they lead. This was where he adapted the Jain concept of *ahimsa*. It was, of course, Gandhi's leadership that gained India its independence from Britain in 1947.

The great wave of searching, discovery and expansion of consciousness in the West in the sixties to mid seventies focussed on the Hindu tradition. I was myself part of that wave. Many, especially in the music and entertainment business - and some were big names - adopted guides or gurus. There emerged at this time of searching a series of spiritual teachers such as Sai Baba, Bhagwan Shree Rajneesh (Osho), Swami Shivananada, Meher Baba, Maharaji ji and Baba Ram Dass with mass followings. In different forms, several still have followers today.

Customs and ceremonies

The Hindu religion gains its flavour from its many customs. The *Vedas* advise Hindus what to do at each stage of their lives. The Upanayana initiation ceremony symbolises a second birth, into the spiritual realm. It is reserved for boys of 8-12 years of the higher Brahmin, Kshatriya and Vaishya castes. The Brahmin priest instructs the boy on how to live a pure and moral life. The new initiate is called a Brahmachari. He is expected to display the qualities of celibacy, truthfulness, obedience and humility.

The boy then takes a ritual bath of purification, after which he becomes a *Snataka*, undertaking to live the life of the householder, carrying out the duties of a family man. All the while he is expected to carry on with his spiritual practice or *sadhana*.

A third phase of life is that of the *Vanaprastha* or forest dweller. For this the older man may take his wife with him to the forest or otherwise make arrangements for her support. The celibate, austere *Vanaprastha* lifestyle enforces a return to the simplicity of living with Nature. Begging is the only permitted means of livelihood.

The final stage of life is that of a *Sannyasin* or wanderer. The person wanders from place to place preaching and begging for food. Some *Sannyasins* are called *Dandins* because they have a stick; others are called *Nagas* because they wander naked and have no possessions.

Marriage of course is considered an important part of the householder phase. Marriages are entirely arranged between two families on the advice of astrologers. A dowry is usually paid by the female's parents. This gives rise to the unpopularity of a female child in India. The astrologer advises on the auspicious day for the wedding.

At death, the body is always cremated so that Agni, the god of fire, can consume the person's sins. The ashes of the deceased person are gathered up and sprinkled on a holy river such as the Ganges. There is a special ceremony in the temple when food and clothes are offered up to appease both the *preta*, the ghost of the person and also Yama, the Lord of Death. On the anniversary of the person's death there is the Shraddha ceremony to appease Lord Yama.

Hindus can attend the temple throughout the day and often make an offering of food to the *murti* or image of the deity or deities of the temple. Worshippers receive this food back as *prasada*, holy food.

Pilgrimage to different spiritual sites is an important part of the Hindu religion. People go on pilgrimages in India for a holy holiday. On my visit to the holy city of Rishikesh on the Ganges close to the Himalaya, I witnessed thousands attending holy shrines as part of the annual Shiva festival. There are other popular destinations on the Ganges such as Hardwar and Varanasi. The Ganges is held as a living goddess. Bathing in its waters is an act of purification, washing away all sins. I witnessed many hundreds of people bathing in the Ganges at Rishikesh and Mathura, a moving sight.

Festivals

Religious festivals in India are part of the fabric of life. The *Kumbh Mela* is a massive festival held every 12 years in Allahabad and three other locations. It celebrates the spilling of immortal nectar by gods trying to steal away a jar of immortality to heaven. Then, every 144 years, after 12 of the *Purna* or complete *Kumbh Melas* celebrated only at Allahabad, there comes the *Maha* or Great *Kumb Mela*. The last gathering, in 2001, was so huge it could be seen from space!

The *Diwali* festival celebrates the goddess of prosperity, Lakshmi. It symbolizes the victory of righteousness and the lifting of spiritual darkness. Diwali is observed as the day Rama returned to Ayodhya to assume his role as the king of India. It is a time when thousands of candles are lit.

Sankranti is the harvest festival, timed for the middle of January. Farmers bathe and decorate their cattle with saffron and turmeric powder and worship them with flowers, since cows are sacred animals to Hindus.

The *Sri Rama Navami* Festival in March and April celebrates the birth of Lord Rama as an incarnation of Lord Vishnu. He portrays the ideal man and Sita, his wife, the ideal woman. Celebrations include reading the great epic Ramayana and staging plays about the life of Rama.

Holi, a major festival in March, celebrates the onset of spring along with good harvests and the fertility of the land. It commemorates the burning of the demon Holika who was burnt alive for trying to harm a devotee of Vishnu. Bonfires are lit throughout India. This festival is best known for the way people throw brightly coloured powder and water over each other.

The *Ganesh Chaturthi* festival in August-September celebrates the birth of Lord Ganesh. He is the god of wisdom, prosperity and good luck and He removes obstacles. The celebration of the birth of the elephant-headed Ganesh in processions and at festive gatherings, symbolised by participants wearing life-sized clay elephant heads, continues for two days.

The *Krishna Janmashtami* festival also in August-September celebrates the birth of Lord Krishna. Artful decorations and lighting bedeck temples and homes. Notable are the cribs and portrayals of the stories of Lord Krishna's childhood. In the evening, *bhajans* (devotional songs) are sung ending at midnight, the auspicious moment when Lord Krishna was born.

The *Maha Shivaratri* festival in February-March is a celebrated in honour of Lord Shiva. It was on this day that Parvati, the wife of Shiva, prayed, meditated and fasted for his well-being, hoping to ward off any evils that might fall upon him. Celebrants fast, spending the day focused on Shiva, meditating and chanting *Om Namaha Shivaya* (homage to Shiva). It is customary to spend the entire night singing the praises of Lord Shiva this way. In the morning, the fast is broken with a feast.

The *Dussehra* Festival signifies the victory of Lord Rama over the demon Ravana. It is often observed with special celebrations and the burning of the effigy of Ravana, said to represent the destruction of the false ego.

Green Hinduism

My time in India travelling, interviewing and researching confirmed for me that Hinduism is permeated with a Green philosophy and intent. With its roots in Nature spirits, Hinduism can be seen as an elaborate series of homages to Nature. It asks its followers to see God in every object in the Universe. For Hindus, noticing the presence of God in air, water, fire, Sun, Moon, Stars and Earth is central to their faith. Each of the many festivals offers opportunities to worship His omnipresence in different, over-the-top ways, which are engaging, freeing and powerfully healing. Hindus consider all life forms on Earth as children of God; they believe that there is soul in all plants and animals as well as in humans.

Their faith gives Hindus a world perceived as being alive with forces, powers, spirits and deities—life energies. All natural phenomena are expressions of these energies. The Deep Ecology outlook of Hinduism is unmistakable: "He whose self is disciplined by yoga sees the Self abiding in all beings and beings in the Self; He sees the same in all beings" (Bhagavad Gita 6.29).

The Brahmans of the Vedas said that high souls reincarnate as cows and therefore cows need to be respected. The sight of cows wandering the streets shocks many first-time visitors to India. It can even be tricky to get past them! I heard they were even taking ageing cows from Delhi for "retirement" in Vrindavan, where Krishna used to be a cowherd!

It is because of the elevated status of cows that their dung and urine feature in certain purification ceremonies. Milk is offered as an oblation to the gods, as cows bestow bliss, happiness and wealth upon humans. Even in Vedic times, to stop a cow grazing was considered an act of murder. Krishna had an ideal relationship with cows, caring for them as a cowherd in his youth. When I visited the ashram in Vrindavan and the Sant Math temple in Mathura, I saw firsthand how both ashrams took tender care of their cows. At the dairy farm all male cattle were kept thriving regardless of their not producing anything that could be used!

Animals are associated with gods throughout Hindu sacred literature. Agni is associated with the bull, Krishna with cows and Ganesha with elephants. Shiva has strong connections with serpents, Saraswati and Brahma with the wild goose.

Flora as well as fauna were protected and revered as shown in the evidence of early Hindu literature. Trees and plants were considered the abodes of benevolent gods and goddesses. Early Hindu scripture was clear that Nature was bountiful and should remain so, saying "as long as this Earth is full of Nature, the human race is going to flourish." (Durga Saptasak 54).

The Hindu scriptures may be thousands of years old, but they do not fail to alert followers to the ills of pollution. The Yajurveda instructs people to keep the Earth free from contamination. The Chandogya Upanishad states "in pure nourishment there is pure Nature" (7, 26, 2) and so encourages believers to keep their bodies pure.

There are examples of Hindus applying their ecological teachings to environmental problems around the world. The New Youth Village Welfare Association, founded in 1990, is a youth-led, volunteer association in northern India. Founded by Laxman Singh to help the Laporiya community revive their degraded soils, barren pastures and ailing livestock, it enlists village youth to work on water conservation, agriculture and health issues.

Through an indigenous method of rainwater harvesting, the organisation has visibly transformed the degraded, barren ecosystem into a lush and abundant one. They have revived local customs and rituals that foster environmental responsibility, water conservation and reverence for Nature among the villagers. Small shrines dedicated to Hindu deities and local guardians of the water reserves adorn the village's many small tanks and wells. Certain trees and plants (such as Peepal and Tulsi, sacred to Vishnu) are worshipped regularly on household altars; seasonal and family celebrations often begin and end by honouring Nature deities; and daily water drawing entails ritual blessings of the Hindu deity, Shiva, at well shrines.

The Chipko movement of the Indian Himalayas follows a tradition of non-violent protest for the sake of truth and purity. The movement, rural people many of them women, is dedicated to ecological protection, especially forest preservation. Named for the practice of 'hugging' trees in order to protect them from loggers, this grassroots movement seeks to prevent socially and environmentally destructive land use and development schemes. Chipko express reverence for Nature; they perceive a sacredness in trees that testifies to the religious dimension of the movement. Its leaders perform Hindu rituals and recite *vedas* during protests.

From this, we can clearly see that with its inspirational outlook on life energies and much else, Hinduism can support us in raising our standards of care for our Planet, if we observe, absorb and practise some of the powerful and ancient wisdom it offers.

Hindu websites

www.hindunet.org
www.religioustolerance.org
www.hindukids.org
www.religion-cults.com
www.hinduonnet.com
www.hinduwebsite.com
www.hinduism.org
http://www.pantheon.org/
http://virtualreligion.net
www.karansingh.com
www.hindulinks.org
www.hinduism.suite101.com

CHAPTER 5 : BUDDHISM

Introduction

Rather than being a religion based on a belief in one or a panoply of supreme beings, Buddhism is a life path involving practices. The practices of this path of spiritual development lead to insights into the true nature of events, the world, one's own life and one's aliveness.

Buddhism is over 2,500 years old. Today it has some 350 million adherents worldwide. Buddhist communities are found in Southeast Asia, India, Sri Lanka, Myanmar/Burma, Japan, Korea, China including Tibet, Vietnam, Thailand, Cambodia and Laos. Since the 1960s there has been a growing number of Buddhists in the West. From just a few prominent seekers during the 1930s this interest in Buddhism swelled with the new consciousness arising alongside the drug culture of the 1960s and '70s. Significant numbers were exploring Eastern mysticism and Buddhist Lamas newly exiled from Tibet after its invasion by China in 1950 began journeying to the West.

Buddhism: a brief history

The historical Buddha is the basis of this spiritual tradition. The birth of the Buddha in Nepal, 2,500 years ago, was hailed at the time as an auspicious event: when the Buddha took his first seven steps, lotus flowers blossomed with each step, it is said. In the traditional accounts, he was born the son of the rulers of the kingdom of the Sakyas and thus a member of the warrior or ruling caste. He grew up as a prince, Siddhartha Gautama, married – some say at 16 - and lived in the luxurious lifestyle of his caste. His father was afraid of astrological predictions that Siddhartha would become a spiritual leader, so he deliberately shielded him from the realities of old age, sickness and death.

One day the prince escaped the palace grounds; he saw a decrepit old man, someone diseased, a corpse being cremated and a *sadhu* (holy man, hermit). This was Siddhartha's first exposure to old age, sickness, and death but witnessing them he realised that people ultimately had little control over their lives. He was changed by the experience. It kindled in him the desire to know why there was old age, sickness, and death and whether there was a way out of this suffering. To this end he secretly stole away from his father's kingdom and began his search for the truth. This took him to a series of eminent teachers. Unconvinced by the mystical states they helped him experience, he took up the ascetic life of a hermit.

For seven years he underwent many privations but he was unable to find the answers to his questions. He finally became disillusioned with asceticism and the Hindu doctrines of his time and one day, the story goes, he accepted some rice from a young girl and felt better.

Still determined to achieve realisation, the prince sat under the Bodhi Tree at Bodh Gaya. There, after just seven days, he finally achieved the enlightenment or *Nirvana* he'd sought for just as many years. This would earn him the title, The Buddha, or enlightened one. With enlightenment, he understood the answers to his burning questions. After achieving *Nirvana* he sat for a further three weeks as he sought to absorb the experience. Then he took some food from two merchants. These two, it is said, became his first followers.

The site where The Buddha set turning the wheel of the dharma or truth is revered to this day and known as the Deer Park in Varanasi. It is where he preached his first sermon. The ascetics he had associated with came to hear him preach. The Buddha told them that there was a middle path between the two extremes of self-indulgence and self-denial. The first followers to join him were called Bikkhus. An adherent who had gained enlightenment came to be known as an Arahant or 'one who knows'. The number of Arahants rose steadily and soon there were sixty such followers.

The Buddha taught his doctrine throughout what today is northern India for the next 40 years. When he died, he left behind many monasteries and monks and also Bikkhunis, or nuns, and nunneries. He did not nominate a successor but said that the dharma (his teachings and those aspects of reality and experience the teachings address) was all that was needed. His last piece of advice was "work out your salvation with diligence."

Buddhism over the next several centuries became fragmented and eventually 18 different schools emerged. King Ashoka (3rd Century BCE) was a major figure in helping to spread Buddhism beyond India to Sri Lanka. Ironically, Buddhism subsequently largely died out in India due to the absorption of Buddha into the Hindu pantheon and persistent persecutions by Hindu kings and by the invading Moghuls who became overlords.

India's Buddhists may have largely perished, but the practice and its path to Enlightenment had spread across the Himalayas - though not initially to Tibet. Via the Silk Road, Buddhism found its way to China in the first century CE. The Emperor Ming gave it imperial support. Buddhism enjoyed an elevated level of acceptance among the Chinese at this time as the mystical teachings of Taoism were on the ascendancy. The mixture of Taoism and Buddhism resulted in a new form of Buddhism called Chan. Then Dogen, a Japanese Buddhist monk (1200–1253 CE), went to China to study meditation. He took what he learned, Chan, back to Japan. There, he developed it into what became Zen Buddhism, which subsequently became established back across the sea in Korea and then in Vietnam.

The spread of Buddhism to Tibet took place in waves during the 7th to 10 centuries CE, culminating in reforms. These gave Tibet's Buddhism its emphasis on the role of the Guru or Lama in guiding the chela or pupil to enlightenment. The major sects had emerged by the 11th Century, the Dalai and the Panchan Lama sect engaged the active involvement of large proportions of the population and assumed temporal as well as spiritual authority over the people.

Tibetan Buddhism owes its remarkable recent uptake in the West to the trickle of knowledge about it that followed the invasion of Tibet by the Chinese in the 1950's. A mass exodus of Tibetan monks to India was followed by tours, visits and establishment of centres and schools in the West. Buddhists claim their faith is the fastest growing religion in the developed world.

Scriptures

For several centuries following the Buddha's death, Buddhism was essentially passed down in an oral tradition by monks memorising whole scriptures. No written records remain from the first 400 years. The earliest scriptures were translated into Pali in Sri Lanka in 29-28 BCE. This three-part work became known as the Pali Canon or Tripitaka. The sutras or discourses of the Buddha describe the practices required to yield results; the Vinayapitaka, describe rules for monks and nuns; and the Abhidhammapitaka has commentaries on the scriptures with a philosophical and psychological bent. These scriptures formed the basis of Theravadan Buddhism, also known as the Hinayana or 'Lesser Vehicle' school of Buddhism.

The Theravadans held fast to the ideas of monastic discipline and withdrawing from the world to practise spiritual discipline, scholarly attainment, and strict adherence to the scriptures of the Buddha. Others saw this as being inflexible and difficult for anyone besides a monk to come to terms with. A movement to bring Buddhism to the 'common people' began and soon gained popularity. This movement eventually lead to the development of Mayahana or the 'Great Vehicle' school of Buddhism with its own set of scriptures.

The Mayahana School differed from the Theravadans in having the ideal of the Bodhisattva monk. The main focus for a Mayahana monk was to develop a 'wisdom heart', volunteering to be reborn to help others rather than seek enlightenment for himself. The Bodhisattvas also took on celestial forms such as Avaolkiteshvara, representing the Buddhist aspect of compassion, or Manjushri manifesting the Buddhist expression of wisdom.

The Mahayana School translated the scriptures into Sanskrit and added other sutras, claimed to be the secret teachings of the Buddha. The Buddha was said not to have been ready to release these teachings in his lifetime so they were left to a time when people were ready for them: the Lotus Scripture, the Heart Sutra, the Diamond Scripture and the Perfection of Wisdom Scripture and others. There was also a healthy growth in works which commented on the Buddhist teachings. The time lapse between what the Buddha said and what was written down has been a recurring source of debate and dispute, leading to the many divisions within Buddhism that ensued.

Doctrine

The Buddha's approach to enlightenment was practical. He discouraged metaphysical discussions. He never discussed the existence of God or a creator. The Agganna Sutra, however, talks of a Buddhist creation legend. The first beings were luminous and full of spiritual joy until greed entered their minds and their luminosity dissipated.

According to Buddhist teachings all beings in our universe are caught in *samsara*, the cycle of birth and rebirth. All beings reincarnate and reappear in different forms. The human form is seen as most precious. Being caught in the cycle means suffering is inevitable as beings are "poisoned by the pig of ignorance, troubled by the snake of anger, and wracked by the cockerel of desire." The only way off the wheel of life for humans is to follow the Buddha's way and attain enlightenment.

The Buddha did not attribute to humans a separate self or soul that could be reincarnated. Instead he claimed it is a person's essence that is reincarnated.

This leads us directly on to the most pivotal teaching of the Buddha, that of *Annica*, the nature of impermanence. The Buddha maintained that there is no static or stable reality. All things are of a transitory nature, in a state of constant flux. To the Buddha, it was illusory to see the self as real and reality as stable.

In his 'middle way' teaching after his enlightenment, the Buddha advised that to find the path between the extremes of austerity and total selfishness we have to observe the Four Noble Truths. These are:

1. The first truth is that life is characterised by suffering or *Dukkha*.
2. The second truth says that the cause of this suffering is desire or cravings or *Tanha*. These cravings cannot be met because everything is subject to impermanence. As the Buddha said, "whatsoever is subject to the condition of origination is subject to the condition of cessation". The Buddha explains the arising of desire thus: cravings give rise to attachment, this gives rise to becoming and this leads to rebirth of a bundle of latent energies. Birth gives rise to old

age, sickness and death. So the wheel of life keeps turning and *dukkha* is recycled.

3. The third truth says there is a method which if followed removes the causes of rebirth.
4. The fourth truth says that in order to find a way out of suffering an eightfold path must be followed.

To tread this path, the main aspects of which are wisdom, morality and meditation, there are but eight requirements asked:

Panna: discernment, wisdom.

1. Right View or Right Understanding of the Buddha's teaching in theory and practice.
2. Right Thought, centred on being of service to others, not on being of service to our egos.

Sila: Virtue, morality.

3. Right Speech requiring that you do not use speech in harmful or unproductive ways. Tell the truth at all times.

Right Conduct

4. The *Panca Sila* or the five major Precepts followed by Lay Buddhists, are the guide to this:
   a) Refrain from taking life.
   b) Refrain from taking that which is not given.
   c) Refrain from misuse of the senses.
   d) Refrain from telling lies.
   e) Refrain from taking self-intoxicating drink or drugs.
5. Have a right livelihood and earn your living in a way which is not harmful to others.

Samadhi: Concentration, meditation.

6. Have Right Effort: promote good thoughts; conquer evil thoughts.
7. Right mindfulness or awareness. Become aware of your body, mind and feelings.
8. Right concentration. Meditate to achieve a higher state of consciousness.

Mindfulness and concentration developed through meditation are fundamental to Buddhist practice. Meditation can transform the mind. Buddhist meditation encourages and develops concentration, clarity, and a positive emotional disposition. Through practise of a particular meditation one learns the patterns and habits of the mind. Daily practice cultivates more positive ways of being. Calm and focused states can deepen into profoundly tranquil yet energized states of mind. Such influences can transform an individual's experience, bringing new perceptions, a new understanding of life.

The ultimate meditation in the Thervada School is called *Vipassana*. It focuses on awareness of the body. This is a powerful meditation, I am able to say, having practised it for ten years. I now practise Zazen, a form of Zen meditation that I find just as powerfully transforming. Through this meditation, the practitioner can develop insight and come to realize the Buddha's words "everything that arises passes away and is not the self". Other schools have other forms of meditation.

The ultimate goal of Buddhism is *Nirvana* or enlighten-ment when there is a release from desire (and consequent suffering) and thus from the continuous cycle of rebirths.

Obstacles to achieving the bliss of *Nirvana* are many. The Buddha taught that our intentional acts of body, speech and mind have consequences. Good deeds have pleasant consequences; bad deeds unpleasant. As 'heirs to our deeds' we must take full responsibility for them. Such moral cause-and-effect is referred to as *Kamma* or *Karma*. "If a person speaks or acts with an unwholesome mind, pain pursues him, even as the wheel follows the hoof of the ox that draws the cart." Again, "Avoid doing wicked actions, practise most perfect virtue, thoroughly subdue your mind." Accumulated *Karma* does not end in death but results in rebirth, which brings another chance to neutralize the effects of bad *Karma*. Bad *Karma* is the result of defilements or *Kilesa*, which hold a person to be reborn. These are; greed, hatred, delusion, conceit, doubt, restlessness, wrong view, a lack of moral shame for actions and a lack of moral dread.

The Mahayana northern school of Buddhism developed the idea of the Bodhisattva. This person is a would-be Buddha in the making who holds back from his final human birth to help others as an act of great compassion. The Bodhisattva tries to generate 'Bodhichitta' or the wisdom heart in order to help others. At the higher level there are bodhisattvas that rescue all beings. They are thought to reside in the celestial realms such as Avalokiteshvara, the Buddha of compassion, Amitabha, the Buddha of light, and Manjushri, the Buddha of wisdom.

Customs and Ceremonies

The monastic ideal became the basis for Buddhist practice. Monasteries were initially temporary dwellings where the monks would congregate in the rainy season when Buddha forbade monks to travel. As time progressed they became permanent residences and even nunneries were built.

Monks and nuns in Theravada Buddhism adopt 227 monastic rules covering every aspect of their lives. At the regular Uposatha ceremony these rules are recited.

In the more liberal *Hyana* Buddhism, monks go out into the community to provide care and support. Traditionally the laity, who seek 'merit' for the afterlife, support the monks by offering food on their daily alms round. At festivals such as *Wesak*, celebrating the birth, enlightenment and passing of the Buddha, the laity gives money to the monks. At the *Kathina* ceremony they provide robes.

At death most Buddhists have a short funeral service and the body is cremated.

Festivals

The Buddha advised his followers that to thrive they should 'meet together regularly and in large numbers'. Festivals provide an opportunity for celebration and the expression of devotion and gratitude to the Buddha and his teachings.

The Wesak Festival is the most universally celebrated festival in the Buddhist calendar. In the orthodox Theravada tradition it is a remembrance of the three most significant events in the Buddha's life, his birth, enlightenment and final passing, all of which took place on the full moon of *Vesakha*.

In Tibetan Buddhist schools the Buddha's birth, enlightenment and passing is celebrated in the fourth month. There is the pre-New Year *Gutor* Festival when all the negative accumulations of the old year are put to rest. *Losar* is the New Year Festival and a prayer festival follows this for three weeks. This culminates in the butter festival where offerings are made to the local deities. The Buddha's first sermon and his ascent into heaven are also celebrated.

Paranirvana Day is when people celebrate the death of the Buddha at the full moon in February. The day is used as an opportunity to reflect on the fact of one's own future death and on people one has known who have recently died. Meditations are focussed on the recently deceased to give them help and support on their journeys.

The *Magha* Festival is held toward the end of February or early March. This festival tells of a spontaneous gathering of 1,250 fully enlightened monks who were direct disciples of the Buddha. They had all quite independently decided to go and visit the Buddha and assembled on the full moon day of *Magha* in the Bamboo Grove at Rajagaha where the Buddha had been living. This has come to be known as 'Sangha day' and is a time when monks gather together to share their knowledge and experiences.

The *Asalha* Festival in July commemorates delivery by the Buddha of his first discourse containing the essence of all Buddhist teachings. This occasion established the order of monks and the new spiritual tradition of Buddhism, hence the celebration.

Ulambana or Ancestor Day is a festival celebrated in the liberal *Mahayana* tradition in August. It is believed that the gates of hell open in this period and the ghosts may visit for fifteen days. Food offerings are made during this time to relieve the sufferings of these ghosts. On the fifteenth day, *Ulambana* or Ancestor Day, people visit cemeteries to make offerings to the departed ancestors.

Green Buddhism

The Buddha himself lived very much in harmony with Nature and his example has encouraged thousands monks nuns and followers to respect life in all forms. His non-materialistic philosophy has encouraged Buddhists to keep their impact on the environment to a minimum. The signal Sigalovada sutra says we should act like a honeybee: take nectar but without harming the plant. We should use from Nature only what we can take without despoiling it.

There is a further dimension to Buddhism's Green spiritual tradition: its teachings about materialism and wealth. Wealth accumulation is seen as a barrier to spiritual progress. Thus Buddhism challenges the very fundamentals of our current economic system based as it is on identity and social status, consumption, material acquisition, ownership, wealth accumulation and encouragement of greed - and the planetary environmental degradation that ensues. In the words of His Holiness The Dalai Lama: "we are burning up ourselves and our world in our intense quest to satisfy unnecessary desires."

The Buddha respected Nature. He would not tolerate pollution.

(We return to this in the chapter on water.) To maintain tranquillity, the Buddha asked a group of monks who were being noisy to leave the monastery. The Buddha's life is the story of a human living at one with Nature. Trees are central to his story: he was born under a tree; he meditated under a jambo tree; and enlightenment came to him under a bodhi tree.

Such a benign attitude towards the environment comes from Buddhism's solid moral foundation with the individual's experience at its heart. In seeing all life forms as parts of the continuous cycle of incarnation and re-incarnation, Buddhism's perspective is truly holistic. Unlike some of the more prescriptive spiritual traditions there is an emphasis on personal responsibility arising from within rather than from rules imposed from without. The Dalai Lama sums this up by saying, "the key point is to have a genuine sense of universal responsibility based on love and compassion and clear awareness."

The awareness and responsibility called for by the Buddha come from learning and practising meditation, the cornerstone of Buddhist practice. The Buddha said, "There is no wisdom apart from meditation. Those in whom wisdom and meditation meet are not far from *Nirvana*".

Thich Nhat Hanh, a Buddhist monk from Vietnam, who has written many books explaining the Buddha's teachings using modern language, says: "Meditation is not an escape from life but a preparation for really being in life." Meditation helps the individual and the environment: it reduces egotism and endless desire, it deepens the appreciation of our surroundings, fosters awareness of the whole universe and it helps develop love and compassion for all beings.

Buddhism gives us the great teaching of *Karma*, of cause and effect. Nowhere is *Karma* better illustrated than in the dangerous consequences of the behaviours that give rise to climate change. But we will understand our part in its causes only by recognising this connection and accepting our responsibility for it.

Through our actions we create the world in which we live. We have the capability to free ourselves from delusion and greed, yet collectively we have created bad planetary *Karma* and put our future at risk.

The cultivation of *Metta* or loving kindness is a central meditation in the Theravada School of Buddhism. The Buddha said "Cultivate loving kindness, a wish for others to be happy. Extend this love to the world without bounds." For Buddhists, to cultivate loving kindness and compassion towards all beings is to develop wisdom.

It is said the Buddha told stories of his previous lives when he had been incarnated in animal forms. This explains why Buddhists are fastidiously compassionate about animals. Zen Buddhists believe firmly that all beings have Buddha nature in them. The Buddha taught the practice of *Ahimsa*, non-injury; butchers and fishmongers did not practise livelihoods conducive to enlightenment, he held.

Lastly, Buddhism has Green credentials through its teachings about the need to share resources fairly. Buddha set up monasteries as models of how to distribute basic material resources equally. He constantly emphasised in his teachings the danger of over-attachment to material things and the need to help the poor through sharing wealth. He encouraged the laity to support the monks.

In Dharamsala, India, I witnessed firsthand the frugality and absolute simplicity practised by the Tibetan monks at Tse Chok Ling monastery. I also stayed at Sera Monastery in Karnataka where there were over 5,000 monks. The monks spend day and night studying texts and debating them. With their modest consumption and minimal draw on material resources the impact on the immediate environment of the presence of so many souls remains minimal.

There are many examples around the world of Engaged Buddhism where Buddhists are active in environmental and social justice works. This has been greatly encouraged in the West by the writings of John Seed and Joanna Macy. The International Network of Engaged Buddhists, founded in 1987 by Ajarn Sulak Sivaraksa from Thailand, links together engaged Buddhists worldwide. Its work is supported by His Holiness the Dalai Lama and the Venerable Thich Nhat Hanh. INEB concerns itself with alternative education and spiritual training, gender issues, human rights, ecology, alternative concepts of development, and activism. It is particularly prominent in offering an alternative education to that based on consumerism.

In 2004 the Association of Buddhism for the Environment (ABE), was formed at a conference attended by about 100 monks from Cambodia, Thailand, Laos and Burma as well as 18 mainly environmental NGOs. It was held with the aim of creating a 'saffron' special interest group to defend green values. Having monks exchange experiences in these efforts was seen as valuable. This has given rise to a 'Monk Watch' with monks collecting information about illegal logging, land rights, abuse of forest land, wrongful action by government or forestry administrators and destruction of wildlife habitats. In their efforts to highlight pirate logging and protect trees from being felled, some activist monks have tied saffron robes around trees.

In Thailand today Ajhan Pongsa is a perfect example of Buddhist environmental principles being put into action. He is the Abbot of Wat Palad and since 1985 monks have planted 170,000 seedlings to counteract the effects of massive deforestation. He has encouraged local people to dedicate a day's labour a month to the project. Now a Dhammanaat Foundation has been formed by a group of monks with the purpose of protecting ecologically threatened sites. Ajhan Ponsa sums up his Buddhist approach to the environment thus: "Nature is the manifestation of truth and when we destroy Nature, we destroy the truth and the teachings." In 1998 in Cambodia Buddhist monks set up a forest protection initiative, Mlup Baitong or Greenshade. The organisation has grown to include public education, training and community projects as well as reforestation projects.

The Dalai Lama is active in applying ecological principles in a Buddhist context. He is encouraging a new project to convert 11,000 ha (27,000 acres) of agricultural land in India, farmed by Tibetans, from conventional to organic methods of production. In 2002 I personally witnessed Tibetan Buddhists working to protect the fragile mountainside environment by maintaining forests around Dharamsala in India. The Tibetan Government in Exile's Environment Department has been researching the environmental problems of Tibet caused by Chinese occupation and seeking to raise awareness of them in the West. I witnessed the only recycling scheme I found in all my travels in India. Tibetan Buddhists set this up.

At a conference held in 2009, attended by the 17th Karmapa, Ogyen Drodul Trinley Dorje Kal, extensive measures to protect the fragile environment of the Himalayas by all monasteries of the Kagyu order were agreed. In 2009 Mongolian Buddhists instituted an eight-year plan to conserve the deteriorating environment of Mongolia through such activities as monks educating local people about the effects of their actions on the local environment.

As we have seen, Buddhism has much to offer the Green movement. We can conclude with an observation on our present consumerist culture and its values from the great Buddhist teacher, Thich Nhat Hanh: "In the name of comfort and short-term convenience, the planet itself is consumed for the personal advantage of a relative few."

Buddhist websites

www.buddhanet.net
www.globalbuddhism.org
www.fwbo.org
www.buddhistthought.org
www.religioustolerance.org
www.buddhism.about.com
www.buddhaweb.org
www.dharmanet.org
www.answers.com
www.thebigview.com
www.accesstoinsight.org
www.aboutbuddhism.org
www.soyouwanna.com
www.thebuddhistsociety.org.uk
www.tibet.com
www.buddhismtoday.com
www.earthsangha.org
www.lotusinthemud.typepad.com
www.mro.org
www.sanghanetwork.org
www.sgi.org
www.religiousfacts.com
www.greenfuse.org
www.engagedbuddhists.org.uk

Chapter 6 : Jainism

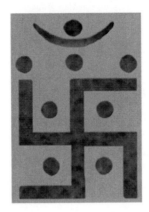

Introduction

Jainism has claims to be the world's oldest religion but it is little known in the West. Its origins in Northwest India date from pre-history as far back as the Stone Age. It has expanded, waned and revived again many times. There are references to Jainism at the time of the Buddha, about 2,500 years ago. There remain today some 4 million Jains in India and small numbers in Europe, USA and Canada whose families had formerly settled in East Africa.

Both Buddhism and Hinduism share similarities with Jainism. Like Buddhism, Jainism holds high humans who are believed to have achieved liberation from the bondage of human life, rather than deities. Jains - who call themselves Jaina -believe humans achieve happiness and spiritual progress through self-endeavour rather than by the intervention of a supreme being, though prehistoric myth stories, creatures and traditions do feature in their faith. Spiritual progress occurs within the framework of the laws of Nature.

History

Of its panoply of major figures, Jainism centres on twenty-four spiritual leaders called *tirthankaras*, from the idea that they form a *tirth* or a ford across the ocean of existence. The first *tirthankara* was Rishabh in the 9th century BCE, or even earlier. He is credited with introducing agriculture, writing and marriage; also with organising society into different classes or *varnas*. Two other *tirthankaras*, Arishtanemi and Ajitanatha feature also in the Hindu Vedas. The *tirthankaras* seem all to have been born into the noble, warrior class families. The last and most influential *tirthankara* was Mahavira, born to a noble family at Patna in Bihar in 599 BCE. He is credited with bringing about a revival of Jainism.

There are two main sects in Jainism, the Svetambaras (wearers of white cloths) and the Digambaras (the naked), though dress codes apply only to the highest order monks and not to other monks nor lay people. The Svetambaras say that Mahavira married a princess called Yosoda and had a daughter. Mahavira worked as an official until his parents died. At the age of 30, Mahavira took the vows of a Jain monk and renounced all his wealth, property, wife, family, relatives and pleasures. In a garden of the village Kundapura at the foot of an Ashoka tree, no one else being present, after fasting two days without water, he took off all his clothes, tore out the hair of his head in five handfuls and put a single cloth on his shoulder. He went naked and was attacked by demons, animals and people, but this did not distract him from his path. The Acaranga scripture describes his *panshaka* or twenty-two endurances and him visiting thirteen towns in the Ganges plain. At the age of 42, while sitting under a tree on the banks of the Rjukula River, Mahavira attained enlightenment. Even a cow and a lion are said to have sat with him in perfect peace. For his first sermon the gods created a *samavasarana* or pavilion with a sacred tree in the centre. The gods are said to have replicated Mahavira three times so that gods and animals as well as people could hear his sermons.

Mahavira's sect is mentioned in the Buddhist scriptures as the Nigrantha or 'the ones who have no ties'. In his lifetime he collected together eleven disciples or *gandhara*s, the most reputed of whom was called Gautam. Mahavira was rumoured to have special marks on his body and it is said he performed miracles such as feeding thousands by multiplying the food available.

Mahavira organized his order into four groups: monks, nuns, male householders and female householders. All those initiated had to take the five vows, which included the four vows of *Parshva* (non-violence, truthfulness, non-stealing and non-possession) plus chastity. At the age of 72 Mahavira gave his last sermon and died at Pava around 527. By contemporary accounts, he left 36,000 nuns, 318,000 female followers, 14,000 monks and 159,000 male followers.

After his death, as in all religious movements, differences arose. Around 360 BCE there was a famine in North India and most of the monks left leading thousands of locals to safety in the South. When, a decade later, the southern monks returned, they found the remaining northern monks had started to wear clothes. This began a split into what became the two sects, the Svetambaras who favoured clothes and the Digambaras who remained naked. Further differences between the two sects arose, the Svetambaras claimed that females as well as males could attain enlightenment and that a female called Malli had been a *tirthankara*. The Digambaras rejected these claims. The sects began producing separate scriptures and adopting distinctive practices. Today the Svetambaras comprise two thirds of all *Jaina* and reside in the North in Gujarat and Rajastan and are mainly merchants and business people. The Digambaras are grouped in the Southern Indian the state of Maharastra and are mainly farmers.

Scriptures

The scriptures of the Jains rest deep in antiquity. Many ancient texts have been lost or destroyed. The Digambara "Scripture of Six Parts," written in the 2nd century BCE, was concerned with the soul and its connection with *Karma*. The other important Digambara text is the 'Treatise on Passions'. The two together are called the Mudbidri texts after the town in southwest India where they are kept. Both texts are considered sacred and worshipped by Digambaras. Soma Deva was a Digambara monk who wrote the "Upasakadhyayana" in the 10th century CE. This work emphasised what duties were to be performed by a lay Jain and made a clear demarcation with Hindu practice by saying that only the *tirthankaras* should be worshipped, not cows, trees, the sun or fire. The main scripture of the Svetambaras is the Kalpa Sutra. This is still read in its entirety at the Pryushan festival, an eight-day event.

Doctrine

Jain cosmology is profound, deep and detailed. Time is eternal and based on the symbol of the spokes of a wheel divided into six ages. The first three ages are said to be golden, with humans six miles high, no old age, no disease and wish fulfilling trees. The first *tirthankara* arrived in the third age; the remaining 23 came in the fourth age. The fifth age is called Kali Yuga. Here, there is a sharp decline, with human lifespans becoming much shorter. By the sixth age - ours - the dharma, sense of duty, has died out altogether. The six-age cycle is continued endlessly for eternity.

Jaina believe that the Universe and everything in it is eternal. Nothing that exists now was ever created, nor will it be destroyed. There is nothing but infinity both in the past and in the future. The universe consists of three realms: the heavens, the earthly realm and the hells. There are seven levels of heaven. The top level, 'the Realm of the *Jinas*', is reserved for liberated souls. The next level down is the realm of the gods; then comes the earthly plane, with seven realms of hell below it.

Jaina believe that all aspects of reality have *jivas* or souls. There are animate entities such as living beings called *jeevs* and inanimate entities such as matter, energy, space and time called *ajeevs*. There are constant and complex interactions between the two *jiva* types. According to the Jain scriptures there are 8.4 million species of *jiva* and they all have some form of consciousness. In Jain thinking, a *jiva* is a soul attached to a body. Beings are also classified according to the number of senses they have: *Tras* beings can move at will but have no senses; *Vaklendriy* beings have two to four senses; and *Pancendriy* beings have five senses.

Each class of beings lives in a different realm of existence. Those that live in the heaven realms live in bliss and peace. Those that live in *Naraki* or hell realms are in perpetual darkness and suffer from great extremes of cold and heat for aeons of time. The human realm is the one of the plants and animals. There are however strange creatures born continuously from impure substances such as semen, urine or faeces; they are less than a finger's width in size and live for only 48 minutes. Humans are at the top of the hierarchy of living beings.

The Jain theory of *Karma* is different to that found in Hinduism and Buddhism: Jaina see *Karma* as ultra fine particles of matter found in the body of a worldly soul. The entire universe is filled with such *karmic* matter and covers every living being. The *karmic* particles become attached to the body through the activities of body, speech and mind, which are readily affected by the four passions of anger, pride, intrigue and greed. A person can prevent the accumulation of *karmic* matter by modifying and regulating their emotional states. When *karmic* matter attaches to the soul, *Karma* will obscure its essential nature and prevent it from attaining liberation.

The Jain concept of divinity is unique. Those rare humans that succeed in reducing to nil their *Karmas* achieve Infinite Knowledge, Infinite Perception, Infinite Power and Infinite Bliss or *moksha*. Liberated souls no longer interact with other beings, matter, space or time and so become gods or *Jina* and are beyond the sufferings of rebirth. In this divine cycle, or *cakra*, birth as a human is exceptional since Jina have no more than eight human lives in succession.

Jainism recommends that to cleanse the soul, followers should avoid worldly activities and adopt ascetic practices such as fasting and non-attachment instead. Powerful ascetic practices remove *Karma* from the soul. Acts of merit or good *Karma* can also offset sinful acts.

The doctrine of Jainism is based on rationalism rather mysticism. Practitioners of Jainism do not follow this path blindly but are expected to study the scriptures and observe their own experience and the workings of Nature to discover for themselves the need and effectiveness of spiritual practice. This rationalism is derived from constant awareness of Jainism's Three Jewels of Perception.

The first of these is *Samyak darshan,* Right Perception. Jainism advocates that one should first try to understand the nature of reality, one's own self, one's religious goal and the path. *Jaina* are taught about the many-sidedness of reality - *anekantavada*. Reality in its totality is beyond our grasp; no individual's own perspective on any issue contains the whole truth. Only an omniscient being would be able to comprehend reality completely. We humans are recommended, therefore, to admit our dependence on others (the concept of universal interdependence) and to accept and value the positive viewpoints of others.

To assist us achieve Right Perception, meditation is recommended. Meditation topics include the impurity of the human body, the transience of beings and the difficulties encountered when trying to accomplish liberation from *samsara*, the endless cycle of suffering.

Svetambara monks engage in some extreme practices. They try to change their perception of reality through following the *Avashyukas* or basic rules. These entail following a series of spiritual exercises such as the practice of *Samayik*, which requires 48 minutes - the exact lifetime of those entities created of impurities - of reciting sacred texts and excluding all worldly thoughts. They are also required to venerate the 24 *tirthankaras* by reciting their names as well as the name of their own *acharya* or spiritual teacher. They further practice *pratikraman*, the casting off and repenting of sins. This can take up to four hours daily. They also perform regular austerities such as fasting and *kansagy*, which involves holding the body in a motionless state for long periods in an attempt to overcome attachment.

The Second Jain Jewel is *Samtyak Jnaan*, Right Knowledge - attaining the correct, proper and relevant understanding of this reality.

The Third Jewel is *Samayika Charitra*, Right Conduct, the requirement to follow ethical codes, rules and disciplines. Mahavira said: "Conquer anger with peace, conquer pride with humility, conquer attachment with simplicity, conquer greed with contentment, feel friendliness to all living creatures."

Today in the West we recognise contentment and equanimity or calm are essential to true happiness. We also recognise how negative emotions can provoke cycles of violence, mental as well as the physical violence than generates much of our news. One of Jainism's contributions in this area is its code, the Five Great Vows (*Maha-vratas*), undertakings to always observe or adhere to:

- non-violence (*ahimsa*)
- truth-telling
- fairness in exchange and trade; no stealing
- purity of body and mind
- temperance in consumption; generously share any surpluses

Monks in the Svetambaras belong to certain spiritual lineages called *Gacchs*. The monks travel continuously throughout the year except during the four-month rainy season, when they might unknowingly harm insects. Monks travel as a group or *parivar*, helping each other follow the rules. They are usually led by an *archarya* or spiritual leader, whose spiritual authority is measured by the number of followers they have. I was privileged to meet Acharya Mahapragya in Gujurat where some 10,000 adherents were attending a celebration of Mahavira's birth, several thousand of them reputed to be followers of Mahapragya himself. At the event, I interviewed a monk who had been ordained 40 years. In a touchingly candid way, he confided to me he still found life as a monk was "very hard" due to the austere rules of conduct.

A *himsa*, the vow of non-violence, is translated into some surprising situations. Even when sleeping, monks are only allowed to lie on a piece of cardboard; and if they move in the night they have to do penance as they may harm insects. Then, when they get up, they are not allowed baths in case they harm insects. They always carry a brush so that when they have to sit down they can always first brush the floor carefully so no creatures are harmed. They even have to keep their mouth covered with a fine net to prevent inadvertent swallowing of insects. They are encouraged to talk little and when they do talk they do so slowly. When they walk they do so very carefully, not swinging their arms at all. Not only are they strictly vegetarian, they never eat root vegetables on account of the *jivas*.

Customs and Ceremonies of Jains

Worship by the laity in Jainism is focussed on the Jain temple, which during my travels in India I witnessed as beautiful, ornate buildings. The temples have a main hall and an inner shrine in which the images of the *tirthankaras* are kept. Anyone entering the temple is required to rinse out their mouth and not to wear leather. Those entering the inner sanctum are required to bathe first, wear special clothes and have their mouth covered by cloth. There is a further emphasis on absolute purity by the total exclusion of those women during menstruation or people grieving after a death in the family.

In Svetambara Jainism, the monks can be worshipped and asked for help at a special *guru puja* or audience. But central to worship of most *Jaina* is the *Namaskara* mantra. In uttering this mantra they are offering homage in turn to the full panoply of holy beings in Jainism. For *Jaina*, making this salutation destroys sin. It is so important to them they may repeat the chanting up to nine times a day.

There are ceremonies that centre on the images and idols of the *tirthankaras* in the inner temple. In the eightfold worship, adherents wash, place oil on and polish the idol, adorn it with flowers and make offerings, all the while uttering devotions and purifying mantras. Fasting is a regular practice of lay *Jaina*. There are six basic fastings, some of which allow drinking and others not. The rare extreme is *santhara* or *sallekhana*, a fast where permission is granted for them to ritually starve to death under the benign guidance of monks. This is reportedly the choice of a few hundred *Jaina* a year, still today, for a range of stated and unstated reasons - suffering from famine, terminal illness, to assuage a sin, old age and just wanting to leave.

Pilgrimages to holy Jain shrines are very much part of the Jain tradition, to Mount Parsvanatha and Mount Parvapunin in Bihar where 20 of the 24 *tirthankaras* achieved liberation. There are also hundreds of temples to visit at Mount Abu in Rajastan and the Givnar temple complex in Gujarat. A major Digambara shrine is the colossus of the Sravana Belgola figures in South India.

Festivals

Festivals also are an integral part of Jain life. The *Paryusava* festival I attended near Ghaninagar in Gujurat where 10,000 *Jaina* gathered in September 2002 takes place over a period of eight to ten days. It is characterised by talks from monks, ritual fasting and repentance and the communal expression of goodwill to all, through chants such as the one that translates as: "I ask pardon of all living creatures. May I have friendly relations with all beings." On the final day, festival goodwill overflows as everyone asks for forgiveness from relatives and friends for all wrong deeds committed in the last year. They see that the pigeons and other animals are fed; they pay for the slaughterhouse to be closed down for the day. Even businesses send out letters asking for a pardon for any sharp practices they may have been guilty of!

The *Mahavira Jayanti* festival in March and April celebrates Mahavira's birth. There are processions through the streets and the symbolic sharing of coconut. *Diwali*, a Hindu celebration is celebrated as a Jain festival as it is the time of Mahavira's enlightenment. This is the start of the New Year and businesses traditionally balance their books.

At the *Kartik Purnima* festival after the rainy season end in November, monks resume their wandering pilgrimages. On this day, the monks are walked out of town in a festive procession; a few people even accompany them to the next town or village.

Green Jainism

My research in India in 2002 revealed to me that Jainism is one of the most environmentally benign faiths on the Planet. Mahavira was Green because he lived in an ecological, sustainable way. He was concerned with social justice and equity as well. Jainism's tradition of non-violence and peace is probably the world's longest. The lifestyle of Jain monks and nuns is entirely non-materialistic. Because they may possess only what they can physically carry, they have a minimal impact on the environment. They act as models to the laity—and to us all - who are inspired by their example to value the temperate life.

Mahavira stated "One who neglects or disregards the existence of earth, air, fire, water and vegetation disregards his own existence which is entwined with them." Among the central tenets of Jainism, the Tatwarth Sutra affirms that all forms of life are mutually supportive. Clearly, *Jaina* see the biosphere as an integrated whole and they discipline themselves to act in accord with life and Nature.

In identifying materialistic accumulation in possessions and in wealth as bad *Karma* and a barrier to spiritual progress, the Jain code honours the environment, including all forms of life. In eschewing consumerism, *Jaina* avoid contributing to the growing pandemic of pollutants that are wreaking havoc with our Earth's ecosystems almost everywhere.

Greens also seek more equity in the world. Jain teachings promote equity, too: wealth creation must have a philanthropic goal rather than simply for individual economic betterment. Furthermore, generous charitable giving in monies and time for community projects is for *Jaina* an obligation.

It is their social responsiveness that has led the *Jaina* to found and maintain countless active institutions in their areas: schools, colleges, hospitals, clinics, lodging houses, hostels, orphanages and relief and rehabilitation camps for the handicapped, the aged, the sick and the disadvantaged, as well as hospitals for ailing birds and animals. Such a list replicated worldwide would end most of the social problems of our day.

Gandhi had a close Jain friend called Srimad Rajachandra from whom he gained insight into the Jain teaching of *ahimsa*. *Ahimsa* is a Green concept because it means the practise of non-violence in all situations; it applies equally to the environment and to all beings within it—including, for Gandhi, the police or army charged with clearing away activists or demonstrators.

Ahimsa is the reason why *Jaina* are required to be vegetarians. Vegetarianism is essential for minimizing physical as well as mental violence. Raising animals for food not only involves significant cruelty towards animals but, as we now know, it also consumes significantly higher natural resources than vegetarian food. Further, the rearing of livestock creates significant environmental pollution locally and as much as one fifth of global warming emissions as well. *Jaina* follow precise and strict dietary rules. Even vegetables are held in high esteem; they are seen as having a sense of hearing and of smell. So Jainism forbids the plucking and eating of the leaves of vegetables. All seeds are to be avoided until they are made into flour. Sugar, ghee, curd and milk are usually excluded from the diet. Limiting the number of ingredients put in the mouth at one time is recommended. Common stimulants such as the betel nut are forbidden as are cardamom and even root vegetables.

So, even from this brief look, we can see Jainism may be one of the world's oldest religions but its philosophy and practices are deeply Green.

Jain Websites

www.environment.harvard.edu/religion/Jainism
www.jainheritagecentres.com
www.jainism.org
www.arcworld.org
www.religioustolerance.org
www.beliefnet.com
www.atmadharma.com
www.san.beck.org
www.religionfacts.com
www.jainworld.com
www.jainsamaj.org
www.jcnc.org

CHAPTER 7 : SIKHISM

History

The Sikh religion places great importance on its historical roots. Its founder, Guru Nanak, was born in 1469 near Lahore in Punjab, India. Aged 16, he began work for a local Muslim leader.

Nanak exhibited mystical qualities early on. It is told that, aged 27, he went to bathe in the local river and was not seen for three days! He returned from what he said had been an enlightening experience of God and declared: "There is only the one universal timeless creator (God) who is at once the creator, sustainer and destroyer... There is neither Hindu nor Muslim."

Nanak claimed that in his conversation with God he was told that he had been given freedom from rebirth; he had attained *Saha Moksha*, the highest level of enlightenment for Hindus. He befriended a Muslim musician called Mardana and over the next 25 years the pair went on five long journeys to teach. Their message was one of humility, love, unity, selfless service and universal truth. He studied Hinduism, Jainism and Buddhism as well as Islam. He returned to the Punjab in 1520 and lived as a peasant farmer at the head of a small spiritual community.

When he died there was disputation as to whether to burn or bury him, meanwhile his body disappeared.

As leader, Guru Nanak was succeeded by his named successor, Guru Angad (1504-1552), who continued the tradition of emphasising the spiritual life of a householder. He made a living twisting grass to make cots. Angad began collating the writings of Guru Nanak. He initiated regular meetings of Nanak's followers in *sangats* or holy congregations. They came to be known as Sikhs. Angad began the Sikh tradition of serving food after meetings. The food was prepared in a *langar* or community kitchen and shared by the congregation.

Angad was succeeded by the third guru, Guru Amer Das, (1479-1574) a convert from Hinduism at the age of 72. He encouraged annual gatherings of Sikhs at Goindwal (Amritsar, Punjab, India) where he lived. This led to its being established as the centre of Sikh authority and learning. Here he created a large bathing area where people could cleanse themselves while reciting the Holy Scriptures.

Amer Das also raised the significance of the *langar*, the communal kitchen. The Guru refused to parlay with anyone until they had eaten with others in the *langar*, including the Muslim Mughal Emperor, Akbar.

As well as collecting together the first Sikh scriptures, Amer Das sought to elevate the status of women. He decried the Hindu practice of *sati* - where widows committed suicide on their husband's funeral pyre - and the Muslim practice of *purdah*, where women had to cover their faces. He lived to be 95.

His son, Guru Ram Das (1574-1581), who succeeded him as fourth guru founded Amritsar where the Golden Temple was soon started, wrote additions to the Sikh scriptures and introduced music into Sikh worship. He emphasised the importance for Sikhs of performing service or *sewa* to mankind.

His son, Arjan Dev (1563-1606), who succeeded as the fifth guru, was the first Guru to be born a Sikh. He constructed a 'Hari Mandar' (house of God) shrine at the Golden Temple Complex in Amritsar and installed the *Adi Granth* or Sikh scripture there. He encouraged Sikhs to give 10 per cent of their income to a common fund to help the less fortunate.

There followed, with the Moghul invasion of the Punjab, a difficult time for Sikhs and Sikhism: Jehangir, the Muslim Emperor, captured Arjan Dev and demanded that he convert to Islam. Despite brutal torture, he refused. Guru Dev became the first Sikh martyr.

By the time the sixth guru, Guru Har Govind (1595-1644), was installed, the Moghuls had become a still greater threat. He became the first militarised leader, asking every Sikh to get a sword and raise a horse. He himself had two swords, one symbolised his spiritual authority and the other his temporal authority. He fought six battles with the Moghuls but eventually had to retreat to the hills to avoid being overrun. He built the Akal Takt (throne of the infinite) building in front of the Golden Temple in Amritsar.

The seventh guru, Hari Rai,(1630-1661) spent most of his time at Kiratpur where he promoted the teachings of the previous gurus. He sent disciples to east and west India to spread Sikhism. Hari Krishnan (1656-1664) was the 8th guru and son of Hari Rai and was given his guruship at the age of five. He died at the age of eight from smallpox after trying to heal Sikhs in Delhi suffering from an outbreak of the disease.

Guru Teg Bahadar (1621-1675) was selected as the ninth guru on account of his contemplative and meditative manner, as a resolution to a dispute over the rightful succession. He travelled widely propagating the message of Sikhism in west India. In 1675 he went to Delhi to plead for religious freedom on behalf of Hindus who were being forced to convert to Islam by the Moghul emperor Aurangzeb. The emperor demanded the guru convert to Islam and when he refused this request Guru Teg Bahadar was executed.

Guru Govind Singh (1666-1708) was born in east India and became guru at the age of nine. Sikhism was under repeated attack throughout his life. Though he excelled as a military leader against the Moghuls and local allies, he and his followers enjoyed little peace. He lost two of his sons to the Moghuls.

Govind is famous in Sikhism for the the *Khalsa* rite which he created on the 13th April 1699. During a dramatic ceremony on this day in 1699, he asked five Sikhs to come to his tent and asked them if they were prepared to lay down their lives for him. Turn by turn, five devotees from different caste (social) backgrounds came forth and vowed to lay down their lives to uphold the ideals of the *Khalsa* or community of 'Saint Soldiers'. The five became the first band of dedicated loyal Sikhs and were called the *Khalsa*. They were encouraged to live a life of high morals and develop military skills to fight oppression, tyrannical rule and injustice.

It was Govind Singh who insisted on having a *langar*, the Sikh communal kitchen in every *gurdwara* or Sikh temple. Meals (vegetarian) were offered to all including non-Sikhs also and prayers were said at every meal.

Govind Singh eventually died from an injury inflicted on him some considerable time earlier by a Moghul spy. Just before he died, he declared he was the last physical Guru of the Sikhs and that the message of Sikh teachings would be enshrined in *Adi Granth*, the Holy Scriptures which would from then on be known as the Guru Granth Sahib, the text to refer to for advice on the spiritual life.

The struggle with the Moguls continued long after Govind Singh's death. They sacked the Golden Temple in 1742 and again in 1757. It was Maharaja Ranjit Singh, who ruled 1799-1839, who defeated the Moguls and who created, then expanded the kingdom of Punjab into Afganistan and Kashmir. Sadly, independence did not last long. The Punjab was annexed into British India in 1849.

By 1909 the Colonial Indian Government was forced to recognise Sikhs as a separate national and religious community. In 1925 the Gurdwara Act enshrined in law the separate Sikh identity and the British Colonial government was compelled to hand over the administration of their *gurdwaras* to Sikhs.

In 1947 the Sikhs suffered a double blow: in Partition (the creation of separate Muslim and majority Hindu states following India's achieving independence from the UK) the Punjab, their homeland, was divided in two; in the chaos that ensued, *hundreds of thousands* of Sikhs on the Pakistan side of the border were massacred, a trauma with later echoes and repercussions.

Sikhs have suffered recurring injustices at the hands of successive Union governments in Delhi. The re-boundarying of Punjab State in 1966 exceptionally did give Punjabi speaking Sikhs more of a say in their state legislature. However, with every move at redressing imbalances between the local Muslim majority and the large Hindu minority, Sikhs lost out, creating a resentment that manifested in support for Sikh separatism. One movement called for the creation of the independent Sikh homeland, Khalistan. This was seen in Delhi as a threat and military moves to thwart it were put in train. Events reached a climax in June 1984 when the Indian state launched a military operation against a small number of committed Sikh separatists (labelled 'extremists' by Delhi) whose vigil in the Sikh's supreme Golden Temple complex was intended to draw attention to the growing demand for independence. Such an attack on a sacred site would have been bad enough, but it came on the major annual holy day with uncounted thousands of Sikh families visiting the Temple. Along with the separatists, many hundreds of pilgrims of all ages were killed within the temple complex. No number has ever been agreed by Sikhs or government.

Then, in November 1984, in revenge for Sikh deaths at the Golden Temple, Prime Minister Indira Gandhi was assassinated by two Sikh bodyguards. This in turn sparked off an orchestrated retaliation by Hindus in Delhi. About 3,000 Sikhs were killed and 50,000 made homeless. Some have estimated that 25,000 Sikhs died between 1983 and 1993 in connection with the movement for a separate Sikh state. Since 1993 a growing number of Sikhs have been peacefully campaigning to have the Punjab made an autonomous region within the state of India.

Scriptures

The scriptures of Sikhism emerged against the background of the dissenting traditions of the Hindu *Bhakti* (loving devotion) movement and Sufi Muslim *Bhagats* or saints during the first half of the 2nd millennium. The Sikh scriptures' rich mix of the writings of the Sikh Gurus and the *Bhagats* constitute some of the most poetic and beautiful spiritual writings in the world. Offering deep philosophical insights into the physical and metaphysical realms, they present an inspiring vision of the order of the cosmos and an exhortation to aspire to a higher life. The Adi Granth is an anthology of spiritual literature compiled by Arjan, the fifth Guru, in 1604. Unusually, though in the Sufi tradition, it includes the wise sayings of 36 holy men from disparate religious traditions. And after being renamed the Guru Granth Sahib, the 1,430-page Adi Granth became - and remains - the source of divine guidance for all Sikhs

Doctrine

Sikhism's founder, Guru Nanak, was exposed to many religious traditions but rejected all in favour of a unified, universalistic ideology. While they fascinated him, he was ultimately disappointed in the way many faiths had been reduced to ritualistic practice and egotism. When he re-appeared after his first experience of enlightenment he said, "there is no Hindu, there is no Mussalman (Muslim) – there is but only one universal truth which I recognise."

Guru Nanak found the ritualistic practices of Hinduism escapist, ascetic and abhorrent. Instead, he saw family life and the spirituality of the householder as having prime importance. A person's moral life acted as the sole barometer of his or her spiritual progress. All humans have equal status in the eyes of God. He rejected the caste and gender divisions promoted and maintained by the dominant Hindu Brahmin tradition. Nanak's commitment to egalitarianism can be most clearly seen in the *langar*, the communal kitchen where Sikhs and non-Sikhs, king or beggar, guru or disciple are–still to this day - invited to dine all together as equals, as one family, even. Yet while Sikhs still welcome all comers in their *langars*, paradoxically, Nanak had no time for begging.

Sikhism is monotheistic, strongly emphasizing belief in one true God. This God is unborn, omnipotent, infinite, formless, all-knowing and all-pervading.

Guru Nanak said God cannot be defined but is an ocean of attributes. He described him as "infinite, unapproachable and imperceptible". God is "the substance of all bliss and those who worship him are ever in a state of bliss". The experience of realising God through consciously recalling his name is called *moksha sahaj*.

Despite Nanak's break with Hinduism, Sikhism retains certain of its beliefs: belief in the forces of good and evil in the world; that the human soul is in essence divine and inherently good; that the fate of a person is determined by their *Karma*.

However, Sikhs reject fatalism and firmly believe in existential free will. So while seeing reality governed by the laws of Nature and cause and effect or *Karma*, Sikh teachings emphasise self-reflection and awareness of ego's role in the creation of suffering.

Sikhs, rather than renouncing the *maya* or the material world as do Hindus, must engage with and navigate through the material world. God is not found on a mountain top but resides in the hearts of all living beings. To serve God's creation is to serve God and selfless service is the only way to remove suffering. This is the means by which one can defeat the ego, which is the source of all suffering in this world.

Sikhs' hope is that they progress over time towards 'absorption', where they leave the body and their soul blends with the essence of God and experiences 'the true reality', regarded as perfect bliss by Sikhs.

The Sikhs like Hindus believe in an individual eternal soul which can never be destroyed as it is "neither born nor does it die." Upon death, the soul transmigrates from one body to another according to the *Karma* accrued from previous lives. Sikhs believe that birth as a human is rare for a soul. Bad *Karma* can result in a descent from human to animal form, a belief shared with Hinduism.

Customs, ceremonies and worship

The homely *langar*, the communal kitchen of every *gurdwara* (temple) encapsulates the wisdom of the founder. Gone are the escapist, ritualistic and ascetic practices of Hinduism Nanak found so abhorrent.

The Guru Granth Sahib text has the pride of place and honour in the *gurdwara*. While in its presence, Sikhs must remove their shoes and cover their heads as a mark of respect. The Guru Granth Sahib is read by the *granthi*, a community member with a deep understanding of the book. He leads the worship but has no special status. The Guru Granth Sahib certainly has, however: during services it is placed on a pedestal of pillows, is opened and closed ceremoniously and it is transported with the utmost care and ceremony. I have witnessed the ceremony of placing the holy book in its special room at the end of the day's worship at the Golden Temple in Amritsar and it is truly moving.

Sikh services consist of singing *kirtan* or hymns and may last up to five hours. All services end with the *ardas* or special prayer. This prayer recalls the ten gurus and appeals to God to help those in trouble.

A Sikh is also asked to rise daily between 3 and 6 a.m., bathe and then intone the *mool* mantra:

> There is one God,
> He is supreme truth,
> He is the creator,
> Is without fear and without hate,
> He is omnipresent,
> Pervades the universe,
> He is not born,
> Nor does he die to be born again.

Daily prayers, the *Nitnem*, include a series of five special hymns and special prayers at sunset and in the late evening.

To mark a birth, the *mool* mantra is chanted in front of the newborn so they may hear wisdom at an early age. At the naming ceremony in the *gurdwara*, the parents present a *rumala*, a special cloth used to cover the holy book.

At the Amrit ceremony, which venerates the initiation by guru Govind Singh of the first five men into the *Khalsa*, a sword is dipped in sweet water and the participants reiterate the five freedoms: from previous religious practices, from past deeds, caste, status and from prejudices. Both males and females can participate in the ceremony. Male Sikhs thereafter adopt the name Singh, or lion. Females adopt the name Kaur or princess. Males make a lifelong commitment to the five K's: hair uncut (hence the turbans); wear a special comb, special breeches and a special bangle on the wrist; and last, to carry a small sword.

Before a marriage, the bride and bridegroom's families exchange gifts. The wedding ceremony itself includes the couple walking around the Guru Granth Sahib four times.

At death the body is wrapped in a white sheet, deceased males decorated with the five Ks. The body is cremated the same day, the ashes scattered in a river. The *Sohila* funeral prayer reminds mourners not to fear death as it is no different from sleep. The family completes the rites, either in the home or in the *gurdwara*, with a daily reading of the entire Holy Granth. It it takes about ten days. Only when all 1,430 pages have been read is the final service held.

Festivals

Of Sikh festivals, *Gurupurbs,* celebrating the lives of the gurus, the most important are two births and two martyrdoms: Guru Nanak and Guru Govind Singh's births and the Martyrdom of Guru Arjan and Guru Teg Bhadur at the hands of the Moguls. Both gave their lives in support of religious tolerance and freedom.

The Vaisakhi Festival marks the lunar New Year, but is important to Sikhs who commemorate the day on 13 April 1699 when Guru Govind Singh gave the Sikhs a new name (Singh) and a new identity as a nation with their distinctive physical appearance and personal behaviour.

Sikhs celebrate Diwali the festival of light, as do Hindus, though for Sikhs it celebrates the occasion in the early 1600's when the 6th Guru Har Govind was freed along with 52 devotees from the Gwalior Fort, having been held prisoner there by the Mogul authorities.

Sikhs celebrate Hola, a *mela* celebrated in Anandpur on the Indian festival day of Holi, but do so in memory of Guru Govind Singh and the many battles he fought against the Moguls. The Guru instituted this day for military exercises, followed by music and poetry contests. The holiday is celebrated with mock battles, displays of horsemanship, swordsmanship and processions with the Sikh flag and the Guru Granth Sahib.

Green Sikhism

To Sikhs existence of Spirit is compatible with existence of matter. Guru Nanak declared that Spirit is the only reality and matter is a form of Spirit, taking on many forms depending on conditions. For Sikhs a concern for the environment is part of an integrated approach to life and Nature. As all creation has the same origin and end, it is important that humans grow to become conscious of their place within creation and their relationship with the rest of creation. Wise humans conduct themselves through life with love, compassion and justice. Only by endeavouring to live in harmony with all of God's creation can we become one with God and be in harmony with Him.

The inspiration of Nature can be found in the gurus' teachings. Guru Nanak saw Nature as a manifestation of the divine that must be respected: God is "seated in Nature, and watches with delight what he creates". A benevolent God provides Nature for the sustenance of man. The inference is that man must take care of Nature and not destroy it or seek to control it.

Sikhism emphasises the importance of respect for the elements. "Air is guru, water the Father, Earth the Mighty Mother of all." Early Sikh rural communities were very respectful of the Earth and did not pollute - unlike the rampant pesticide pollution of watercourses found in the heavily farmed Punjab today.

Unfortunately, the Indian Punjab today has been largely stripped of its forest cover. Native species are in sharp decline. Now, in an initiative in celebration of the 300th anniversary of the founding by Guru Govind Singh of the Khalsa Panth (the Sikh path) in 1699, Sikhs are engaged in restoration of Nature and are establishing a wildlife Nature reserve near Chandigarh, where Indian deer and lions along with other native species are to be protected.

The traditional Sikh way of life is ecologically benign, its non-materialistic ethic is clear. Ideally, meditation and remembering the name of God take priority over making money.

With its strong sense of social justice, Sikhism adds Green credential. Sikhs are implored to raise their voices against social injustice, especially the tyranny of their rulers, the corruption of bureaucracy and caste prejudices and rivalries. Sikhs exposed the Hindu priestly class for its greed and hypocrisy and pushed for social reforms, particularly ones aimed at abolishing injustices and cruelty such as the fate of the *Dalit*, infanticide and *sati*, where widows burned to death in their husbands' funeral pyres.

Women's rights, anti-poverty drives

Equality for women has been a Sikh ideal from the founder's time. He insisted that spirituality was equally for women as for men. In the late 19th century, Sikhs initiated colleges and schools for women, part of the drive to improve education among Sikhs overall.

Sikhism advocates helping the poor and unfortunate. Sikhs are traditionally required to allocate 10% of their income to good causes. In India I saw a shining example of Sikh *sewa* when I visited the Pingalwara (respite) community in Amritsar, supported entirely by charitable donations. Today it cares for the needs of 70 mentally ill, mentally or physically handicapped or orphaned members. A printing press they operate prints free literature on environmental problems.

The gurus' Green credentials are evident in the way the many towns and cities they founded were created around a *gurdwara*, with a lifestyle based on community and sharing. This promoted equity among people and optimum utilization of resources. *Gurdwaras* have for centuries exemplified Green principles, the larger ones having always maintained water tanks to collect and share water as a community resource. They also have land set aside for growing trees and plants to provide a habitat for Nature to thrive and to produce fuelwood sustainably. And *gurdwaras* show the true Green community spirit as community centres offering medication, education and accommodation and sustenance for travellers.

The gurus themselves were Green activists. Recognising the hazards posed by water contamination in the Beas River, Guru (1552-74) Amar Das constructed a well at Goindwal to provide clean water. He planted trees nearby for shade. Arjan Dev, fifth guru (1581-1606) had a well dug in Cheharta village in Amritsar when the villagers were suffering from drought.

The seventh guru, Hari Rai (1630-1661), ran a herbal treatment centre in Kiratput Sahib. He developed the town into one of parks and gardens. He planted flowers and fruit-bearing trees over the entire area to sustain wildlife. Today there is an effort by local Sikhs to re-establish the plantations.

The Sikh community in India today still offers meals to about 30 million people a day in total. For example, the five great *gurdwaras* of Delhi feed more than 10,000 needy people daily. As well as delivering *sewa* (being of service) Sikhs today are very conscious of the energy they use in cooking and its contribution to global climate change.

The first steps, in an initiative to reduce fossil fuels used in 28,000 *gurdwaras*, involve Delhi's eight largest *gurdwaras* where a part of the fossil fuels used for heating, lighting and cooking will be substituted by the use of solar energy. Later, *gurdwaras* in rural areas will be fitted with fuel-efficient cooking equipment, reducing energy consumption in these *gurdwaras* by up to 15 per cent.

The Punjab today is suffering environmental blight: water tables are plummeting and pesticides are poisoning people. Now the Sikh Defenders of the Environment and Ecology of Punjab (DEEP) based in the UK is trying to raise awareness within the Sikh Diaspora of the Punjab's crises. They also promote sustainable living to Sikhs in the UK by installing solar panels, developing rainwater harvesting and adopting green building methods.

Lastly, Sikhs abroad have planted a wood: Khalsa Wood was created in 1999 by 600 members of the Sikh community in the UK to celebrate the 300th anniversary of Vaishakhi. The wood is located within Bestwood country park, Nottingham.

Compared to other spiritual traditions, Sikhism may be considered a 'young' religion but it has much to offer us in how to build both community service and care for our Planet into our everyday lives.

Sikh websites

www.sikhseek.com
www.sikhfaces.com
www.realsikhism.com
www.sikhs.org
www.khalsa.com
www.sikh.net.com
www.sikhspectrum.com
www.sikhnetwork.org
www.religioustolerance.org
www.beliefnet.com
www.allaboutsikhs.com
www.religionfacts.com
www.sgpc.net
www.info-sikh.com
www.sikhiwiki.org

CHAPTER 8 : TAOISM

Introduction

Westerners might be forgiven if they have not heard of Taoism by name (it's pronounced 'Dowism'), but unknowingly they will have encountered some of its concepts and practices: the yin and yang symbol, acupuncture, Tai Chi and Qi Gong now permeate Western life. The 'natural order of things' is a concept fundamental to Taoist understanding.

Taoism left an unmistakable imprint on the Orient, especially on China, its land of origin, where it influenced history and culture and left a legacy of profound wisdom. Taoists view the universe as an interconnected, organic whole where nothing exists separately from anything else.

The Taoist universe is governed by a set of natural and unalterable laws, which manifest themselves as a flow of continuous change. This natural order and flow is referred to as the Tao, or the Way. By recognizing and aligning ourselves with these laws, we can attain a state of being which combines the experience of total freedom with one of complete connectedness to life's processes -being at one with the Tao.

Today, Taoism has some 20 million followers, mainly in Taiwan.

There are about 30,000 Taoists in North America and it enjoys a rising following in the People's Republic.

History

The founder of Taoism was Lao Tzu, a mystical and enigmatic figure who lived in the province of Hunan in China about 600 BCE. His real name was Li Erth or Lao Tom and he was employed as an archivist at the court of the King of Chou. His thoughts were dictated to a frontier guard before he retired to the mountains and compiled them in a book called the Tao Te Ching, the basis of Taoism.

In the 4th century BCE, with the publication of a treatise on internal medicine called the 'Yellow Emperor', Taoism became associated with longevity and the achievement of immortality. Later, in the 2nd century BCE, a formalism was added to Taoism's practical emphasis: gods, goddesses, rituals and magic spells were introduced in 142 by Zhang Das-Ling with a movement called the Way of the Celestial Masters.

Zhang developed the Taoist church and introduced the role of the libationer, who became an intermediary between the parishioners and the spirit world, by making decisions about which specific gods and spirits were useful to particular individuals. Zhang was so influential that he established a state in what is now Shaanxi province and governed it on Taoist principles. This entailed the banning of alcohol, the rehabilitation of animals and the stockpiling of food for the poor.

In the period 960-1279 CE, under the Song Dynasty, Taoism became the official religion of China. This was the time when the Taoist pantheon was developed including immortals and gods such as the Jade Emperor, Yellow Emperor and Lao Tzu, the author of the Tao Te Ching.

By now Taoism had developed two main schools. The northern school was concerned with monastic ideals and withdrawing from the world to develop asceticism. The southern school concentrated on practices to achieve immortality.

When the Imperial religion switched to Buddhism in the period 1279-1368 CE, Taoists became persecuted and never again enjoyed widespread popularity. From 1949 communists in China actively persecuted Taoists until 1979 when it was tolerated under a reformed constitution, by which time its focus had shifted to Taiwan where Taoism remains an active religion.

Scriptures

Li Erth compiled the Tao Te Ching around 600 BCE. It is, after the Christian Bible, the second most translated work in the world. It can be used as a guide to the cultivation of the self as well as a political manual for social transformation at both the community and nation state levels. The Tao Te Ching provides the basis of the doctrine of Taoism. There were various rewrites of a Taoist canon based on the Tao Te Ching. A third and final version was produced in 1016 CE.

'Five Talismans of the Sacred Spirit,' an important work on Taoism, formed the basis of the later Taoist scriptures which were finalised in the 12th century. It contains detailed guidance on achieving longevity through ritual canons, spells and meditation.

Doctrine

Taoism at its core is the understanding of the Tao. Taoists believe that the world that we experience is the manifestation of the unmanifest Tao. It is here that the dualism, logic and (pre-quantum) science of the Western trained mind stumbles into an abyss: words cannot actually define what the Tao actually is. In general terms we can say that the Tao is a path or way of doing things. It is a primordial cause from which the entire universe derives. It is formless, imperceptible, indescribable, devoid of all that exists, non-being and pure Spirit. Taoists believe the Tao to be the cosmic, mysterious and ultimate principle underlying form, substance, being and change.

Taoism's central principle is that all life, all manifestation, is part of an inseparable whole, an interconnected organic unity that arises from a deep, mysterious and essentially unexplainable source, which is the Tao itself.

Taoism views the universe and all of its manifestations as operating according to a set of unchanging, natural laws. As an inseparable part of the Tao, human beings can gain knowledge of these laws and become attuned to them. It is these natural laws that constitute the core principles of Taoism. Aligning ourselves with these principles provides a universal perspective and understanding and allows life to be lived in harmony with the Tao. Our true self is an expression of the Tao, because it is intrinsically connected with the power of the universe. Here are some descriptions of the Tao from the Tao Te Ching.

The greatest wisdom is to follow the Tao.
The Way is one of joyfulness and open hearted acceptance of
life, which regards the Universe as basically good.
Nothing can produce Tao, yet everything has Tao within it.
We achieve the joy of the Tao by returning to our original
nature.
To live in harmony is to follow the Tao.

This is certainly an enigmatic teaching which needs interpretation by another essential ingredient in Taoism, the sage. The sage, according to Taoist teachings, is the Chen Jen, a person of pure potency who accomplishes things without having to act. Generally he realises the Tao within himself through unity, simplicity and emptiness. He is not seen as a man of intellect; he instructs us to "banish knowledge and live a carefree life". The sage works with his heart and his instincts. He is beyond life and death and accepts things as they are and "follows the nature of things" (Chuang Tzu). He "takes things as they come and is not overwhelmed" (Chunag Tzu). He can express Tzu Jan or show the ability to express his thoughts and feelings in a spontaneous way. He shows great virtue because "virtue is the realisation of the Tao". He shows compassion because "the Tao forever favours the compassionate and wise". He expresses peace because he can "follow the Tao and cultivate its ways and be at peace". All in all he displays our original nature because he can "return to the root from which we grew". The sage expresses the three jewels, or characteristics, that all Taoists should live by: compassion, moderation and humility.

Compassion ultimately leads to courage, moderation leads to generosity and humility leads to leadership. All three are necessary to return to the Tao.

The Sage dwells in Wu Yu or the void. He practises emptiness and advises, "in one word, be empty". Taoists demonstrate the central importance of emptiness using the illustration of a wheel. At the hub where all the spokes meet there is nothing. The sage says "identify yourself with the infinite, make excursions into the void".

The sage dwells in the void. He acts only when necessary and when he does, it is only in accordance with the Tao. These actions are described in Taoism as Wu Wei or 'actionless activity'. Really, the idea is to go with the flow around you and not struggle against the tide. By adhering to the principle of Wu Wei, a person is thought to be closely following the Way, to have returned to his or her original nature.

Lao Tzu believed that living by Wu Wei would lead to a society of peace and harmony. As the Tao Te Ching says. "Tao does nothing but nothing is left undone". Actions are Wu Wei because their motivation is free of desire, attachment or sensual gratification. Effortless action may be illustrated by the conduct of water, which unresistingly accepts the lowest level yet wears away even the hardest rock.

The sage sees the world around him as exhibiting Usiang-Sheng or mutual arising. Events are interdependent, nothing happens in isolation but in relation to something else. To the sage seeing Li, the natural organic order, the totality of the cosmos, reality is a perfect system: "Nature goes on without consulting books"; all things will harmonise if left alone. The sage does not see the Universe working in a mechanical way, but as a series of patterns such as trees, clouds and water.

The Taoist concept most present in contemporary Western popular culture is that of Yin and Yang. Yin and Yang symbolise the primordial state, the belief that the universe arises as opposites such as light and dark, coming and going, opening and closing, being and non-being. There is nothing which does not contain the germ of its opposite. Yin is dark, female, cold, solid, wet and the primordial darkness. Yang is light, male, fiery, strong, active, ethereal, dry and hard.

The tension between the two forces is held in harmony by the mutual play of creation. The dynamic energy between Yin and Yang releases energy or Chi that permeates all life. The Sage's skill is to act without disturbing the balance that keeps the two powers in harmony. As the Tao Te Ching says, "knowing the male but keeping the female, one becomes a universal stream". The sage builds up his power or Chi but only through living skilfully, since Chi eludes all but those who "do not seek power and who do not use force".

Beyond the flux of Yin and Yang lies the great ultimate or Wu Chi, an enlightened state, shown as an empty circle.

Taoists do not hold the position of good against evil; rather they see the interdependence of all dualities. In Taoism there is no concept of sin. Punishment for wrongdoing falls naturally on the perpetrator as they violate the harmony of the universe. Not living in accordance with the Tao is simply seen as ignorance.

Taoists see desire as a major obstacle to living in the Tao. "Seek simplicity and grasp the essential, overcome selfishness and wasteful desires", the Tao Te Ching explains. "Great conflict arises from wanting too much." The antidote to desire is simplicity and frugality, the hallmarks of the life of the sage. This is the essential message of Taoism.

In terms of cosmology Taoism sees the universe in terms of a triad. Heaven represents the spirit or essence, Earth represents substance and mankind is a synthesis of Earth and Heaven. Therefore mankind has Heaven and Earth in its Nature and thus can demonstrate the Tao in action.

Taoism is a polytheistic religion. Each of the gods is believed to be a manifestation of some aspect of the Tao. As the Taoist pantheon developed, it came to mirror the imperial bureaucracy in Heaven and Hell–and in its complexity!

The head of the heavenly bureaucracy was the Jade Emperor or Yu-huang, who governed spirits assigned to oversee the workings of the natural world and the administration of moral justice. Although Yu-huang is the High God, there are other abstract deities above him. He rules; they simply exist and instruct. First and foremost is Yuan-shih T'ien-tsun - the First Principal. He has no beginning and no end. He existed "before the void and the silence, before primordial chaos." He is self-existing, changeless, limitless and invisible, contains all virtues, is present in all places and is the source of all truth.

In the spirit realms there are immortals. These are people who have reached a state where they are able to enter Heaven. It was said that often a Taoist master would die and when they looked in his coffin there would only be a sword or a bamboo cane - 'proof' that they had gone to Heaven.

In Taoism there are also etheric beings on Earth such as Tsao-Chun the Kitchen Lord. Taoists worship him because he makes sure that the fires are lit and there is enough food in the house. He is reputed to observe the family's activities and report his findings to the Jade Emperor of Heaven annually on New Year's Day.

Toaists believe in Hell, which is ruled over by Lord Yama or King Ch'in Kuang. He judges people on entry to Hell. If they are good then they go back to Earth to be born in another form. If they are judged as bad then they are sent to suffer in one of the ten realms of Hell according to the category of their misdeeds. Some of the tortures on offer include being burned alive or torn apart.

Worship and ceremonies

In Taiwan, where Taoism is a living religion, it is believed that the whole destiny of a person's life is in the hands of deities and spirits.

Making offerings at shrines, reading the scriptures and chanting all display devotion to these deities. The Taoist priest's main function is to intercede with deities on behalf of his congregation. Priests play a central role in all ceremonies as they have to purify the Taoist temple and all the objects used in rituals. There are many Jao or offerings to different gods and deities, some very public events that draw large crowds.

Meditation is also seen as a means of making contact with spirits and deities. The method advocated in the Tao Te Ching is by "emptying your mind of all thoughts" and control of the breath. In this way the gods can be visualised and invited to come within, thereby giving the meditator a chance to experience the oneness of the universe. This helps to unify and harmonise Shen-Chi and Chung or spirit, breath and vital essence.

At a birthing, the mother makes offerings to Tai Shen - the guardian of the spirit of the unborn child. At four months there are ceremonies of thanksgiving and further offerings. At one year of age there is a banquet held for the whole neighbourhood as a celebration. Rice cakes are offered to the young child to encourage it to turn its thoughts to Heaven.

At death, Taoists believe that the spirit hangs around the body until burial. The pure essence of the person is said to go to be judged by the gods. The funeral service can last up to three days and is conducted by a special 'blackhead' Taoist priest. Children place the favourite things of the deceased in their coffin. Prayers are written on pieces of paper and then burnt to help the person rise to Heaven. The day of burial is chosen according to the Taoist calendar. In a special procession to the graveyard, people play instruments and recite traditional spells.

Weddings are officiated by the Taoist priest. The ceremony involves an exchange of gifts and a visit to the burial sites of both families' sets of ancestors to obtain their blessing. There is also a ceremony of Universal Salvation to offer comfort to lost souls who wander from place to place because they have not been given a proper burial.

Another ceremony focuses on petitioning the deities to ask forgiveness for past sins. This involves fasting by Taoist monks and prostration by followers as an act of repentance.

Festivals

Of all the Taoist festivals the Chinese New Year is the most important. The street processions with the dancing dragon celebrate the birth of yang, which is seen as the positive force in the Universe.

In the seventh month of the year there is the celebration of the Earth God and Earth Spirits. Floating water lamps on the river liberate the spirits and guide them back from Hell.

In the tenth month there is a water spirits festival to celebrate the birthday of the God of Water, when the reign of the water spirits begins. A banquet celebrates the release of souls from the watery regions of the underworld.

Green Taoism

As well as being a pragmatic philosophy, Taoism offers a spiritual perspective, born from looking at the natural world. It therefore has much to offer in Green awareness. Taoism always stresses the importance of harmony between human beings and Nature as a key aspect of the protection of Nature. Taoism is always opposed to the violation of natural laws. It denies any human right to conquer Nature, or wage a war against Nature. Taoist scriptures make constant reference to Nature. It is taken as an expression of the spiritual dimension of existence:

- Humanity follows Earth, Earth follows Heaven, Heaven follows the Tao and Tao follows what is natural.
- When you know that Nature is part of yourself, you will act in harmony.
- Realise that we live in Nature. But we cannot possess it. We can guide and serve it but never control it. This is the highest wisdom.
- We must obey the laws of the Earth if we wish to know the truths of the Spirit.
- Those that dominate Nature and seek to possess it will never succeed.

It is clear that the Taoist approach to the self and the environment is based on a deep analysis and understanding of the ways of Nature and the universe.

Taoists see throughout the natural world symbols that show us how to live right. Nature is seen as Mother Earth from which all things are born and to which all things return. Trees represent strength in weakness and weakness in strength .The bamboo tree is strong and upright but its strength comes from its hollow centre. The white crane is a symbol of innocence, purity and transcendence. Its flight mirrors that of the soul from the body upon passing. The butterfly, being the result of a miraculous metamorphosis, symbolizes rebirth and immortality.

Taoism's vision of a society based on social justice and peace is another Green attribute. This society is characterized by equality and fraternal love between members. It opposes extremes of wealth and exploitation by governments and the powerful. Lao Tzu saw that excessive farm taxes and excise taxes resulted in famine. He saw the ruling nobles as little better than robbers. To realize a Taoist society its members reconnect with their original inner nature and then work at perfecting it. Only by this means can the moral balance of society be restored.

Taoism's Green thinking emphasizes self-reliance and reduced dependence on and intervention by government. It advocates relying instead on individual development to reach society's natural harmony. Taoist political doctrines state that the ruler's duty is to minimise government intervention, while protecting his people from experiencing dire material wants or the unwanted effects of excessive passions. Nature with its order and harmony has far greater stability and endurance than either the state or even civilizing institutions born of human learning. The whole Taoist way of life is in fact Green. Consider these guidelines from the Celestial Masters of how to live in the Tao.

- Give assistance to the poor and oppressed.
- Live modestly without coveting wealth or fame.
- Be humane, loyal and just to all.
- Never pollute or divert rivers. Close up wells. Light fires in open land and do not disturb birds.
- Respect animals.

The Tao Te Ching teaches a life of simplicity, frugality and of overcoming the ego, assuredly benign to the environment and an antidote to a materialist culture producing large amounts of waste. "The Tao person helps others. So no one is lost. And uses things wisely. So nothing is wasted," says Lao Tzu.

Taoism displays its Green credentials by emphasising the need to help others rather than pursuing selfish individualism. The Tao Te Ching states, "people of the Tao transcend self through loving compassion. Through loving service they attain fulfilment." How can a teaching be more timely today?

Taoists still pay their doctors when they are well and withold payments if they become unwell. Taoism is Green because of its non-invasive, minimal intervention approach to health and medicine. This developed because of the worship of ancestors, which precluded ever having human cadavers for surgeons to examine internally. We benefit today with these 'complimentary' medical approaches, such as acupuncture, shiatsu and kinesiology which can be used in diagnosis.

Today throughout China, Taoist temples often establish clinics and hospitals and provide natural medicine to patients. Recently the Chinese Taoist Association importantly announced that traditional medicines that were collected through suffering or endangering species could not be used for healing, as they violated the Tao, or natural way of the world.

As we will find from future chapters, China is facing a plethora of environmental problems. The ruling Chinese Communist Party now finds itself with a nation hell bent on growth and consumerism and with a corresponding loss of a sense of community and responsibility. Concerned with loss of what the CC Party has called "spiritual culture" – meaning higher values and a sense of wider environmental responsibility - an invitation has been extended by some government officials to Taoism and Buddhism to help reinstate a sense of a purpose beyond just self and consumerism.

There are thousands of Taoist temples in China. Taoist monks and nuns representing ten temples in Shaanxi and Gansu provinces recently signed a commitment, known as the Qinling Declaration to protect the environment around their sacred lands and buildings. The Taoist monks and nuns also decided to form a 'Taoist Temple Alliance on Ecology Education' and agreed to send representatives regularly to workshops and to share their experiences in protecting China's sacred Taoist landscapes. They have already rebuilt a Taoist temple destroyed in the Cultural Revolution to act as an ecological centre to provide education for other Taoists in China.

In 2009 Taoists attended a meeting in the UK of faith leaders seeking ways to combat climate change. Taoist leaders have put together an eight-year plan, to run from 2010 to 2018, which will hold Taoism's founding figure, Lao Tzu, as the 'God of Ecology'. Having 26,000 temples in China run on solar power is a major goal of its plan to put ecology at the heart of Taoism.

As well as itself being good for the environment, this revival of

Taoism signals the germination of a new seed of awareness, concern and positive action.

Taoism Websites

www.religioustolerance.org
www.askasia.org
www.uga.edu
www.weber.ucsd.edu
www.religiousworlds.com
www.clas.ufl.edu/users/gthursby/taoism
www.daoiststudies.org
www.edepot.com
www.taoism.net
www.truetao.org
www.beliefnet.com
www.chebucto.ns.ca
www.taoistarts.net
www.eng.taoism.org
www.sacred-texts.com
www.infoplease.com
www.arcworld.org
www.chinadialogue.net
www.stanford.edu

Chapter 9 : Shamanism

Introduction

If man invented religion, then Shamans were his original explorers. Shamans were among the earliest humans to engage in the quest to understand the existential meaning of life and to seek to intercede with Nature and her forces. Evidence suggests Shamanism dates back 40,000 years. And, amazingly, Shamanism is still found today - among the indigenous peoples of the Arctic regions, Southeast Asia, Australasia and of North, South and Central America - and is in demand for what they can teach us about ourselves today.

In this chapter we will focus mainly on Shamanistic practices found in the tribes of Arctic regions and North America.

Shamanism is the work of the shaman, deriving from an Evensk word from the Tungus region of Siberia. According to the man acknowledged in the West as a world authority on Shamanism, Michael J. Harner, the word 'shaman' means either 'one who sees in the dark' or 'one who sees with eyes closed'. Though rarer, there are female shamans too.

Shamanism is based on the premise that invisible forces or spirits that affect the lives of the living pervade the visible world. Shamanism is not a system of faith. Shamans know and use specific techniques for altering consciousness so that they can access spiritual realities normally invisible and undetectable to people whose consciousness is focused on the ordinary reality of daily life. Some anthropologists and scholars of religion define a shaman as an intermediary between the physical and the spiritual worlds. He, or she, enters a trance state and travels between these worlds.

Divination, clairvoyance, trance, music, song, dance and ecstasy are skills, states and influences in everyday use by the shaman. The shaman follows a path of knowledge: s/he is a visionary, mystic, healer and magician. S/he often follows a family tradition and is chosen to serve the community as a healer and teacher.

Basic beliefs and the work of the shaman

Many shamanic traditions see the world being created by an all embracing and powerful Great Spirit. The myths of creation of the Native American Omaha tribe are typical of this idea. In the beginning all creatures were spirits seeking a place where they could come into bodily existence. So the god Wakonda descended to Earth, but found it full of water. Then a rock rose up and burst into flames and then floated up into the clouds. Dry land then appeared and grass began to grow on it. Eventually the spirits became flesh and blood.

The Buryat tribe of Siberia believe the gods created man but the evil spirits created disease and sickness. The gods decided to give mankind a shaman to combat disease and death. So God sent an eagle that saw a woman under a tree and had intercourse with her. She gave birth to the first shaman.

Native Americans see in Nature an all-pervasive giver of life, often called the Great White Spirit, who breathes life into everything. The Apache call it Manitou or Life Giver, the Cherokees call it Papagos, the giver of breath; the Crow call it the Earth Mother.

The shaman sees the natural world imbued with spiritual energy. The Kiowa tribe believe everything in the cosmos has a power or spirit force called *dwdw*. Earth, moon, mountains and other natural forms possess souls and express this power through natural phenomena such as lightning and tornadoes. In world of Nature, *dwdw* power is gifted to creatures according to their status in the spiritual hierarchy, giving predators power over their prey. *Dwdw* is available to man only if he keys into it through questing, visions and encounters with the supernatural.

Native Americans treated animals such as beavers, eagles, bears and deer with great respect and reverence. They performed elaborate ceremonies before hunting them. The Cherokee shaman thought that if a brave failed to ask forgiveness of a deer before killing it he would be visited by disabling joint stiffness -rheumatism.

A shaman might either inherit his or her position or might be 'chosen' - by a series of events or a condition. For instance, a shaman may be chosen because s/he suddenly experiences strange states of consciousness or experiences lucid dreams of being reborn when all their organs are replaced; or they are given to episodes that we know as epilepsy. In the Yakut tribe of Siberia, one who is destined to become a shaman shows signs such as losing consciousness, withdrawing to the forest, flinging himself into fire or water, or cutting himself with knives. Among the Tungus tribe of Siberia, the would-be shaman has a dream about a dead shaman who orders the dreamer to succeed him. To seek to become a shaman is a rare calling. Candidates face death-defying challenges. Many succumb and die. Survivors of the gruelling tests of initiation are the exception.

There are common initiation themes found in shaman cultures throughout the world: enduring long periods of seclusion, often in conditions of great physical hardship is one. Harsh ordeals are commonplace, which can include amputation of fingers, beatings and having feet held very close to red-hot fire. These tests of physical and mental endurance are designed to sever the shaman's link to his previous life. Initiations almost always have a death theme. They will often undergo a ritual death and resurrection. In the Siberian shaman there is a symbolic dismemberment of the body.

Would-be shamans of the Manchu tribe of the Arctic regions go through gruelling physical hardships. To prove themselves in their initiation they are asked to walk barefoot over burning coals and if the spirits are with them they will not come to any harm. The initiate then cuts nine holes in the ice and dives through each one in turn. In the Ammasalik initiation of Inuit boys into shamans they are required go to a snow hut and experience temperatures as low as minus 40^0 C. Over a three day period the initiate is not allowed any food and only two to three drips of water. Usually this results in physical collapse, but the would-be shaman is rescued from the ordeal by the female spirit Pinga.

Once initiated the shaman then has to develop his spiritual power and become recognised as a leader, healer and adviser in his or her community. To gain this power initiates seek intimate contact with supernatural beings in natural surroundings. Some Native American tribes engage in what they call a vision quest as a rite of passage for would-be shamans.

Vision quest preparations involve a time of fasting, the guidance of a tribal Holy Man and in some cultures ingestion of natural hallucinogens. The quest itself usually involves a solitary journey into wilderness and is a quest for personal growth and spiritual guidance. Within a particular landscape certain spots are thought to be especially good for spiritual attunement, as they lie at an interface with spiritual realms. Both the Navajo and the Hopi thought for instance that Mount Taylor in New Mexico was a sacred place. Other sacred places were burial grounds, graves, purification sites such as sweat lodges, springs and rivers and healing sites such as hot springs. Places where animals congregated, especially animals such as deer, elk, wolf, buffalo, moose and eagle were also seen as sacred.

During the quest, participants often receive guidance from totem or spirit animals. To help re-access the power provided by any vision or encounter afterwards, the initiate might seek a physical representation of the vision or message such as a feather, fur or a rock and add it to his medicine bag.

The Lakota vision quest began with a sweat lodge session, smoking a peace pipe and praying. Questors would then be directed to climb a hill, find a stone circle and go within and remain there for four days - without food or drink. Those that experienced visions would go down to the sweat lodge and share them with others. They would be given a new name and invited to join a secret medicine lodge. Those that had visions of thunder beings were obliged to become Heyoka or a sacred clown and spend the rest of their lives doing things the wrong way round.

The shaman's close relationship with supernatural forces is dependent on his ability to go into a trance at will, even if this involves certain techniques to intensify the state. The soul of the shaman is believed to leave the body and ascend to the sky (heavens) or descend beneath the earth (underworld). His complete focus on this ecstatic trance state is the distinguishing characteristic of shamanism. His 'out-of-body' trance puts the shaman in communication with spirits of the dead and Nature spirits without his being controlled by them. It is the very foundation of this spiritual tradition.

Trance techniques vary: in Siberia, the beating of a drum made with reindeer, elk, or horse skin, is used as a focussing device; a 180-cycles-per-minute rhythm helps; it may be accompanied by "power" songs to summon spirits. Others employ breathing techniques, fasting, reduced sleep or reduced sugar intake.

Most shamanic cultures include use of drugs, with tobacco being used by the Native Americans, marijuana and fly agaric mushrooms by Siberian and other Arctic shamans.

In his journey to other worlds the shaman may seek help and guidance from animal spirits. He will identify with one or magically transform himself into one. Native American shamans have the horse that helps the shaman fly through the air and reach the heavens; the eagle has power to see clearly over long distances and possesses speed in the spiritual realms. The mouse sees what the eagle misses and warns of coming danger. The grizzly bear can show the shaman where to find hidden treasure. The frog is the totem of water and helps the shaman to adapt to change. The turtle helps the shaman maintain balance and represents Mother Earth. The hawk brings messages from the spirit world and is a totem of power. The wolf helps the shaman see the truth and represents loyalty. The owl helps him see inner truths.

Shamanic cultures also have deities that aid the work of the shaman. The Navajo have Big Fly who can sit on someone's ear and advise them what to do. The Inuit have Sila the Sky God who can foretell the future and make prophecies. They also have 'Mother of Sea Beasts', who lives at the bottom of the ocean and determines how many animals are killed in hunting.

An important role of the shaman is that of a healer. The shaman has often been referred to as 'the wounded healer'. Such a shaman has passed through a life-threatening illness or other crisis, or has even been to the land of the dead and has returned intact.

Sickness arises in a person because of their separation from Nature. Traditionally, the shaman looks for either of two specific causes: the patient has something inside which should not be there (an unwanted power intrusion), or is missing part of their soul.

So the shaman's work is to travel to where the lost part of the soul is hiding out and attempt to retrieve it. They may travel to the underworld by going to a hole in the ground, or to the upper world by climbing a tree, mountaintop or jumping into a fire. Siberian shamans practise exorcism. They may extricate an unwanted spirit from a person's body and take it into their own to deal with it.

Ceremonies and Worship

The lives of Native American tribes revolved around ceremonies and ritual but these were of a life enhancing nature. It has been estimated that the Hopi tribe spent a third of their lives in prayer, ritual dances, songs and preparations for ceremonies. Most tribes had a deep kinship with every form of life. Many ceremonies were offerings to Nature in thanks for the gifts given by her. All beings were seen as sharing the life force emanating from the Great White Spirit.

Its presence would be invoked by many Native North and South Americans with an altar and natural objects placed upon it. The skull of a dog is an aid to find people, the skull of an eagle to help spiritual vision and diagnosis of illness and the skull of a serpent, to help balance light and dark are typical ritual objects imbued with powers.

For some Native American shamans, a Medicine Wheel drawn on the earth grounds worship and ceremony. This elaborate drawing has the four directions marked on it. The Lakota used the wheel as source of power and a vehicle for contacting the Great White Spirit. For them the Medicine Wheel is a symbol of wholeness, perfection, balance and completeness. Each direction of the Lakota wheel is associated with different energies and characteristics.

To Native Americans the peace pipe is essential for communicating with the Great White Spirit and making an offering to him. Before smoking the pipe, permission is sought from the Great White Spirit. The smoke from the pipe is a vehicle for prayer used in many ceremonies.

Smoke from burning dried herbs and plants such as sage, sweetgrass and juniper are used in smudging a space, a purification ceremony to clear negative energies.

In the Sweat Lodge ceremonies common to many Native American tribes, the lodge provides an enclosed sacred space with a central fire pit. With great care and in ritual manner, extremely hot stones are placed in the pit. The lodgers prepare themselves with ceremonies then crawl in, crowd around the pit and all openings are closed. In the confined, heated space the participants sweat profusely. Ceremonies vary, but typically consist of prayers and chanting, often as a means of personal purification. I myself have taken part in a Sweat Lodge ceremony which I found to be challenging and thought provoking.

In the ancient past Native Americans had many ceremonies centred on giving thanks to Nature for providing life's necessities. In mid-summer the Plains Indian tribes of the Arapahoe, Cheyenne and Dakota performed the Sun Dance ceremony in honour of the Buffalo upon which they depended for their survival. The practice lasted eight days: four days preparation for a four day ceremony. Special, dances such as the Buffalo Dance, the War Dance and the Sun Gazing Dance were carefully choreographed and performed afresh each season.

In an autumn thanksgiving ceremony the Pueblo Indians perform the deer dance. They mime elk, deer, bison and mountain sheep. Then a sacred tree is brought in and showered with symbols of food and riches. The spruce and fir trees represent the life-giving properties of the Earth and its strong female energy.

The Delaware give thanks with the Big House Ceremony. "We thank our Mother Earth who we claim as mother because the Earth carries us and everything we need." All then pray for mercy for the year ahead. In the evening two cedarwood bonfires are lit, one in the east and one in the west. There are further prayers to the creator, Manitou, in a special evening banquet. Women and children are then invited to share their visions, concluding with further thanksgiving prayers.

Shamans contact the Spirit World through ceremonies. In the Crescent Moon ceremony the Kiowa and the Comache tribes seek to make contact with the spirit world through taking peyote. In a ceremonial journey towards the spirit world overseen by the Roadman, a button of peyote is placed on an altar shaped like a crescent moon. Having taken the peyote the shaman or celebrant will offer spontaneous teachings under its influence. This ceremony continues to this day - and with legal dispensation - under the auspices of the Native American Church.

Green Shamanism

The sanctity of Nature and of Mother Earth is the essence of Shamanism. This is borne out in the worldview of shamans and in their prayers and inner practices. They see their surroundings as the home they share with its wildlife. Cultures with such values woven into their fabric seldom over-exploit the natural world. Rather they cohabit with the untamed universe; when their livelihood demands they take life, they say a prayer. They prize what Nature yields and show this by avoiding waste as a matter of course.

This is reflected in these statements:
- Black Elk: "with all beings and all things we shall be relatives."
- Grandfather David Monogye: "we are all flowers in the Great Spirit's garden, we share a common root and the root is Mother Earth. "
- Intiwa, a Hopi Indian: "The whole universe is enhanced with the same breath: rocks, trees, grass, earth, all animals and men."
- Chief of the Blackfoot on land ownership: "It was put here (the Earth) by the White Spirit and we cannot sell it because it does not belong to us."

There is great dignity in the humility with which Shamanic societies express their gratitude and deep respect for their food and shelter and the wondrous powers that provide it. Prayer rituals and ceremonies to tend their inner landscape were matched by hunting and farming practices to provide all life's necessities. They hunted to meet only their own needs. They practiced rainfed seasonal agriculture that kept soil healthy and free from erosion. Through such minimally intrusive practices, they lost no valuable topsoil, they endangered no species and they secured sustainable sources of food.

Today we marvel at how simple, how balanced, how integral with Nature such a way of life must have been. Unburdened by materialism, opportunism and selfish exploitation but sensing a spiritual power all around them, Native Americans saw life as a journey to attain 'medicine power' or spiritual insight into the deeper reality around them. In their Vision Quests, ceremonies and prayers they sought communion with the realms of the supernatural and the spiritual.

Material wealth had value in shamanic cultures but limited to the extent it delivers life's necessities. To indulge in the accumulation of wealth would be aberrant. True wealth was seen as non-material. For instance the Navajo tribe saw wealth in terms of the number of songs an individual owned. Nobody could sing a song unless they had proof of ownership. And among the Arctic communities the shaman's wealth was seen in terms of the wealth of his experience in travelling to different worlds.

These cultures were sustainable because they maintained a profound awareness of the physical resources on which their lives depended.

Unlike the European culture that came and quickly overwhelmed them, they chose to limit themselves in what they took to what Nature could provide, season by season. This is why the Native Americans thrived across the North American continent for thousands of years until the Europeans came. It meant, too, that the tribes of the Arctic could survive in a harsh and inhospitable environment.

The sustainability of their relationship with their environment was a mirror of the shaman's wisdom: we are all part of the Great Mother who feeds us all and to whom we owe our deepest gratitude which we show throughout each day. Practiced as shown by shamans, such a value system assures a viable culture indefinitely, provided, that is, another altogether more exploitative one does not want your land or what lies beneath it.

Shamanism Websites

www.hornedtree.org
www.shaman-center.uk
www.wicca.com
www.buryatmongol.com
www.haldjasfolklore.com
www.sacredhoop.org
www.shamana.co.uk
www.pathofthefeather.com
www.barbelith.com
www.important.ca/shamanism
www.shamanism.info
www.shamanelders.com
www.shamanlinks.net
www.shamanbeats.com
www.urbanshamanism.com
www.celticshamanism.com

CHAPTER 10 : PAGANISM

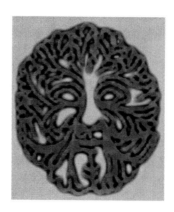

Introduction

Paganism has been described as the ancestral religion of the whole of humanity. It includes several distinct paths and traditions which all share a veneration of Nature and the worship of many deities.

The Paganism we look at here originated in ancient Europe in pre-historic times. The ancients believed there were spiritual forces present all around and that they could be placated only if treated with reverence. Though the many different gods and goddesses they worshipped were part of everyday life, they took great care to placate and honour them through ritual and prayer.

Modern Paganism is an umbrella term covering a range of beliefs with some or all of the following in common: Nature-centred spirituality, the honouring of deities and personal belief systems, a quest to develop the self, the acceptance and encouragement of diversity; also freedom from hierarchies.

Here, we touch on three: Heathenism, Druidism and Wicca. Many Pagans believe in more than one god or goddesses - often supporting polytheistic spiritual practices that refer to ancient cultures - while others have a single main god and one main goddess. Pantheistic Pagans believe that everything around us and within us is sacred.

History

Paganism has a long history as an oral tradition, written records tending to be second-hand. As Christianity became dominant, Pagans were persecuted as "heretics" and their practices all but died out in Europe in the 1200s. So the revival of interest in Paganism in modern times may seem surprising. With small beginnings in the 18th century, Paganism has grown in significance, particularly since the 1960s and the expansion of consciousness, perhaps a reaction to the overwhelming cultural dominance of marketing and materialism.

Paganism describes what is known of the religions of the Celts, whose origins remain a mystery. As they settled widely throughout Europe they spread Paganism. Archaeological evidence provides most of what we know today about Pagan practices. Boundary ditches have been excavated to reveal enclosed open spaces, which might have been used for Pagan worship. We also know that important people had their treasures and provisions buried along with them to ensure enjoyment of their next life.

An outstanding ceremonial burial mound found seventy years ago at Sutton Hoo in East Anglia in the UK yielded a wealth of detailed background on the society and its belief system. Further clues come from artefacts such as the richly decorated silver Gundestrup Cauldron (2 - 3rd century BCE) which depicts Pagan gods and goddesses. Votive offerings to gods and goddesses such as axes, coins, ladders, yokes, ploughs, spades, saws and wheels have been found in rivers and healing springs.

Rare written accounts of aspects of Paganism do exist, for example the Roman author Tacitus, who describes how they sought contact with other worlds through dreams, signs and divination. But we have gleaned more from archaeological digs.

Common beliefs of Pagans

Modern day Paganism comes in varied forms but there are certain core principles most share. One often quoted is the statement "if it harm none then do as you will." Paganism is one of the so-called "mystery paths," where each individual seeks direct experience of the divine. Individual experience of divinity remains the primary objective for most practicing Pagans even though Pagan priests and priestesses are increasingly administering rites to a group .

Pagans generally seem never to have pondered on creation theories or consistent cosmology, being more concerned with their immediate setting. However, the Norse Pagans did develop a complex cosmology quite of their own. They believed that there were nine worlds, which were all linked to a universal tree called Yggdrasil. Our world was called Midgard. These other worlds were located above and below the earth. Each world was purported to be populated by two types of being: Desir beings involved with sovereignty, magic and warfare and Vanir beings concerned with fertility. At the base of this tree were three sisters called Norns and they represented the past, present and future and they determined people's Wyrd or fate.

Paganism is a religion of Nature, home of Gods, Goddesses and Nature spirits. Pagans see the divine as immanent in the whole of life and the universe. They seek connection with it. Pagans today worship gods and goddesses, male deities looking after the community, female deities linked to landscape and the forces of Nature. Godesses are seen as the embodiment of natural forces, particularly the creative force displayed by the sexual polarity of the gods and goddesses.

More than any group, the Celts have left us clues on their worship and sacred practices. Yet the Celts had no single religion nor political unity. Their tribes spread across half of Europe. Among finds, as many as 374 Celtic deities have now been identified. However, over 300 occur only once in the archaeological record; they are deities of *place*. This suggests that for each group of Celts, the spirits of their own locality had greatest power vested in them.

Many Celtic deities were worshipped in triune (triple aspect) form. The Triple Goddess is a concept in which the Goddess is split into three aspects - Maid, Mother and Crone. These aspects correspond to the three phases of the moon - waxing, full and waning.

Since the worship of deities is central to understanding all aspects of Paganism we'll look now at the gods and goddesses that in their main aspects have come to be accepted as representative of the different traditions found throughout Europe.

- The Mother Goddess is central. She represents Mother Earth. She was worshipped because she provided the bounty of Nature and she sustains life. To primitive peoples, dependent on each year's crop for survival, having a good relationship with the Earth was crucial. The importance of this Goddess to Celts is evident from 50 inscriptions found on archaeological artefacts dedicated to her.

- The Moon Goddess controlled the weather, seen as an extension of the Earth Goddess. The Greeks worshipped Hecate as the Moon Goddess; many rituals honouring her at harvest. Sender of nocturnal visions to some modern Pagans, she has special significance in the Wicca tradition.
- The Star Goddess - associated with the Pole Star and northern heavens, she was seen as the shining beacon that guides spiritual destiny. The Druids used to worship this goddess. Some modern Pagans also.
- Cailleach - an important Celtic goddess worshipped for her wisdom; she controlled the weather.
- Cerridwen - another important goddess in Celtic times, known as the Mistress of Mysteries and Keeper of the Pathway of Initiation into the Higher Wisdom. Said to possess the Cauldron of Rebirth, she was a shape shifter, could appear in many guises and thus magical.
- Helen of the Roads - worshipped by Celts as a goddess of tracks and ways. She was the Ruler of Dreams, could guide seekers to attain arcane knowledge, hence much sought after.
- Morrigan - Goddess of Battle and Death, chose who died in battle, who passed to the Otherworld. Great importance attached to her by Druids; often appeared in form of a raven.
- Epona - the Horse Goddess, worshipped by the Celts because she represented fertility and sexual prowess; also associated with death and regeneration.
- Freya - worshipped by Norse Pagans, an important goddess of fertility, also of beauty and love; patroness of magic and protector of the land.
- Frigga - worshipped by Norse Pagans, another goddess of fertility, more important as Goddess of the Sky and Mother of the Gods; often associated with marriage; ability to predict future events, so her council sought.
- Brigit or Brigid - Celtic Goddess of Fire, patron of artists, blacksmiths and healers; her blessing invoked for preparation of forged items, food and other commodities requiring fire; also a fertility deity.

It is clear from these descriptions that for early Pagans the world was imbued with goddesses. A source of comfort, support and counsel in troubled and uncertain times, their goddesses were part of Nature and an integral part of the cycle of their lives.

The gods of Paganism were of an entirely different nature from goddesses. Several were found throughout Europe, including many of Norse origin.

- The Green Man - worshipped by the Celts, promised fertility and growth - remains perhaps the best known Celtic deity in our times. He was son and lover of the Great Mother Goddess; he is worshipped by present day Pagans.
- Pan or Cemunnos - worshipped by Celts, represented the Spirit of the Earth; associated with cultivation;had the body of a man, also had hooves and antlers which could rise up into the heavens and capture the power of the sun; represented male sexuality as suggested by phallic nature of horns, virility and strength. Seen as Lord of the Underworld.
- Woden or Wotan - Anglo Saxons worshipped him as a god of wisdom and knowledge; seen as enabling others to see different worlds.
- Mercury - God of Light and Trade, he too guided people into the mysteries of the unseen worlds; also Patron of Wisdom and Learning.
- Thor - worshipped by Norse Pagans as Controller of the Weather, with interests in agriculture and war.
- Loki - a deity who clung to Thor's belt and retrieved his hammer when it was thrown but he was a trickster and not to be trusted.
- Odin - favourite deity of the Norse, god of battle; also ruled the Land of the Dead. Odin's trial of being hung from the tree of knowledge gave him formidable knowledge including of the Runes, sacred stones that could reveal potent secrets.
- Frey - a God of Yule, of peace and plenty, bringer of fertility and prosperity.

Each Pagan religion has its own beliefs around an afterlife and reincarnation. Not all believe in the afterlife. There is a strong affinity with the idea of life arising in cyclical patterns that do not cease with the death of the physical body. The Norse believed that on death people entered the hall of Odin called the Valhalla where food and drink abounded. The Celts believed that when people died they went to a sort of paradise filled with food, drink and birdsong. Most Druids today adopt the belief of their ancient forebears that the soul undergoes a process of successive reincarnations—either always in human form, or in a variety of forms that might include trees and even rocks as well as animals. The Wiccans of today believe that on death people enter 'The Summerlands'; a place where souls find rest before being re-born into the physical world.

The Druids

In Celtic times Druids were respected leaders of their societies. They acted as judges, doctors, advisors, magicians, mystics and religious scholars. They were the keepers of knowledge for their culture, a spiritual link between their people and the gods. To become a Druid involved lengthy trainings in each field: as Bards responsible for safekeeping the traditions of the tribe through writing and performing poetry; as Ovates, native healers of the Celts specialized in divination, prophesy and conversing with ancestors.

In adverse times, Druids were mistrusted by the authorities of the day and held ceremonies in secret using secluded groves. They were banished by the Romans from Gaul (France). With the advent of Christianity the persecution of all 'heathens' was unrelenting and Druids almost died out in Europe. Only in the 18th century was Paganism re-established with the forming (in secret) of *An Druidh Uileach Braithreachas*, the Druid Circle of Universal Bond in England. In 1834 Henry Hurle established the Ancient Order of Druids and in 1902 a number of national orders became united under the International Grand Lodge of Druidism which to this day holds gatherings of which one is scheduled for 20 November 2010 in the UK Midlands.

The Celtic mystical tradition accounts for the great majority of those following the Druid religion in modern times. They worship the Celtic deities we describe and follow an eight-fold cycle of festivals.

Heathens

Heathenry is a term used to describe the religious practices of two main groups of people, one historical and one contemporary. The original Heathens were north European peoples who lived a thousand and more years ago in the lands around what is now called the North Sea; their religion can in turn be traced back to the start of the Bronze Age in Scandinavia. At its widest spread its followers included the peoples of Scandinavia and the Norse colonies in Greenland and Newfoundland, southern Scotland, Anglo-Saxon England, Frisia (coastal Friesland in Netherlands), Germany, eastern France, northern Italy.

Modern Heathen groups around the world are reviving these old practices and call their religion by a variety of names, of which Heathenry is the most universally accepted, but including Asatru (North America and Iceland) and the Northern Tradition (UK).

Our knowledge of the original Heathenry is mostly drawn from two Icelandic documents, the poetic Edda and the prose Edda, from the Icelandic Sagas, from Christian chronicles and from archaeological fieldwork.

Modern Heathens form groups they call Hearths. In keeping with the original Heathens, a Hearth is run on democratic lines and honours the contributions and status of women and men equally. In ancient times worship included animal sacrifice, with the meat often being cooked and eaten in ceremonial feasts. Modern Heathen rituals are still called *blots* - after the Norse word for blood - though they no longer involve blood sacrifice. Blots include ritual drinking of mead from a horn accompanied by prayers or oath-taking, though neither is essential. An oath taken is considered sacrosanct; to be an oath-breaker is considered the ultimate disgrace.

Heathens strive to live the Nine Noble Virtues: courage, truth, honour, fidelity, discipline, hospitality, industriousness, self-reliance and perseverance. Their worship includes gods and goddesses mentioned earlier such as Odin, Thor, Freyr and Freyja and Frigga, but also honours the spirits of each place, known as Wights, their ancestors and the three Norns or Wyrd Sisters. Many Heathens use Runes for divination or guidance - a set of straight-sided characters drawn on cards, wooden discs or stones, an occidental I-Ching.

Wicca

The modern form of Wicca began in 1939 when Gerald Gardner was initiated by a coven of witches in the New Forest in the UK. In 1954 he wrote his authoritative work *Witchcraft Today*. Wicca is one of the most influential traditions of modern Paganism. It is an initiatory path, a mystery tradition that guides its initiates to a deep communion with the powers of Nature and of the human psyche, leading to a spiritual transformation of the self. The core philosophy of Wicca is contained in the Wiccan Rede, "An It Harm None - Do As Ye Will", thus emphasising the need for personal responsibility. Wiccans worship together in Covens. They focus their worship on Arcadia, the goddess of the moon, and her horned consort Cernunnos. The four elements of Air, Fire, Water and Earth play an important part in ceremonies. The elements are always invoked at the four cardinal points of the Magick circle to guard it during ceremonies.

The uninitiated first join the Coven's Outer Court, a training platform, for a year and a day, before entry into the Inner Court. All Wicca's rituals, which involve dancing and chanting inside the Magick Circle, are encoded in Gardner's *The Book of Shadows*.

Pagan worship and ceremonies

In ancient times, with survival uncertain, ceremonies often concerned the fertility of the soil and protection from malignant forces. With written accounts of ceremonies so rare, there is a heavy reliance on archaeological evidence and conjecture. Digs have uncovered cups and chalices. It was thought that these were used in ceremonies with a consecrated libation. Finds also include cauldrons - evidence suggests that these may have been used in ceremonies of rebirth - and swords. Some accept that these were used in ceremonies as magical wands, as symbols for the penis.

In modern Pagan ceremonies they still use the chalice, sword and cauldron. Every object used in a ceremony has been consecrated. A space is rendered safe and sacred by placing candles covering the Four Directions. Rock salt for cleansing along with an altar set up with a bowl of water and incense placed upon it readies the space for worship. Only once the space has been cleansed will they invoke their favourite deity. The cleansing actions in reverse close the space when the ceremony is completed.

In marriage ceremonies modern Pagans form a circle and offer gifts to the deities, to the cardinal directions and to the ancestors. Then the couple exchange rings and kisses and there is a physical binding of their hands together. The ceremony ends with saying farewell to the ancestors, deities and the Four Directions.

Modern Pagans have ceremonies to honour the birth of the child and to initiate them as Pagans. The child is placed in the middle of the circle and washed and anointed with oil. The congregation then ask the child to be blessed by their chosen deity. The child may then be given gifts.

In Wicca initiation ceremonies the initiate meets the Goddess and then experiences a ritual death and rebirth. The initiate is given a new name and made a priest or priestess. After a year and a day there is a further initiation again focussing on death and rebirth. A year after that there is the final initiation ceremony where in some circles full acceptance is displayed with the initiator and the initiated engaging in sexual intercourse.

Wicca ceremonies use Wicca Magick defined as the art of causing change to occur by the application of will. The purpose of Magick was to discover the self and will through a process of transmutation and realisation.

Finally, the Norse Pagan tradition originally included animal sacrifice but this has been replaced by beer, juice or mead as offerings to the Gods. Afterwards, those present are either sprinkled with the liquid, or drink it in sequence. Sometimes they hold a Sumbel where a filled horn is passed. As they prepare to sip, each person gives a toast to the gods, ancient heroes, or their ancestors - some will voice a poem, song or story.

Festivals

Pagans see the divine manifested in Nature and are attuned to the changing patterns of the seasons as expressions of their different spiritual deities. Pagans become known in the areas where they are active by their festivals, during which they commune with Nature. And many of the festivals were celebrated by Pagans long before the advent of Christianity, which often rebranded the events on the "if you can't beat 'em, join 'em" principle. The Pagan Samhain festival became All Saints Day; the Pagan Midsummers Day Festival evolved into the Feast of John the Baptist; and the Imbolc Festival gave rise to the Candlemas purification of the Virgin Mary. These original festivals are still celebrated by modern Pagans.

Such familiar festive trappings as the Yule Log originate in the Pagan festival of Yule, which honours the darkness from which light comes. It is the cycle of the goddess in her dark aspect when she gives birth to the divine son who will reign throughout the coming year. This sun child will become the God of Spring. On 21st December the festival is celebrated with an exchange of gifts; people decorate their homes with greenery they have gone out to collect.

Next in the cycle comes Imbolc, a festival concerned with fertility and gaining wisdom - and which marks the start of the lambing season. This is symbolic of the true goddess who is invited to leave the underworld and come to the Middle World. Brigid, daughter of the Irish god Dagda is invoked. There is a quickening of life in the Earth Mother, so the Mother Goddess also is worshipped at this time. On 2 February there is a fire festival at which pagans contemplate their own purification. Some people celebrate by spring-cleaning their home.

Following this there is the festival of Ostara or the Spring Equinox, which begins on the 21st March. This celebrates the young god bursting forth with new growth. He meets his maiden bride and starts the cycle of life again. The celebration of the Christian Easter comes from honouring the goddess Oestric at this time, whose symbol is the egg.

Beltane is the next festival, associated with the god Belenus. It comes from the Irish name 'Bright Fire'. Traditionally this is a pastoral festival held about 30 April, ideally at full moon. In the past cattle were taken through lanes of fires to the fields. This is a celebration of the union of the goddess and the god, bringing forth blossoming and fertility. There is the traditional dancing round the maypole and the crowning of the May Queen escorted by the Summer King. Couples are encouraged to go 'a maying' and make love in the open as an offering to the Earth. Often the Green Man appears and dances joyfully to encourage new spring growth. Modern Pagans enjoy this festival and will often stay up all night around a bonfire and in the morning dance on its embers!

Next in the Pagan calendar is the Festival of Litha or the Summer Solstice starting on 21 June. This is the celebration of the Sun god at the height of his powers. The goddess is also seen as pregnant with the mystical child, which she will bear at Yuletide. This festival is also connected with the Irish god Lugh or God of Light. Some Pagans try to make contact with elves and fairies at this time. In modern times Pagans often have night vigils and sit around bonfires all night.

Then comes the harvest festival, Lammas, celebrated on 31st July. This was connected with the Corn god worshipped by ancient Celts and celebrated by the making of corn dollies. It is also a celebration of feminine transition of the Goddess through the seasons. Modern Pagans emphasise the inner journey - the need to let go and move on. In Ireland at this time there is Celtic Sunday, celebrated while lifting the potato crop. In ancient times the Celts celebrated this festival over a period of a month with great assemblies, mock fighting, horse racing and feasting.

The next celebratory festival is Mabon or the Autumn Equinox starting on 21 September. A time of reflection on birth, death and decay and the need for harmony and balance, this was a harvest celebration as well. Modern Pagans take time at Mabon to reflect on their spiritual lives and inner journeys.

Samhain is another autumn festival that celebrates the departure of the Sun and also the departure of god, with his transformation into Lord of the Underworld. It celebrates the traditional Celtic New Year on 31 October in the Celtic month of Yew. Samhain is what has been popularised as Halloween. It is said at this time the veil between the living and the dead is very thin. The Celts believed this was when the spirits emerged from their dwellings in the hills, springs, lakes, rivers and ancient burial mounds. They honoured the dead, acknowledging death as part of the natural cycle. The Celts honoured the deceased they held as important by displaying their skulls. They dug a hole in the ground and placed food in it for the gods. There was at this season the slaughtering of meat for the winter and much feasting. However, there was always one extra place set at table – an invitation to the dead to join in.

Green Paganism

Paganism has to be among the Greenest religions. It sees the whole environment as imbued with sacredness. Pagan religions being Nature-centred, their values push us to rethink the way we relate to the Earth. Rather than seek dominance over the environment, modern Pagans seek to live as a part of Nature, seeking a genuine balance between the self, the biosphere and society. Paganism emphasises connectedness between mankind and the immediate environment via spiritual forces.

Modern-day Pagans see the Earth as a living entity with bands of power called ley lines, which are equivalent to meridians in oriental acupuncture. A spot where ley lines intersect forms a centre of power, referred to as an Earth chakra. It is thought that where ley lines are particularly strong, settlements of spiritual significance often arise, such as Glastonbury and Avebury in the UK.

As Celts believed that there was no separation between the physical world and the spiritual world, the example of reverence and respect for Nature they set is a good one. To them, natural features such as springs, lakes, rivers and mounds were homes to Nature spirits. In fact each Celtic tribe had its own places sacred to Nature spirits. Pagans of the Norse tradition in Sweden and Iceland worshipped land spirits, thought to bring prosperity to the land and good hunting. Was this not instinctive care for Nature's bounty?

Because water features were the dwelling places of Nature spirits, Pagans in ancient times would have been careful not to pollute or waste water, just as Modern Pagans follow this same reverence for this most vital of natural resources.

Evidence suggests Pagans of the past showed respect and reverence for many animals and plants and were therefore the protectors of biodiversity. Their reverence for trees is evident in the ancient Druids always carrying out important ceremonies in oak groves. Modern Pagans are also active in protecting animals and landscapes from over exploitation by man.

The Pagan calendar of festivals is testament to the Pagans' perception of the environment as sacred. The festivals honour Nature and show a true insight into natural cycles. They are a celebration of the spiritual aspects of our surroundings. While holding the environment in such high regard, Pagans are certain not to knowingly despoil it.

Modern pagans follow the example of the past in how to relate to Nature. I have direct experience of this in running a Green Spirituality Group. They emphasise the need to respect Nature, as we are not masters of it but humble parts of it.

There are, in fact, many modern Pagan organisations concerned with Nature and ecology such as Tree Spirit who advocate tree planting; to them the tree is sacred. The Pagan organisation Hammarens Ordens Sallskap promotes self-sufficiency and organic farming. The UK Eco-Pagan Dragon Environmental Network was founded in 1990. Founder members, including Wiccans and Druids have sought a practical expression of the Pagan belief that the Earth is sacred. Dragon organises public protest rituals as a form of political action. Some would call themselves Eco-Pagans as they are environmental activists who are either members of contemporary Pagan traditions or who practice "de-traditionalised, but Pagan-like, spiritualities". Starhawk, a modern Pagan writer sums it up when she says: "The Earth is our mother and we will take care of her. The Earth is our mother she will take care of us."

Pagan Websites

www.igld.org http://druidnetwork.org/en/conference
www.paganfed.org
www.fatheroak.com
www.rary.thinkquest.org
www.bellaonline.com
www.religioustolerance.org
www.crystallinks.com
www.isle-of-avalon.com
www.pagans.org
www.religionfacts.com
www.avalonia.co.uk
www.paganwiccan.about.com
www.altreligion.about.com
www.storm-crow.co.uk
www.pagan-alliance.com
www.druidry.org
www.wicca.com
www.wicca.org
www.dragonnetwork.org
www.geocities.com/hammarens
www.eco-action.org
www.paganassociation.co.uk

CHAPTER 11 : SPIRITUALISM

Introduction

Spiritualism is essentially concerned with communication with the spirit world. Spiritualists believe that those that have passed on into the spirit world can communicate with us and guide us in our lives. Some see it as a modern religion; others say it is more a philosophy. Whichever the case, Spiritualism claims roots in ancient history, citing parts of the Christian Bible as evidence that Spiritualism is thousands of years old, for example. Here, we take the Spiritualist perspective on life and the afterlife.

History

Many of the examples of Spiritualism that Spiritualists cite are from the Christian Bible's Old Testament. To them it is clear that God, Angel and Spirit are used interchangeably; spiritual leaders in the Old Testament had psychic gifts. Abraham's many visions and direct exchanges with God feature large in Genesis (Gen 17:1-16). To Spiritualists, Abraham's visions were appearances by his Spirit Guide. Abraham displayed the gift of clairaudience or the hearing of spirit voices, a powerful gift that to Spiritualists marks a person out as special.

Our dreams are gifts, too, as is the art of interpreting them. Joseph had dreams that enabled him to foretell the future, which meant he evidently had the gift of clairvoyance. Moses saw a burning bush because of his psychic vision and he heard the voice of the Spirit because he was clairaudient. Moses also had a "tent meeting" attended by the 'cloudy pillar' (Ex 33:7-10) because he wanted the assembled Israelites all to see the Spirit Guide, Yahweh. This could be seen as the holding of a séance.

Psychic events occur in the New Testament, too. There are many sightings of spiritual beings - called angels. The angels appeared to Mary before the birth of Jesus (Luke 2:14). Mary Magdalene saw two men in shining garments at the Holy Sepulchre (Luke 2:4).

Jesus possessed highly developed psychic abilities and healing skills. His powers meant he did not even have to touch people to heal them. A cripple of 38 years was cured when Jesus said to him "rise to your feet take up your bed and walk"(John 5: 1-9). A Roman centurion's son was paralysed but Jesus cured him when he told the centurion that his faith in the ability of Jesus to heal was enough to cure his son (Matthew 8: 5-13). Jesus said "your eyes are opened" and a blind man was healed (Mark 8:22-26). He cured one blind from birth: Jesus spat on the ground, made a paste and rubbed it over the man's eyes (John 9:1-7). Jesus often healed through touch, so when a leper touched his garment he was automatically healed (Mark 1:40-45).

Jesus brought people back from the dead: a girl presumed dead came back to life when he said "Get up my child" (Mark 5: 21-24). In another instance, a widow thought her son had died, but when Jesus touched the boy and said, "Young man, rise up", he came back to life.

Mental illness was often seen as a case of spirit possession. Jesus cured a woman who had been ill for 18 years when he laid his hands on her and said "You are rid of the trouble." In another instance, Jesus told the spirits inhabiting a man to vacate and live in a herd of swine. Subsequently the herd ran over a cliff and were all drowned. At this instant the man was cured (Mark 5:1-20).

These stories illustrate that spiritual healing has a very ancient history. They also show that Jesus came from a tradition where people saw psychic events as a natural occurrence - as would those who wrote the gospels.

The psychic aspects of Jesus's story became distinctly less acceptable in the early centuries after Jesus's death as the Church became hierarchical and institutionalized and the priest became the central figure and sole interpreter of religious experiences for the congregation.

Canon or church law outlawed the cultivation and use of psychic powers, considered heretical and the work of the devil. A single verse in Exodus (22:18) states "Thou shalt not suffer a witch to live." These eight words were taken to justify persecution of suspected witches included in the Roman Catholic Inquisition with execution of many innocent victims by burning at the stake. There was 1,500 years of persecution. In a 200 year period in England, 30,000 witches were burnt at the stake. Between 381 at the First Council of Constantinople, which declared Arianism to be heretical and the beginning of the 19th century it has been estimated that 25 million heretics were executed. It is no wonder that Spiritualism did not come into being as a religion until religious tolerance was guaranteed in law which happened in the 19th century in both the US and UK.

The Swedish mystic, theologian and scientist Emanuel Swedenborg (1688-1772) is credited with being the first significant practitioner and promoter of the central tenets of Spiritualism. Swedenborg claimed to be able to communicate with spirits and travel through the spirit world. His followers held him as a highly skilled medium.

Modern Spiritualism came into being in 1848 at Hydersville, New York state in the USA with the psychic events surrounding the Fox sisters. It was noticed that rapping sounds were continually being heard around Margarita Fox. When the raps were noted down and checked, it was found they gave out a coded message and said that they were from a peddler who had been murdered and his body was to be found in the cellar. To everybody's amazement a body was duly found. The rappings continued and by 1850 both sisters were giving public demonstrations, proving that there was life beyond the grave. Spiritualism became fashionable with the middle classes and spread to Europe.

Among the lower middle class and the working class in parts of the mid-nineteenth century Britain and elsewhere, there was an explosion of radical thinking and free thought with the advent of Owenism, Feminism and Socialism. This occurred in the newly industrialized areas of Lancashire, Yorkshire and the Midlands in the 1830s to mid-1860s. A variety of Spiritualism came about with the spokesperson James Burn. He said that each person's soul was their own. He was anti-establishment in that he challenged the way the established churches laid claim to people's souls.

Meanwhile Christian Socialism began to emerge as a movement among the wealthier of the middle classes. They embraced Spiritualism and took proof of life after death as a confirmation of their own faith. The Rev Stainton Moses, who had psychic gifts - which included levitating tables and producing spirit hands - became a leader of the movement. In producing his book *Spirit Teachings* in 1883 he claimed he'd had the help of the spirit world. *Spirit Teachings* became the bible of British Spiritualism. Spiritualism's following swelled. When it added influential recruits, the latitude it had enjoyed vanished as Establishment Christians turned on it and called Spiritualism the work of the devil.

In 1882 Moses helped found the Society for Psychical research. Such was the interest in all things spiritual that even Victorian luminaries such as Gladstone and Alfred Lord Tennyson joined. The National Spiritualists Association of America was formed in 1893.

In the 1920's Arthur Conan Doyle, the creator of Sherlock Holmes, spent a quarter of a million pounds promoting Spiritualism in lecture tours, particularly in America. He claimed personal validation through automatic writings he had received from his son, Kinsley and his brother, Innes.

The Greater World Christian Spiritualist League (later Association) was founded in 1931. The inspiration for this movement came from the medium Winifred Moyes, who worked with her spirit guide Zodiac, a purported teacher in the temple at the time of Christ. Its mission was to spread the teachings of Jesus Christ as relayed from the spirit world by the spirit guide Zodiac.

Spiritualism struggled to gain widespread acceptance, not helped by the exposure of many fraudulent mediums. Most mediums in the beginning used a cabinet to sit in, but there were shameful incidents in which mediums appeared dressed as a ghostly figure impersonating spirits. Sometimes special aluminium telescopic rods were used to manipulate objects, such as musical instruments. At other times mediums wore special shoes, which would allow them to make rapping sounds undetected. Other mediums visiting a new town would memorise names on gravestones so that they could use them in their sessions. Certainly the great magician, Houdini, did much to debunk fraudulent mediums by exposing hidden means they were using in séance rooms to cause objects to move. For instance he exposed the famous Boston medium Mina Crandon of making the sound of bell ring in the séance room by the skilful movement of her ankle.

In England, in 1950, the Spiritualists National Union was formed and recognised as the official body of spiritualism. In 1951 the Witchcraft Act was repealed and replaced by the Fraudulent Mediums Act, which meant that true mediums could practice unhindered. Public demonstrations of psychic abilities became popular.

Beliefs and philosophy

The philosophical basis of Spiritualism rests on establishing a scientific basis for the existence of the spirit world rather than blind faith. Unlike most other major religions, Spiritualism does not tie its adherents to a creed or dogma. The Spiritualists National Union in the UK is similar to spiritualists' organizations elsewhere that adhere to basic principles and these are:

1. The Fatherhood of God.
2. The Brotherhood of Man.
3. The Communion of Spirits and the Ministry of Angels.
4. The continuous existence of the human soul.
5. Personal responsibility.
6. Compensation and retribution hereafter for all the good and evil deeds done on Earth.
7. Eternal progress, open to every human soul.

The first principle is central: a majority of spiritualists believe in God, though by names such as Infinite Intelligence, Mother-Father God, or most often the 'God of your understanding'. Purposely, Spiritualism leaves the defining of God to the individual. A general consensus might be that God is an ever-present, positive force in the universe. A belief in Spiritualism often does not require you to change your view of or definition of God. Spiritualism has been called a "religion of conviction not conversion".

The second principle is that all of humanity is part of the same family. Divisions between people on the grounds of wealth, colour, race or religion are unfounded and unhelpful. Spiritualism is egalitarian.

The third principle is that there is a spiritual reality, with which we can communicate and from which ask for help. Spiritualism gives substance to its promise of eternal life through the revelations of mediumship.

The fourth principle is that Spirit is indestructible. When the physical body dies, the Spirit continues as an integral part of a world which interpenetrates ours, but which is in a different dimension, the spirit world.

The fifth principle reflects the importance of personal responsibility: where we end up in this life and the next is dependent on our own actions. We must all individually take responsibility for our spiritual progress. Spiritualists do not depend on God or higher spiritual entities to address their unresolved life issues.

The sixth principle shares much with the law of *Karma*: For every action there is a reaction in the universe. Bad deeds result in bad consequences for the individual.

The seventh and last principle establishes for spiritualists that it does not matter where a person is in their spiritual development, they can make progress. We all have the potential to overcome obstacles we find in front of us.

Those who are in the Christian Spiritualist tradition would adhere to the principles listed below, which come from the Greater World Christian Spiritualists Association.

1. Believe in one God who is Love.
2. Accept the Leadership of Jesus the Christ.
3. Believe that God manifests through the power of Holy Spirit.
4. Believe in the survival of the soul and its individuality after physical death.
5. Believe in Communion with God, with His angelic ministers and with souls existing in conditions other than the Earth Life.
6. Believe that all forms of Life created by God intermingle, are interdependent and evolve until perfection is attained.
7. Believe in perfect justice of the Divine Laws governing all Life.
8. Believe that sins committed can only be rectified by the sinner through the redemptive power of Jesus the Christ, by repentance and service to others.

The Spiritualist Cosmology is a universe comprising vibrations. This includes everything and everyone. Vibration levels range from low (and slow) to high (and rapid) frequency. The Medium is a person who can tune into the higher vibrations. The way a person lives their life determines the level of vibration on which they function. Positive thoughts promote more positive (higher) vibration, negative thoughts a lower rate of vibration.

Sir Oliver Lodge (died 1940) and Sir William Crookes (died 1919), were pioneer physicists of radio and television who believed the universe is filled with a material called *ether* which conducted vibrations of a range of types rather as radio and television signals rely on waveforms. The ether vibrated at much higher frequencies, however. Spiritualists claim, but many scientists dispute, that ether is continuous throughout the universe, as it acts as a connecting medium to everything. Ether holds atoms together and transmits vibrations from one piece of matter to another. It is the transmitter of every kind of force in the universe, especially light, electricity and magnetism. To some Spiritualists, recent discoveries in quantum mechanics and the behaviour of certain sub-atomic particles support this theory.

Spiritualists perceive the universe as composed of mind and matter without limit. Mind is the cause of the vibrations and matter is its effect. Physical matter is just a motion at a fixed rate of vibration. So mind acts upon matter, with mind being positive and matter negative.

Some spiritualists also see the universe as one big thought. Other Spiritualists say that the mind substance is in fact the Universal Mind, which is seeking to express itself. In a hologram analogy, some say that each atom must hold within it part of this great Mind. Other Spiritualists say that the universe is a collection of past minds, which have been strengthened by knowledge and spiritual values. All things in the universe are servants to this Universal Mind. The mind of man is seen as capable of evolution: as we attain finer and finer planes of consciousness we gain more of the capabilities we imagine for ourselves. The ultimate goal is to find total affinity with divinity. Other Spiritualists claim that when we return to the vibrations we came from we return to God. However, most people remain toward the gross end of the vibration spectrum, given that we inhabit the level to which our minds and bodies are attached.

The essence of Spiritualism is mediumship. The medium has the skill to tune into the vibrations of the Other World, which has a higher vibration. Mediums tune into this and are able to translate communications from the spirit world to others, through their ability to see, feel, or, more commonly, hear messages from spirits. They seek to demonstrate the continuity of life after death.

It is said by Spiritualists that when people pass to the spirit world they enter the realm which is most suited to their vibrations. Some are fortunate enough to go to 'Summerland' described by Native Americans as the 'Happy Hunting Ground' or the 'Isle of the Blessed' by the Celts. In the higher realms of the spirit world, colours are more vivid, rivers pure, natural beauty pervades all. One Spiritualist described his Heaven as "the indescribable unity with the divine whole that is joy and upliftment beyond description".

In this realm the last attachments to our world are severed and the last vestiges of personality are dissipated. Beings travel anywhere at the speed of light and communicate soul to soul. They can move objects by willpower. There are no human forms, just beings radiating an inner aura of light, as the soul is clothed in a body of light. Beings meet their spiritual soul family, some of whom they may not have met on the Earth plane and often consult them before reincarnating on the Earth plane.

On this plane any work is voluntary and is for the sheer joy of it. Each calling has its rightful place, as halls of music, halls of fabrics, studios and libraries. There are doctors who work in the Great Hall of Rest where they help people make the transition to the spirit world. Doctors also help healers on the Earth plane. Children grow up in the spirit world if they die young. They inhabit the reality most suited to them and their teachers bring them up and educate them.

Spiritualism has a place for the negative aspects of being, too. Those who have missed out on doing good deeds and works on the Earth plane are likely to gravitate to the dark realms of 'Winterland', colder, dimmer and less colourful than its counterpart. Foul odours permeate the air, people hold their heads in their hands with despair. Some take on the appearance of monsters, which can torment fellow inmates. Some particularly evil people can spend centuries in this realm until they resolve to progress to higher realms.

Now we have outlined the world of spirit, we can look at how Spiritualists see humankind. The human body is seen as a biological energy system but essentially it is driven by spiritual energy. The centres of psychic energy are seen in the seven vortices of energy called charkas, which are sited opposite ductless glands in the endocrine system. Their function is to draw in the life force and stimulate the glands' hormonal output. When these vortices of psychic energy spin quickly, then the person is well; if they slow down then the person is or becomes unwell.

Next comes the aura: it has two 'layers' of physical electro-magnetism interwoven with etheric substance. The first protrudes from the body 37 mm (1 ½ inches). Our inner aura emanates from the core of our body and spreads to about 600 mm (2 feet) from the body. The colour of the aura shows the state of health of the individual as all life is embedded in the aura. With Kirlian photography the aura can be photographed. A medium has a special aura because there is no barrier between her aura and the spirit world.

Human beings also possess an etheric body, which is an exact copy of the physical body, but the atoms on the etheric plane vibrate at a different frequency. At death the etheric body hangs around the physical body for about three days and then dissolves. The soul then uses the vehicle of the astral body to journey to the astral world.

Anything on Earth may be replicated in the astral world, only at a higher vibration. The astral body is a complete replica of the physical body but vibrates at a higher rate. This astral body, which you occupy when you die, lives in a realm governed by thought, as in the saying, "as you think, so you are". The conditions a person finds himself or herself in at death are governed by the quality of thinking that person has engaged in during their life. Astral body travel and near-death experiences by the living are the result of a suspension of physical functions.

Mediumship

Making contact with the souls of the deceased is the function of the Medium, the central figure of Spiritualism. Mediumistic abilities can be cultivated with proper training. For spirit communication mediums often rely on spirit guides, which are spirits that have a particular affinity with the medium; they may have known each other in previous incarnations. Guides facilitate and act as intermediaries in exchanges between the medium and the spirits who want to communicate. Spiritualists say that there is a Guide for each of us. Guides inhabit a special realm in the spirit world, where some are said to have remained for centuries.

The spirits themselves view mortals as the 'shadow people'. Compared to the great light they bathe in, we live in partial darkness. Spirits say there is but one power in the universe: God. We are all part of God but we each function as a separate consciousness. Our materiality separates us from higher consciousness. Our egos and personalities can be dissolved in the realm of the spirit, opening a higher plane of consciousness to us.

Mediums vary in their techniques and abilities in contacting spirit.

A clairsentient medium can feel the presence of the spirit using their emotional body and mind. For instance spirits will often bring with them the condition of which they died, such as a heart attack or cancer; such a medium may physically feel these conditions - as strong emotions or feelings of empathy - when they sense the spirit.

In physical mediumship the medium can manifest objects from the spirit world. The audience or congregation would see things appear. A century ago this was the most important type of mediumship. Typically it involved the materialisation of people or objects - or levitation. Sometimes spirit hands would manifest; cones would fly through the air with spirit voices speaking through them. In one process, transfiguration, the physical mediums would have spirit faces superimposed on their own. Sometimes there would be full materialisations of Spirit and they would wander round the room and talk to people. There were also *apports*, objects transported from the spirit world and given to a specific person. In one recorded séance, Red Cloud, a guide of one of the mediums, gave a jewel to each participant.

Some mediums used automatic writing. The Spirit Guide uses the pen of the medium to write down messages. A famous case of this was Madame Blavatsky (1831 - 1891) who founded the Theosophical Society; she had whole books dictated to her by Spirit masters and wrote *Isis Unveiled* and *The Secret Doctrine* by this means.

Another type of mediumship is trance. Here the breathing of the medium becomes spasmodic, heartbeat increases and there may be some involuntary movements. They can then become a vessel of communication for Spirit. I personally have known a medium, Ray Brown, who goes into a trance and then becomes Paul, a friend and contemporary of Jesus Christ. He is then capable of healing work. I have witnessed him, while in trance, despite no medical training, successfully diagnose and treat a friend of mine.

A further technique used by mediums is a process called channelling. Spirit communicates directly through the medium, a process popularised in books by Shirley MacLaine and Helen Cohn Schucman among others.

Some mediums carry out healing, but more often than not from my experience as a spiritual healer in a spiritualist church, people can specialise in healing without becoming a medium. Healers are basically channellers of spiritual energy. Healers allow the energy from the higher realms to flow through them. The spiritual healers in the UK are governed by law and I can personally vouch for the thoroughness of the training. Absent healing is when an individual healer or group send out healing energies to the patient elsewhere.

Spiritualism has a long tradition of healing, one of the most famous practitioners, Harry Edwards, received as many as 9,000 letters a year and is said to have cured people of tuberculosis and even cancer. Modern day healers include Betty Shine, Matthew Manning and Ray Brown.

Ceremonies and worship

Some Spiritualist Churches follow services of worship, which are similar to Christian ones. There is praying to God and singing hymns. However, unlike Christian services, the central part of the service is where the medium relays messages to the congregation from their relatives and friends. There is usually spiritual healing offered before or after the service. If the Spiritualist church is a Christian one, they will follow the usual Christian celebrations and festivals such as Christmas and Easter.

Green Spiritualism

The spiritual teachings found in Spiritualism are Green in nature because they are founded on the acceptance of personal responsibility for every aspect of our lives. The consumer society feeds into a narcissistic individualism blind to our responsibilities in the wider context of a shared world. Marketeers are constantly pushing us to consume but - with only certain exceptions around legal requirements on health and safety - discourage us from thinking of the consequences of or taking responsibility for the planetary consequences. Spiritualism teaches that we are responsible for our actions individually and collectively.

This emphasis on responsibility even stretches beyond the physical plane to the wider context of our own spiritual journeys. In terms of leading a Green lifestyle, this philosophy is a good fit: Acting while taking a shared responsibility for each other and the whole planet is the way to be Green. Therefore being party to social injustice - through exploiting the poor in sweatshop labour, creating poverty or ignoring climate change implications of our actions -would be self-evidently unacceptable to Spiritualists because of the karmic implications.

Spiritualism is also Green because of the brotherhood of man, a collective it recognises to encourage us to realise we are all part of a global community. This approach is an antidote to selfishness. It means that all global environmental and social problems, wherever they are happening on Earth, are the concern of Spiritualists.

Spiritualists take a Green approach to life because their faith highlights how important their thoughts are as motivators to action. Since "you are what you think", when we change our thinking for the better we change ourselves as well. Spiritualism teaches that your thoughts and your way of thinking are the basis for your being and your vibration. As we shall see, being truly Green is, after all, little more than being thoughtful, being aware and taking individual responsibility.

For the Spiritualist, what happens after death is dependent upon how you live your life on Earth; there is complete accountability. Selfless service to humanity is a very prominent theme in Spiritualism and is seen as a high ideal. Living a moral, caring life yields good results in the next world

The descriptions of Summerland show clearly the pristine quality of the natural environment. Spirits always emphasise that we need to try and maintain such an environment on Earth. Spiritualists see Nature as an expression of the Spirit.

Spiritualist churches even organise themselves in the Green way. A democratically elected committee headed by a president usually runs a church. They embody the Green principle of democratic representation. The structure tends to be less hierarchical than in other faiths, where spiritual authority is often invested in a single person. In a Spiritualist church, authority is given to those who have spiritual experiences rather than book knowledge. If there is any spiritual authority, it is invested in the medium, but they are only in that position because of their special gift.

Spiritualism also adopts a Green approach to healing which uses natural means rather than being totally dependent on high-tech medication. Spiritual healing is an integral part of the Spiritualist way of life. The philosophy embodies the idea that healing is natural, can be done by all and is free. There are no experts.

The cultural perception and value system Spiritualism offers is markedly different from that of the faith-free culture that prevails in the West today.

Spiritualist Websites

www.thespiritualist.org
www.spiritualism.org
www.survivalafterdeath.org
www.christianspiritualism.org
www.spiritualplatform.org
www.pathwaystospirit.co.uk
www.spiritlincs.com
www.snu.org.uk
www.answers.com
www.spirithistory.com
www.spiritualism.meetup.com
www.graterworld.com
www.paranormalreview.com
www.arthurfindlaycollege.org
www.isfederation.org
www.spiritualistchatroom.com
www.netdoctor.co.uk
www.spiritweb.com
www.spiritlearn.com

CHAPTER 12 : BAHÁ'Í

Introduction

One of the most modern religions is the international faith of Bahá'í, which has now grown to be the seventh largest religion in the world. The majority of Bahá'ís live in Asia (3.6 million), Africa (1.8 million), and Latin America (900,000). According to some estimates, the largest Bahá'í community in the world is in India with 2.2 million Bahá'ís; next is Iran, with 350,000; and the USA with an estimated 150,000 members.

History

Bahá'í originated in the nineteenth century in Persia, modern day Iran in reaction to what was seen as a nation in chaos in part due to a corrupt Shi'ite Muslim priesthood.

The Bahá'í story begins with Siyyid Ali-Muhammad, who was born in 1819 in Shiraz in southern Iran, a city steeped in ancient Persian culture. The title Siyyid means that he was a descendant of the prophet Muhammad. Ali-Muhammad practised as a strict Shi'ite Muslim and made an extended pilgrimage to the holy shrines in Iraq in 1841, resulting in some deep spiritual experiences. He returned home, married and settled down. Soon after he began to have powerful, recurring visions. He felt God was permeating his whole being. He recorded his mystical experiences in his book *Qayyúmu'l-Asmá'* which was written (in Arabic) in a similar style to that of the Qur'an. The Prophet Muhammad's writings foretell that there would come forth a new prophet after him called the Mahdí who some Shia thought would be the return of the 'twelfth Imam' who had disappeared centuries earlier.

Then, in 1844 Siyyid Ali-Muhammad went to Mecca and there publicly declared that he was the Báb or gate to God, in other words the Mahdi of whom The Prophet had spoken. His claims were promptly dismissed by the ulamá, the intellectual, elite Shi'ite priesthood. They said that the Báb had not shown the signs of his coming indicated in the Qur'an, such as the raising of the dead. In 1845 the Báb was put under house arrest in Shiraz.

Despite imprisonment the Báb had gathered round him some 18 disciples and they started to spread his message to other parts of Iran. In 1846 the Báb's house arrest ended when he was taken under the protection of the governor of Isfahán. But by 1848 the Grand Vizier (prime minister) had arranged for the Báb to be imprisoned in a remote fortress. This is understandable as he was regarded as a threat to the authorities: he claimed to be a manifestation of God, who had come to help mankind to love God. He further threatened the *status quo* by publishing a second book. In it he advocated changes in the Islamic law, calling for justice for non-believers and an end to the practice of beating children and animals.

The Báb's influence grew further as by 1848 he had written half a million verses and 100,000 of these had been widely circulated. Central to the Báb's message was that a new world religion was about to appear.

Despite constant persecution through burnings, beheadings and the massacre of 313 followers at Tabarsí, the Bábi religion spread. Finally, in 1850, the Shah's minister, Mírzá Taqí Khán, ordered the execution of the Báb, which was carried out the same year. He was just 31.

The Báb's life was ended, but not his story. Further persecutions of the Báb's followers came in 1852 when they were accused of an assassination attempt on the Shah.

Bahá'u'lláh was born two years earlier than the Báb. He was the son of a government minister, yet received a very basic education. Despite this, from an early age, he displayed great intellectual gifts, for example when discussing theology with the clergy as a boy. By the age of 22, when his father died, he was already renowned for his wisdom and learning and was even offered his father's position in the government, but refused it. Instead, he became a follower of the Báb.

In 1852 he was arrested as a suspect following the same attempted assassination of the Shah. He was imprisoned for four months in Tehran. In a visionary dream whilst in the 'Black Pit' of the prison, a divine figure told him, "Verily we shall render thee victorious by thyself and by thy pen."

This had a profound effect on Bahá'u'lláh. Though he told no one about his experience it provided him with the inspiration he would need in his mission to see the Bábí movement grow into a new faith for all. Difficult times lay ahead. In 1853 the Shah forced him to flee, first to Baghdad then the following year to Kurdistan. There for two years he lived the life of a dervish. During a visit to a seminary, he impressed the most prominent scholars of the day with his wisdom and understanding.

In 1857 Bahá'u'lláh returned to Baghdad and for the next seven years he worked hard to revive the Bábí movement, which had suffered years of repression and persecution. He gathered round him a group of faithful disciples who spread the Báb's message to the masses. His own writings were more accessible. In his *Book of Certainty*, he wrote extensively about the manifestations of God and the fulfilment of prophecy. He described his mystical experiences in his writings in the form of poetry, which became very popular.

All this time in Baghdad he was not a free man but under the control of the Ottoman Emperor who in 1863 called him to the imperial capital, Istanbul. Just before leaving Baghdad, Bahá'u'lláh made a significant announcement. Although he had hinted at his mission, it was in a statement in the garden of Ridván that he first made clear that he was the World Teacher or Universal Manifestation of God that other prophets, including Jesus, Krishna, the Buddha and Muhammad, had foretold.

The Emperor and his ministers saw Bahá'u'lláh as a threat and exiled him again, to Adrianopole, Edirne in western modern Turkey. Still the mullahs felt their authority was threatened by the presence of Bahá'u'lláh and demanded he was given a life sentence at the penal colony of Akká, then in Syria.

The majority of the followers of the Báb recognised Bahá'u'lláh as the one promised by the Báb and from then on they became known as Bahá'ís. Bahá'u'lláh continued to write and communicate with his followers and in 1877 he was allowed to move out of prison in Akka to a house in the country, referred to as the 'Mansion of Bahjí'. He died there in 1892 aged 75.

Bahá'u'lláh named his son `Abdu'l-Bahá as successor. He was always close to his father and known by those around Him as the "Mystery of God" or the "Master." From an early age he visited mosques, visited the sick, answered letters from around the world and continued to develop and support the expansion of the Bahá'í faith. He toured extensively and in 1911 visited the UK, France and Egypt. In 1912 he visited 38 US states, as well as France, Germany, Hungary and Austria. During the First World War he was very active in Palestine, ensuring food supplies for the destitute, efforts which were recognised by the British government in a knighthood. His contributions to world peace after WW1 included correspondence with the Central Organisation for a Durable Peace based in The Hague. He died of a fever in 1921 aged 77.

`Abdu'l-Bahá named his grandson, Shoghi Effendi, as his heir. He became known as the 'Guardian of the Cause of God'. He was a natural organiser and took the Bahá'ís to an international dimension by establishing the International Bahá'í Council. In 1951 he established the organisation called the Hands of the Cause of God to assist national Bahá'í assemblies with their work. There were in 1953 only twelve national spiritual assemblies and a ten-year campaign was announced to boost growth. It worked. By 1963 there were 56 national spiritual assemblies and 4,500 local spiritual assemblies, with Bahá'ís gathering in 120,000 different locations.

Shoghi Effendi's sudden death in London in 1957 aged 60 posed a problem for the movement as no successor had been chosen. The Bahá'ís went back to the writings of Bahá'u'lláh and `Abdu'l-Bahá which stated that the Bahá'ís should be governed by an elected body called the Universal House of Justice. In 1963 the national spiritual assemblies elected nine people to represent them in the first Universal House of Justice. This body acted as the official interpreter and promoter of the Bahá'í movement. Today Bahá'í is certainly one of the most international of the religions: 11 percent of its members come from the West, 31 per cent from Southeast Asia and India, 28 per cent from sub-Saharan Africa and the remaining 30 per cent spread across other parts of the world.

Doctrine

`Abdu'l-Bahá, defined a Bahá'í very succinctly saying, "To be a Bahá'í simply means to love all the world; to love humanity and try to serve it." The purpose of life on Earth is for each individual to develop the spiritual and moral qualities that lie at the core of his or her nature. Bahá'u'lláh stated, "The purpose of God in creating man hath been, and will ever be, to enable him to know his Creator and to attain His Presence".

The cosmology of the Bahá'ís developed from the writings of Bahá'u'lláh (1817-1892) and his son, `Abdu'l-Bahá (1844-1921). According to Bahá'í teaching, the present universe is a perpetual emanation of the First Cause, namely God. The Bahá'ís accept evolution as scientific fact. They see the elements in the universe as stable but taking different forms at different times. As `Abdu'l-Bahá said "The existence of God is everlasting and eternal." Creation is then seen as an expression of the attributes of the one God.

God is seen as something that cannot be directly known but He can be described by His attributes. So God is the "unknowable essence" but can be recognised by his manifestations. The manifestations of God evoke in people a love of God, which gives them a source of everlasting joy and happiness. `Abdu'l-Bahá summed this up when he said, "What an infinite degree of love is reflected by the divine manifestations towards mankind". The love that people seek is attained through knowledge of God. The aim of our life is to become the perfect lover of God, seeing things with a pure heart and seeing the face of God in all. As `Abdu'l-Bahá said, "The more we love each other, the nearer we shall be to God".

The Bahá'í religion pivots around the life and teachings of Bahá'u'lláh. Bahá'ís see him as a manifestation of God and the current messenger for mankind. So obedience to his teachings is synonymous with obedience to God. As Bahá'u'lláh put it, "Faith in God and knowledge of Him cannot be fully attained except by practising all that He hath commanded."

Bahá'u'lláh (1817-1892) and his son, `Abdu'l-Bahá (1844-1921), both had the gift of prophecy. Bahá'u'lláh predicted that Napoleon III would fall from power, which came about – in 1870. In 1912 `Abdu'l-Bahá prophesied the First World War and even the rise of Communism - and its eventual fall. He foretold the Nazi holocaust in the Second World War. Bahá'u'lláh foresaw the decline of influence of the priesthood in both Islamic and Christian societies. They both foretold the explosion of scientific knowledge and the advent of nuclear weapons.

Another Bahá'í claim of Bahá'u'lláh's divinity lay in how his teachings about the need for world peace were very advanced for the 19th century. It was not until 1963 and Pope John XXIII's Peace Declaration that another world figure made a similar call. Bahá'ís add that Bahá'u'lláh was exceptionally gifted, for instance his mastery of Arabic and the exceptional quality of his written work without the usual thorough grounding. Bahá'u'lláh saw his writings as the "outpourings from the clouds of the Divine Bounty". Bahá'u'lláh had a talent that is seen as miraculous: he could quote extensively from religious scriptures he apparently had never studied.

Those in Bahá'u'lláh's company said the divine emanation coming from Bahá'u'lláh was palpable; it made them feel serene and exhilarated, even one intending assassin. The fanatical Muslim saw it as his religious duty to assassinate Bahá'u'lláh and came armed. The assassin approached Bahá'u'lláh, gun at the ready, yet he could not bring himself to shoot. In fact handed his weapon over to the son, 'Abdu'l-Bahá. The assassin thereupon became so upset that Bahá'u'lláh sent someone to make sure he got safely home! Bahá'u'lláh came from a wealthy family. His generosity 'knew no bounds'; he was always giving food to the poor.

During his house arrest in Baghdad Bahá'u'lláh was asked by the mullahs to perform miracles as a proof of his divinity. In response, he made clear his view that the performing of miracles is not actually a prerequisite for a prophet. However, he did agree to perform one miracle, one which they would have to choose—on the condition that if he performed it they would accept him as the true manifestation of God. The mullahs did not take up his offer - for fear, presumably, of the implications for them if Bahá'u'lláh somehow managed it.

The Bahá'í faith accepts as valid all the great religions, their teachings and their teachers. Bahá'ís see each age as having its spiritual master. So in one age it might be Buddha and in another Jesus but in this age it is Bahá'u'lláh. They believe that there is only one true religion and all of the Messengers of God have progressively revealed its nature. This one religion is continually evolving and each particular religious system represents a stage in the evolution of the whole. So, to its followers, the Bahá'í Faith represents the current stage in the evolution of religion. Together, the world's great religions are expressions of a single unfolding divine plan. Bahá'ís see their own doctrine as an extension of all the previous doctrines. Bahá'u'lláh said: "Let all religions agree, [and] make the nations one so that they may see each other as one family and the whole Earth as one home." He also said "True religion is a source of love and agreement among men." According to the Bahá'í writings, the process of revelation will continue indefinitely into the future and humankind will see the coming of a great many more Manifestations.

The emphasis of the teachings of the Bahá'ís is to serve the cause of mankind, in essence to study the cause, practise the teachings and then spread the message. Bahá'u'lláh said, "God made it incumbent upon every soul to deliver his cause according to his ability." Serving humanity is an important aspect of this, as "service is prayer." 'Abdu'l-Bahá' said, "To serve mankind is to minister to the needs of the people". Work is seen as a form of prayer and it is incumbent on each Bahá'í to earn their own living if they are able to.

The teachings of the Bahá'ís emphasise the need to live a moral life. Bahá'u'lláh said, "Let integrity and uprightness distinguish all thine acts." Speaking the truth is important as Bahá'u'lláh said, "Truthfulness is the foundation of all human virtues." Other qualities are being "fair in judgement and guarded in thy speech". Other virtues are practising "forbearance, mercy, compassion and loving kindness towards all peoples." Sexual relations are only allowed within marriage and homosexual practices are not permitted. Drugs and alcohol are to be avoided.

The need to practise prayer is given great prominence. Bahá'u'lláh said that all Bahá'ís should "commune with God every day through prayer." 'Abdu'l-Bahá said "The impulse to pray is a natural one, springing from man's love of God."

At death Bahá'ís believe the soul leaves the body and continues its journey in the spirit world. But deeds done in this world produce consequences in the hereafter. In the final analysis, heaven can be seen partly as a state of nearness to God; hell is a state of remoteness from God. Each state follows as a natural consequence of individual efforts, or the lack thereof, to develop spiritually. The key to spiritual progress is to follow the path outlined by the Manifestations of God.

Ceremonies and Worship

Bahá'ís may worship in any building and many Bahá'ís worship in their own homes. In fact, each continent has its dedicated Bahá'í temple. The movement's world centre is in Haifa, in Israel. Worship centres on readings from the Bahá'í scriptures and on prayer. For daily use, a Bahá'í will choose one of three obligatory prayers. The long obligatory prayer must be said once every 24 hours, the medium obligatory prayer three times a day and the short obligatory prayer is said during the afternoon.

There are also special services such as the marriage service where the people marrying have to promise to "abide by the will of God". The Bahá'í law is that both sets of parents have to give permission for a marriage to take place.

Festivals

Festivals punctuate the Bahá'í year. There are nine Holy days a year and ideally it is recommended that these Holy days be used for activities benefiting mankind, such as charitable works. The Bahá'í year includes fasting in March, an April new year celebration, the Ridván festival in late April, a series of festivals celebrating key dates in the faith's history and the lives of its leaders, two in May, one in July and the birth of the Báb's in October and Bahá'u'lláh's on 12 November.

Green Bahá'í

The Bahá'í faith's outlook is perhaps one of the most Green. Bahá'u'lláh stated, "Nature is God's Will and is its expression in and through the contingent world." For Bahá'ís, Nature and all of creation reflect the qualities and attributes of God, to be cared for and maintained by mankind. They see Nature as an interdependent whole with co-operation and reciprocity its main characteristics. Man cannot be separated from Nature; as 'Abdu'l-Bahá says, "We cannot separate the human heart from the environment." He said the way man relates to the environment depends on "His inner life which moulds the environment and is itself also deeply affected by it."

The Bahá'ís have always shown a signal commitment to the environment. They have an explicitly Green agenda and have engaged local communities everywhere. Their international involvement includes a presence in Nairobi at the United Nations Environment Programme headquarters where they maintain a staffed office. They fund an office of Social and Economic Development; and they had an organisational role in the Rio Earth summit of 1992.

Bahá'ís were very much in evidence when I attended the 2002 UN Conference on Sustainability in Johannesburg. Bahá'í development projects have grassroots origins and application but they address both material and spiritual needs. Outside help, both financial and technical, is available to local projects (see www.bahai.org). All projects are open to everyone and for the good of everyone, regardless of religious belief.

Bahá'ís have always focussed on the importance of agriculture. The Bahá'í International Community, a UN-recognised non-governmental organization (NGO), is eager to advise local Bahá'í communities attempting to develop sustainable agriculture.

Since the 1992 Rio Earth Summit, Bahá'ís have been involved in many of its Agenda 21 sustainability projects. Local Bahá'í communities in the UK have become active proponents of the Local Agenda 21 initiative, working with partner groups and with local authorities. In Japan, the Tora project is researching solar energy collection. In Malaysia Bahá'ís operate a recycling scheme. The Bahá'í Vocational Institute for Rural Women, located in India, helps Indian women grow vegetables and develop skills in making clothes. In rural Kenya, a Bahá'í-sponsored development project encourages and empowers village women to develop their own entrepreneurial weaving businesses. Bahá'ís in the United Kingdom, the Philippines, Singapore and Taiwan have all organized and/or sponsored arts and educational activities geared to creating awareness of the fragile environment and conservation.

Whereas with many faiths followers' representatives are appointed, those of the Bahá'ís are elected democratically—another example of the Green credentials of Bahá'í. The way the Bahá'ís should organise themselves was described in the work of Bahá'u'lláh called the *Kitáb-i-Aqdas*, which was completed in 1873. If there are nine or more Bahá'ís in an area then they can elect their Local Spiritual Assembly. Anyone who is a Bahá'í and 21 or older can vote in the annual elections. There are no nominations or canvassing.

The local assembly governs the affairs of the local group and helps promote the Bahá'í religion locally. Delegates are also elected who vote for candidates to sit on National Spiritual Assemblies, each of which votes for nine candidates to serve on the Universal House of Justice, with its seat in Haifa. This is the body that governs the affairs of the Bahá'í religion worldwide. This Green structure allows people not only to govern the affairs of their local assembly but also have a voice on the faith's world stage. Latest figures suggest that there are 11,740 local spiritual assemblies and 182 national spiritual assemblies - as compared with 192 member states of the UN.

"The Earth is but one country, and mankind its citizens", said Bahá'u'lláh. He believed there was a need for a new form of world government. This could only function effectively when people had evolved spiritually. The oneness of humanity is, for Bahá'ís, the fundamental spiritual and social truth of this age - another example of its Green thinking. World citizenship encompasses the principles of social and economic justice, both within and between nations; non-adversarial decision making at all levels of society; equality of the sexes; racial, ethnic, national and religious harmony; and the willingness to sacrifice for the common good.

It was over one hundred years ago that Baha'u'llah called for an international legal system, a sharing of the world's resources, a re-alignment of the world's economic and inter-governmental relations, and moderation in human consumption. Today his vision makes sense to almost everyone.

Bahá'ís view of global economics is also Green: a common world currency, universal weights and measures and the lifting of trade barriers. In the workplace they hold that relations between employer and employee should be based on spiritual principles and should involve profit sharing. Bahá'ís believe that the most important industry is agriculture and this should be prioritised and properly supported.

Bahá'ís take a pro-peace and an anti-war stance. They promote the idea of arms limitations agreements. They seek to prioritize and promote world peace.

Social justice requires equitable sharing of wealth and obliges those who can to help the disadvantaged of the world community. This can be seen quite clearly in Bahá'ís development work in poorer developing countries.

Bahá'ís have a particular emphasis on equal treatment for women. As a practical result of this, for example, in India great importance is placed on the empowerment of women, through programmes where they can improve their literacy, learn skills to increase household income, as well as learning about nutrition, health and preserving the environment. When they go back to their villages they become agents for change.

Bahá'ís are Green because they focus on the community. 'Abdu'l-Bahá described a sense of community as in: "Co-operation and mutual helpfulness is the basis of human society". Education is an expression of that sense of community involvement as all members of the community have a right to education. Bahá'u'lláh said, "The acquiring of knowledge is praiseworthy when it is coupled with ethical conduct and virtuous character." Unlike the clergy of some other religions, Bahá'ís see the advancement of scientific knowledge as no threat to their faith.

At a gathering of faiths at Windsor in the U.K., in 2009, to discuss the challenges of climate change prior to the Copenhagen conference, the Baha'i Faith leaders presented a plan that focuses on using a system of regional training institutes to encourage within the worldwide Baha'i community "acts of service related to environmental sustainability."

It seems abundantly clear that Bahá'ís have much to offer the world in terms of Green values, thinking and activism.

Bahá'í Websites

www.bahai.org
www.bahai.us
www.bahai.com
www.answers.com
www.manvel.org.uk
www.bahaiglobe.com
www.bahai-liobrary.com
www.statements-bahai.org
www.bupc.montana.com
www.media.bahai.org
www.bahaiindex.com
www.bcca.org
www.arcworld.org
www.ncf.ca
www.netcomuk.co.uk
www.origin.org

PART 2

GLOBAL ENVIRONMENTAL PROBLEMS AND WORLD POVERTY

CHAPTER 13 : THE WATER WE DRINK

Water shortages

Water makes up 81 per cent of our bodies and so for us fresh, uncontaminated water is the single most important resource on Earth. As well as drinking it, we use it for personal needs, to produce food and as a primary resource for industry, which consumes an amazing two thirds of our fresh water supplies. More remarkably, though, fresh water was a scarce resource on our Planet *before* we began overloading it with a population doubling so rapidly to almost 7 billion today.

Water is a finite resource and the water cycle on Earth is essentially a closed system—we always have the same amount of water. There's no shortage of water, *per se*: the oceans occupy two-thirds of the surface of the globe; but their water is saline. It's fresh water supply that is a problem - because it is so unevenly distributed around the globe. As a result of this anomaly, six countries benefit from half the world's supply of fresh water, five in the developing world and only Canada in the developed world.

We already have fresh water shortages in hotter countries, as opposed to temperate regions and this is now exacerbated by the effects of climate change. In poorer countries of Africa people, usually women, travel long distances daily to obtain fresh water. Even then it can be riddled with waterborne diseases. In a large percentage of newly industrialising countries, 'fresh' water becomes polluted beyond re-use. Over the last 100 years fresh water use per capita has increased six-fold against a three-fold increase in world population. Between 1960 and 2000, world fresh water use doubled from 1,800 km³ (cubic kilometres) to 3,600 km³. Future demand increases will come from the developing world where 90 per cent of the world's population growth is occurring at a rate that is exceeding the capacity of the Earth's water cycle to provide. By 2025, water withdrawals are predicted to increase by 50 per cent in developing countries and 18 per cent in developed countries. Unbelievably, one tenth of the world's major rivers no longer reach the sea due to withdrawals.

- **China's urban domestic water demand will increase from 50 billion tonnes to 80 billion tonnes a year, an increase of 60 per cent, says the World Bank.**
- **China's current annual rate of use of water in industry stands at 52 billion litres, but will increase to 269 billion litres within two decades.**

Already 2.8 billion people, 40 per cent of the world population, live with some sort of water scarcity. Water scarcity may even exist in water-abundant areas if there is heavy population pressure, excessive pollution or unsustainable consumption levels. According to the UN-backed World Commission on Water, coping with water scarcity will require global investment of $100 billion per year. The situation is set to get a lot worse because by 2025 two out of every three people on the Planet will face a level of water scarcity in one form or another. By 2050 4.2 billion people (45 per cent of the projected global population) will live in countries where there will be less than 50 litres per person, per day, which includes water needed for agriculture (20 litres a day is deemed the minimum for drinking, cooking, washing and sanitation). Yet to live a healthy life a person must have access to a minimum of 100 to 200 litres each day. This level of water scarcity raises the possibility of water wars in the future where the blue gold of water will replace the black gold of oil. It also highlights the possibility of widespread famine in those countries that cannot secure water supplies for growing the crops to feed their people. Disparity in the consumption of water throughout the world is massive.

- **75 per cent of the global population survive on approximately 50 litres a day, half the World Bank recommended minimum.**
- **In Africa annual per capita water withdrawals for personal use average 47 litres per day, whereas in the USA it is up to 400 litres per day.**

You can see from the statistics above that the need for water, on an individual basis alone, is huge, outstripping the world's water resources available. We must wake up and recognise now that existing sources and supply of fresh water for industry and agriculture in the near future is not sustainable.

Water for agriculture

Agriculture accounts for a boggling 70 per cent of water consumption globally - up to *95 per cent* of consumption in some developing countries. Irrigated agriculture accounts for only 20 per cent of cultivated land but produces over 40 per cent of the global harvest. This has significant implications for the future of water availability and food security worldwide.

The irrigated land area nearly tripled between 1950 and 2003, growing from 94 million to 277 million hectares globally. This growth, however, is tapering off as the water resources become stretched. Yet, if delivery to crops were more efficient, existing irrigation could produce far more food.

Water losses in agriculture are huge — down to archaic irrigation systems. So up to 60 per cent of the water never reaches the crop! It is quite possible for modern technology to provide more efficient irrigation systems such as the 'surge' type, which can cut losses in half.

Given the scale of the crisis, there is a strong case for donor nations to prioritise funding of irrigation upgrades everywhere. The charity Water Aid has done much to highlight this issue and organises practical projects around the world to deliver clean water and enhanced irrigation.

Irrigation can use 'blue' water, sources of water that the natural action of precipitation replaces. Water run-off from rainfall may renew water lost from rivers or the water table, just below the surface of the soil, aquifers or wells. The problem arises when irrigation systems use non-renewable water supplies which are not easily replenished through rainfall.

Aquifers can shrink or disappear with deforestation and in coastal areas aquifer over-exploitation leads to intrusion of salt water from the sea. A good friend of mine, an agricultural engineer and reliable source of information in this area, has visited the Punjab in India over many years in succession. His findings are that they are drilling their tube wells (wells sunk into the ground to gain access to aquifer water) several metres deeper each year. It is estimated that by 2025 the aquifer under the Punjab may be completely depleted.

Similarly, on the North China plain, they are using non-renewable water sources and as a consequence the water table is dropping at an average of 1.5 metres each year. There will be an impact of immense proportions on world food security as water supplies dry up, since the North China plain produces 40 per cent of that nation's grain.

All over the USA, aquifers feed water to 21 per cent of the country's irrigated land at rates faster than they recharge naturally. The Arabian Peninsula relies on 75 per cent of its water supplies coming from non-renewable sources for food production and experts have estimated that this supply will run out in approximately 50 years. There are also demands from the urban population for non-renewable water supplies from surrounding rural areas, which could otherwise be used for growing food.

- **Roughly 2 billion people—in both rural and urban environments—rely on non-renewable groundwater for daily water consumption.**
- **30 per cent of China's urban water supply is fed from non-renewable groundwater.**

Such a generalised shortage of water will impact on food security for the world before long. It takes a thousand tonnes of water to grow a tonne of wheat. World wheat production was predicted to reach 635 million tonnes in the 2009. Although total production has edged upward, this was thought unlikely to bring prices down as wheat stocks were low. It is now highly questionable whether future water resources will meet demand for irrigation on the scale needed. Water demand for agriculture is also fuelled by trends for 'fast food', rising meat consumption and a more varied diet across the expanding middle-class populations of Asia. Then, there are the land-grabs to grow bio-fuels.

Unless we address our global water shortage problems now and attempt to solve them by providing money and resources to developing countries so they may develop and manage their water resources more effectively, disastrous famines will return as regularly in our current century as they occurred in the last.

Water Wars

Spiritual Insights

We are entering a period when scarcity of water could increasingly become the flashpoint for conflict between peoples and nations. Here, we can take a moment to reflect on the wisdom of spiritual leaders and what the faith traditions have to say about the use of violence to steal, rather than share with others Nature's finite resources. They highlight, quite definitely, the need for an adequate sharing of water resources through practising compassion, love and co-operation.

Islam

Muhammad lived at a time of frequent conflicts in the Arabian Peninsula where tribal groups used armed aggression to establish territorial supremacy. In what is a beacon for us all today, He brought peace to the region through introducing laws about conservation and sharing of water resources. Water was seen as *mawat* or common property and the Islamic states realised that ethically and morally, water should be shared out according to need. Disputes were always settled by peaceful means, yet modern-day Muslim states have ignored their own religious heritage and threatened to go to war over water.

Resolve dissensions through discussions - Muhammad

Bahá'í

Bahá'u'lláh, in his lifetime (1817-1892), called for establishment of a world organisation similar to the UN to arbitrate in international disputes. He urged that the love of humanity should be put ahead of national self interest.

The highest of created beings fighting to obtain the lowest form of matter, earth - 'Abdu'l-Bahá, describing the futility of war.
The divine purpose is that men should live in unity, concord and agreement and should love one another - 'Abdu'l-Bahá

Christianity

But I say this to you who are listening: Love your enemies, do good to those who hate you, bless those who curse you, pray for those who treat you badly - Jesus Christ (Luke 6:27)

Taoism

Taoism is opposed to taking wealth by force. Taoism advocates non-aggressive, non-violent, peaceful coexistence of states.

Great conflict arises from wanting too much - Lao Tzu.

Sikhism

The highest religion is to rise to universal brotherhood - Guru Nanak.

Only those who love can find God - Guru Granth Sahib

Buddhism

Meditate on love so that you long for the welfare of all, even your enemies - Buddha

Who is the greater enemy ... the man outside or your evil thoughts within? - Buddha

One who can turn conflict into collaboration is the Buddha - Buddha

We can share the Earth and take care of it together - Tenzin Gyatso, the 14th Dalai Lama

Riverine squabbles

Sharing a river system with neighbours tests any country's patience. No fewer than 214 of the world's major river systems are shared by two or more countries. As water shortages become ever more acute, tensions will increase and the possibility of armed conflict - and the massive environmental degradation war brings - will be an ever-increasing risk. Historical precedents are numerous:

1960: Syria attempts to divert the Jordan River's headwaters, affecting Israel's water supply. Israel planes bomb the diversion project.

1967: During the Arab/Israeli war, Israel took and secured by occupation the vital water resources of the Jordan's headwaters and valued West Bank land. Thereafter, it imposed fixed quotas for water in favour of the Israelis, leaving Palestinians with depleting water supplies.

Now, some scholars estimate, at least a third of Israel's maintainable water yield is from the occupied territories. Satellite images clearly show that Israel's and the parts of the occupied territories it has settled are largely green—from growth of crops, trees and grass - while the Palestinian territories are mostly brown or desert.

1987: Iraq accused Syria of restricting the flow of the Euphrates and as a response to what they called theft, amassed troops on its borders to deal with the threat. Armed conflict was only avoided by the intervention of Saudi Arabia. Since then, disputes over water have arisen between Turkey and both Syria and Iraq.

1989 and the mid-nineties: the Turkish Prime Minister used water as a political weapon. He threatened to cut off the supply of water to Syria from the Euphrates if Syria continued to support the Kurdish rebels. Now Turkey intends to use more of the headwaters of the Tigris and Euphrates for irrigation at the expense of Syria and Iraq, both of which have rapidly growing populations.

Egypt is the most vulnerable to water shortages because 95 per cent of the run-off of the Nile originates from outside its borders. Ethiopia intends to divert approximately four billion cubic metres of water away from the Blue Nile. This must be a recipe for disaster, since Egypt has a rapidly increasing population and will need all its water to produce food for its own people. This is a conflict waiting to happen, especially now Egypt has enhanced its combat capability with advanced weapons purchased from the West.

A 2009 report from the US National Centre for Atmospheric Research warns that due to climate change, flow in some of the Planet's largest rivers is shrinking, including the Ganges, the Niger and the Yellow River in China. Flows in 925 rivers over a half century to 2004 were studied. Climate change impacted on a third of the major rivers. Though other major Asian rivers remained stable, their dependence on Himalayan glacier melt makes them susceptible to shrinkage in years to come.

Water Pollution

Spiritual Insights on water pollution

With its pollution, we have reached one of the most important issues concerning water. But before we discuss this, let us reflect on what ancient spiritual teachings tell us about our attitude towards the pollution of this most essential of resources. These are some of the more poignant sayings taken from spiritual scriptures highlighting the importance of conservation of fresh water in its pure state.

Hinduism

Water was considered to be sacred and vital to the ecosystem; as the Rig Veda states, "Water in the sky, water in the rivers, water in the well, whose source is the ocean; may all these sacred waters protect me" (Rig Veda 7, 49.2). Water is described as the foundation of the whole world, the essence of plant life and the elixir of immortality (Satapatha Brahmana VI 8, 2.2; III 6, 1.7). Water is seen as giving vigour, potency and vitality (Yajurveda 29, 53). Water is definitely not to be polluted, as the Atharva Veda states: "May all water on Earth remain pure and unpolluted". One ancient scripture said that a person who polluted ponds, well and tanks would go to hell (Bhoomukhanda 96, 7-8).

> *May the Water bring us well being!* - Atharva Veda II, 3.6
> *The rivers are the veins of the cosmic person; trees are the hairs of His body* - Bhagavad Gita II.1.33-34

Islam

In the Qur'an God says, "We made from water every living thing" and "By means of water, we give life to everything" (Qur'an 21:30)

To desert people, water is life. There are 900 references to water in the Qur'an. Muhammad said, "People share three things: water, pasture and fire." Extravagance in using water was forbidden; this applied to private use as well as public and whether the water was scarce or abundant. It is related that the Prophet passed by his companion Sa'd, who was washing for prayer and said, "What is this wastage, O Sa'd?" "Is there wastage even in washing for prayer?" asked Sa'd; and He said, "Yes, even if you are by a flowing river!"

Water conservation was practised in the Prophet's time in that large rivers were decreed for use by all; and with local rivers, the rights of people living upstream were more restricted than the rights of those downstream. With naturally-occurring springs ownership was deemed to be held in common. If a person discovered a spring, then the water rights of that person would be assured. Yet, significantly, even when a spring was someone's property, the owner was expected to allow others to use it to water their livestock. Wells were also carefully managed. Generally the priority of usage was granted to those with livestock and crops. If a person dug a well then they had the right to the water but it was expected that any surplus would be available to the livestock of others. If a well was of a temporary nature then the person who dug it had the right to the water, but if they abandoned the well then anybody had access to it. The Qur'an also prohibited the misuse and pollution of water, declaring that those who did so would suffer on the day of judgement. The Prophet forbade that a person relieve himself in a water source or on a path, or in a place of shade, or in the burrow of a living creature.

Finally, the Qur'an states "The whole Earth has been created as a place of worship for me, pure and clean." Accordingly, Muslims are charged with the religious duty of treating the Earth, including water, with the respect due to a place of worship and with keeping it pure and undefiled.

Christianity

Christian teachings state that water is an aspect of the divine, hence its use in the baptism ceremony. These quotes point to a reverence in attitude towards water.

> *For the Lord our God is bringing you into a good country, a land with streams of water, with springs and fountains welling up in the hills and valleys* – Moses, Deuteronomy 8:7
> *Be praised, my Lord, through Sister Water; she is very useful and humble and precious and pure* - St Francis of Assisi.
> *Water is now not drinkable. It is contaminated with pesticides and fungicides* - Father Superior, Justin Thundumennil, Bethany Ashram, Trivandrum, India.

Judaism

The first Jewish state of Israel, in pre-Roman times, instituted laws to punish people severely for any form of water pollution. Anyone who caused environmental damage by polluting water was to be punished severely.

Buddhism

The Buddha forbade his monks from disposing of their rubbish in the rivers and streams.

> *Every human should have the idea of taking care of the environment, of nature, of water. So when using too much water or wasting it we should have some kind of feeling or sense of concern. Some sort of responsibility and with that, a sense of discipline* - Tenzin Gyatso, the 14th Dalai Lama

Jainism

The *anarth dand tyag* vow prohibits unnecessary or excessive violence and excludes participation in occupations that involve violence. Any feeling of ill will, even, is seen as a form of violence. So Jains see the polluting of water as well as any other environmentally destructive activity as forms of violence. Polluting water would create bad karma, as water beings are part of the eternal self or *Jiva Tattva* and keeping faith entails treating these life forms as sacred.

> *Water itself has been propounded as a living being* - Bhasyam Sutra 53

> *Industries grow more and more, but do not pay attention to the pollution they create* - Acharya Mahapragya, head of the Jain Terapanth sect

Paganism

The Celts revered all kinds of water habitats, rivers, springs, lakes and seas, and so they would never despoil them. Among their numerous riverside deities, Coventina was the water nymph at the sacred spring at the Roman fort on Hadrian's Wall near Carrawburgh, Northumberland in England. Thirteen altars discovered there along with some 13,000 roman coins attest to her popularity. Springs were thought to be places of spiritual power, especially hot springs. At the spa town of Buxton in Derbyshire, England, they found evidence of a whole healing cult, with people immersing themselves in the water and drinking it. There are few written records, but the clear archaeological evidence of offerings near springs and rivers suggests that water's life-giving qualities were not just recognised but actively honoured and water held as sacred.

Spiritualism

Spiritualists believe in cause and effect, or the law of karma. Their view is that to knowingly pollute waters that others use creates bad karma, resulting in suffering in the after-life.

Taoism

"Never pollute or divert rivers." This is advice given by the Taoist celestial master who viewed water as part of the Tao and therefore sacred.

> *The highest good is like water. Water gives life to the ten thousand things and does not strive. It flows in places men reject and so is like the Tao* - Tao Te Ching, Chapter 8.

Sikhism

Guru Amar Das recognised the polluting of water as an ill; he built a *baoli*, a type of well, at the holy town of Giondwal to protect its water supplies from the polluted waters of the river Beas.

Air is the Guru, water is the Father and Earth is the Great Mother of all - Japji Sahib prayer in the Guru Granth Sahib
Pollution is the burning fire, which is consuming the world. Pollution is in the water, upon the land and everywhere. O Nanak, people are born and die in pollution. By Guru's grace, they drink in the Lord's sublime elixir - Guru Granth Sahib, p.413
The water teaches us cleanliness and purity - Guru Granth Sahib

Shamanism

Shamanism teaches that the landscape and waters are alive with spirits and therefore to pollute water is unthinkable to them.

We call upon the waters that rim the Earth, horizon to horizon, that flow in our rivers and streams, that fall upon our gardens and fields and we ask that they teach us and show us the way - Chinook Indian Blessing
We should be as water, which is lower than all things yet stronger even than the rocks - Oglala Sioux Proverb
The rivers are our brothers, they quench our thirst and feed our children - Chief Seattle of the Suquamish and Duwamish Native American tribes
They shall offer thanks to the Earth where all people dwell – to the streams of water, the pools, the springs and the lakes - Iroquois saying

Water pollution from agriculture

It is an irony that even when countries do have sufficient fresh water supplies for their needs, they pollute them in such a way as to endanger the health of their own people, most often with chemicals. Pesticides are biocides, substances used to prevent, destroy, repel or mitigate damage from pests ranging from insects, animals and weeds to micro organisms such as fungi, moulds, bacteria and viruses. In the 1990s world production of pesticides grew at a rate of 12.5 per cent per year and now 1.5 million tonnes are manufactured annually. Pesticides sales earn companies more than $30 billion a year, more than 80 per cent of it shared by just eight corporations: Aventis, BASF, Bayer, Dow AgroSciences, Dupont, Monsanto, Sumitomo and Syngenta.

Little recognised is the fact that as much as 85 to 90 per cent of pesticides applied to crops never reach their targets. Instead, this 1.3 million tonnes disperses into the air, soil, waters and rivers and into the bodies of insects, animals and people nearby. Once ingested (e.g. by insects), pesticides can be transported enormous distances—by migratory birds or fish, for instance. Seemingly isolated and remote Canadian Inuits, who eat mainly fish and marine mammals show pronounced immune system deficiencies, particularly among breast-fed infants and children. This has been traced to the heavy pesticide contamination accumulated in the wildlife they eat. Meningitis and inner ear infections occur at rates 30 times that of North American children. There is pollution of watercourses of this sort worldwide and consequent risks to health for millions of people are great but till recently went unrecognised. This is a hidden cost paid by the public for the freedom to pollute given to agribusiness and the chemical corporations that supply them.

- **In the USA, pesticide pollution of even rural watercourses is a significant problem, since 75 per cent of rural Americans rely on local groundwater for domestic use.**
- **In USA during the early 1990s, pesticide residues were found to contaminate groundwater in 34 states.**

It has since been established by some experts that many pesticides are carcinogenic. Some scientists believe the greater use of pesticides has contributed most to an increase in cancer cases in the USA and Europe.

- **Childhood cancer increased 0.6 per cent a year from 1975 to 2002 according to the US Center for Disease Control. It is now the second leading cause of death in children.**
- **Breast cancer incidence in developed countries in 1960 was 1 in every 20 women, yet by 1993, this had risen to 1 in 8 women.**
- **Rates of testicular cancer in developed countries (US and Europe) have tripled and prostate cancer has doubled in the last twenty years.**

We have witnessed grave effects in less developed countries, too. In the former Soviet Union, the use of pesticides has been proven to have a catastrophic effect on groundwater, in the Aral basin, for instance. Thirteen per cent of all water supplies are polluted with pesticides, with inevitable health problems. Likewise, in Uzbekistan, infant mortality has increased fifteen times, with oesophageal cancer increasing from seven to ten times. There are heightened rates of throat cancer, as well as respiratory and eye diseases. Deteriorating conditions have also been tied to increases in leukaemia and liver and kidney diseases. Pesticides have been found to reduce the numbers of white blood cells and disease-fighting lymphocytes and impair their ability to overcome unhealthy bacteria and viruses.

Water pollution from industry

Spiritual insights

The quest for a 'higher standard of living' continues in the developed countries despite the fact that most people have all the material means necessary to live comfortably. This obsession is not only at the root of our soul destroying materialism and Planet-damaging consumerism in the West but it is the cause of its spread to countries such as China and India. Their cultures are losing their strong spiritual and cultural traditions in their people's rush to emulate the materialism and mass consumerism of the West.

My interviews with many spiritual leaders in India showed me that they considered there to be a gradual erosion of India's spiritual outlook. The younger generation is now more fully under the influence of television, telephones and the media, popularising a Western influenced lifestyle of casual coolness and shallow consumption totally foreign to their culture. The consumer society emerging is one based on industrial output, inevitably leading to more water pollution that, in turn, will cause severe health problems for millions. Different spiritual traditions point to the costs and dangers of desiring greater riches, material comforts and distractions such as day-long music, taking us far away from a spiritual path.

Christianity

> *Thou shall not trade thy soul, the priceless gift of a loving God, for the riches of the world, which are seeds sown on stony ground, having no root in themselves and enduring but a little while* - The Ten Commandments from the Essene Book of Moses
>
> *What then, will anyone gain by winning the whole world and forfeiting his life? Or what can anyone offer in exchange for his life?* - Jesus Christ (Matthew 16:26)

Sikhism

They do well who have destroyed the five evils of lust, anger, greed, covetousness and pride. They shall be known as the inheritors of the kingdom of God - Guru Granth Sahib

Judaism:

They shall have no other Gods before me - The Ten Commandments

Buddhism

In the name of comfort and short term convenience, the Planet itself is consumed for the personal advantage of a relative few - Thich Nhat Hanh, Zen Buddhist monk and international writer on Buddhism

Islam

There is no such wealth as contentment - Ali ibn Abi Talib, son-in-law of Muhammad

At least until the global recession, industry was expanding at a meteoric rate in certain developing countries bringing on a step-change in demand for water. Globally each year roughly 450 cubic kilometres of wastewater are discharged into rivers, streams and lakes. To dilute and transport this dirty water before it can be used again, another 6,000 cubic kilometres of clean water would needed - an amount equal to about two-thirds of the Planet's total annual useable freshwater runoff. For instance it takes up to 80,000 litres (26,400 US gal) of water to make one tonne of steel. Signs are that costs are finally pushing industry into conserving water. However, a UN study found that the production of a complete computer and monitor took 1,500 litres of water. In 2000 alone, industry pumped out some 468 *billion* tonnes of effluent into waters around our Planet.

- **Total municipal and industrial use of water has grown twenty-four times in the last century alone.**
- **According to the UN, water consumption by industries will double by 2025 which will lead to a fourfold increase in industrial pollution overall.**

The trouble is that industry's water discharges are invariably polluted and are seldom cleaned up for reuse as they should be. Even in developed countries like the USA, industry has a shabby record on clean-up:

155

each year polluters dump about 110,000 tonnes (120,000 short tons) of toxins into US waterways. As much as 40 per cent of the nation's surveyed lakes, rivers and estuaries are too polluted for such basic uses as drinking.

Yet, control over pollution of watercourses by industrial effluent is stricter in the developed world than the majority world. It is too often the case that developed country-based TNCs relocate their dirty, effluent dumping industries to developing countries to circumvent environmental laws operating in their home territories. This makes it a social justice issue as well as an effluent dumping issue.

The worst example of this practice is in Mexico in Maquiladoras, an area conveniently close to the border with the US. Here there are close to 3,400 factories taking advantage of Mexico's lax regulatory framework. Most are owned by multinational companies from north of the border. Toxicologists found that in zones where these US companies operate 75 per cent of the industries dumped industrial effluent untreated. Toxins then find their way into public water supplies, exposing the local population to health threats of cancer and birth defects, acts that within US jurisdiction would meet with hefty fines.

In developing countries three-quarters of all industrial wastes are discharged into surface waters without any treatment whatsoever. In 2008, of China's seven major rivers, fully 70 per cent were severely polluted, 80 per cent of its rivers failed to meet standards for fishing and 90 per cent of the country's cities suffered from polluted water supplies to some degree of severity. As a result, over 700 million Chinese drink water of a quality well below World Health Organization standards. According to data from 30 cities and 78 counties released by the Chinese Ministry of Health in 2006, airborne and water pollution, mainly the latter, have made cancer China's top cause of death. Cancer expert Chen Zhizhou of the Chinese Academy of Medical Sciences blamed fertilizer and pesticide runoff from croplands for contaminating groundwater and industrial effluents for contaminating rivers. Death rates from cancer have risen to 19 per cent of total mortality figures in cities and 23 per cent in rural areas closest to where all the agrochemicals are applied. But there is trouble where they are manufactured, too.

Unfortunately for us all, 'effluent' is industrialists' euphemism for a cocktail of substances, including the 50,000 different compounds used in the manufacture of agrochemicals each year. Production of chemicals is set to increase 85 per cent in the next 20 years. The most hazardous effluents contain heavy metals such as arsenic, mercury, lead, chromium, cadmium, selenium and copper.

Heavy metals are naturally found deep within the Earth's crust where Nature buried them safely out of harm's way for living organisms in the biosphere. In minute amounts, certain metals - Iron, cobalt, copper, manganese, molybdenum and zinc—are essential for human health. We obtain these from foods, drinking water and air. However, at higher concentrations they lead to poisoning. Heavy metals are dangerous because they tend to bio-accumulate, increasing in concentration in an organism over time. Compounds will accumulate in living creatures any time they are taken up and stored faster than they are broken down (metabolized) or excreted. Many cannot be metabolized at all.

Arsenic is a known poison. Yet mining, waste incineration and coal combustion emit the metal in the form of an invisible gas that is later trapped in raindrops deposited on the ground. From there it seeps into wetlands, rivers and lakes; here, microbes convert it into methyl mercury, a persistent compound that via insects works its way up the food chain into fish and ultimately into the fat tissue of mammals including humans. A 2001 report on arsenic found that men and women who daily consume water containing 20 parts per billion of arsenic have a significantly increased risk - about a seven in 1,000 chance - of developing bladder or lung cancer during their lifetime.

Mercury, a highly toxic metal, is used in things ranging from dental fillings to watch batteries. Mercury is a neurotoxin which affects the brain and nervous system; developing foetuses and young children are the most vulnerable to its debilitating affects. A loss of physical coordination and mental retardation are among the impacts from chronic exposure to mercury. The term 'mad hatter' comes from the common occurrence of dementia among hatters in nineteenth century England who used mercury as a coating on hats. The US EPA recently reported that a third of the country's lakes and nearly a quarter of its rivers are now so polluted with mercury that children and pregnant women are advised to limit or avoid eating fish caught there. Some 630,000 US babies born during a 12-month period in 1999-2000 had potentially unsafe levels of mercury in their blood — about twice as many babies as previously estimated.

Lead is the most widely used non-ferrous metal and has numerous applications. Since lead ceased to be used in gasoline in the 1980s, its largest industrial single use worldwide is now in the manufacture of batteries (60-70 per cent of total annual consumption of some 4 million tonnes). Lead is also used in paints, glazes, alloys, radiation shielding, tank lining, roofing and piping. Lead at high levels can cause convulsions, coma and even death. It is a powerful neurotoxin that builds up in the skeleton. Its effects are most serious in infants, young children up to the age of six years and pregnant women. As well as being toxic to the nervous system, lead interferes with Vitamin D metabolism and can cause anaemia and possible cancers from long-term exposure. Even low levels of lead can cause adverse health effects on the central nervous system, kidney and blood cells.

Because foetuses, infants and children are so vulnerable to lead exposure, its damaging effects include lower IQ levels, shortened attention spans and increased behavioural problems. Half a century on, these effects were finally recognised in the 1970s and its removal from gasoline began in the 1980s and was 80 per cent complete by 2002.

The greatest use of chromium is in metal alloys such as stainless steel, decorative electroplating, magnetic tapes, paint pigments, cement, paper and rubber. Its soluble forms are used in wood preservatives. Chromium has the potential to cause the following effects from a lifetime exposure at low levels: damage to liver, kidney, circulatory and nerve tissues and skin irritation. Chromium often accumulates in aquatic life, adding to the danger of eating fish that may have been exposed to high levels of chromium.

Cadmium, used in tens of millions of NiCad rechargeable batteries over four decades, most now in landfill, is both a deadly poison and carcinogenic. Unbelievably, dumping NiCad batteries to landfill, outlawed in some European countries for decades, is still permitted in the UK and most US states. It is also used in electroplating, pigments and plastics manufacture, in welding, brazing and painting operations. Long-term, it can do in your kidneys. High exposure can lead to obstructive lung disease and has been linked to lung cancer and damage to respiratory systems.

Selenium is a toxic metal discharged into bodies of water by coal mines and coal-fired power plants. Another source is mining and smelting of copper and nickel. At Sudbury, Ontario, Canada, 2 tonnes are released per day. High levels of exposure can cause severe reproductive impairment and even death in fish, birds and other wildlife. In humans, selenium is linked to kidney and liver damage and damage to the circulatory and nervous system.

Copper is used for electrical cable and piping. At trace levels, the element copper is essential to human life, but in high doses it can cause anaemia, liver and kidney damage and stomach and intestinal irritation.

Aluminium is not a 'heavy metal' but is a typical pollutant of heavy industry. Evidence suggests high aluminium intake leads to bone disease and Alzheimer's, a disease that severely affects brain function. Independent studies performed in Norway, the UK, France and Canada, show a direct correlation between the prevalence of Alzheimer's disease and aluminium concentrations in drinking water. In fact, one British study reported in the medical journal *The Lancet*, showed the risk of developing Alzheimer's disease to be 50 per cent greater where drinking water contained high levels of aluminium.

Chlorine is perhaps the most pervasive highly toxic pollutant. It is found in effluents of scores of industrial processes especially paper production, antiseptics, dyestuffs, foods, insecticides, paints, petroleum products, plastics, medicines, textiles, solvents and thousands of consumer products. In lower concentration, it is used to clear bacteria and other microbes from drinking water supplies. Though a totally chlorine-free (TCF) pulping process pioneered in Sweden has been taken up there and in Finland, it was never adopted elsewhere because of a lack of tight environmental legislation. However, due to pressures from environmentalists over dioxin emissions and other organochlorines in effluents in North America and elsewhere, the industry has gone half-way by replacing some or all of the 'elemental' chlorine with chlorine dioxide, moving to what is known as the ECF (elemental chlorine-free) process. German consumers' greater awareness and preference for totally chlorine-free TCF paper products has given the Nordic TCF mills a market, but elsewhere the pollution from ECF process mills continues, albeit at reduced intensities.

It is disturbing to realise that known poisons, classified as solvents, cyanides and phenols, continue as common constituents of industrial effluents. The major sources of cyanides in water are discharges from mining and processing of some metal ores, manufacture of cyanide-containing pesticides, iron and steel plants or manufacturers and wastewater treatment facilities - often publicly owned. Exposure to high levels of cyanide even for a short time damages the brain and heart and can cause coma and death. Long-term exposure at low levels has the potential to cause weight loss, thyroid effects and nerve damage.

Phenols are used in the manufacture of textiles. Repeated exposure to low levels of phenol in drinking water has been associated with diarrhoea and mouth sores.

A solvent is any compound capable of dissolving a given substance, forming a solution. Solvents have a wide variety of industrial applications, including the manufacture of paints, inks, cleaning products, adhesives and petrochemicals. Solvents may damage the liver, kidneys, heart, blood vessels, bone marrow and the nervous system. They do require a lot of water to dilute them to safe levels. For instance, to render harmless the industrial solvent *trichloroethylene*—a CFC formerly used by dry cleaners and once sold as 'Dab-it-Off' before its ozone damaging power was recognised—it would take 60 million litres of water to dilute every 200 litre batch. A study in Japan in the late nineties found that 30 per cent of the groundwater was contaminated with solvents used in manufacturing processes. This is the result of Japan having a high density of population in a small geographical area with limited water resources to deal with the pollution. The implications of so much irresponsible industrial pollution may make us question whether industrial companies can be candidates for ethical investment at all.

Pollution from sewage

In developing countries, on average, 90 per cent of all domestic sewage is discharged into surface waters without any treatment whatsoever. Only 2 per cent of spending in developing countries goes towards low-cost water treatment and sanitation. Asian rivers are the most polluted in the world. They have three times as many bacteria from human waste as the global average. For instance, all of India's 14 major rivers are badly polluted. Together they transport 50 million cubic metres of untreated sewage into India's coastal waters every year.

I attended the Johannesburg World Summit on Sustainable Development in 2002 where the UN set a millennium target to halve the people not having access to sanitation and clean water by 2015. We still have a long way to go.

- **Over 1 billion people lack access to safe water supplies.**
- **An estimated 3 billion people - 4 out of every 10 - lack a sanitary toilet.**

Until a century ago in Asia, human waste or 'night soil' was used to fertilise fields in fallow. Today, in developed country communities focused on reducing the impact of humans on the environment, there is a growing interest in composting toilets. Not only are they safe, they yield an exceptionally fertile compost. And among innovative gardeners, a growing number are meeting their plants' need for nitrogen with liquid human waste, carefully applied. Some see such alternative approaches making inroads as the water pollution, food security and soil fertility problems converge.

Spiritual insights on water contamination

As we have seen, water is considered sacred in many spiritual traditions and to pollute water with human waste is seen as an act of sacrilege. No doubt for thousands of years observers noted that, left out of harm's way and in contact with the soil, human waste dissipates harmlessly within weeks, whereas dumped in a watercourse, it can be the cause of severe problems for thousands. Let us reflect on the spiritual teachings.

Hinduism

A law in the book of Manu states that water should not be polluted by urine, stools, blood or poison; if people disobeyed this law, they would be punished. To Hindus, the Ganges is a living Goddess who came down to Earth from heaven. One devout Hindu has spent his whole life seeking a solution to the growing problem with sewage pollution of the Ganges. In 2002, I came across the work of Professor U. K. Choudhary at the Banaras Hindu University in Varanasi. His Ganga Laboratory was dedicated to his lifelong goal of finding a solution.

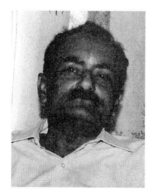

Professor U.K. Choudhary

Buddhism

The Buddha forbade his monks to pollute the local watercourses with faeces and resort to more sanitary forms of disposal. There are even instructions in the rules for monks on how to build safe toilet facilities.

Practicalities and costs of wastes

Solid human and animal waste is riddled with pathogens including unhealthy bacteria, viruses and protozoa. If not rendered harmless by the interaction with benign bacteria such as found in the soil, these pollutants enter waterways through untreated sewage, storm drains, septic tanks, runoff from farms and particularly from boats and ships that jettison untreated sewage. Though microscopic, these pollutants have a devastating effect evidenced by their ability to cause cholera and chronic sicknesses in humans. The lack of sanitary waste disposal and of clean water for drinking, cooking and washing is to blame for over 12 million deaths a year.

- **Each year 250 million people are debilitated by diseases caused by water-borne pathogens found in contaminated water.**
- **Cholera, dysentery and diarrhoea, coupled with pollution from water-spills and dumping, kill 25 million people annually.**
- **In 2005 an estimated 4 billion cases of diarrhoeal disease occurred, causing 3 million to 4 million deaths, mostly among children.**
- **According to a Water Aid report, each day, water related diseases claim the lives of 6,000 children, 2.2 million children a year.**

Pollution of water may seem an intractable problem. However, if development-aid commitments by the wealthy countries were met regularly and if influential world leaders declared it as a priority goal, then our chances of solving it would be transformed. As with poverty, our leaders need an education, a political will - and more courage.

However, as mega cities continue to expand world wide, it is evident that safe sewage systems remain a low priority. Perhaps effort would be better placed on making the alternative low-cost solution workable which could also go some way to offsetting losses to erosion of topsoil and fertility.

Conclusion - spiritual and physical solutions

As we have seen here, the problems of water affect all of us: we are all in this together. Climate change and rising population are only going to exacerbate the problem. Water shortages, water pollution and disease-ridden water are all global problems but require us to find local solutions. To me, this suggests what we need to change is the self-interest mentality inherent in us individuals and in our governments.

One antidote to the selfishness generated by the materialist consumerist culture is that of spirituality. If others are suffering in the world, the spiritual teachings say that we must help them through co-operation and providing the required resources. If the essentially human qualities like compassion, love and understanding that flow out of the faiths' teachings were once again to become guidelines for political leaders, we could together bring an end to these the direst of human problems.

The physical solutions to the problem of water shortages lie in part at the feet of the wealthier nations. They have the resources to provide efficient irrigation systems, water management and sustainability, which they need to offer freely or at minimum cost, rather than in the exploitative ways with privatisations that have been imposed recently under WTO and IMF rules. The richer nations also need to take effective actions to honour their promises to cut their carbon emissions—after two decades of talk while emissions rise ever upward—and thus tackle climate change so that water scarcity in areas of Africa, Asia and South America does not deteriorate further. Poorer nations have their part to play in that they need to address the problems associated with rapid population increases. They also need to find ways to avoid conflict by sharing out water resources equitably. We need to empower the United Nations to play its role in bringing this about.

The problems of pollution are a product of the way we live. In agriculture we could solve the problems of pesticide and chemical pollution by exploring less polluting and more sustainable, 'no-till' or 'direct drill' and perhaps organic ways of growing food. Food bills, though, might rise, unless we grow some of our own facilitated by making land available within parks, for example, as is beginning to happen. Direct distribution of food from farm to homes, as being pioneered in the UK by the Soil Association, could in fact lower costs of certain foods. Increased pressure from discerning consumers could result in less polluting goods. And if as consumers we limited our rates of consumption, we would ease industrial pollution levels which could, at the same time, be curbed through enhanced laws and regulatory systems. And the export of pollution by migrating TNCs needs to cease. They must face the same penalties abroad as they face in their home jurisdictions.

The problems of disease from water are closely associated with a separate problem, poverty, to which we devote an entire chapter. National poverty would be eased if richer nations ceased their farm subsidies and agreed fairer terms in world trade so poorer nations can earn enough from their commodity exports to undertake things like controlling sewage pollution. Wealthier nations could also lend resources, expertise and experience to poorer countries to treat sewage cost-effectively. As well as population growth, poorer countries need to address the problems in mega cities with better planning and development of water supply and treatment.

Personal actions we can take on water

It's not all down to governments. We each have a part to play. Here are a few practical tips and suggestions any of which you are free to implement today to alleviate the emerging water crisis that will affect us all.

1. To become fully aware whenever you are using tap water in kitchen, bathroom or garden, train yourself to ask: is this the right way, the best way? If it is, can I re-use it somehow?
2. Re-use water from washing-up or the bath to water your plants during the growing months. Watering in the early morning or in the evening means more reaches your plants, less evaporates. www.waterwise.org.uk/ www.greenandeasy. co.uk
3. Get onto water metering. Unless you have a family and/or a swimming pool, it will lower bills even before you optimise water usage.
4. If you have a garden, collect rainwater. Lawns and plants prefer chlorine-free rainwater. www.waterbuttdirect.com
5. Ensure you are not losing water through wastage from a poor plumbing system or dripping taps.
6. Consider a dual flush water cistern or a Peterton retrofit to cut down on use - www.peterton.co.uk. If you run a business, consider a waterless urinal. www.smartflush.com

www.greenbuildingstore.co.uk/air-advantages.php www.hippo-the-watersaver.co.uk

7. Always insert a full load wash when you use the washing machine.

8. Use natural cleaning materials in the home and avoid the water pollution of bleach-based and other chemical ones. www.ecosafeproducts.com www.planetnatural.com www.greenpeople.co.uk www.soorganic.com

9. Clean your teeth without letting the water run.

10. Use spray taps and showerheads: they save water; aerating ones save even more: www.tapmagic.co.uk www.ecocamel.co.uk

11. Have a shower rather than a bath; showers use less water.

12. Try cutting back on consumer goods that create excessively high levels of water pollution during manufacture, such as cotton, beef and new electronic gadgets (try low impact second-hand instead).

13. Campaign to have water utilities do more to cut the worst leakage rates. Eat organic food, support local producers wherever possible.

14. Grow your own vegetables, preferably organically by using companion plants instead of pesticides and artificial herbicides. www.kitchengarden.org www.veggiegardentips.com www.gardenorganic.org.uk www.global-garden.com

15. Walk, cycle, skateboard, rollerblade, run or take public transport instead of using your car, especially for local trips to cut down on your greenhouse gas emissions, the cause of climate change which exacerbates the global water crisis.

16. Donate to a charity which will alleviate water shortages in poor countries. www.wateraid.org www.waterscape.com www.justgiving.com www.worldlandtrust.org

17. Campaign actively—write to your representatives and water supplier for more monetary and logistical aid from your local utility and your national government to support developing nations' investment in water treatment and especially improved efficiency in farm irrigation systems.

CHAPTER 14 : THE FOOD WE EAT

Introduction
The next meal may for many of us be assured, if not something to look forward to, but for 3 billion of those with whom we currently share this Planet, that next meal is what I have to struggle for the rest of the day to pay for, if I am able.

However, as well as a physical necessity, food is a source of spiritual, social and cultural nourishment. Too often in our hectic Western lives, with ready-meals and a proliferation of commercial eating establishments including fast food, we lose all touch with the ancient wisdom and spiritual teachings about how our food nourishes us, about our relationship with the land and about all that went into the growing of our food. Is there, as some suggest, a link between the West's growing problem with obesity and our spiritual starvation?

Spiritual Insights on our relationship with the earth
Islam
Land was recognised as a primary resource. It is mentioned 485 times in the Qur'an and was carefully and wisely controlled in Islamic law. Land was classified into three types:

- Developed land, or *Anuit*
- Undeveloped land, or *Maivat*
- Protected land, or *Havin*

The Qur'an states that God has granted human beings the responsibility of stewardship (*khilafah*) of the Earth as "He who appointed you viceroys of the Earth." (Qur'an 6:165) "The world is sweet and verdant green and Allah appoints you to be His regents in it and will see how you acquit yourselves..." (Sunnah of the Prophet) "It is he who has made you his agents, inheritors of the Earth: He hath raised you in ranks some above others: that he may try you in the gifts he hath given you." From these words it is clear that mankind represents the interests of God on Earth. Man is thus entrusted with its maintenance and care and, as a trustee, he must care for it within the limits dictated by God.

Judaism

Judaism sees the Earth as belonging to God. "For the Earth is mine." (Lev 25:33) God saw the Israelites as tenants of the land and they were told to have a loving attitude towards it or face dire consequences (Deut.11 13-17).

Paganism

Pagans of the past viewed land not as a thing to be exploited for profit but as a living organism, rather as Permaculture does today. When the Irish King was crowned he had a ritual marriage with the Land Goddess who was called Sovereignty. The caves of the River Boyne were seen as evidence of the womb of Mother Earth. In Wales the milky substances coming from springs was seen as proof of the Mother Goddess's breasts! In fact most goddesses of the Celts were concerned with fertility. The Mother Goddess represents Mother Earth. She is worshipped as the provider of the bounty of Nature. Her importance to Celts is evident from 50 dedicated inscriptions to her found on archaeological artefacts.

The Green Man, perhaps the best known Celtic deity in our times, is associated with fertility and new growth and still worshipped today. He is the son and lover of the Great Mother Goddess. Freya was a goddess of fertility but also of beauty and love. She was the patroness of magic and protector of the land.

Christianity

Christians learn that land belongs to God: the Bible implies that the Earth is not Man's, but God's. "The land must not be sold permanently, because the land is mine and you are but aliens and my tenants." (Lev 25:23) and "...the Earth is the Lord's and everything in it." (Psalms: 24) Christians believe that God has commanded them to take care of his creation by respecting and honouring it. The Bible gives clear instructions of how man should relate to the earth, as quoted in Genesis; "...work it and take care of it," (Gen:2:15). All farmers received instruction to tend to their land for six years, but that they must leave it fallow or rested in the seventh. This not only restored fertility, but also meant that the less privileged in the community could use the fallow land for food provision. The Bible even advocates 'set-aside:' the advice of the wise was not to harvest the crop too near to the edge of the field *so that wildlife, too, could make use of it*. This suggests that for the ancients, the wisdom of respecting all of creation was innate. Modern man has to legislate to preserve what little bio-diversity remains.

> *We should practise stewardship as we trust that God has given us to care for Nature* - Dr. Andreas De Souza, Director of the Henry Martyn Christian Institute, Hyderabad, Andhra Pradesh, India
> *God gave human kind the environment to be managed and it should not be destroyed* - Vincent Concessao, Archbishop of Delhi

Hinduism
In Hinduism the earth itself has divine meaning, as it is the abode of the earth goddess Bhumi. She is described as being dependable, patient and conscious of human activity and can easily be offended by destructive and disrespectful activities.

> *Mother of plants and begetter of all things, firm far-flung Earth, sustained by Heavenly Law, kindly and pleasant is she. May we ever dwell on her bosom, passing to and fro* - The Hymn to the Earth, Atharva Veda
> *May she, the ruling Mistress of what has been and what will come to us, spread wide a limitless domain - Rig Veda*
> *Impart to us those vitalizing forces that come, O Earth, from deep within your body, your central point, your navel; purify us wholly. The Earth is the mother; I am son of Earth* - Rig Veda
> *The root cause of our problems is exploiting Nature because of lack of God consciousness* - Vedanta Chaitanya, President, Hare Krishna Temple, Hyderabad, Andhra Pradesh, India

Sikhism
In Sikhism the scriptures say that the Earth should be seen as the Mother and provider of life and therefore should be held in deepest respect.

> *The air is the Guru, Water the Father, and Earth the Great Mother -* Jap Ji Sahib-Salok, Guru Granth Sahib
> *The Earth teaches us patience and love* - Guru Granth Sahib

Taoism

When you know that Nature is part of yourself, you will act in harmony - Lao Tzu

Realise that we live in Nature. But we cannot possess it. We can guide and serve, but never control. This is the highest Wisdom - Lao Tzu

In Taoism, Nature is symbolised by Mother Earth from which all things are born and to which all things return.

Shamanism

Native Americans lived off the land. Respect for all of creation was so important to them they recognised Nature as the source of deepest wisdom and guidance for their ways. They saw everything as interrelated. For instance the Cherokees and the Creeks had ceremonies to mark their interactions with plant spirits. They sought to co-operate with the spiritual forces of nature to ensure a successful harvest. The Green Corn ceremony and the Bread Dance, held in springtime, were to ensure a successful growing season.

We thank our Mother Earth who we claim as Mother because the Earth carries us and everything we need - Prayer of the shaman of the Delaware tribe

The Earth does not belong to man, man belongs to Earth - Seattle, Chief of the Suquamish and Duwamish, territories now in Washington State, USA

Bahá'í

Bahá'u'lláh recognised that growing food was one of the most important occupations in a society and he gave farmers high status.

Man is organic with the world. His inner life moulds the environment and is itself deeply affected by it - Bahá'u'lláh

Our population issues

One of humanity's greatest problems today is that we are already too many for our Planet and we are creating around 1,700 more mouths to feed *every minute*. This is not balanced by a similar increase in food production. The population explosion is nowhere brought home better than by the minute-by-minute rising estimate shown on the website of the Optimum Population Trust (www.optimumpopulation.org/).

- There were approximately 6.8 billion people living on Earth in 2009.
- Lowest UN estimates calculate that the population will increase to 9.2 billion by 2050 and 11.6 billion by 2100.
- By 2050 there must be a doubling of food production.
- In the 22nd century it has been estimated that for every person born in the North, 60 will be born in the South, leaving a ratio of 9:1 in favour of the people of the South.

The big unanswered question is whether the world can supply enough food for all these extra mouths. During the 1990's it seemed world food shortages were looming, as agricultural production increased by 0.9 per cent whereas the population grew 1.6 per cent. One real problem is that starvation risks rise with the price of food and prices have been pushed upward by the 2007-08 spikes in oil prices and by the demand from bio-fuels. On top of that, the total land available to grow food is decreasing. We'll examine why. So in 2009 we were definitely in a crisis with world food security, but perhaps in a less strident phase.

Urbanisation and loss of productive cropland
The problem of food shortages is exacerbated by the growth of mega cities in the developing world. Sixteen of the 24 cities with over 10 million inhabitants are in developing countries, the swell due to mass migration of rural poor. Some are migrants forced off their land due to modern methods of farming. Most are unemployed and destitute, unable to buy food ending up dependent, begging or starving.

Fifty years ago 18 percent of people lived in cities whereas in 2009 it exceeed 50 per cent. As cities expand to absorb new migrants, productive cropland is constantly being lost.

- Urbanisation in China up to the 1990s has led to 435,000 hectares of land being built on, enough land to feed 10 million people.
- Globally the expansion of the urban infrastructure consumes approximately 0.5 per cent of prime agricultural land each year.
- The process of urbanising agricultural land is set to continue as it has been estimated that by the end of the 21st century an extra 5 billion people in the South will need

an extra 280 million hectares of land for non-agricultural use.

Desertification—expanding uncontrollably

Desertification is defined as the long-term degradation of biologically productive land ultimately to wasteland through overuse, mismanagement—deforestation for example - or climate change or a mixture of all three. Rates of desertification have been known to be increasing since the 1970s. As the area of viable forest, agricultural or grazing land diminishes, there is less productive soil per person. Land degraded to the point where it cannot produce food—or even wild plants—is considered desert. Large-scale desertification—so far - is concentrated in Asia and Africa, two regions that together contain nearly 4.8 billion of the world's 6.5 billion people. Soil is a very precious resource and not easily replaced. On average it takes between 100 and 200 years to form two and a half centimetres.

Spiritual Insights on maintaining the fertility of land

Islam

In early Islam land reclamation or revival (*ihya'al-mawat*) was encouraged in Islamic law. Any person who brought life to unowned land by undertaking its cultivation or reclamation acquired it as his private property and according to Muhammad would be rewarded in heaven. Only those actions that brought new life to the land conferred ownership; mere exploitation did not constitute revival. Thus *ihya'* gave people a powerful incentive to invest in the sustainable use of the land and avoid desertification and so provide for their welfare and the welfare of their families and descendents.

Judaism

Farmers followed *Mishnah* rules which told them they were allowed to grow on land for six years but on the seventh year it had to be rested to conserve its fertility. There were laws to limit grazing rights to avoid soil erosion. For instance people were encouraged to graze their flocks in uninhabited areas.

Hinduism

Ancient though the Hindu texts are, they incorporate warnings of the dangers of soil erosion which is so rampant today. The Hindu scriptures stated "Oh pure earth, may we utilise your soil well without causing you injury or harm or disturbing any vital element in you." (Hymn to the earth in the Atharva Veda)

Bahá'í

Putting into practice the high value their faith places on the role of the farmer, Bahá'ís working at the Environmental Studies Centre in Bolivia are helping local farmers find ways to prevent soil erosion. Other examples are a community gardening project in Mongolia, which helps to improve nutrition by providing fresh vegetables. There is also an organic farming project by the Bahá'ís community of Japan where people are taught how to grow organic food.

The ills of soil erosion

If it weren't for plant cover, much more of the Planet would turn to desert. When plant cover is removed, as with over-grazing or when converting to farmland, many fertile soils suffer erosion from wind and rainwater runoff and the land becomes infertile desert.

- **Soil erosion causes the loss of between 20,000 and 50,000 km² of productive land per year, especially in Africa, Latin America and Asia where rates are two to six times higher than elsewhere.**
- **Each year, 20 billion tonnes of topsoil is lost through soil erosion; that's about 750 tonnes per second.**
- **The USA has lost half its topsoil since 1960 and loses it at a rate 17 times faster than Nature can create it!**

Intensification of crop production is one major cause of desertification. This usually happens in conventional agriculture where there may be high artificial fertilizer inputs but little organic matter added to the soil. Organic matter is vital in maintaining not only sustainable fertility but more importantly the actual soil structure which protects the soil from erosion. As productive agricultural land is lost, pressure on existing agricultural land to produce more food increases. But such intensification of production is not sustainable long-term on fertile soils, let alone degraded lands.

Another cause of soil erosion—via soil degradation and desertification that follows - is over-grazing: too many animals grazing at a rate higher than the re-growth capacity. In the Sahel region it has been estimated that there are 8 million more cattle than the carrying capacity of the land. When the vegetation that binds the soil together is removed through over-grazing, soil is blown or washed away. This is complicated by expansion of cropping onto former grazing lands and also by cultural values: in Sahel and other areas of the world, status accrues to those with most cattle.

A less well known cause of loss of productive soil is the process of salinization. This is the result of poorly managed irrigation. Crop-toxic salts found lower down in the soil (particularly sodium chloride) migrate to the surface. When the roots of crops take up moisture with the high level of salt they die or give negligible yields.

- **In the last three centuries poor irrigation practices have resulted in 1 million km² of land becoming desert and another 1 million km² of land having diminished productivity.**
- **20 per cent of irrigated land is salt affected.**
- **Between 2,500 and 5,000 km² of agricultural land is lost each year through salinization.**

Salinization is therefore a large-scale global problem and one that seems to be getting worse, being further exacerbated by the effects of climate change.

The area of deserts grows each decade. The UN estimates that more than 250 million people are already directly affected by desertification and around one billion people in more than a 100 countries are at risk from famine and malnutrition as a result of the rapid decline in the area of fertile lands available for growing crops for human consumption. The International Food Policy Research Institute (IFPRI) predicts that if land loss continues at current rates an additional 150 to 360 million hectares could go out of production by 2020.

- **Desertification affects 30 per cent of the world's land surface. Thirty per cent of China's productive land is affected by desertification.**
- **Drylands are most under threat of desertification and they occupy 40 per cent of the total land area of the globe. Two billion people depend on drylands for their livelihood.**
- **About 2 billion hectares of land, that is 15 per cent of**

the Earth's area, larger than USA and Mexico combined, have degraded soils.

- 60,000 km² of productive land is lost each year losing farmers $42 billion in revenues.
- Nigeria, Africa's most populous country, is losing 351,000 hectares of rangeland and cropland to desertification each year.

The dire effects of desertification were all too often seen on television screens in the 1980s with the tragedies of the famines in the Sahel region of Africa. Half of the people in the world who are affected by desertification live in the Sahel. An area twice the size of India is under direct threat of turning from drylands into full desert, now recognised as likely to be down largely to climate change.

China may be the new industrial power but expanding deserts are seriously compromising its food producing capacity. In China there has been a doubling of areas under threat of desertification between 1949 and 2000, affecting the lives of 170 million people: over 15 per cent of its land area is undergoing desertification; 90 per cent of its grasslands are considered degraded. The Eastern Desert is now only 70 km from Beijing and it was only due to China's good fortune—and a $6 billion 'green wall' tree plantation for protection - that the 2008 Olympics escaped the debilitating dust storms that are desertification in process.

The USA fares little better. One third of its croplands have been abandoned since 1950, down to intensive agriculture and over-grazing. Desertification is accelerating, with 2,500 km² of land lost to deserts each year.

The frightening result of desertification is its effect on the production of staple foods. The area of grain lands has shrunk from 0.23 ha per person globally in 1950 to 0.11 ha per person in 2000. This figure could fall to 0.07 ha of grain land per person by 2050. Worldwide loss of productivity due to soil erosion is equivalent to losing 20 million tonnes of grain. This has hit grain reserves which made for the volatile grain prices and food riots of 2008. In 1999 there were grain reserves to feed the world for 116 days and in 2006 that figure was down to 57 days, the lowest for 25 years. 2006 was the sixth time in seven years there was not enough grain produced to feed the world population. Countries which cannot produce enough food to feed their populations struggled to purchase grain supplies. Increasingly, the spectre of famine hovers over us.

Meat eating in a food scarce world
Spiritual insights on vegetarianism

There have of course been ethical grounds for not eating meat for millennia. Now with our Planet so over-crowded and food scarcity having reached crisis levels we are hearing more and more about how as a regular meat eater we are taking twice the resources of someone who eats a vegetarian diet. The comments below on diet from different spiritual traditions should be considered when reading the next section on the environmental impacts of a meat based diet. The spiritual traditions that recommend vegetarianism on ethical grounds include Jainism, Hinduism and Buddhism. Going wholly vegetarian will halve the land use of your diet—but part-way helps, too. Having had a totally non-meat diet since 1975, I would recommend it because it also keeps you healthy.

Jainism

Jainism begins with a serious concern for the human soul in its relationship with the laws governing existence in the universe, with other living beings and its own future state in eternity. First and foremost, it is a religion of the heart. The golden rule is *Ahimsa* or non-violence in all parts of a person - mental, verbal and physical. Jains have deep compassion for all forms of life. Jains are required to be vegetarians on moral grounds as it is considered an act of violence to kill animals. They follow strict dietary guidelines and are expected to have a minimal effect on the natural environment in all areas.

Hinduism

Many Hindus are vegetarian on the grounds of non-violence. India is a paradise for vegetarians. *Ahimsa*, the law of non-injury, is the Hindu's first duty in fulfilling religious obligations to God and God's creation. All of our actions, including our choice of food, have karmic consequences. By engaging in the cycle of inflicting injury, pain and death, even indirectly by eating other living creatures, one must in the future experience in equal measure the suffering caused.
He who desires to augment his own flesh by eating the flesh of other creatures

lives in misery in whatever species he may take his birth - Mahabharata 115.47

> *When a man sees that the God in himself is the same God in all that is, he hurts not himself by hurting others. Then he goes, indeed, to the highest path* - Bhagavad-Gita 13.28
> *You must not use your God-given body for killing God's creatures, whether they are human, animal or whatever* - Yajur Veda 12.32
> *Aside from all the compelling moral and spiritual reasons, one can now say that vegetarianism is the only responsible choice in terms of waste and ecology* - Swami Chidanand Saraswati, Head of Parmarth Niketan Ashram, Rishikesh, Uttarakhand, India

Sikhism

Sikhs are encouraged to be vegetarians as their faith comes out of the Hindu tradition.

> *Our saints said that we should eat simple and live high* - Dr Inderjit Singh, Director of the Pingalwara Institute, Amritsar, Punjab, India

Dr Indergit Kaur

We humans use up much less land and water if we eat crops directly rather than through the intermediary of an animal. This is because farmed animals consume much more protein than they produce, most of the protein from their vegetable feeds is used for the animals' bodily functions and not converted to meat, eggs or milk. Yet a massive 70 per cent of all agricultural land is used for rearing farm animals, including the land needed to grow all the feed they consume. World meat production has quadrupled in the past 50 years. Livestock now outnumber humans by more than 3 to 1! Any contribution to reducing livestock levels helps, even a reduction of meat consumption by one or two meals a week.

The West's meat-intensive diet brings global warming, deforestation, topsoil loss, desertification and water pollution. It also causes health problems. Half of all Americans die of heart disease or cancer and two-thirds are overweight. The American Dietetic Association says that vegetarians have "lower rates of death from ischemic heart disease; ... ... lower blood cholesterol levels, lower blood pressure and lower rates of hypertension, of Type 2 diabetes and lower rates of prostate and colon cancer."

Now, because of the rise of a new middle class in developing countries - where the eating of meat is seen as a sign of wealth - more people there seem to be adopting a high meat diet. China's emerging middle classes have increased their nation's consumption of meat by 150 per cent since 1980. So while there is growing demand for meat we have less and less land to raise it on.

Livestock production is responsible for 70 per cent of the Amazon deforestation in Latin America, where the rainforest is, by the hour, being cleared to create new 'burger pasture.' Deforestation increases greenhouse gas emissions by releasing carbon previously stored in the soil and the trees—accounting for *one fifth* of global emissions. Deforestation is also a major driver in the loss of biodiversity—a pressing concern when one considers the fact that just a few species of livestock now account for about 20 per cent of total terrestrial animal biomass.

- **World livestock production exceeds 21 billion animals each year.**
- **276 million tonnes of meat were produced in 2006, four times that of 1961.**
- **Globally, one third of all grain harvested is fed to animals.**
- **Demand for cereals *to feed livestock* will double in developing countries in the next generation.**
- **Meat demand is projected to double between 1995 and 2020.**

There are issues around the relative merits of factory-farmed, grain-fed cattle versus grass-fed free grazing animals that we cannot discuss here. Whichever the mode of livestock rearing, cattle are fed from productive land which could support many more human lives. Cattle are notoriously bad converters of food to protein: it takes 14kg of grain to produce just 2kg of beef. Globally, one third of all grain harvested is fed to animals. And livestock production contributes massively to climate change: 16 per cent of methane caused by humans comes from farmed cattle. Soya is also used in cattle feed and growing this crop in Brazil has contributed enormously—and still is - to the ongoing daily destruction of the Amazon rainforests. Brazil now produces 38 per cent of world soy output. Some 2.5 million hectares (6 million acres) of land in Brazil is being used to grow soy beans for animals in Europe alone, while at the same time, 20 million Brazilians suffer from malnutrition. Manure from cattle fouls many rivers.

As food demand soars, farmland and harvests shrink

For much of the century just past, meeting the food requirements for an ever-increasing population meant bringing new lands into productive use. But by the 1980s expansion of agricultural land had ceased altogether and in fact more land went out of production than was newly opened up—for reasons we don't usually hear about. Population pressure is forcing the poor onto unsuitable marginal lands (or forest), where soils are being quickly exhausted; they then move onto other lands to repeat the process. So we now have a situation where the supply of new, potentially productive land is shrinking while the area of non-productive land is growing. As the area of productive land cannot be substantially increased, it will mean that in the future each hectare needs to double its yield even to maintain the already inadequate diet of the developing nations.

- **Even now the world average number of hectares per person is 0.27, whereas 0.5 hectares per person is the minimum to maintain an adequate diet.**
- **World wide, about 420 million people live in countries that no longer have sufficient cropland to grow their own food. By 2025 the people in countries that must import food will to rise to 1 billion.**

Now countries that cannot feed themselves have to buy in food to survive but on the open market staple foods are declining in availability due to decreasing yields and to increasing demand from wealthier developing nations such as China and India.

- In 2006 grain production fell short of consumption by 61 million tons, marking the sixth time in the last seven years that production has failed to satisfy demand. In 2007 world grain reserves stood at 57 days. In 2008 US grain reserves were 2.7 million bushels of wheat, enough to make 1/2 of a loaf of bread for each American.
- According to the Food Policy Research Institute we have to produce 40 per cent more grain by 2020 to meet extra demand.
- People in the rich North consume five times as much food as people in the poor South.
- For people in poor, developing countries to have the same standard of nutrition as those in rich developed countries, agricultural output will have to increase by a massive 430 per cent!

It's surprising therefore that even with declining yields and desertification there could be enough food to feed the world. According to the UN Food and Agriculture Organization, there *is* enough food in the world to supply everyone with a daily 3,500-calorie diet of grains, fresh fruit, beans and nuts, vegetables, dairy and meat. But because we lack a fair food distribution system and they lack income to pay for it, poor people go hungry. The sad fact is that a minority eats very well - even to the extent of causing an epidemic of obesity - whereas the majority scrape by on a meagre and inadequate diet. People in the rich North consume five times as much food as people in the poor South.

What results is malnutrition and death for millions. Hunger manifests itself in many ways other than starvation and famine. Most poor people who battle hunger face chronic under-nourishment and vitamin or mineral deficiencies, which result in stunted growth and mental capacities, weakness and heightened susceptibility to illness. According to WHO, poor nutrition and calorie deficiencies cause nearly one in three people to die prematurely or have disabilities. In the developing world, 20 million children are born each year with a low birth weight, leaving one in three hindered by chronic malnutrition. According to the Global Health Council, in 2009, an estimated 10.1 million children under the age of five die each year—nearly 28,000 per day or 19 every minute. If current trends continue, some 1.2 billion people could be chronically hungry by 2025, 600 million more than previously predicted.

- **More than 840 million people in the world are malnourished — 799 million of them live in the developing world.**
- **14 million children die every year in developing countries from hunger- related diseases. That is equivalent to three jumbo jets crashing every hour of every day of the year.**

Food aid

One way of solving food crises in countries affected by desertification is food aid, but this relies on having surplus production of grain in the world. Australia and the North America have been the main providers. Between them they have a 60 per cent share of the international grain trade. But the sobering fact is that grain surpluses are declining, with grain yields per hectare having fallen 15 per cent in 30 years and projected to drop by a third by 2030. Meanwhile the projected cereal demand in developing countries is set to increase by 80 per cent by 2020. As the food and now bio-fuel policies of the major grain producing countries have greatest influence on grain prices in international markets, there is a growing risk that poorer nations will no longer be able to purchase grain to feed their starving peoples and food aid will have to be increased, further exacerbating price rises.

Trade injustices in agricultural commodities

The way international markets operate has left developing country exporters at a huge disadvantage for decades. Because they depend for revenues from the low-value, bulk commodities they export, their combined exports amount to only 10 percent by value of global trade. As a result, developing countries find themselves up against a wall of mutual self-interest from the buyers of the rich north over terms of trade. Buyers both play the markets and set the rules. So these markets are operated under close to cartel conditions, conditions that have long been ruled unfair and are illegal in a majority of sovereign jurisdictions. These unfair trading conditions are a frequent contributor to the food supply problems that certain developing countries repeatedly suffer.

Global world trade has increased 2.6 times since 1987 but poor countries benefited rather little. The domination they confront in the global marketplace is by rich countries but predominantly by their TNCs (trans national corporations). They alone control 85 per cent of world trade. The World Trade Organisation (WTO) still establishes the rules for trading. This international body awards votes by country in proportion business volumes, creating an overwhelming built-in bias in favour of the richer countries. Because it suits the richer nations, WTO rules require poor countries to cut support for farmers and open up their home agricultural markets to rich country producers. But do the European Union and the United States cease to heavily subsidise their farmers to protect their own home markets? No! What is worse, some richer country farm subsidies are so high their food can be exported to developing countries at below-cost prices.

- **In 1961 developing world farmers had 40 per cent of the world trade in agricultural commodities, now it is 35 per cent.**
- **Agricultural subsidies in OECD countries in the period 2001-2003 totalled $324 billion.**
- **An EU cow gets a subsidy of $2.50 a day, which exceeds the daily income of most Africans.**

Poor countries aspiring to greater levels of food self sufficiency are hobbled because often the best land and resources are owned by TNCs. These corporations have no brief to feed local people; answerable only to shareholders, they are geared to maximising profits by growing cash crops for export.

The threat of global food shortages loomed larger with the 2008 spike in oil prices, but there is a knock-on effect that could be worse. Following the food riots that struck some 30 countries in 2008—along with raised demand for bio-fuels and for foodstuffs from within India and China - several major agricultural export countries including the US, Canada, Brazil and Thailand put restrictions or stops on their export volumes, measures aimed at ensuring adequate supplies at affordable prices at home. Unsurprisingly, these restrictions made it even harder for impoverished importing countries to finance the food they purchases from abroad.

Conclusion—possible spiritual and physical solutions

It's a truism that our actions bear out the personal values to which we subscribe. Spiritual traditions place a very high value on and have a deep respect for the land. The focus of modern agricultural production reflects an attitude that the land is a free resource, a commodity to be 'mined' rather than seeing it as a valued resource to be cherished and nurtured. So a shift in values, a change of attitude towards a spiritual perspective might inspire agribiz execs and farmers recognise there are solutions to the problems of declining crop yields, diminishing growing areas and desertification. Spiritual teachings also address the need for respect and social justice if we are to make our world work—fairshares, as Permaculture puts it. They all point to the injustice of the present food trading system and the values we need in our hearts to help us address these wrongs.

Physical solutions lie in transforming conventional agriculture to being truly sustainable. This would take imagination and commitment, but there is no shortage of inspired pioneers, many within the growing organic food movement. The United Nations defines organic agriculture as a 'holistic' food system that avoids the use of synthetic fertilizers and pesticides, minimizes pollution and optimizes the health of plants, animals and people. This form of agriculture is reliant on inputs from the local environment such as use of compost in place of artificial fertilizers. Higher fertility gives stronger plants better able to resist pests. Increasing the variety of crops means smaller colonies of pests, some of which can be tempted elsewhere by 'companion' plantings. Such 'novel' methods combined with traditional practices could become vital in the coming years as climate change starts seriously to affect the ability of farmers to grow crops using conventional methods.

The UN already sees organics as a means to combat world hunger. The FAO held an International Conference on Organic Agriculture and Food Security in Rome in May 2007. Organic farming is now commercially practised in 120 countries and represents a $40 billion a year market. One study produced by the University of Michigan predicts that a global shift to organic agriculture would yield at least 2,641 kilocalories per person per day, just under the world's current production of 2,786 and could rise to as many as 4,381 kilocalories per person per day. One recent study, possibly the largest of its kind on organic agriculture, looked at more than 280 projects in 57 of the world's poorest countries. The team of international scientists conducting the four-year project found that the farmers enjoyed improved crop productivity while reducing their use of pesticides and water. Scientists elsewhere discovered that techniques such as crop rotation and organic farming increased crop yields by an average of 79 per cent without risking future harvests. This must surely be bad news to the agrichemical giants and their shareholders - or will we see 'dung futures'?

Poorer countries have to address the problem of their expanding populations and the loss of land to urbanisation and desertification. Developed countries can help them with these problems by providing more of the right resources. Along with organic growing there is also the very sustainable system of growing called Permaculture. Permaculture works by careful planning so there is a minimum disruption to Nature's poorly understood systems for nutrient distribution within the soil. Food is produced without massive inputs of energy or resources. Once a Permaculture system is established it is truly sustainable over time. In a world where oil-based aids will soon no longer be viable this makes a lot of sense. Examples of organic agriculture and food production by Permaculture feature in our final chapter.

It's abundantly clear that radical change is coming—*has* to come - to how we feed ourselves. We have only scratched the surface here; it's clear that the sooner we all recognise the changes needed and are prepared to help them along, the sooner we will address the challenges ahead. Applying some of the wisdom of the ages might be a good place to start.

Personal Food Action Ideas

We've assembled here some of practical things you can do to help address, on a personal level, some of the food issues raised in this chapter:

1. Buy food with the "Fair trade" mark on it; at least you know more income is going to the producer and not to a middle-man or a multi-national. www.fairtrade.net www.fair-trader.info www.getethical.com
2. Avoid food containing any GM (GMO) ingredients. Always demand GM-free. Tell your political representative you want GM (GMO) foods banned or limited. www.howstuffworks.com www.foodfuture.org.uk www.gmwatch.org www.truefood.coop/node/1055 www.responsibletechnology.org/GMFree
3. Buy food that is locally produced, which cuts food miles and its pollution, supports local farmers and avoids unnecessary packaging. www.farmersmarkets.net www.

information-britain.co.uk www.bigbarn.co.uk www.localfoodworks.org

4. Avoid all forms of junk food: it's bad for you; it's bad for our Planet; if it doesn't destroy rainforest it has a large energy footprint. www.healthyeating.net www.healthyeatingdirectory.com

5. Campaign for your government to step up its international aid in areas such as combating desertification and helping countries effectively develop their agriculture. www.globalissues.org www.practicalaction.org www.wdm.org.uk/

6. Eat organic food and encourage traditional agricultural methods. www.whyorganic.org www.growingwell.co.uk www.purefood.org www.soilassociation.org

7. Campaign for your government to support the development of organic agricultural production. www.efrc.com/ www.gardenorganic.org.uk/

8. Grow as much food as you can in your garden, allotment or window box. www.gardenorganic.org.uk www.kitchengardens.org www.goodhumans.com www.permaculture.org.uk

9. Aim raise your awareness in what you eat, how much and when. Join a campaign like Sustain: www.sustainweb.org/

10. Experiment with vegetarian dishes; decrease your intake of meat products. If you do eat meat, ensure it is produced without undue suffering to the animals. www.vegsoc.org www.vegansociety.com

11. Fish: support sustainable fisheries: look for the international MSC 'fish check' logo of the Marine Stewardship Council before you buy–see www.msc.org. For farmed fish, make sure it is farmed organically, check at www.fishonline.org Marine Conservation Society UK www.mcsuk.org/ www.marineconservationalliance.org/

12. Buy only line-caught tuna, a system that does not ensnare dolphins.

13. Campaign against the use of toxic chemicals in modern agricultural production. www.pesticideinfo.org www.pesticidescampaign.co.uk www.soilassociation.org/

pesticides Pesticide Action Network UK www.pan-uk.org North America www.panna.org

14. Support the work of OXFAM and similar charities by donating unwanted goods to them so that they can be sold to raise funds for agricultural development.

15. When disaster strikes, remember your donation via Disasters Emergency Committee www.dec.org.uk, American Red Cross www.redcross.org, or other national fund pooling agency.

16. Be aware of the impact of food miles in your food shopping basket. Locate you local Farmers' Market. Develop a preference for locally, grown 'in season' foods (they're cheaper). If not local, then try and buy foods grown in your region or country. If not national, then Fair Trade. USA: www.localharvest.org. UK: www.farmersmarkets.net www.fairtradefederation.org

CHAPTER 15 : THE AIR WE BREATHE

Death by polluted air

We all breathe in about 10,000 to 20,000 litres of air per twenty-four hours to stay alive. You would think that it is a basic right to have clean air to breathe, but for more than half the world population air pollution is a constant threat to health. In fact is has been estimated that 1.6 *billion* people in urban areas may now be at risk from poor air quality throughout the world. The World Health Organization states that 2.4 million people die each year from causes directly attributable to air pollution, with 1.5 million of these deaths attributable to *indoor* air pollution. Polluted air is blamed for four increasingly common disorders: cardio-pulmonary disease, cancers of trachea, bronchus and lung and acute respiratory infections in children. WHO estimates that 2 per cent of all deaths in urban areas worldwide are from cardio-pulmonary disease, 5 per cent from cancers of trachea, bronchus and lung and 1 per cent from acute respiratory infections in children. We can conclude from these figures that there is a strong correlation between poor air quality and the incidence of life threatening respiratory diseases.

Of the 800,000 premature deaths attributed to urban outdoor air pollution every year, about 65 per cent occur in the developing countries of Asia. WHO estimates that 1 billion people in Asian countries are exposed to air pollution that breaches WHO safety limits, leading to the premature death of 500,000 people every year or 1,400 every day.

The problem is not confined to developing countries. In 2005, a study by the European Commission estimated that air pollution was responsible for an estimated 310,000 premature deaths in Europe each year. Air pollution reduces the life expectancy of the average European by 8.6 months. In the UK, it has been estimated that 18 common diseases involving perhaps 149,000 deaths a year could be caused by industrial air pollution. In 2009, a report by the London Assembly stated that 107,000 people of the capital had their health affected by air pollution and in some cases this shortened their life expectancy by one full year. Air pollution costs the UK economy an estimated £19 *billion* a year. Health implications are greatest however in developing countries, where in-home smoke inhalation is especially rife.

The worst affected are countries such as China and India. SEPA, the Chinese Environment agency, has predicted that within 15 years China's GDP will double and at the same time the pollution load will increase by four to five times, judging by present resource consumption rates and levels of pollution controls. The study, conducted by the Chinese Academy on Environmental Planning in 2003, found that 300,000 people died from outdoor air pollution, while 111,000 people died from indoor air pollution each year.

Poverty condemns half of humanity to cook with solid fuels such as dung and crop residues as well as charcoal, coal and wood. Without a proper flue, chimney or outlet, the smoke these fuels produce creates indoor air pollution that kills. Indoor air pollution is the fourth greatest risk factor for death and disease in the world's poorest countries and is linked to 1.6 million deaths per year, particularly from bronchitis and emphysema. For example, in India where 80 per cent of households use solid fuel, an estimated half million children die annually from indoor air pollution, especially from acute respiratory infections. It seems that young children are twice as likely to contract acute lower respiratory infections and women are three times more likely to suffer from chronic bronchitis, if exposed to indoor air pollution from solid fuels. Because of these high mortality rates, some NGOs have prioritised cooker hoods, chimneys and windows as practical solutions, but funding the outreach initiatives needed has remained a serious limitation.
(See www.practicalaction.org/?id=smoke_ahd)

Mega cities "on 40 a day"

The Planet's direst air quality is predictably found within the great mega cities of the developing nations. People still migrate to them in their millions and urban settlements swell year on year. In 2008, fifty per cent of the world's population was for the first time estimated to live in cities. In part as a result of swelling local populations, these cities suffer from horrendous air pollution problems, caused by little regulation of emissions and phenomenal increases in traffic and industrial activity.

For instance if you live in Beijing, Kolkata, Mexico City, Shanghai or Tehran, air pollution is so bad in some places that people are involuntarily being exposed to air pollution levels equivalent to smoking 40 cigarettes a day!

No motorised transport without fumes

The car is seen everywhere as a great symbol of prosperity and wealth and, increasingly in the developing world, one that people aspire to. I have seen huge changes even in my lifetime where, in the 1950s, my father had to wait ten years to buy an old, second hand car, yet my daughters purchased newer cars in their early twenties. The car in developed countries has long been a necessity to get to work or to do business. In America vast suburban hinterlands were built on the assumption that oil would always be plentiful and make commuting by car cheap. Not any more, it isn't. The car not only consumes finite resources, it acts as a "pollutermobile" belching its noxious fumes to be breathed in by unsuspecting lungs. At least until the 2008-09 financial crash, the car's population had since the 1960s been growing faster than the human population. It is estimated there are 600 million cars, globally, increasing pre-2009 at 45 *million* cars per year.

- **The number of motor vehicles in the world was expected to reach about 1.3 billion by 2020, more than doubling today's number. The fastest growth has been in Latin America and Asia.**
- **In 2008, the number of motor vehicles in China was 168 million well over a 30 per cent increase from the 2004 figure.**
- **In 2006 there were 250 million motor vehicles in the USA.**

While vehicle populations have grown in both the developed and the developing nations, the greater increase is in the developing countries where the worst of air pollution occurs.

Our industries all pollute

The other main source of air pollution is industry. Pollution levels rose in step with increasing rates of growth in industrial production pre-crisis. Since 1900 the world economy has expanded by a factor of 20 whilst consumption of fossil fuels has increased by a factor of 30. Industrial production has increased by a factor of 50, four fifths of this increase occurring since 1950. This industrial expansion has been underwritten by availability of abundant, cheap fossil fuels, the main contributors to urban air pollution, starting with coal. The situation is getting worse with the emergence of India and China as the 'smokestack' industry giants of the world economy: they both use 'dirty' coal as a primary fuel for manufacturing and to generate massive amounts of electric power.

Spiritual teachings about air
All spiritual traditions recognise air as a vital, life-giving force.

Hinduism
Ancient Hindus saw air as "His breath" (Srimad Bhagwat 2.1 32-33) and the sky is identified as the Father in the Vedas. Air is seen as medicine for the body, which should be kept pure (Artharveda 4.25 1-7). The Rig Veda describes air as the storehouse of the elixir of life, a panacea for all diseases and friend of the world (Rig Veda 10.185 1-3 and 10.186.3). There is a mantra in the Rig Veda, which praises the oxygen content of air and says, "do not destroy it" which implies that air pollution of any sort is wrong (Rig Veda 6.37.3). In Yoga, air is seen as being permeated with *prana* or spiritual energy.

> *The air is His breath, the ocean is His Waist* - Bhagavad Gita II. 1.33-34
> *The three aspects of the environment: land, water and air, have been regarded by the Rishis as Gods* - Professor Y. Shastri, Lecturer in Philosophy, University of Amedabad, Gujarat, India
> *In the shastras people were punished for polluting the water, cutting down trees and bringing impurity to the air* - Professor V.D. Randu, Friend of Shivananda Ashram, Rishikesh, Uttarakhand, Northwest India

Judaism
In the second century the Jews had *Mishnah* rules to prevent urban air pollution. Under these rules the siting of threshing barns or furnaces near residential areas was forbidden so as to avoid exposure to fouled air.

Sikhism

In Sikhism air was considered divine and referred to as Guru in the scriptures.

> *The air is the Guru, Water the Father and Earth the Great Mother* -
> Jap Ji prayer Sahib-Salok in the Guru Granth Sahib
> *The Air teaches us mobility and liberty* - Guru Granth Sahib
> *Sikh spirituality is to live a simple life, use resources carefully and not to spread pollution* - Dr. Mavinder Singh, Lecturer at the Department of Guru Nanak Studies, Guru Nanak University, Amritsar, Punjab, India

Dr. Mavinder Singh (right) with the author

Jainism

Transport is a very significant cause of air pollution worldwide. Jain monks set an example in that they do not use any form of motorised transport. Lay Jains are encouraged to make a vow limiting travel in the four directions and to limit how far they will travel from their home. In taking the *deshavakashik vrat* vow Jains are encouraged to set an actual limit to the area within which they physically move around. The *anarth dand tyag* vow prohibits unnecessary violence and participation in occupations that involve violence. Jains see air pollution creating bad karma, as air beings are part of the eternal self or Jiva Tattva.

> *Without air we cannot live* - Puiya Manibhadra Muni, Jain Monk at the Parshwanath Vidyapeeth Institute, Varanasi, Uttar Pradesh, India
> *Pollution of vehicles and factories means there is no fresh air* –
> Acharya Mahapragya, Head Monk of the Jain Terapanth Sect, Ghandhinagar, Gujarat, India

Christianity

There is air pollution from traffic and from undeveloped factories because they do not give importance to ecological concerns - Father James Thattanparamba, Asirvanam Monastery, Bangalore, India

Father James Thattanparamba

Islam

Islam teaches that we must always strive to keep the environment clean and this must extend to keeping the air clean.

> *Here, there is no mechanism of control of air and noise pollution* - Abir Mirz, Secondary School Teacher, Kolkata, West Bengal, India

Buddhism

Buddhism teaches the karmic results of actions. Any action that causes ill health to others is considered bad karma and poor moral conduct.

> *The Buddhist way of living is conducive to not hurting people* - Dr. P.C. Candasri, Theravada Buddhist monk, Bodh Gaya, Bihar, India
> *Refrain from harmful activities and develop loving kindness and practise contentment* - Lobsang Dakpa Geshe, Tibetan exile, Senior Buddhist Monk, lecturer in philosophy, Namgyl Monastery, Dharamsala, Himachal Pradesh, India

How common air pollutants impact on health

As we burn more and more fossil fuels (oil, gas and coal) we produce a great variety of air pollutants. Each has its impact on health. Even burning wood, if it is not dried to 18 per cent moisture, produces noxious irritants in the air. It is quite clear from the health risks described below that we do not recognise clean air as precious and a requirement for good health. Let us now look at the effects of each of these common air pollutants found most in urban areas.

Particulates

Airborne suspended particulate matter is made up of smoke and soot from diesel engines, from burning and industrial processes, dust and liquid droplets from fuel combustion. The two most hazardous groups of particles (particulate matter or PM) are known as PM 10 and PM 2.5, which are minute, invisibly fine particles which measure less than 10 microns (1/100 of a millimetre) in diameter and 2.5 microns. Of special concern in the protection of lung health are the very fine PM 2.5's. These mainly come from motor vehicle exhausts, particularly diesels. Fine particles are easily inhaled deeply into the lungs where some remain embedded for long periods of time, some even absorbed into the bloodstream. A recent study showed a 17 per cent increase in mortality risk in areas with higher concentrations of PM 2.5's. The WHO estimates that outdoor particulate pollution overall accounts for 800,000 premature deaths in the world annually, including 500,000 in Asia alone.

The problem of particulate pollution is found throughout the world, particularly within the great mega cities. By one estimate, 57 million tonnes of suspended particulate matter are produced globally each year. In a survey of cities by the UN, twelve out of 20 of the cities surveyed did not meet the WHO guidelines on particulate matter levels. Bangkok, Bombay, Cairo, Kolkata, Delhi, Jakarta, Karachi, Manila and Shanghai were found to be breaching the WHO safety guidelines.

Particulates irritate the throat, bronchus and lungs, PM 2.5s lodging in the deeper parts of the lungs. This can lead eventually to chronic bronchitis. And there is evidence that breathing them in weakens people's immune system. Because particles can penetrate deep into lung tissues there is a greater risk of contracting lung cancer. There can also be decreased pulmonary function, causing extra strain on the heart.

- **From 1997 to 2004, 23 to 45 per cent of people living in urban areas world wide were exposed to levels of particulates above the *minimum* safety standards set by the EU.**
- **In China smoke particles from burning coal cause 50,000 premature deaths and 400,000 new cases of bronchitis a year.**

- A 1995 US study showed that PM 2.5 exposure led to premature death by two years and was linked to lung cancer and cardiopulmonary problems.
- In 2000 a thorough study of toxic air pollution in Southern California showed that motor vehicles and other mobile sources accounted for about 90 per cent of the cancer risk from toxic air pollution, most of which was from diesel soot (70 per cent of the cancer risk).
- According to estimates for 18 cities in Central and Eastern Europe, 18,000 premature deaths a year could be prevented and $1.2 billion a year in working time lost to illness could be regained by achieving EU pollution standards for dust and soot.

Heavy metals

These are often released into the air through the incineration of municipal rubbish and industrial processes. Incinerators have spread throughout Europe as an alternative to use of vanishing landfill sites. However, research has since shown that people living near incinerators are exposed to greater health risks, especially from heavy metals. The most common heavy metals to be released as fumes into the atmosphere by incinerators are arsenic, lead, cadmium, chromium, manganese, mercury and nickel, all of which are toxic, many carcinogenic.

Arsenic is released into the atmosphere from many industrial sources like pesticide manufacture and smelting. It is a highly carcinogenic substance and a proven cause of cancer of the lungs, liver and skin.

Cadmium is released into the air from steel plants, waste incineration and zinc production. When incinerators burn waste they often end up burning paints and plastics, which may contain cadmium and NiCad batteries which certainly do. Inhalation of cadmium fumes can lead to it accumulating in the kidneys, lungs and heart. Since Cadmium is known to be carcinogenic it can cause cancer in the organs affected.

Chromium can be released into the air through incinerator plants and cement kilns. At lower levels of exposure it leads to skin irritation and skin rashes. Since it is known to be carcinogenic at more repeated high levels of exposure, lung cancer can develop.

Manganese is released into the atmosphere mainly through the smelting of ores and combustion of fossil fuels. When inhaled it can give rise to aching limbs, backache and drowsiness.

Mercury is released into the atmosphere through activities such as mining and smelting ores, burning fossil fuels and incineration. This is a very toxic substance as just one seventieth of a teaspoon of atmospheric mercury can contaminate a 20-acre lake for a year. Mercury is the heavy metal present in the atmosphere at the highest concentrations. Incinerator plants are not always selective of what they burn and materials with high mercury content such as batteries, fluorescent light tubes and paints are incinerated routinely. Exposure to this metal can gravely effect the development of the central nervous system leading to arrested development and mental retardation in children.

Nickel enters the atmosphere through the burning of oils, nickel mining and municipal waste incineration. Exposure to this heavy metal has been associated with cancer of the sinus and lungs.

You'll notice from the descriptions that a lot of heavy metals are emitted from incinerators. There is no doubt that many European countries have failed to raise their recycling rates and have opted for incinerators to avoid EU penalties for extending landfill. Those in favour of incinerators claim that they produce energy from waste, but more energy would be saved through recycling the waste. In the UK, the government is trying to force through the expansion of an incinerator programme despite the known health risks to its population. I myself have heard convincing statistical evidence that there is a rise in cancer rates in the immediate vicinity of an incinerator plant ten years after construction. I learnt this from an engineer who'd lost both his wife and son to cancer. He was convinced it was from their exposure to a nearby incinerator. Surely no just government can rightly choose to expose its people to health risks in the name of saving money. Every proposed site has its campaign against (see end chapter listings).

Dioxins

These man-made chemicals known as polychlorinated dibenzo-para-dioxins or PCDDs are toxic, pervasive, persistent and carcinogenic. They are so pervasive they are found in all meat products on Earth and even in Antarctica penguins. The sources of dioxin pollution are smelters, those same incinerators and chemical factories. Significantly, Dioxins have been identified both in the smokestack emissions of incinerators as well as in the waste fly ash they produce often used locally.

Dioxins are one of the most toxic substances on Earth: they can have an adverse affect on the human body—and of any mammals, birds,

194

and fish - even when they are measured in parts *per trillion*. Dioxins are known carcinogens and they are a known cause of birth defects. Cancers associated with exposure are soft tissue sarcoma and Non-Hodgkin's Lymphoma.

The most widespread dioxin poisoning resulted from Agent Orange, used as a defoliant in the Vietnam War between 1965 and 1970. During this period 13 million gallons were sprayed which has resulted in as many as 400,000 deaths and disabilities and perhaps 500,000 children suffering from birth defects that continue to destroy quality of life to this day. Lawyers argue still over the numbers.

The Missouri Shenandoah incident in the USA also highlights the dangers of dioxins. In Shenandoah County, waste oil containing dioxins was accidentally sprayed as a dust suppressant between 1971 and 1984. Animals were the first to suffer with the immediate death of birds, horses and cats. Later people contracted bone tumours and the incidences of leukaemia increased dramatically, whilst many suffered from liver and kidney problems.

The most infamous dioxin pollution incident was in Seveso, Italy in 1976. Here, a chemical plant blew up releasing 2,900 kg of organic matter containing dioxins. This resulted in 81,000 animals being destroyed and the evacuation of thousands of people. Overall about a quarter of a million people were affected by the incident.

Oxides of Nitrogen–asthma and worse

Oxides of nitrogen, which though not poisonous can cause asthma and trigger more severe conditions, are formed during any high-temperature combustion process such as in vehicle motors and jet engines. Because air is two-thirds nitrogen gas, the nitrogen oxidises during burning and comprises a major emission. There is a whole group of these gases, including Nitrogen Dioxide (NO_2) and Nitrous Oxide (N_2O) grouped together and referred to as NO_x or NOx. In 2005, 40 million tonnes was produced worldwide with 64 per cent coming from fossil fuel combustion, 14 per cent from other burning and a surprising 22 per cent from soil.

The UN found in its survey of air pollution in mega cities that Los Angeles, Mexico City, Moscow and Sao Paulo all had moderate to heavy pollution of oxides of nitrogen. China's NO_x pollution has grown 50 per cent between 1996 and 2003. Twenty-five per cent of the EU urban population were found to be exposed to oxides of Nitrogen beyond acceptable safety limits. NO$_x$ is a known hazard in and around airports and traffic bottlenecks everywhere.

Upon inhalation, 80 to 90 per cent of NO$_x$ can be absorbed; it is very soluble and tends to enter the blood quickly. At low doses it can cause irritation, inflammation of the deep lung tissue and asthma. Nitrogen Dioxide increases the onset of asthma by triggering allergic reactions to dust and house mites. Whereas asthma was a very rare occurrence before the First World War, it is now a disease of all industrialised societies and is on the increase. It is characterised by spasms, which lead to attacks of breathlessness, in some cases hospitalisation and premature death.

- **In Britain, 1 in 12 people now suffer from asthma.**
- **In 2004, according to the American Lung Association, 20 million Americans have asthma or 1 in every 14 people.**
- **Six times more children are treated for asthma now than 25 years ago.**

In children, NO$_x$ exposure leads to immune system debilitation and consequent increased susceptibility to lung infections such as bronchitis. In higher doses it can cause pulmonary swelling, decreased pulmonary function and broncho-pneumonia. Very high exposure can result in sudden circulatory collapse and sudden death. Yet, despite so many known, serious and widespread health problems associated with NO$_x$, this form of pollution has till recently received little public attention. In the 1990s, the European Union, however, called for its monitoring and has set increasingly stringent levels which member countries are obliged to meet. It was these EU measures that had placed UK government plans for a third runway at London's main airport in doubt before the scheme was cancelled by incoming coalition government in 2010.

Ozone

In the lower Stratosphere, 10-50 km up, this substance is very important in protecting the Planet from deadly UV radiation; but at near-surface levels, ozone is harmful to human health. Low-level ozone pollution is often associated with cities that lie in basins where air circulation is poor, such as Los Angeles, Sao Paulo, Tokyo and Mexico City. Motor vehicles are the main contributor as they provide 48 per cent of the nitrogen oxides and 37 per cent of the hydrocarbons needed for ozone to form. Ozone forms in the presence of sunlight when there is an interaction between nitrogen oxides with volatile hydrocarbon compounds. Formation is thus more likely during sunny, high-pressure weather and often spreads from large urban centres into the surrounding countryside and beyond. Significant levels of ozone pollution can be detected in rural areas as far as 250 miles (400 km) downwind from urban industrial zones. Ozone levels typically rise during the summer (May to September in Northern hemisphere) period when higher temperatures and the increased amount of sunlight combine with the stagnant atmospheric conditions associated with ozone air pollution episodes.

On examination, low-level ozone is far nastier than billed: it can limit the ability to take a deep breath and it can cause coughing, throat irritation and breathing discomfort. At a mere 200 parts per billion, the bronchial passages and the lungs' delicate alveoli cells can be damaged permanently. There is also evidence that ozone can lower resistance to respiratory disease such as pneumonia, damage lung tissue and aggravate chronic lung disease such as asthma or bronchitis. Ozone causes serious damage to plants as well.

- **Studies in Mexico City, where the ozone rate can exceed the WHO guidelines on 300 days a year, show an increase in the number of people with asthmatic symptoms.**
- **In Los Angeles one survey suggested that if ozone pollution levels were lowered it would save 1,600 lives a year.**
- **In the USA nearly 9 million people with chronic bronchitis or emphysema and almost 7 million children and adults with asthma live in areas that exceed the Federal health limits for ozone. Nine US cities, home to 57 million people, are considered "severely" polluted, experiencing peak ozone levels that exceed safety standards by 50 per cent or more.**
- **Ozone smogs are costing Europe's farmers more than six billion Euros a year, according to the most detailed assessment to date.**
- **By 2050, in China, the urban pollution is expected to increase ground-level ozone levels by at least 25 per cent.**

Like NO_x, ozone has received little more than lip-service attention as a malevolent pollutant, perhaps because, as car drivers or users of public transport, a majority of people in Western countries contribute to these pollutants on a daily basis. Armed with awareness of the life threats it poses, we could as a society cut back on vehicle use and perhaps do more to pressure technicians to devise alternative forms of power that avoid creating these pollutants.

Carbon monoxide

This gas does not occur naturally. Formed from the incomplete combustion of fuels that contain carbon, it is colourless and odourless but far from harmless. Ninety per cent of all this gas comes from motor vehicles; other sources are tobacco smoke, heating systems and wood stoves.

Usually your muscle cells receive oxygen through haemoglobin in your blood that carries it from your lungs throughout your body. Happily, haemoglobin is unstable in that it is equally happy to take up oxygen in the lungs as it is to give it up in the muscles. However, when exposed to carbon monoxide, haemoglobin changes into a stable substance that no longer absorbs or yields up oxygen. And its affinity for carbon dioxide is 300 times stronger than for oxygen, even more so at altitude. This is why even at low concentrations, CO is always harmful; and if the amount absorbed rises it very soon can be lethal: exposure to CO results in a rapid drop in available oxygen levels, affecting the functions of the heart and the central nervous system.

Classic mild symptoms are dizziness, tiredness and headache, which people might experience after being stuck in traffic. Continued exposure can cause cardio-vascular problems and an increased risk of a stroke. Nervous system exposure leads to impaired learning, limited dexterity and sleep problems. Smoking produces CO. Pregnant women and foetus are at risk as exposure can result in babies with low birth weight and retarded mental development. In the developing world where pollution controls are less stringent, much higher levels of carbon monoxide are found, especially in cities such as Sao Paulo, Cairo, Mexico City, Bangkok and Jakarta. But there are still CO exposure problems in the developed world, where WHO safety limits are breached in London, New York, Moscow and Los Angeles. At higher exposure levels there is a risk of convulsions, coma and death.

- **Motorists are vulnerable as readings of 100 parts per million are common when they enter a tunnel. Officials** working in the tunnels in New York suffer a 35 per cent increased mortality rate. Tunnels at altitude, such as under the Alps or the American Continental Divide, require super-efficient ventilation to counter special hazards from CO.

- Researchers observed an approximately 10-20 per cent increase in the risk of premature birth and low birth weight for infants born to women living near high traffic areas in Los Angeles County.

- The US Center for Disease Control estimates that each year 1,500 Americans die from carbon monoxide poisoning. About 900 of these deaths occur in homes and are preventable.

Photochemical smog

When all the pollutants from vehicle exhaust fumes—and jet plane exhaust - including numerous oxides and ozone are mixed together in the presence of sunlight, you get that strange orange-brown grey haze which is photochemical smog. Smog episodes occur whenever air pollutants are trapped in still air at ground level in sunlight. A temperature inversion that prevents vertical mixing of the pollutants from the boundary layer into the free troposphere keeps an episode going longer. Smog forms most readily in and around cities that lie in basins. Los Angeles's smog was so severe it led to the pioneering of catalytic exhaust systems—which allowed more cars. In Mexico City at one time the problem was so bad that special oxygen producing equipment had to be installed.

When people are exposed to this noxious mixture of air pollutants their health can be severely affected. Exposure ages the lung tissue at an increased rate and this can lead to fibrosis of the lung. Repeated high concentrations lead to emphysema, characterised by a shortness of breath and swelling of the lung tissue. Eventually repeated exposure leads to decreased pulmonary function leading to stress on the heart and sometimes sudden death through heart failure.

Conclusion - possible spiritual and physical solutions

We tend to take air for granted in our lives as long as it is clean enough to breathe. The real problem lies with our blasé attitude towards air, and to all the polluting activities we engage in, such as jumping in the car, too often for needless travel, engine on in jams. The spiritual traditions clearly state that air is precious and a valued part of Nature and even a medicine for the body. Certainly Jainism and Hinduism see air as a living spiritual force and believe that to pollute it in any way is an act of sacrilege. The founders of the different traditions lived in times of pristine unpolluted environments yet they still pointed towards the need to preserve air in its purest form. We would do well to adopt the same attitudes in our lives today.

Spiritual traditions such as Sikhism, Hinduism and Buddhism point to the law of karma or cause and effect. If personally we are to avoid polluting the air we would have to radically reappraise how we live. We might also seek to become more aware of the impacts of our actions on others. For instance every time we use a car we are adding to the pollution of the air for, say, a cyclist sharing the same space. Every time we consider buying a product, we could become more aware of the potentially massive air pollution caused to produce it; we could ask, do I *really* need this? Are there lower polluting alternatives? Could I buy second-hand? Could I share with family or friends? Until reminded, we tend to forget the consequences of our actions; recognizing just what they are can support us in changing our behaviour.

We might start with our travel and transport choices. We can reflect on the impact on the environment of our lifestyle choices and transport modes. What we choose makes a big difference to our overall personal environmental impact. How many journeys a week could we switch to a lower impact mode? From air to surface? From road to rail? From rail to bus? From bus to cycle or to foot? Each downshift reduces our personal impact. We could switch to hybrid or all-electric for the car, though pollution cuts will remain modest in re-charging an electric car until our mains power sources are cleaned up. Also, beware first generation bio-fuels, which have pushed up food prices and trampled rainforest. There remains the used chip fat option for diesels.

More effective monitoring of known sources of urban air pollution is urgently needed and the use of communication, ingenuity, technology, laws and enforcement to reduce them. For example, to cut down on pollution in Delhi and Mumbai in India, the government has decreed that only reduced emission LPG (liquefied petroleum gas) fuelled taxis are allowed in city centres. Emission standards for industry could be tightened further and factories not meeting them closed down. But the most effective way of dealing with pollution is to change to sustainable, non-polluting alternative energy sources. This is why massively increased funding is needed to boost research and development into alternative energy systems.

Personal actions to cut our air pollution

1. Examine ways you might cut down on or even avoid motorised transport: as often as possible, cycle or walk. Be sure to consider your options, their emissions and plan longer, one-off journeys, at www.transportdirect.info Try http://walkit.com the UK National Cycle Network: www.sustrans.org.uk/ www.whycycle.co.uk www.lowflyzone.org/alternatives-to-air-travel-2/ The man in seat 61: www.seat61.com/ www.bettertransport.org.uk/

2. Use public transport as much as possible to minimize pollution. Some governments are trying to integrate public transport by assisting journey planning, so search for what may be available in your country. For the UK try the useful government Journey Planner site: www.direct.gov.uk/en/TravelAndTransport

3. Join the campaign for better public transport. www.bettertransport.org.uk/ www.cpre.org.uk www.bettertransit.com

4. Join a local car club (community or commercial) or other car sharing scheme www.carplus.org.uk/ www.carclubs.org.uk/ www.carsharing.us/ http://worldcarshare.com/ www.liftshare.com www.shareajourney.com www.nationalcarshare.co.uk OR give your car away (proceeds to charity): www.giveacar.co.uk/

5. Consider converting your car to run on cleaner LPG gas rather than petrol. www.greenfuel.org.uk www.ewossuk.com

6. Consider buying a hybrid vehicle, which produces less air pollution. www.hybridcars.com www.green-car-guide.com www.earthenergy.com

7. Consider buying an electric vehicle, which slightly reduces air pollution overall. www.electriccars.com www.evworld.com www.whyfiles.org

8. Consider converting your diesel car to a Planet friendly bio-diesel which is less polluting—but this might limit

you to used chip fat. www.biodiesel.org www.biompu.com www.bio-pod.com www.dieselsecret.com

9. Campaign against the building of incinerators. www.foe.co.uk www.greenaction.org www.anti-incinerator.org.uk www.ukwin.org.uk/map/

10. Recycle as much as possible so preventing the need to build incinerators. www.recyclinginfo.com www.recyclingconsortium.org www.recyclenow.com www.recycle-more.co.uk

11. Service your central heating boiler so it causes less pollution and if it's over 12 years old, consider upgrading to super-efficient condensing type. www.energysavingtrust.org.uk/

12. Invest in wind and solar energy for your home, which will mean less reliance on fossil fuels for heat and light, now with attractive in-feed tariffs in UK. www.urbanwindenergy.org www.renewabledevices.com www.resourcesfinder.net www.diy.com www.microgeneration.com www.solarpanelinfo.com www.solarenergy.com

13. Think before buying manufactured products of the air pollution in their manufacture: do I *need* this? Could I buy second-hand? Could I borrow or share one with family or friend? www.newsociety.com/bookid/4015 http://depletion-abundance.blogspot.com/2008/01/low-energy-seed-starting.html

CHAPTER 16 : THE CLIMATE WE CHANGE

Introduction

The year I was born, 1950, marked a widely recognised departure for the citizenry of the rich global North: the start of a prolonged, six-decade rise in our standard of living. It marked another departure for the Planet that we're only beginning to recognise today: a rise in levels of consumption—of manufactures and of natural resources. It's important we distinguish between *standard of living* and *rate of consumption* because today, as we enter the second decade of the 21st century, we learn that we of the North need to bring down our rates of consumption. And we seek to achieve this without a significant overall lowering in our standard of living.

We have learned over the past decade that we can significantly reduce our rate of consumption - our global environmental footprint - without putting in serious jeopardy our overall high standards of living, by curbing only our excesses; oh, and our massive wastages in materials and energy.

It is our excesses of consumption and our massive wastages that have been bringing the biosphere to its knees: magnificent hardwood trees standing hundreds of feet high in Tasmania's forests felled to produce what? Chips that end up as garden mulch in Korea; just one obscene example of the pathological logic that flows from having a virtually-free source of highly concentrated stored energy known as petroleum—a pathology only magnified by the free-market economy. Other symptoms include giving low priority to pricing for transport by modes that perversely favours flying over rail. Flying is the most polluting, the most carbon-intensive mode. Rail produces one third of the warming effect for a given journey. We fly too much, we drive too much in too many vehicles for the fine balance of our planetary systems to remain undisturbed. Disappearing bird species, for one, provide conclusive evidence for that. Our fundamentalist obsession with free markets ensures we remain free to continue these insanely destructive behaviours.

As much as anything, it is this gross imbalance in the availability of cheap energy that has brought on man-made global climate change. I and others who live in the more prosperous countries of the world are responsible for the greater part of man-made climate change. If we choose to see things from a spiritual perspective, then we in the West must now take a stand to take responsibility and to respond with effective measures in our own lives, in our local communities, our own nations' policies and internationally as well.

To express my alarm, I attended week-long climate camps in the UK in 2006, 2007 and 2008 at Drax Power Station, Heathrow Airport and Kingsnorth Power Station, protesting against coal fired power stations and aviation as accelerators of climate change. Denial is no longer a meaningful option, though the most desperate cling doggedly to that illusion. Climate change is the single most important environmental challenge we face in the 21st century—the single most threatening challenge to life for 95 million years, says Mark Lynas in his *Six Degrees*. For economic and financial instability, Peak Oil may match it on the natural resources front.

Climate: situation outline

With climate change we have concerns on two timeframes: short-term and medium- long-term. While it's important we continue to lay plans and devise policies for the medium- and long-term, short-term we need to guard against abrupt climate changes. So while we should definitely redouble our efforts to bring about political consensus on appropriate and effective carbon-curbing actions; we should redouble our scientific searches for a better understanding of Earth's many complex systems; but in the short-term we also have to closely monitor for the risks of abrupt destabilising climate changes. These could come from positive feedback mechanisms such as further loss of polar ice cover, from ocean warming, from increased wildfires, from deforestation, from undersea methane venting and a few other known potential causes of destabilisation. Hopefully, the scenarios with abrupt changes will not be realised, but not to look at them in the hope they will 'go away.' That seems unwise in the extreme.

All the signs are that what we most urgently need to change is the continuing *rise* in our global GHG emissions. The step increase in emissions from new coal-fired stations in China and India more than counteracted any moderation in emissions elsewhere due to the 2008-09 global economic recession. So human GHG emissions continue *upward*, when we know we need them to be turning *downward*.

What is becoming clear is that both the causes and the effects of climate change are cumulative and will last for hundreds of years into the future. How we handle climate change in the coming few years will determine whether we will actually make it much past the end of this century. We have, according to one respected UK campaign, but 100 months, from August 2008 - till 30 November 2016 - in which to bring under control the inexorable growth in CO_2 in the atmosphere, currently rising at around 3 parts per million each year and steepening. Following the failure of the UN Climate Negotiations in Copenhagen in December 2009 there is much more work ahead to achieve a new global pact to share the burdens of emissions controls and mitigation measures such as flood protection. Our options narrow with each month. It is the world's poorest who are at greatest risk, but it is the polluters making the rules—or rather delaying on agreeing them.

Physical causes of climate change

The temperature of Earth's atmosphere is the result of the continuous exchange of incoming and outgoing radiated energy: the Earth's atmosphere is warmed by heat from the Sun in an entirely natural phenomenon on which life in all its forms has depended for much of the last billion years.

When too little of the incoming heat is able to escape back into space, then the equilibrium changes, producing a rise in temperature of the atmosphere. This is what people mean by 'global warming'. But this term can be used to mislead: while the *average* global temperature is seen to be rising, some world regions can experience cooling. It is for this reason that the term 'climate change' has come to be favoured over 'global warming'.

Make no mistake, without the basic warming process, Earth would be a much, much colder—and probably lifeless - place. The many influences that have acted to maintain atmospheric temperatures within benign ranges for the past 10 - 15,000 years are only beginning to be understood by science. However, it now seems the in-built stability of Earth's atmosphere came to an end in modern times, starting with industrialisation in the North 250 years ago.

Earth's ability to keep its temperature average within—spikes apart - a range of less than 15° Celsius has relied on influences that are called feedbacks. A negative feedback will return temperature towards the average level. It is thanks to negative feedbacks that a cooling trend would itself trigger warming influences; and a warming trend would trigger cooling influences, each restoring the equilibrium. Living mechanisms - plant and animal growth on land and marine lifeforms - tend to *release* atmospheric carbon when concentrations fall too low and *absorb* it when they rise above the balanced level. With CO_2 levels stabilized in this way, temperatures, too, have been maintained to within a 15 degree band.

What we have today is 'positive feedback.' Positive feedback is climate destabilising—potentially irreversibly so. This is the danger of which we are being warned and of which we must—literally - not loose sight. This is what is unprecedented about the situation today—one that has been building since the Industrial Revolution which began in the 1740s. The last time positive feedbacks took over control of the climate was 95 million years ago when around 90 percent of lifeforms on the Planet were extinguished.

Man's fossil fuelled industrial era brought massive demands for energy. This was obtained by burning coal and oil in ever larger quantities. It is this that is returning our atmosphere to its primeval hothouse state as it was before the rainforests and the microbes extracted most of the atmospheric carbon. Industrialisation has brought us back to the brink of what scientists see as a possible re-run of the massive extinction event.

With today's high—and rising - levels of greenhouse gases, average air temperatures have risen. Along with a warmer atmosphere we get warming of the world's oceans, melting of the polar icecaps, loss of glaciers almost everywhere and a thaw spreading to the Arctic's 'permafrost' regions. In the Arctic Ocean, open water absorbs much more warmth from the sun than the reflective sea ice that melted; bare rocky mountain valleys absorb more heat than glaciers. In addition, when the frozen ground of a permafrost area thaws, that ground releases methane, a greenhouse gas with a warming effect 23 times as powerful as the principal GHG, carbon dioxide.

These are all examples of 'positive feedback.' like monetary inflation, a little need not be a worry, but if it's uncontrolled it can become a 'runaway' situation, one that would, many scientists agree, signal another 'end-Permian' extinction event, an end to life as we know it on Planet Earth.

Preventing that runaway situation with so many positive feedback loops waiting to be triggered is the main challenge faced by the industrialised and industrialising countries of the world today. The 100-month timeframe for peak emissions is based on recent rates of GHG build-up and estimates of maximum 'safe levels.' The crisis on climate has not been retarded even by the recession. The rates of carbonisation in India and China as new coal-fired industrial capacity balloons more than cancel declines elsewhere.

So what are these greenhouse gases? The main greenhouse gases are carbon dioxide, oxides of nitrogen, methane, CFC's, surface ozone and water vapour. Of these, by far the most influential is CO_2, produced from fossil fuel burning, followed by deforestation.

Climate in brief

It is by burning fossil fuels we re-release that primordial carbon back into the atmosphere as carbon dioxide gas. As it and other gases accumulate they alter the atmosphere's 'heat trading' so that the atmosphere lets go of less heat than it receives. So Earth's atmosphere experiences a heating effect. Each square metre on Earth receives 390 Watts of solar energy, but the proportion going back into space is a mere 237 Watts, leaving a surplus of 153 Watts/m². It is this surplus retained in the atmosphere that is the cause of atmospheric warming and climate change.

Spiritual causes of climate change
Advertisers, 'haviness,' greed and materialism

Reflect upon the values which give rise to us altering the world's *climate*. The developed world has evolved a lifestyle driven ultimately by ownership, consumption, status and greed, not real need. These values have rubbed off on us all. Cunning advertisers exploit man's base nature, creating in us a dissatisfaction that compels us to consume more and more. Misguided, we have come to equate happiness with *having* rather than with *being*—'haviness' we could say. Like an addict, the consummate consumer is constantly looking for the next fix.

Apparently, our consumption provides us relief from the 'pain of being', of facing uncomfortable personal issues. Worse—and for the advertiser 'best' - what little relief we do find doesn't last: we just keep on searching in the vain hope of finding the thing—or service or partner or holiday or second home—that gives lasting relief from the dreaded 'pain of being.'

Then come our lifestyle choices in living in over-heated, poorly insulated homes (often in tee-shirts in winter) and in unlimited travel down to the shops as well as to all points around the globe, as fiendishly promoted in every newspaper and magazine we see. To imagine we could continue such energy-hungry habits without an impact on our Planet is sheer fantasy. Each item we buy, each powered journey we take, each day we over-heat our home, we are each contributing to the growing imbalance with Nature, with Gaia. Is it so surprising that Nature is letting us know about it?

Christianity
Jesus was the model non-materialist. He concentrated on his relationship with God, not on the accumulation of wealth. He spent his days on walkabout preaching: he totally depended on God for his material needs. In terms of being carbon-aware, treading lightly on the Planet, his life was exemplary.

> *What good will it be for a man if he gains the whole world, yet forfeits his soul* - Matthew 16:26
> *If you want to be perfect, go, sell your possessions and give to the poor and you will have treasure in heaven. Then come, follow me* - Matthew 19:21
> *The love of money is the root of all evils and there are some who, pursuing it, have wandered away from the faith and so given their souls any number of fatal wounds* - St. Paul (Timothy 6:10)
> *No one can be a slave to two masters: he will hate one and love the other; he will be loyal to one and despise the other. You cannot serve both God and money* - Jesus (Matthew 6:24)
> *Watch out! Be on your guard against all kinds of greed; a man's life does not consist in the abundance of his possessions* - Luke 12:15
> *Do not save riches here on Earth, where moths and rust destroy and robbers break in and steal. Instead save riches in heaven, where moths and rust cannot destroy and robbers cannot break in and steal* – Jesus, Matthew 6:19-20
> *There is a whole emphasis on consumerism in contrast to the simple way of life* - Archbishop of Delhi Vincent Concessao, India

A spiritual man is one who is filled with the spirit of God - Father
George Koovackal, Delhi, India
*There is no need for creating more things if you follow the teachings of
Jesus* - Father Sebastian, Delhi Cathedral, Delhi, India
*We must attempt to return to a proper relationship with the Creator
and the creation. This may well mean that just as a shepherd will
in times of greatest hazard, lay down his life for his flock, so human
beings may need to forego part of their wants and needs in order
that the survival of the natural world can be assured. This is a new
situation—a new challenge* - statement by the Eastern Orthodox
Church
*Future generations should not be robbed or left with extra burdens.
Those who are to come have a claim to a just administration of the
world's resources by this generation* - Joint Statement on Climate
Change by the Roman Catholic Bishops of Australia

Judaism

*You shall not set your heart on your neighbour's house. You shall
not set your heart on your neighbours spouse, or servant, man or
woman, or ox, or donkey, or any of your neighbour's possessions* - Ten
Commandments
You shall have no other gods to rival me - Ten Commandments

Islam

Muhammad was the "perfect man" who lived frugally and gave all his
wealth away to the poor. Like Christ, he led a life that in our terms was
non-materialistic and consumed a minimum of the Earth's resources.

Happy is the man who is content with what he has - Muhammad
*When we are able to be content with non material things we are
a spiritual person* - Maulana Wahiduddin Khan, Mullah and
international writer on Islam
The whole thinking of Islam is based on the concept of contentment -
Maulana Wahiduddin Khan
Once you are religious you will no longer believe in consumerism
- Professor Mohammed Iqbal, Lecturer, Jamia Hamdard
University, Delhi, India

Hinduism

The ideal of the Hindu in later life is to become a *sannyasin* or holy
wandering man. The Naga type of sannyasin does not have any clothes

let alone any possessions! They display a lifestyle which does not use much energy, walking from place to place, often sleeping outside and depending on people to give them food. The *sannyasin* learns from the guru who also practices non-attachment to the material world. He or she lives a non-materialistic lifestyle focussing on God consciousness and in consequence uses very little energy.

> *If one is a slave to his passions and desires, one cannot feel the joy of real freedom* - Swami Vivekananda
> *Man has to turn inside knowing that this makes him contented, peaceful and satisfied* - Swami Chidanand Saraswati, Head of Parmarth Niketan Ashram, Rishikesh, Uttarakhand, India
> *The human being is greedy - after all, if there is no peace in their heart, they will be* - Swami Jivanmukhtananda, Rishikesh, Uttarakhand, India.
> *The main purpose of life is to realise yourself* - Professor Chandrashekara, Lecturer in Philosophy, Mysore University, Karnataka, India.
> *Everybody has the seeds of happiness in them but this happiness is not found in the body comforts, it is in the state of mind* - Swami Swatantranand Ashram, Rishikesh, Uttarakhand, India
> *The more you want, the more you destroy the environment* - Nanda Kishore, monk, Sri Kesavaji Gaudiya Matha Ashram, Mathura, Uttar Pradesh, India

Swami Swatantranand

Buddhism

The Buddha was non materialistic. His focus was on achieving enlightenment. Even when he achieved that, he spent his life teaching people how to achieve it for themselves. Buddhism teaches that the cause of our suffering is rooted in desire. One reason that energy use is so high in developed countries is that people desire more and more material comfort and this material prosperity is founded on using vast amounts of cheap energy. Buddhism reminds us that it is wisest to live in the 'middle way' between extremes of wealth and poverty. Acting on this wisdom would significantly reduce our energy use and enhancing our self awareness would help us recognise in our lives the consumption we could easily do without.

End greed, hatred and delusion - Buddha
Not to do any evil, cultivate good, to purify one's mind, this is the teaching of the Buddhas - Buddha
The more we possess, the more we want - Buddha
Follow the middle path. Neither extreme will make you happy - Buddha
Desire does not create problems. Our attachments to desire do - Buddha
Everything arises because of more craving and because people have much more craving there is more destruction of the environment - Geshe Charaaps Tenzin Choosan, Teacher of Philosophy, Sera Monastery, Mysore, India

Geshe Charaaps Tenzin Choosan

Once we understand our innate power to purify ourselves and our surroundings, we will act properly - Shunryu Suzuki, Zen Master
If we have luxuries we have to pay the price for them - Dr. Bhikkhu Bodhipala, Research Scholar and Bhikku in Charge of the Mahabodhi Mahavirhara Temple, Buddhgaya, India

Dr Bhikkhu Bodhipala

Jainism

Jainism teaches seventeen types of internal restraint that can enhance personal serenity. The ideal way of life in Jainism is that of the Jain monk and Nun. I have myself witnessed that, following ancient Jain teachings, they possess no more than they themselves can carry. Theirs is a life of minimal consumption and energy use. This restraint is an embodiment of the attitude of non-attachment, to which Jains commit when they take the vow of *apagraha* or non-possession. The restraint of this vow serves to interpose a pause to think twice before indulging in the acquisition of material goods - one of the root causes of our climate crisis. Since fewer goods are bought, fewer goods are made, use of finite resources and pollution are reduced. There are limits on the amount of furniture one has and the number of clothes, ornaments, soaps, food, creams and powders possessed. Even the number of baths taken is limited. Jains are encouraged to give up luxuries, which of course helps the environment.

> *Jainism teaches us limitations* - Dr. Purishma Metha, Lecturer in Jain studies, International Centre for Jain Studies, Ghandi University, Ahmedabad, Gujarat, India
> *Spiritual and religious life is renunciation and not acquiring* - Satish Chand, Assistant Commissioner for the Delhi Government, Delhi, India
> *The instinct of getting more and more is one of the biggest causes of environmental problems* - Saddavi Pramukha Kanak Pharbhaji, Chief Nun of the Terapanth Sect

Saddavi Pramukha Kanak Pharbhaji

To abandon attachment is the art of living as it is also the art of dying
- Acharya Shri Mahaprajna, Head of the Jain Terapanth Sect
Spiritual life automatically stops the accumulation of things -
Acharya Shri Mahaprajna.
The first rule of ecology is limitation - Acharya Shri Mahaprajna

Sikhism

The Sikh gurus lived simple and frugal lives; they focused on their relationship with God. They saw the gaining of riches as a distraction from the process of God Realisation. They gave an example of a non-materialist lifestyle, which was focused on God.

Riches cannot be gathered without sin - Guru Nanak
Lust and wealth are poisons—heavy and hard - Guru Granth
Sahib, p.1187
Then why get attached to what you will leave behind. Having
wealth, you indulge in pleasures but, from that, tell me, who will bail
you out? - Guru Granth Sahib
The causes of global environmental problems lie in selfishness -
Dr Surjeet Kaur Chahal, Lecturer at University of Pune,
Maharashtra, India
We should not be greedy and all the time remember God - Dr
Indergit Kaur MD, Director of the Pulgalwara Institute,
Amritsar, Punjab, India
Sikhism teaches us to live a simple life - Dr Mavinder Singh,
Lecturer Department of Guru Nanak Studies, Guru Nanak
University, Amritsar

Taoism

Taoism idealizes the sage, a man who lives a frugal, simple life and who therefore consumes minimal energy. Being, rather than possessing, is the key to the Tao.

> *When a man seeks for external things, he is going away from the Great Tao, which is also a process of going away from his inner nature, or Virtue. The wisest person trusts the process, without seeking control; takes everything as it comes; lives not to achieve or possess but simply to be all he or she can be* - Lao Tzu

There is a warning in the Tao Te Ching of the corruptions of greed and materialism when it states, "great conflict arises from wanting too much."

> *Seek simplicity, grasp the essential* - Lao Tzu

Shamanism
The shaman remains the ideal spiritual person. As specialists in the sacredness of the elemental forces of earth, wind, fire, water, they never did accumulate things but valued the imponderable such as visions and connection with the supernatural world. For instance, one measure of wealth for the Navajo tribe was in how many songs a person knew by heart.

Spiritualism
Spiritualism places value on the ability to contact the spirit world. Material possessions are of no significance. Spiritualists think that this world is a place to learn and not to simply accumulate material comfort, which cannot be taken to the next world anyway. A person's progress and value is not measured in material accumulation but in how they behave towards others.

Bahá'í
If carried to excess, civilisation will prove a prolific source of evil as it had been of goodness when kept within the restraints of moderation - Bahá'u'lláh

The main purpose of the Bahá'í faith is to serve the cause. This means practice the teachings of the Bahá'í and spread its message—which is replete with Earth wisdom - rather than accumulate material possessions.

Karma: the cost of being human

As we have seen, karma is simple to define but immense in its implications. It simply means cause and effect. If we want to accumulate good karma, we have to be more aware of the results of our actions. For around 25 years scientists have been clear that burning fossil fuels is the major cause of climate change, in other words creating bad karma for all of humanity. Despite their having warned us about this, world emissions have risen—along with rates of consumption - ever faster and with economic recovery continue their upward spiral. The way we have as a global community avoided awareness of our actions looks like denial by unspoken consensus. This principle of cause and effect, or karma, is common to many spiritual teachings. They powerfully underscore our innate sense of good balance which industrialisation and materialism have disturbed.

Christianity

> *Do not be deceived: God cannot be mocked. A man reaps what he sows* - St. Paul to the Galatians 6:7
> *There is no dark place, no deep shadow, where evildoers can hide* - Job 34:22

Islam

> *Act in your life as though you are living forever* - Muhammad
> *And truly the Lord will repay everyone according to their works for he is well aware of what they do* - Sura XI, verse 113

Spiritualism

Spirits on the other side are always pointing out to people how their behaviour affects others. One of the seven principles of Spiritualism is that there is compensation and retribution hereafter for all the good and evil deeds done on Earth. Spiritualists believe it is not on what a person accumulates in their life that they will be judged when leaving the Earth plane, but on how they have lived their lives according to spiritual principles.

Buddhism

In Buddhism the need to be fully aware of karma or cause and effect is paramount.

If you should speak or act with mind defiled, suffering will follow just as a wheel follows the hoof of a drawing ox - Buddha

Avoid doing wicked actions, practice most perfect virtue, thoroughly subdue your mind - Buddha

The universe we inhabit and our shared perception of it are the results of a common karma. Likewise, the places that we will experience in future rebirths will be the outcome of the karma that we share with other beings living there. The actions of each of us, human or non-human, have contributed to the world in which we live. We all have a common responsibility for our world and are connected with everything in it - Tenzin Gyatso, 14th Dalai Lama

The core of Buddhist teaching is cause and effect - Lobsang Dakpa Geshe, Tibetan exile, lecturer in Buddhist Philosophy at Nam Gyl Monastery, Dharamsala, Himachal Pradesh, India

Hinduism

Hinduism shares the same philosophy about karma as Buddhism.

There is nothing mightier in the world than karma: karma tramples down all powers as an elephant tramples down lotuses - Hindu Scriptures

The world is like a river and our acts are like its ripples - Hindu Scriptures

They say that this world is unreal, with no foundation, no God in control. Following such conclusions, the demoniac, who are lost to themselves and who have no intelligence, engage in unbeneficial, horrible acts meant to destroy the world. They believe to gratify the senses is the primary necessity of human civilization - Bhagavad Gita 16.4, 7-16.

Sikhism

According to one's own actions and deeds, they will get near to God or they will get far away from him - Jaap Ji Sahib-Salok, Guru Granth Sahib

If we do good or bad all our actions are narrated before Dharam Raj and those that have done good will be sent to Heaven and others to Hell - Jaap Ji Sahib-Salok, Guru Granth Sahib

As are one's deeds, so will one become - Dhansari Mahalla I, p.662

Jainism

A person of right world-view reflects on karma and its results - Bhasyam Sutra 53

Balance

Balance is the state of stability toward which Nature always restores things. Like karma, we ignore it at our peril. Over and over, we humans have disturbed the balance of Nature by our exploitative attitude towards it. We lack respect for Nature. The lack of balance and harmony within ourselves is reflected in our behaviour towards the Planet, causing imbalances in natural systems and now we are paying the price. These spiritual teachings remind us of the need for balance in all that we do.

Islam

> *And the firmament He has raised high and He has set up the balance;*
> *in order that ye may not transgress balance* - Qur'an 55:5-9
> *Verily, all things have We created in proportion and measure* -
> Qur'an 54:49
> *He is raised high and set up the measure, that ye may not exceed the*
> *measure* - Surah-Al-Rahman, Ch 55 v 8-10
> *This world is a universal guest house given to us by God. We have*
> *to live here like a guest and not disturb the house* – Maulana
> Wahiduddin Khan, Delhi, India, Mullah and published scholar
> on Islam

E Maulana Wahiddudin Khan

Hinduism

Hinduism describes a Universal Order in the cosmos called *rita*. Its laws of being and Nature contain and govern all forms, functions and processes in the earth. In disturbing these processes we humans are breaking 'Universal Law'.

> *God has made the balance of Nature perfect* - Hindu scriptures
> *The world is a living whole, an interconnectedness of cosmic harmony* - Hindu scriptures
> *The maintaining of the ecological balance is part and parcel of Hinduism* - Professor Maheshwari Prasad, Director of the Parshwanath Vidyapeeth, Varanasi, India
> *Because of our development we have disturbed the whole thing* - Swami Jivananmuktananda, Rishikesh, India
> *A large number of man's activities are polluting the physical environment around him and creating an imbalance in the ecological situation, which is difficult to restore or cannot be restored at all* - Swami Smarananda, General Secretary of the Ramakrishna Mission, Kolkata, India

Christianity
According to the book of Genesis, God made the world for mankind to inhabit and that world was in balance.

> *There are limits to which we can make use of the resources of Nature* - Archbishop of Delhi Vincent Concessao. India

Jainism
A famous Jain aphorism states, "All life is bound together by mutual support and interdependence." This implies that there is a need for balance.

> *If we free ourselves from the notions of uselessness and instead try and understand the concept of usefulness, ecological balance would automatically be maintained* - Acharya Shri Mahaprajna, Head of the Jain Terapanth Sect
> *No life can exist if there is thoughtless imbalance* - Ramesh Chandra, Jain ex Director of the *Times of India* newspaper

Taoism
The ideal of Taoism is the sage who lives in harmony with the Tao by not interfering with the natural order. In this way the balance of Nature is not disturbed. Nature ensures that the essential balance be maintained between the pairs of opposing forces of yin and yang, male and female, light and dark, hot and cold etc. Yin and yang being out of balance is

considered an unstable situation that Nature will already be restoring to balance. The task of mankind is to accept the balance of yin and yang and to recognise the inescapable inter-dependence of all things. Heaven, Earth and Mankind must be in balance. This is particularly poignant when we think of the causes of the climate crisis.

When you know Nature is part of yourself, you will act in harmony - Lao Tzu

Bahá'í

For every part of the universe is connected with every other part by ties that are very powerful and admit to no imbalance - Abdul Baha

Judaism

Joel was a prophet of Nature who warned if the Lord's way was not followed there would be dire consequences, with fields being devastated, granaries failing and animals searching vainly for fresh pasture. But if the way of God is followed there would be vats full of oil, trees bearing fruit and animals having plenty of pasture. The Jewish rules were introduced to train souls to love that which is good, useful and creative and refrain from all destructive activities. God also warned of this in the Talmud when he stated: "Look at my creations. See how beautiful and perfect they are. Do not desecrate or corrupt my world. For if you corrupt it, there will be no one to set it right for you."

Redressing the vast accumulated imbalances that mankind has heaped upon Nature will of course not easily, if ever, be 'put right.' Even if we severely curbed carbon emissions tomorrow, because carbon dioxide gas has a 50 to 1,000 year life, its effects will last for centuries. From a Judaic perspective this suggests that mankind's covenant with God has definitely been broken.

Losing our connection with Nature

In the West, it has taken only about five generations - the Industrial Revolution heralding the advent of materialism and consumerism - for people to have largely lost their connection with the natural world. Such is the disconnect from Nature created with our urban lifestyles, some people believe food is manufactured in a supermarket and milk in a carton. From this loss of connection stems our blindness to how Nature actually works, to its delicate networks and interdependencies and to just how dependent on Nature mankind remains. What emerges is alienation from Nature, a loss of respect, our brutish exploitation. Yet, defended by our imagined separation, we fail to register any serious regret as we push ahead with our despoliations. Many spiritual traditions originated in natural settings. So to reflect on what they say about how we are intrinsically connected with Nature is at once poignant, humbling and illuminating.

Hinduism

An attitude of respect for Creation is reflected in Hinduism as all beings are seen to emanate from God. Also, because of their belief in transmigration of souls, Hindus believe that human beings have taken animal and plant forms in previous lives. Their belief that all living things in Nature are connected is mirrored in the new understanding of Nature's web of life that is emerging with our growing understanding of her subtle ways such as the miracles of symbiosis.

> *For the world is a living whole, a vast interconnectedness of cosmic harmony, inspired and sustained by the One Supreme -* Bhagavad Gita X.20.
> *He on whom the sky, the earth and the atmosphere are woven and the wind, together with all life-breaths, Him alone knows the one Soul -* Mundaka Upanishad 2.2.5
> *We came from a source of pure consciousness and everything is connected with this -* Professor Yaineshwar Shastri, Amdebadad University, Amdebadad, Gujarat, India
> *Hinduism teaches us to understand the laws of Nature and respect them -* Swami Dharammanda, Rishikesh, India

Buddhism

The Buddhist view of Nature is helpful in terms of ecology and sustainability. Buddhism teaches that the idea of separateness is an illusion. The health of the whole is inseparably linked to the health of the parts and the health of the parts is inseparably linked to the health of the whole. Buddhist practice makes one feel one's own existence has no greater importance than another's.

> *Our Planet is our house and we must keep it in order and take care of it if we are genuinely concerned about happiness for ourselves, our*

children, our friends and other sentient beings who share this great house with us - Tenzin Gyatso 14th Dalai Lama
Buddhism sees everything as interdependent - Kalsag Phutsok Lama, M.A., Tibetan Buddhist, Dharamsala, Himachal Pradesh, India.

Paganism

Ancient Pagans were very connected with Nature. They saw spirits, gods and goddesses in their immediate natural environment. Their festivals expressed their connection with Nature throughout the year. Today, Paganism has been revived from its ancient roots and my Pagan friends are deeply committed to the Green movement. Rather than seek dominance over the environment, modern Pagans work to live as a part of Nature, finding a balance between the self, the biosphere and society. Paganism emphasises connectedness between mankind and the immediate environment via spiritual forces.

Shamanism

Shamanism stands out as a spiritual tradition both for its ancient origins but also because of its deep connection with the natural world. Shamanism is perhaps unique in its attitude of sacredness towards all life, which is born out of its intimate relationship with the untamed universe.

With all beings and all things we shall be relatives - Black Elk
We are all flowers in the Great Spirit's Garden; we share a common root, and the root is Mother Earth - Grandfather David Monogye
The whole universe is enhanced with the same breath, rocks, trees, grass, earth, all animals and men - Intiwa, Hopi Indian

Sikhism

Sikh gurus exemplify how to stay in contact with Nature. The whole of Sikh spiritual literature is imbued with descriptions of Nature as an expression of God.

By divine prompting, look upon all existence as one and undifferentiated - Guru Granth Sahib, p 599
I perceive Thy form in all life and light; I perceive Thy power in all spheres and sight - Guru Granth Sahib, p 464

Christianity

I desire that, on the part of everyone, cooperation intensify to the end of promoting the common good, development and the safeguarding of creation, returning to the alliance between man and the environment, which must be a mirror of God the Creator, from whom we come and toward whom we are journeying - Pope Benedict XVI, 2007, on the 20th anniversary of the ozone saving Montreal Protocol. *Whether you like it or not, whether you know it or not, secretly all Nature seeks God and works toward him* - Meister Eckhart, Christian mystic

The spiritual causes of greed, materialism, bad karma and lack of connection with Nature can be seen manifest in the physical causes of climate change which we will now explore, beginning with the greatest of man's impacts: energy use.

Energy use in the world

Carbon dioxide's concentration in our atmosphere is so tiny it is measured in parts per million. Yet this invisible gas has truly remarkable powers of heat-retention. And with all the activities of growing numbers humans—industrial, energy production, deforestation, transport, agriculture and domestic heating—the level of CO_2 and other greenhouse gases are up by almost one third over pre-industrial levels. This rise is in step with world output of goods and services, which increased eightfold between 1950 and 2004. That growth rate increased by over 5 per cent in 2004, its fastest rate in three decades, helped by China's 9.5 per cent and India's 7.3 per cent. In 2009, however, world output registered shrinkage by 0.5 percent, its first move into negative territory in the past 40 years. But in early 2010 there began a move back into expansive growth as steep as the declines of 2009.

World energy use is set to soar in the coming decades, for several reasons: high growth rates, rising living standards for billions in Brazil, India, China and the relentless energy demands to maintain them. Two problems underlie these dangerous trends. First, the rich world's consumerist lifestyle is seriously damaging the Planet yet it is serving as the model that many majority world people aspire to follow. The second is that America continues to put its economic interests ahead of world concerns over climate. This approach was expected to change with the Obama administration. Its success with the USA's first climate legislation in June 2009 was short-lived. Questions remain: when will it be enacted? Will it be soon enough? Will it work? Is there the political will within America to change?

Taking all these factors together, it is now recognised that our Planet's atmospheric temperature is set to continue rising for much of the coming ten decades. The most we can hope to influence is the *rate* at which temperatures rise and, possibly, the maximum it reaches before levelling off - possibly late this century. All the measures to reduce emissions from known sources are directed to limit: the rate of temperature increase and the Planet's final maximum temperature.

Just how the future unfolds will be determined by what follows the impasse at the 2009 year-end negotiations in Copenhagen and follow-ups in Bonn and Cochabamba, Bolivia in early 2010, the latter attended by an estimated 35,000 people making it the largest event of its kind ever, so far.

- **Demand for energy is projected to grow by 53 per cent by 2030. Electricity use was set to increase by 48 per cent in the period 1991-2010.**
- **Coal and energy use in developing countries was projected to double between 1991 and 2010.**
- **Energy consumption in developing countries from 1973 onwards has increased at least at a rate of 6 per cent per year.**
- **Coal consumption in China equalled that of the US in 1990 and is now about twice that of the US and growing, fast.**

International action to combat climate change

Governments were first urged to act 'without further delay' on Climate change 18 years ago at the Earth Summit in Rio de Janeiro in 1992. Emissions rises have been accelerating ever since. So this section could be titled 'International *inaction* to combat climate change'. However, at least up until 2009, the UN never ceased in its efforts to overcome the inertia and susceptibility to the pressures and rewards from business interests of its member states' governments. The UN process suffered a blow at Copenhagen. I went to the alternative ' Klimaforum' in Copenhagen, which was held at the same time as the Copenhagen conference, in attempt to present the world citizen's view of solutions to climate change. I found this international gathering and the subsequent protest march of 100,000 people truly inspiring.

The Inter-governmental Panel on Climate Change (IPCC) was set up in 1988 under the World Meteorological Organisation and the UN Environment Programme to provide an objective source of information about the causes of climate change, its potential environmental and socio-economic consequences and the adaptation and mitigation options to respond to it. As many as 2,000 scientists have contributed to its work. Every four years they have updated their alerts and recommendations for prevention of dangerous, runaway climate change. The latest, IPCC 4 in May 2007, had had to be further revised before the fruitless Copenhagen negotiations in 2009. Its estimates on Arctic ice melt appeared to have been overtaken by events when in that same year (2007) the melt reached levels seventy years ahead of forecast. The IPCC brought us the much maligned Kyoto Protocol. There is a correlation between resistance to Kyoto and GHG emissions. The largest emitters put up the longest campaigns of resistance. This could be said to account for the failure of Copenhagen, too.

With such a display of a lack of political will to set limits, especially on behalf of both the USA and China, the gap between IPCC based targets and the reductions promised has widened to a gulf. This comes despite the fact that scientists have been closing in on agreement over the long disputed 'point of no return' on GHG levels. This is the date by which, to avoid a high risk of runaway warming, annual emissions levels would have to have levelled off. Most disturbing is that as the scientists close in on consensus, the date by which we reach the 'no return' point is ever closer. Unbelievable though it may seem, that date may now be less than seven years off—how old will you be in 2017?

US in multiple stand-offs over climate laws

The Democrats, sole supporters of legislation on climate and clean energy, lost their majority in the House of Representatives in November 2010 and with it the chance of climate change legislation being passed. It seems America's powerful interests will ensure the fossil *fool* party carries on until the 11th hour. To those aware of the hazards of runaway warming, America seems like a sleepwalker still determined to ignore all attempts to wake it to action. But while the US sleepwalks, there is little the rest of the world can achieve toward limiting global emissions other than to prepare, to implement and to demonstrate the Green market benefits of responding to the imperatives of our atmosphere.

Europe loses its climate halo

Europe's reputation as world leader in addressing climate change has been severely dented, too: by the failure to impress with its emissions trading scheme, by its misguided bio-fuels policy and by its support of socially unjust carbon sink forestry projects in poor countries. Its emission cuts targets remain in place, though little is said about tracking progress.

Even beyond its initial 2005 - 2007 'no-load' trial the theoretical advantages of the EU emissions trading scheme failed fully to materialise - it has been bedevilled by scams, junk-value certificates and profiteering - yet the carbon reductions it yielded to 2009 were next to trivial. Nevertheless, it was to be continued - and in expanded form. "A triumph of business lobbying but not of carbon reduction," said one critic.

The EU's target reduction in carbon emissions agreed by 27 member states in 2007 of 20 percent from 1990 levels by 2020 remained, along with the aim of achieving one fifth of EU energy from renewables by 2020. Some states intend to go further: Norway had set its sights of becoming carbon neutral and Sweden on phasing out all oil imports.

Its bio-fuels policy has dragged the EU through thorns of criticism. Launched in 2006, its plan to have 10 per cent of all transport run on bio-fuels by 2020 immediately evoked the harsh criticism of those who knew where the (first generation) biofuels would come from: food crops and, via the incentive to expand oil palm tracts, rainforest destruction. So, two years in, the EU in 2008 announced: "new rules under way". Another two years on and the original target still remains in place, though they are 'working on it'.

Balancing these regressions, to a degree, was the 2008 UK Climate Change Act which was finally signed into law in November. Importantly, it demands an 80 per cent emissions cut by 2050, not the 60 per cent cuts proposed by the government's bill. And, contained within it are other hard-won clauses that include aviation and shipping and demand annual assessments of progress toward the 80 per cent goal. This was the world's first legislation of its type from a major industrialised country. Yet climate received little mention during the 2010 UK general election campaign.

Global agreement on climate brings in the issue of fairness between the historical culprits who still pollute most and those countries where per capita emissions are measured in grams instead of tonnes. Aubrey Meyer and the Global Commons Institute (GCI) have met with slowly increasing acceptance of 'Contraction and Convergence' (C&C) which they put forward as a means of fairly apportioning global carbon emissions 'rights'. C&C allocates global carbon emissions on an equal per-capita basis, each country's emissions entitlement phased in over an agreed convergence period.

GCI asserts that by setting higher rates at which historical polluters cut emissions, this global solution would permit poorer countries to expand emissions during an initial decade while overall global emissions are kept on a downward curve and within limits for an agreed maximum temperature rise. By meeting developing countries' need to improve their living standards as the developed world has done, this solution responds to their legitimate aspirations.

Rising carbon dioxide levels

Around 85 per cent of the man-made CO_2 emissions come from burning of fossil fuels. CO_2 is accumulating in the atmosphere twice as fast as natural processes can remove it. Eight billion tons of CO_2 was released in 2006 that is nearly a million tons an hour. Of all the CO_2 produced, 45 per cent remains in the atmosphere; biotica (living organisms) and the oceans take up 55 per cent. The absorption of CO_2 by the oceans can now no longer be relied upon. The disturbing fact is that as the oceans get warmer through global warming they will act less efficiently as a 'sink' and will eventually reverse the process and *add to* global warming by releasing carbon dioxide into the atmosphere.

- In 2009 CO_2 atmospheric concentration reached 387 ppm, the highest level for 650,000 years.
- The Stern Report has advised that we should aim for an upper ceiling of 550ppm CO_2 equivalent (total GHGs, of which 450 ppm CO_2), yet in 100 years, at the current trends, CO_2 equivalent would be 1,300 ppm.*
- The CO_2 level in the atmosphere could double by 2025.
- US per capita CO_2 emissions are 19.8 tonnes compared to the world average of 3.9 tonnes per year.
- Every week or 10 days, another coal-fired power plant large enough to serve a major city comes online in China.
- The increase in atmospheric CO_2 equivalent concentrations (all GHGs) is now almost 3 ppm per year.
    * CO_2 *Equivalent concentration or* CO_2E

This CO_2E measure incorporates the effects of all the GHGs by calculating their warming effect in terms of CO_2 and totalling them all to give us a substantially higher figure, usually around 100 ppm more than the CO_2 alone.

So far we have talked only about CO_2. So that we can understand the overall picture a little better, we will now look at the other principal greenhouse gases (GHGs) and their heat-retaining properties,

Methane

Methane is a greenhouse gas that concerns us. Its warming effect is 20 to 30 times that of CO_2 Its concentrations in air have been rising in recent years. Methane has been - and still is - produced through natural decay of biomass in the absence of oxygen. Major 'fresh' releases include landfill sites, livestock, deforestation, thawing permafrost and leaks from oil and gas wells. Natural gas, piped to users all over the globe, is methane. Added up, methane leakages world wide (at 85 billion m^3 or 3 trillion ft^3 per year) are equivalent in warming power to over half of the coal-fired plants in the US. Methane formed eons ago also occurs at depth beneath the ocean margins in a highly significant crystalline ice structure called methane hydrate As ocean temperatures rise, the hydrate has begun to melt, releasing, so far, 'still negligible' amounts of methane. Other naturally occurring methane sources are peat bogs, tundra permafrost zones and pockets within coalfields. Another form of methane is biogas, a renewable fuel that can be produced, captured and piped by fermenting organic matter including manure, wastewater sludge, municipal solid waste including landfill, or any other biodegradable material, in enclosed, oxygen-free conditions.

Since 1950 there has been a high correlation between the increase in methane emissions (and CO_2 emissions) and the growth of human populations, largely because of the increase in municipal landfill waste and increased consumption of meat. Annual methane emissions are now 150 per cent above that of the 19th century levels and the highest for 800,000 years. Here is how recent methane emissions break down: after wetlands (22 per cent) and extraction of oil, natural gas and coal (19 per cent) come livestock (16 per cent), rice paddy (16 per cent) and biomass burning (8 per cent), landfills (6 per cent), sewerage (5 per cent), animal wastes (5 per cent), termites (5 per cent) and hydrates (3 per cent).

The world cattle population of 1.5 billion animals contributes 70 million tonnes of methane a year to the atmosphere and are responsible for 16 per cent of all methane emissions. Surprisingly, our meat eating habits mean that cattle have an impact on global warming as great as all forms of transport put together. The rate of increase of methane is four times higher than that of carbon dioxide. In 50 years methane could overtake CO_2 to become the principal greenhouse gas because of its powerful warming effect.

Concerns over the rise in methane emissions is compounded by the fact that rising atmospheric and sea temperatures are resulting in increases in the rates of release of the gas from those ocean-bed methane hydrates. The US Geographic Survey estimates that methane hydrate deposits hold 10,000 billion tonnes of methane gas trapped under pressure in crystalline structures under continental shelves. The release into the atmosphere of the methane in these deposits would powerfully accelerate global warming. It is on avoiding just this eventuality that all emissions limitations are focused. Reports from a research ship in the Artic Ocean in September 2008 indicated methane gas release rates have recently increased markedly and scientists are monitoring developments each summer season.

And, as if that were not enough, vast areas of the Arctic region in Siberia and Canada are tundra, a rudimentary vegetative carpet covering permafrost with a layer of peat beneath it. Thawing of the permafrost was first recorded in 1981 due to rising global temperatures and has been releasing methane from the underlying peat. A study in 2006 in the Siberian Arctic found that permafrost was melting five times quicker than had been predicted previously. There is significant potential for rates of methane release to rise significantly further, since 14 per cent of all global organic carbon is stored in peat.

Oxides of Nitrogen

Earth's atmosphere is composed mainly of nitrogen gas (78 per cent) and oxygen (21 per cent). Nitrogen gas is thought of as inert, but it becomes reactive at high temperatures, such as in almost any form of combustion, when it, too, will oxidise. The main oxide is Nitrogen dioxide, NO_2, an orange-red gas. The sources of this gas are transport emissions, spreading nitrogen fertiliser and land clearance and deforestation for agriculture. Nitrogen dioxide emissions are increasing rapidly which is worrying: NO_2 has *200 times* the warming power of carbon dioxide. Worse still for our climate is its residence time in the atmosphere: 120 years.

The modern human's dream of owning a car is turning into a climatologist's nightmare. In developing countries the car is a symbol of prosperity and personal freedom. Now billions more aspire to this First World 'necessity.' Today there are about 45 million new cars produced each year; by 2010 there were 885 million cars on the road around the Planet and over a billion by 2020. These cars all produce NO_2 as well as the CO_2 we've all been focused on.

Our intensive agriculture requires massive inputs of nitrogen fertiliser to maintain high yields. Yet to maintain the same level of yield, more fertiliser is required each year. Annually about 70 million tonnes of nitrogen fertiliser is applied to crops, contributing 10 per cent of all nitrous oxide emissions. As fertility declines and more fertiliser has to be applied, this figure could double in the next 30 years.

Unit for unit, Nitrous oxide gas, N_2O, is almost 300 times as powerful as CO_2 in retaining heat. Land clearance is newly recognised a major source of GHGs, CO_2 as well as N_2O. Land clearance is driven by rising population which needs to be fed. Nitrous oxide is released as a by-product of the activities of de-nitrifying bacteria, which become more active when land is converted to agricultural production. At least half a million tonnes of Nitrous oxide each year is released by rainforest clearance alone.

Temperature rises

The global average atmospheric surface temperature now is 0.6° Celsius above pre-industrial readings. Despite regions experiencing one 'colder-than-recently' winter, the Planet continues to warm faster than it has for 10,000 years. NASA's chief climatologist concluded a March 2010 paper with the following "We conclude that there has been no reduction in the global warming trend of 0.15—0.20° C per decade that began in the late 1970s."

The main reason the effect of so much heat uptake has so far been muted is that the oceans have absorbed about 30 times more heat than the atmosphere but have warmed less. Water's capacity to absorb and retain heat is one of its characteristics. The oceans are warming, but slowly. Yet it is their currents that drive the world's climate system. So the changes are being 'stored' in the oceans. It's not easy to foresee how they will play out, but they will.

- **The IPCC says if we do little about curbing greenhouse** emissions in a "business as usual" scenario, then temperatures are likely to rise 0.3° Celsius per decade, putting us 1°C degree above current levels by 2025 and 3°C above by the end of the century. The now outdated fourth IPCC report of 2007 stated that an upper range of 6.4°C is a possible worst-case scenario. But on current trends, with greater GHG inputs, faster-than-forecast impacts and signs of 'positive feedback loops' such as methane and Artic ice loss, this is a limit that would be exceeded—if emissions continue up.

- **Even if we were to have stabilised emissions now, a 0.2°C rise per decade will occur for the next few decades. Ecosystems adapt increasingly poorly to rises above 0.1°C per decade.**

Glaciers have been shrinking due to warming for much of the past 100 years. In many regions, people rely on glaciers for water. Where glaciers are disintegrating at higher rates, they already face dire water shortages. This is already happening in Andean countries like Chile, Argentina, Bolivia, Peru and Ecuador. The 15,000 glaciers of the Himalayas provide water for 500 million of Asia's population in India, Pakistan, Bangladesh, Myanmar/Burma and western China. After the Polar caps, this is the largest ice store on the Planet. No reliable predictions have been made as to its rate of shrinkage, though some glaciers are affected, even at the highest altitudes.

The table below shows how effects of temperature increases at each stage of the process differ widely between regions. In Polar Regions temperature rises will be up to three or more times as great in the equatorial belt. While quoted rises in degrees Celsius are in global average atmospheric surface temperature, warming is far from even:

If global average surface temperature rises by Then effects considered likely include:

Projected 1°C rise	• Melting affecting all glaciers threatening 50 million people with water shortages. • 300,000 people die from climate change related diseases such as malaria. • Coral reefs around the world wiped out as ocean surface waters warm.
Projected 2°C rise	• Loss of further 30 per cent of the world's remaining forests. • 10 million people affected by coastal flooding. • Polar bear and walrus become extinct.
Projected 3°C rise	• 550 million people would be at risk of starvation. • More than half the world's forests die out. • Up to 4 billion people face water shortages. • 100 million people affected by coastal flooding. • 30 per cent of remaining animal and plant species face extinction. • Extreme weather increases.
Projected 3.4°C rise	• Amazon rainforest disappears. • North pole ice-free for first time in 3 million years.
Projected 4°C rise	• Sub Saharan Africa and the southern Mediterranean suffer up to 50 per cent decrease in the availability of water. • West Antarctic ice sheet collapses 5m rise in sea levels. • Up to 35 per cent decline in crop yields in Africa. • 80 million more people exposed to malaria.

Projected 4.4°C rise	• 100 million people in Bangladesh displaced by sea level rises. • Permafrost melts in Siberia releasing large quantities of methane. • More than 50 per cent of species are wiped out in the worst mass extinction since the end of the dinosaurs. • Agriculture in Australia collapses.
Projected 5°C rise	• London, New York and Tokyo flooded. • Summer shrinkage of Himalayan glaciers accelerates, resulting in seasonally erratic water supplies to 25 per cent of the world population. • Much of world becoming uninhabitable.
Projected 6.4°C rise	• Most species wiped out. • Firestorms sweep Planet as methane hydrate fireballs ignite. • Constant super hurricanes.

Extreme weather

From experience of our own local climate, we know it is changing. I look at daffodils appearing in mid February in the UK whereas when I was a child they were not seen until the end of March. The world's climate system is highly complex. Even with massive computing power our best experts are stretched to understand its complex systems and the ranges of weather they can unfurl. Illustrating just how sensitive the global weather system is, a small rise in temperature has disproportionate effects. Warmer air holds more water vapour, which precipitates more intensely when it collides with cold air; hence more flash floods deluges and blizzards; warmer oceans mean more hurricanes, typhoons, missed monsoon rains, heat waves and droughts. Weather patterns are becoming less predictable, more extreme. The US National Climatic Data Center has reported a definite increase in extreme weather events recently. For instance, the number of intense tropical storms has doubled in the last 35 years. Weather disasters have increased by 160 per cent between 1975 and 2001, killing 440,000 people.

- 1999 - India, a super cyclone killed up to 10,000 and made 1 million homeless.
- 2000-2001 - Mozambique, flooding left over half a million homeless. Floods now affect 140 million people a year in total.
- 2003 - The European heat wave killed nearly 45,000 in two weeks.
- 2004 - Japan experienced a record 10 typhoons that caused $10 billion worth of losses.
- 2004 - Four hurricanes hit USA generating insurance claims of $22 billion.
- 2005 - Hurricane Katrina destroyed many coastal towns and made New Orleans part-uninhabitable; estimated cost of the damage, $200 billion.
- 2008 - Typhoon Nargis hits Burma, 130,000 killed with two and half million homeless.
- 2010- Floods in Pakistan affecting 20 million people and droughts in Russia worst for 100 years.

Shifting climate belts

Climatologists are registering a definite movement of climatic belts towards the poles: in the last 25 years the equatorial region has expanded polewards by about 275 km (172 *miles*). The estimated expansion rate in the next 30 years is 50 to 70 km (31 to 43 *miles*) per decade. It has been estimated that by 2050 the 'meteorological equator' will have shifted northwards 5° to between 10° and 12° north. The new 'meteorological equator' will run in a line through northern Nigeria, southern Ethiopia, across the tip of India and through the Philippines.

Tragically, such a shift spells a death sentence for millions of species of plants and animals because the rate of movement of the climatic belts will be too rapid for them to adapt to. And as groundcover withers, populations are forced out, which means mass migrations of wildlife. The predicted movement of climate belts is at a rate 10 times faster than plants have been known to adapt to in the past. For instance if there was a 0.4° degree rise in temperature per decade, forest areas will have to move in response to a shift in climate belt at a rate of 600 km per century, instead of the 20 km per century maximum plants can achieve. Historical evidence suggests that at the end of the last ice age all species struggled to adapt to the climate changes. In consequence 32 species of mammals became extinct.

If we follow the advice of the IPCC and stabilize at 550 ppm GHG levels, the die-back of natural vegetation will be 1 million km² as a result of the movement of climate belts. The UK's Institute of Terrestrial Ecology has warned that if emission levels continue on the business-as-usual model, "there could be a die-back of 4 million km² of vegetation within a century; that is an area the size of the Amazon basin." The die-back could well be in the Amazon basin as drought starts to take hold, as began happening in 2005. If the Amazon forest were destroyed its biomass would contribute massive further GHG emissions as it rots or even burns. Added to this, its disappearance would further exacerbate climate change as its function as a carbon sink for 10 per cent of carbon emitted each year was lost.

Rainfall patterns

As climate belts shift, rainfall patterns are altering. Many scientists believe that future rainfall patterns will mean greater precipitation in winter and more droughts in the summer for many regions. Meteorologists predict that rain may come on fewer days of the year but with greater intensity and may result in flooding becoming more widespread. The 0.6^0 of warming has increased evaporation leading to average global rainfall rising by 10 per cent during the 20th century. As a result of a warmer world, precipitation will also increase at higher latitudes.

Some regions will get more rainfall because tropical rains will be squeezed between 12° and 20° north. As a result, in some currently arid areas in Sudan, the Sahara and Mexico, we may see develop more lush tropical vegetation. Generally, precipitation will increase in the northern hemisphere in its winter and in the monsoon areas of Southeast Asia during the north's summer.

Conversely, other places in the world will have less rainfall, particularly in the desert regions around both tropics. Desertification, a process described in the previous chapter on food, will increase; the Kalahari, Sahara and deserts of the southwest USA will expand. Meanwhile parts of Brazil, Central Africa, Malaysia, New Guinea, northern Australia, southern Europe, Central America and southern Africa will have drier summers, which will increase the risk of wildfires and may even result in partial desertification locally.

- Scientists at the Scripps Institution of Oceanography predicted that Lake Mead, which supplies water to Los Angeles and Phoenix, Arizona, could dry up by 2021. California was in 2009 in its third year of drought. Some models show its water supply declining 24 per cent to 30 per cent over the century, mostly after 2050, affecting water supplies for 12 to 36 million in Southern California alone.
- Most of the south of Australia is gripped by unprecedented 12-year drought. Even with the modest temperature rises now seen as unavoidable, drought severity is expected to intensify by a further 70 per cent in New South Wales, reduce water supplies to Melbourne by more than a third and dry up the Murray-Darling river system by further 25 per cent. In 2009 over 200 people died because of wild fires.
- A 10 percent growth in desalinated and re-cycled waste water world wide in 2009 alone points to the advance of the water crisis looming for growing numbers of communities, as one third of the world goes thirsty, say analysts Global Water Intelligence.

Food Supply

Little escapes the impacts of climate change. Changes in rainfall pattern will, it has been foreseen, redraw the political map of the world: it will curtail some countries' capacity to produce surplus food. By the 2080's a pattern will emerge whereby crop yields in the mid- to high latitudes will increase whereas nearer the equator it will decrease. America's historic intransigence over responding to climate change could cost it its leadership in world agricultural exports. Parts of the Great Plains may become too dry in summer to grow grains. As currently the export of surplus from the North American grain belt serves to meet many of the world's food shortages, the risks of starvation from famine on a massive, global scale can only rise.

Extreme drought is likely to expand from under 3 per cent of productive land today to 30 per cent by 2100. By 2080 there will be a decrease of 11 per cent of land suitable for rain-fed agriculture. Africa will suffer further and even more intensely from drought, which will result in a marked drop in its food production. Tragic pictures of the

Ethiopian famine of 1984 may come back to haunt us again with Sub-Saharan Africa set to suffer a 20 per cent decline in food production and expose an additional 300 million people to starvation. However, shortfalls in food may be in small part offset by those producer countries enjoying increased rainfall and the capability to increase harvests. These countries are set to gain more political prominence in world affairs.

Ocean currents

Ocean currents operate as a vast, trans-global conveyor belt taking warm water from the equator to the poles and cold water back to the equator. It has been estimated one complete circulation takes around 1,000 years! Even with state-of-the-art instrumentation and the brilliance of scientists there is still much to learn about the ways and effects of this Ocean Conveyor. Trade Winds are normally steady, seasonably reliable air movements with their associated weather. Disturbances to such patterns are known, but now with increasing frequency. One such disturbance is El Niño, active in 2009-10.

El Nino is a reversal of the flow of ocean currents in the Pacific caused by an invasion of warmer waters by cooler waters. This leads to a change in the direction of the Trade Winds in the east and central Pacific, which in turn results in some regions experiencing violent and destructive tropical storms and heavy rainfall. El Nino has knock-on effects across the Pacific and elsewhere: Australia, Brazil and parts of Africa suffer from droughts. Some scientists have suggested a warmed atmosphere could even create a permanent El Nino effect.

Warming of the oceans could severely disrupt the Ocean Conveyor, the thermohaline ocean circulation current and impair its capacity to transport the vast amounts of warm water from tropics towards both Polar Regions. Part of this system is the North Atlantic Drift or Gulf Stream, which keeps most of northern Europe around 10° warmer than it would otherwise be. It's said to carry the latent heat energy of a million power stations.

The Ocean Conveyor is driven as cooled water, made more salty and dense by evaporation, on reaching the poles sinks to the depths of the ocean allowing the warmer water from the tropics to flow in. The thermohaline current could be shut down if polar ice formations fail to cool the water or if the salty water is diluted by large amounts of fresh water from the melting polar icesheets, preventing the cold current from sinking. Models suggest it might take a temperature rise of as little as

2.5° Celsius to trigger. If this happens the Gulf Stream would become less and less effective in heating the coastlines of northern Europe and subsequently temperatures in the North Atlantic would drop by 6° Celsius. When it last failed, 12,700 years ago, the British Isles were covered in ice and permafrost for 1,300 years.

Spread of disease
While plants and forests struggle to up sticks and shift with climate belt movement, diseases are only too happy to extend their areas of operation. As the climate belts shift polewards pests and diseases will follow, putting millions more at risk. WHO estimates that 160,000 already die each year as a result of climate change and this is forecast to run into millions in the future. Large parts of southern and central Europe, USA and Australia are likely to be affected by malaria, to cite but one of six debilitating diseases ready to migrate.

Sea level rises
One cause of sea level rises is expansion as ocean waters warm. More dramatic is the rise from the melting of glaciers and polar ice sheets. The melting of sea ice, which floats on seawater, does not contribute to sea level rise other than through the additional warming its disappearance triggers.

In the Arctic, the Greenland ice sheet melt water is running off at a rate equivalent to the annual flow of the Nile. Arctic sea ice has thinned 40 per cent since the 1950's and since 1979 the ice cover in summer has diminished by 33 per cent. An area one and a half times the size of Wales is lost each year. In 2007 scientists were predicting that by 2080 the arctic will be ice free in summer. Eighteen months later observations and new modelling had brought that forward by four decades. Tragically, this delivers an imminent death sentence to the polar bear.

The situation in the Antarctic is more complex yet less studied. There have been 'disastrous' losses of floating ice *shelf*: in March 2002, 500 billion tonnes of ice shelf, the Larsen B, disintegrated. In fact 10,000 km² of ice shelf have been lost from both sides of the Antarctic Peninsula. UK and US scientists have found evidence that Antarctica is already losing 470,000 tonnes of ice each year. Though this current melt rate is plainly serious and poses threats to centres of human population that are potentially great, there is still little certainty over their scale or timeframes. If the West Antarctic continental ice *sheet* melts it would raise sea levels by 5 metres—this is the more likely but less deadly of the two. If the East Antarctic ice sheet melts entirely it will possibly lead to a 30-metre rise in sea level—which is less likely, further off in time, but potentially much more deadly.

Overall, today's sea levels are rising at a small but accelerating rate.

- **In the period 1993 to 2003 the sea level rose on average 3.1mm a year compared to 2mm a year in the previous century.**
- **If there is a 'business as usual' approach to greenhouse gas emissions then sea level rise will increase to 60mm per decade, reaching 100mm per decade by the end of the century.**
- **The 2007 IPCC report linked an average rise in temperature of between 3 and 4°C with sea level rises of between 200 and 800 mm, though climate scientists put it at 1,190 mm after adjustments.**
- **By 2030 there may be a 200 mm rise in sea level.**
- **By 2050 there may be between 400 - 600mm rises in sea level.**

Because coastal areas are on average twice as densely populated as inland areas, rising sea levels are seen bringing some of the worst of climate change impacts. These impacts will be highly disruptive, permanent and long term. Over two billion people, one third of the entire world population, lives within 100 metres of the sea. At present 1 billion people live in low lying delta areas, especially in Southeast Asia. This is set to increase to 2 billion by 2050. One hundred million people (100,000,000) live on land which is only 1 metre above mean sea level.

Many of the world's major conurbations close to the sea risk being completely flooded, affecting millions of people in cities such as New York, Shanghai, Bangkok, Jakarta, Bombay, Manila and Buenos Aires. The last five cities alone have a combined population of between 200 and 220 million people. In China, cities near the sea are home to 40 per cent of the population and they are growing at a rate of 10 per cent per year. Overall sea level rises will affect 100 million people in China, Bangladesh, Egypt and Nigeria.

The loss to sea level rise of land for agricultural production will be massive and very serious and has not adequately been foreseen. For every 1 cm rise in sea level, 1 m of beach is eroded. If there is a 10 cm rise in sea level, the boundary between salt and fresh water moves 1 km inland, rendering a 1 km strip of land too salty to farm. This represents a massive loss of agricultural production.

There will also be a loss of production of food from the sea. Of the 13,200 species of fish, 80 per cent of them live in coastal areas. Two thirds of the fish caught for human consumption depend on coastal marshes or mangrove swamps for part of their life cycle and many of these areas will be destroyed through flooding. The implications, should we even keep the impacts to the best-case scenario, are devastating indeed.

Conclusion: Spiritual and practical responses to climate change

It seems clear to many that the challenge we face would be easier if we had a spiritual culture, one where we replace the pursuit of material possessions to derive a momentary sense of satisfaction with genuine happiness from engaging in our local communities and in a quest for meaning through exploring our spirituality. Such a culture change will bring a change of emphasis from the quantity of life to the *quality* of life. By downshifting we may lower our standard of living but gain a greater quality of life. We satisfy our physical, emotional and spiritual needs not our insatiable greed. In our final chapter, we describe many communities that already live just these ideals.

With the cultural transformation comes more awareness of the effects of our actions. A recent survey in America has shown that despite people having twice the buying power as in the 1950's they are no happier. So what are we waiting for?

Whatever cultural and systemic changes we'll need, the practical solution to climate change involves cutting back on our carbon footprint, individually and collectively. In the developed nations we need to find ways, through legislation and through local community initiatives, to cut back on our carbon emissions along the lines of Contraction and Convergence or something better—and soon. The developing nations need to agree to limits on how much additional carbon they emit. We need an international agreement to cut back on carbon emissions, which has to include the US. We have the technology in terms of carbon-free energy production. Political will, however, seems wilfully absent.

Programmes of government spending to revive the economies through investment in upgraded Green energy infrastructure should create win-win situations. In power, most politicians hitherto have thought only of their re-election. Now we need leaders who think of the long term and make painful but statesman-like political decisions that may be unpopular with lobbyists and party backers and with short-termists among the electorate.

What's true is, in the last 50 years the world has become totally reliant on oil for food production, for transport and heating. It is now recognised that more oil price spikes are inevitable. To address both this and the challenge of climate change, the Transition Towns movement brings people together in their local communities to anticipate the challenges of escalating prices for food and oil and climate change. By collaborating, people find creative solutions to these challenges at a local level. I myself am a member of the Leamington Spa Transition Towns initiative, one of over 150 in a dozen countries. Its creative potential is enormous.

The challenge we face is to realise that it is the values which arise from our capitalist culture that lead us to behave in a destructive, unsustainable and complacent manner towards Nature, the Earth and ourselves. Without a reconnection with our spirituality as individuals and as a society we are poorly equipped to make a fundamental reappraisal of our core values or carry through the changes in our lives essential to address the impacts of climate change. But without our climate challenge, none of us might ever have realised this.

Personal climate change action ideas

1. Check (audit) your house for energy efficiency, fully insulate roof spaces, install wall insulation, install double glazing, draught-proof doors, windows, loft hatches, ceiling openings, chimney flues, calk under-skirting gaps, floorboard gaps, get an energy efficiency audit, check for free/subsidized insulation schemes. www.managenergy. net www.energyhog.org www.eere.energy.gov www. energysavingtrust.org.uk www.greenbuildingstore.co.uk www.nationalinsulationassociation.org.uk

2. How efficient is your home heating system? When was it last serviced? How old is your boiler? If it's a decade or more old, consider the payback with a replacement

condensing boiler, which can make important savings in outlays and emissions. www.lowcarbonbuildings.org.uk www.energysavingtrust.org.uk/

3. Cut energy use in the home: Switch off lights, change to energy efficient bulbs, minimize electrical goods on standby, boil only as much water as needed, use lids on cooking pans, launder at 'cold' or 30⁰, defrost the freezer regularly, draw your curtains or drapes at dusk, lag your water tank well, turn thermostats down, tee-shirts for hot weather, jumpers for cool, fleeces when it's cold outside. www.foe.co.uk/living www.ecokettle.com www.osram.com

4. Consider replacing major appliances older than 10 years with an A- or AA-grade appliance . Consider buying a Savaplug to make fridges up to 20 per cent more efficient. www.savawatt.co.uk www.sust-it.net

5. Check whether at your address a wind turbine would effectively cut down on your use of electricity. www.urbanwindenergy.org www.bwea.com www.cat.org.uk www.renewabledevices.com www.resourcesfinder.net www.diy.com

6. Consider passive solar hot water or even pV panels to reduce your carbon footprint: www.microgeneration.com www.solarpanelinfo.com www.solarenergy.com www.solartradeassociation.org.uk www.navitron.org.uk

7. Check the new UK Feed-in Tariffs for pV solar, wind, mini-hydro and other generation methods for investment, payback and carbon gain figures at www.energysavingtrust.org.uk/Generate-your-own-energy/Feed-in-Tariff-Clean-Energy-Cashback-scheme

8. Switch to a green electricity supplier: www.ecotricity.com www.good-energy.co.uk www.jeeko.com www.greenpower.gov www.uswitch.com www.whichgreen.org www.ethicalconsumer.org

9. Use your car as little as possible, use public transport, join a car club, cycle or walk. www.bettertransport.org.uk/ www.carplus.org.uk www.commonwheels.org.uk/ www.whycycle.co.uk www.sustrans.org.uk www.seat61.com www.transportdirect.info

10. Consider powering your car with LPG gas to cut down on emissions. www.greenfuel.org.uk www.ewossuk.com
11. Consider a low-emission hybrid car: www.hybridcars.com www.green-car-guide.com www.earthenergy.com
12. Consider buying an electric car; use green electricity to recharge:.www.electriccars.com www.evworld.com www.whyfiles.org
13. Reduce your meat consumption or consider vegetarianism: www.vegsoc.org www.ciwf.org.uk
14. Grow more of your own food and buy local food. www.farmshopping.com www.farmersmarkets.net www.soilassociation.org www.sustainweb.org
15. Favour good quality, longer lasting products. www.ethicalconsumer.org www.greenamericatoday.org/
16. Compost your kitchen waste for less landfill and emissions of methane. www.compost.org www.recyclenow.com
17. Reuse items so that they do not require energy to be made again. www.raceagainstwaste.com www.globalfootprint.org
18. Reduce your consumption of goods: www.simpleliving.net www.newdream.org www.earthwatch.unep.net
19. Go along to a march or a rally with a local FoE group or the Campaign against Climate Change to stop new coal-fired power, airport expansion, unneeded nuclear power or unjust carbon sink programmes. www.campaigncc.org www.greenpeace.org/climate www.protectingcreation.org www.foe.org.uk www.planestupid.com www.tni.org/ctw
20. Learn how we CAN as a society respond climate change. Read the Zero Carbon Britain 2030 report from CAT: http://www.zerocarbonbritain.org/ Find your nearest Transition Towns initiative:.www.transitiontowns.org www.transitionnetwork.org

CHAPTER 17 : THE SPECIES WE EXTERMINATE

Variety of Species

If evolution is the survival of the fittest, then it is questionable whether *Homo sapiens* will remain the most successful species on Earth for many generations to come. Our success as a species now poses a threat to the ecological balance of the entire Planet. We use 40 per cent of all photosynthetic production and we consume two fifths of all food resources, leaving less and less to support Earth's miraculously myriad bio-diversity of millions of other lifeforms.

So far, science has identified nearly 2 million species and estimates of the total number of species range from 5 to 30 million, some as high as 100 million species, plants representing the greatest number.

Certain ecosystems have exceptionally high concentrations of bio-diversity. Rainforests cover only 7 per cent of the land surface area yet contained over 50 per cent of all species on Earth. Coral reefs occupy only 0.17 per cent of the ocean floor yet support 25 per cent of all marine species.

If we narrow it down even further, there are 34 biological hotspots that occupy only 2.3 per cent of the Earth's land area yet are home to 50 per cent of all the vascular plants and 42 per cent of land vertebrates. The biological hotspots include: Madagascar, the Philippines, Borneo, Java and Sumatra, the Brazil Atlantic forest, the Caribbean, Costa Rica, Indo-Burma, the Ghats of Western India, Sri Lanka, the Eastern Arc forests of Tanzania and Kenya and the tropical Andes forests of Brazil, Ecuador and Colombia. Despite our knowing that these are areas vital to maintaining global biodiversity, in 2000 only 62 per cent of their area had legal protection. This leaves vast swathes of the Planet's lifeforms under imminent threat of extinction.

There are some regions, or zones in which particular species occur that are found nowhere else on Earth. Such species are referred to as *endemic.* A high proportion of endemic species have been sentenced to an extinction that is under way or threatened due to terminal gene pool shrinkage.

- **In Madagascar, of the 190,000 known animal species on the island 60 per cent are found nowhere else.**
- **In South Africa, 73 per cent of plant species are endemic and in some cases only represented by 500 individuals.**
- **Sri Lanka occupies 1 per cent of global land area yet has an estimated 10 per cent of all Earth species.**
- **Costa Rica has 5-7 per cent of the all world species.**

Lost bio-diversity in plants? What's the worry?

Some might say that this vulnerability is not a serious problem because the disappearance of species is a natural part of evolution. But let us reflect for a moment: we humans are dependent on the gene pools found in plants and animals for *all* our food. In 10,000 years of agriculture, 75,000 edible plants have been discovered or bred, yet just 15 food crop species provide 90 per cent of our world population's food energy intake. Of the 250,000 known plant species, fewer than 150 are commercially significant. The danger is that we rely on too narrow a genetic base for our food supply. Remarkably, 80 per cent of our food comes from two dozen species of animals and plants. Wheat, rice and maize are the main staple foods for 4 billion people. The sobering fact is that since 1900 about 75 per cent of the genetic diversity of domestic agricultural crops has been lost.

This process is being driven by the destruction of habitat as a gene pool resource, widely publicised only in recent years. Scientists say that domestic food crop plants each need to be improved and invigorated every 15 years by interbreeding them with plants found in the wild. If wild food crop species are destroyed our plants will become more susceptible to disease, drought and salinity and their yields decline.

One biologist has stated that one plant species useful to medicine will be discovered every 2 years until 2050. Before the advent of modern pharmacy people relied on plants in the wild for health cures. Even today 3 - 4 billion people in the developing world rely on medicinal plants and 80 per cent of these people rely on traditional medicine to maintain their health. Only in 2003 it emerged that 80 per cent of chemicals which were introduced as drugs could be traced back to or were inspired by natural products. In the USA, 25 per cent of all prescriptions contain compounds from higher plants. Most new drugs are developed from the vast biodiversity of the great rainforests, for example the Madagascar periwinkle plant: thirty thousand lives have been saved by an anti-cancer drug developed from it. With each animal or plant species we allow to become extinct we lose a potential cure for serious illnesses such as AIDS. Some may remain unconvinced but are you?

Species decline and the spiritual perspective
Let us reflect on some of the spiritual teachings on this issue from world spiritual traditions.

Islam
Islam shares roots in the Old Testament with Judaism and therefore sees all species as God's creation. The Qur'an sees all creatures as living beings in their own right., The teachings of Islam imply that the absolute destruction of any species of animals or plant by man can in no way be justified; hunting and fishing, forestry and woodcutting for timber and fuel, grazing and all other utilization of living resources should all be kept to within the capacity of nature to regenerate. The Qur'an states, "The merciful are shown mercy by the All-Merciful. Show mercy to those on Earth and He who is in Heaven will show mercy unto you."

It's a little known fact that the Prophet Muhammad developed the first conservation zones where wildlife could thrive. He instituted laws to create *Havin* lands, reserves set aside for wildlife. Within such reserves, development, woodcutting, grazing and hunting were prohibited or restricted in accordance with the special purposes of each reserve. Muhammad encouraged the creation of habitats for wildlife by stating "whosoever plants a tree and looks after it will be rewarded in the hereafter".

Animals were considered Allah's children and cruelty towards them of any kind was illegal. Muhammad said, "There is a reward in doing good to every living thing." We are to respect animals: "there is not an animal on Earth, nor any being that wings its flight but is as people like unto you" and "whosoever is kind to creatures is kind to God." There were specific laws about animal protection: animals are not to be worked too long, be given sufficient water and food and camels are not allowed to have rings put round their necks. It is forbidden to use them for fighting or target practice, they are not to be eaten whilst still alive and only be slaughtered with sharp knives. God punishes with the fires of hell any person who causes an animal to die of starvation or thirst.

In his own life The Prophet actively demonstrated the importance of all creatures. He forbade that a fire be lit upon an anthill. He related that an ant once stung one of the prophets, who then ordered that the whole colony of ants be burned. God addressed him in rebuke, "Because an ant stung you, you have destroyed a whole nation that celebrates God's glory." He once ordered a man who had taken some nestlings to return them to their nest where the mother was trying to protect them. Muhammad also forbade the killing of bees and any captured livestock.

Christianity

The Bible begins with Genesis, in which the creation of all species is described as the 'work of God'. This being so, then surely by implication Christians are meant to take care of these species. Christians who see this as a form of stewardship on behalf of God cite Bible verses to support the case that we are duty bound to care for God's creation.

Do not destroy trees by taking an axe to them - Deut:20:19

A righteous man cares for the needs of animals - Proverbs:12:10

If you come across a bird's nest beside the road, either in a tree or on the ground and the mother is sitting on the young or on the eggs, do not take the mother with the young. You may take the young, but be sure to let the mother go, so that it may go well with you and you may have a long life - Deut 22:6-7

A man is truly ethical only when he obeys the compulsion to help all life which he is able to assist and shrinks from injuring anything that lives - Albert Schweitzer, Christian missionary, theologian and philosopher

World dominion over Nature means that we should nurture Nature and not destroy it - Adreas DeSouza, Director of the Henry Martyn Christian Institute Hyderabad, Andhra Pradesh, India

Human kind has to assume responsibility as Stewards of Gods creation - Vincent Concessao, Archbishop of Delhi, India.

By destroying the Kingdom of God we are destroying ourselves - Brother Jerome Naduvathaniyil, Asirvanam Monastery, Bangalore, Karnataka, India

Brother Jerome Naduvathaniyil

Love thy neighbour, and the whole of creation is our neighbour -
Father Valentine Kumar, Lecturer in Christianity, Mysore
University, Mysore, India

Judaism

Followers of Judaism, too, see living creatures, plants and fish as
expressions of God's creativeness. There is acknowledgement in the
Old Testament that there are different species and they each have the
right to exist, as there is a "rightness of God's patterns". So farmers
were instructed not to mix two crops of the same type in the same field.
Also according to Jewish law, animals of different species should not be
interbred out of respect for the divine order.

Jewish law encourages people to preserve wild species and
biodiversity: foragers should take either some of the young or the mother
bird when seeking wild food, not both (Deut 22:6-7); Noah followed
God's instructions in saving all species from the great flood; and in a
clear exhortation to protect habitat, an ancient Jewish farming tradition
advised farmers not to harvest the crop too near the edge of fields, as this
would destroy habitat beneficial to wildlife. One of the Commandments
stated that animals should not be worked on the Sabbath day (Deut
5:14). For Jews, instructions not to be cruel to animals generally are
clear. Specific instructions not to muzzle an ox when threshing and not
yoking together animals of different sizes are noted, too. Although the
Jews eat meat, Jewish law forbade the killing of a calf and cow on the
same day.

Hinduism

The world is considered by Hindus to be divine in all its aspects, being the work of Brahma, the supreme creator. Krishna modelled the attitude to be adopted towards animals when he cared for the cows. Cows are holy because higher souls are supposed to be reincarnated in them. Here is the key: because of reincarnation, every beast may be reborn a human and therefore must be respected. Indeed the Veda Holy Scriptures forbid the killing of animals. (Yajurveda 13- 47) Trees were considered the abodes of deities and it was forbidden to cut them down. The Vedas state that the "Earth belongs to all" and there needs to be a deep respect for all creation. (Atharvaveda 12 1-45).

In this cosmos, whatever exists - living and non-living, all that is - is pervaded by one divine consciousness - Isa Upanishad 1
The Reality behind all these things of the universe is the Brahman, which is pure consciousness. All things are established in consciousness, work through consciousness and their foundation is consciousness - Aitareya Upanishad
He whose self is harmonized by yoga seeth the self abiding in all beings and all beings in the self; everywhere he sees the same - Bhagavad Gita VI.29
Look upon deer, camels, monkeys, donkeys, rats, reptiles, birds and flies as though they are your own children - Srimad Bhagavatam 7, 14-19
The wicked person who kills animals which are protected has to live in Ghora Naraka (Hell) for the days equal to the number of hairs on the animal killed - Yajyavalkyasmrti Acardhyagasth, verse 180
Let your love be all-embracing, like the sky - Hindu Scriptures.
To live in harmony with the whole of existence; this is what we call environmental religion - Swami Shatrananda, Rishikesh, Uttarakand, India
We do not want to defeat Nature; as Hindus we worship it - Swami Shatrananda, Rishikesh
The root cause of suffering is exploiting Nature because of a lack of God consciousness - Vedanta Chaitanya, Vice President, Hari Krishna Temple, Hyderabad, Andhra Pradesh, India
Trees are our friends. Protect them and ensure their proper growth - Rig Veda 8.11.13
Hinduism teaches that if you plant one tree it is equivalent to having ten children - Professor Shashtri, Professor of

Philosophy, Ahmedabad University, Ahmedabad, Gujurat, India

If you cut the tree, you cut the human being also - Swami Dharammanda, Rishikesh

Swami Dharammanda (left) with the author

Buddhism

Buddhism can be seen as the religion of compassion and non-violence. The Buddha always implored his followers to practice *Metta* or loving kindness towards all beings. This attitude rests on the awareness that all fellow creatures are like us suffering in *samsara*, caught on the wheel of life. It is wise to be compassionate towards them. The Buddha taught that all life is interconnected because all beings undergo reincarnation and any form of violence is, after all, the ultimate denial of our interconnectedness, the furthest remove from acting in harmony with reality.

Buddha was so concerned about life in all forms that he forbade his monks to travel in the rainy season in case they inadvertently stepped on insects. One of the rules of the monks was to refrain from taking life as much as possible. Today, most Buddhists are vegetarian. Budda was an outspoken critic of Hindu Brahmans who made animal sacrifices. He instructed that cows should never be milked dry. He encouraged the practice of letting go those wild animals caught in traps. Monks were forbidden to eat wild game or cut down any trees. In one story from his life he admonished some travellers who having sat down under the shade of a banyan tree proceeded to try and cut it down when leaving.

Let everyone cultivate boundless love for all beings. Let him cultivate

this towards the whole world, above, below, around a heart of love unstained; standing, walking, sitting or lying let him devote himself to this mind - Buddha

A person of great wisdom does not intend harm to the self, harm to others or harm to both self and others. Thinking in this way, such a person intends benefit for self, benefit for others, benefit for both and benefit for the whole world - Buddha

Life is dear to all living things. You should think of others as yourself and neither kill nor allow killing - Buddha

Abstain from injury to seed life and plant life - Buddha

Why should we cherish all sentient beings? Because sentient beings are the roots of the tree-of-awakening. The Bodhisattvas and the Buddhas are the flowers and fruits. Compassion is the water for the roots - Avantamsaka Sutra

Just as each one of us wants to live and does not wish to die, so it is with all other creatures in the universe - His Holiness Tenzin Gyatso,14th Dalai Lama.

Destruction of Nature and natural resources results from ignorance, greed and a lack of respect for the Earth's living things - 14th Dalai Lama

Many of the Earth's habitats, animals, plants, insects and even micro-organisms that we know as rare may not be known at all by future generations. We have the capability and the responsibility. We must act before it is too late - 14th Dalai Lama

Meditating on the path of enlightenment means practising non-violence and kindness - Geshe Thupten Palsang, Nam Gyl Monastery, Dharamsala, Himachal Pradesh, India

If you pluck one flower it is sinful, as a flower has life - Tenzing Dorge, Dharamsala

The Buddha said that it was an offence even to cut grass - Serge Tashi, Dharamsala.

Refrain from harmful activities and develop loving kindness and practise contentment - Lobsang Dakpa Geshe, Tibetan exile, lecturer in Buddhist Philosophy at Nam Gyl Monastery, Dharamsala.

Lobsang Dakpa Geshe

Jainism

In Jainism all animate and inanimate objects have consciousness or *jiva*. Progress towards enlightenment consists in reincarnating in many souls. Not only this, but since all souls are interchangeable it is wise to minimise violence towards them. This is why all Jains take the vow of *ahimsa* or non-violence. In fact the *anarth dand tyag* vow prohibits unnecessary violence and participation in occupations that involve violence. For observing Jains, to hurt any being results in the thickening of one's karma, obstructing advancement toward liberation. The destruction of one form of life or another as food is essential for life. However, Jain belief states that a living being with a greater number of senses feels more pain than lower lifeforms such as vegetables. Therefore, the destruction of higher sense lifeforms - exploiting or killing of animals, birds and fish - for food is considered to be a crueller act because it inflicts more pain on them. It also causes greater destruction to environment. Jains believe that vegetarianism is the first essential feature of the culture of non-violence. Vegetarianism not only helps eliminate intentional and avoidable physical violence of animals but also the violence of self.

> *All things living, all things breathing, all things whatsoever should not be slain or treated with violence, or insulted, or injured, or tortured, or driven away* - Mahavira.
> *Let not anyone injure life, but be as assiduous in cherishing the life of another as his own. For Ahimsa is the highest religion* - Mahavira
> *Knowing the equality of all beings of the world, one should desist from the weapon of violence* - Bhasyam Sutra 3
> *The non-violent person does not kill living beings, nor does he get them killed, nor does he approve of the killer* - Bhasyam Sutra 46

Sikhism

Sikhism sees Nature as sacrosanct as it is an expression of the divine and therefore to be respected and treasured. According to Sikh metaphysics, Sikhs are related to the whole universe. So God is seen as caring for all creatures. This belief requires that Sikhs avoid harming all creatures as it is against God's will. Guru Hari Rai ran an animal clinic caring for sick animals and he even sent out hunting parties to collect sick animals in the wild so he could treat them. He also planted trees and flowers, purposefully creating habitats for wildlife.

> *He is omnipresent, pervades the universe* - Guru Granth Sahib.
> *With his blessings all creatures of the universe may prosper* - Guru Granth Sahib
> *We should respect all creatures because of the presence of God in them* - Dr Indergit Kaur, Director of the Pangalwara Institute, Amritsar, Punjab, India.
> *God dwells in Nature and I have no right to exploit Nature* - Dr Chalal, Lecturer at Pune University, Pune, Maharashtra, India.
> *Every human being in the universe is duty bound to live in co-existence with Nature as required by the Guru Granth Sahib* - Information Officer at the Golden Temple, Amritsar, Punjab, India

Taoism

Lao Tzu's dates are given anywhere between 600 and 300 BCE but he is known to have lived close to Nature. He set out his teachings using symbols from Nature. One of his basic principles is that we should all show compassion and empathy towards all beings. This compassion is clearly shown from the early days when Taoists actively protected wild animals. They would buy caged animals so as to set them free. By the 3rd and 4th centuries CE, protection of wildlife was enshrined in Taoist thinking, as humans came to be seen as only a part of the microcosm of Nature. Later, Taoism developed its own gods - of rivers, earth and mountains. Even to-day Taoists go to the mountains to be closer to the Tao.

> *Display deep love, care and compassion and penetrating empathy towards all living things* - Lao Tzu
> *The man in whom the Tao acts without impediment harms no other being by his actions* - Chuang Tzu

Shamanism

Shamanic traditions assert that the natural world is permeated with supernatural power; it is a source of visions and all kinds of spiritual experiences. This attitude breeds the highest respect for the natural world. Native Americans thought that the 'Great Spirit' had given each creature a "piece of his heart". Even before killing a single animal, they would go through elaborate ceremonies to appease the spirit of the animal. Since the shaman works with animal spirits, within the culture there is an unwritten rule not to destroy animals unnecessarily. Certain animals such as eagles, grizzly bears, buffalo and hawks were seen as sacred. It is interesting to note that, despite the Apache being totally reliant on the bison, the numbers they took did not impact bison populations. It was Europeans with their rifles that decimated the buffalo. Respect for animals was and remained inherent in the life of shamanic peoples.

> *The whole universe is enhanced with the same breath, rocks, trees, grass, earth, all animals and men - Intiwa, Hopi tribe*
> *We are part of the Earth and the Earth is part of us. The Earth does not belong to man, man belongs to Earth. Whatever befalls the Earth befalls the sons of Earth. Man did not weave the web of life; he is merely a strand in it* – Chief Seattle, of the Suquamish and Duwamish people

Paganism

Paganism has its roots in Nature. From Nature came the gods and goddesses that pagans worship. Mother Earth was the source of divinity. To the early pagans only working with Nature ensured survival. Out of this came a deep respect for life in all its forms. Modern pagans have a passion for the protection of all living species; I have witnessed personally pagans' active participation in today's Green movement. Gods such as Morrigan could transform themselves into animals, such as from a young girl to a crow. Horses were revered as Gods: Apollo, Mars and Epona all appeared escorted by horses. Horses were worshipped for their fertility, vigour, their use in warfare and in work. The humble dog was revered as a source of healing. This can be seen from the remains of hunting dogs found at burial sites. The Bull was worshipped for its strength, ferocity, virility and power. Boars were given supernatural qualities, as they were a symbol of food, hunting and battle. The Stag was perceived as the spirit of the forest for it displayed speed, agility and sexual vigour. Also because it shed its antlers each year it symbolised seasonal death and rebirth. Ravens and crows were seen as representatives of the underworld. Eagles were associated with the ability to escape the limitations of the Earth. Trees also were seen as having supernatural power; the rowan protected people from evil, whereas the hazel bestowed wisdom.

Spiritualism

Spiritualists consider all animals to have souls and to inhabit the afterlife, as I have witnessed in my experience with mediums. Also, information that has come through clearly indicates there is retribution in the afterlife to those who deliberately kill animals. I assume that this would apply to all species. Again, my experience with Spiritualists points to their having a deep respect for Nature.

Bahá'í

Bahá'í is a modern, environmentally conscious religion. Bahá'ís believe in the protection of the diversity of species. Richard St. Barbe Baker was a fine example of a Bahá'í environmentalist. In 1945 he created the International Tree Foundation, dedicated to reforestation, which grew out of the organisation 'Men of the Trees' which he first founded in Kenya around 1924. To date, the Bahá'ís have been involved in forestry projects in California, Kenya, Palestine, Canada, Iceland, Pakistan, Uganda, Brazil, India, Australia, Benin and Laos.

> *To love God means to love everything and everybody* - Bahá'u'lláh
> *Show loving kindness to every living creature* - 'Abdu'l-Bahá

Extinction of species

Ever since industrialisation began its spread from Europe around the globe in the 1800s, the rate of extinctions of species has been rising. Between 1600 and 1800 one species of bird or mammal became extinct every 5.7 years, yet in the first 50 years of the 20th century this rate had increased to one species becoming extinct every 1.1 years. There is now virtual unanimity among scientists that mankind's activities have precipitated a period of mass extinction not seen since the demise of the dinosaurs. This emerging global crisis is already affecting our future food supplies, our ongoing search for new medicines and the supply of fresh water we drink as well as exacerbating global climate change through deforestation and decimation of life in the seas and oceans.

Distinguished scientists estimate an average of 137 species of life forms are driven into extinction every day. That is one species exterminated every 10½ minutes, or 50,000 each year. Rates of species loss are now 100 times higher than the highest shown in the fossil record. With climate change, this rate could increase to 1,000 to 10,000 times, scientists predict. This extinction event is only the sixth in the Planet's 4,500 million year history but it is the first brought on by a creature living on the Planet.

- **In 2008 a study by WWF concluded that biodiversity had declined by fully one third in the last 35 years!**
- **A study by Leeds University in the UK predicts a loss of a further 25 per cent of all species of land animals and plants in the next 50 years.**
- **According to a United Nations report on the state of the global environment, almost a quarter of the world's mammals face extinction within 30 years:**
- **30 per cent of fish species are likely to become extinct;**
- **One third of all plants are threatened with extinction;**
- **One out of every 8 bird species is threatened with extinction;**
- **20 per cent of reptiles are likely to become extinct.**

The impact on ecosystems of species decline is most clearly evident when we look at specific habitat types. Research shows us that to kill off half the species in a given habitat, all you have to do is reduce that habitat's area by 60 per cent—not a shot need be fired. So we see that even habitat break-up spells a death knell; total loss of habitat brings numerous local extinctions. Compound habitat destruction with climate change and you have Earth's sixth Extinction Event, now playing throughout the tropics, and in a threatened woodland near you.

Ocean species

The oceans supported the earliest forms of life but today's sea creatures are experiencing a devastating onslaught, as the 2009 film *End of the Line* illustrates. Twelve percent of the land species are protected in some way but less than 1 per cent of the marine species share the same status. The great whales have come to be seen as a symbol of conservation thanks to organisations like Greenpeace and WWF. There were originally around 250,000 Blue whales, yet now they are estimated to have declined to as low as 10,000 in number. There were 10,000 Wright whales in the North Pacific and now the numbers are down to 2,000.

Coral reefs are the ocean's equivalent of the tropical rain forests. They only occupy 0.17 per cent of the ocean floor yet are home to 25 per cent of all marine species and contain some 9 million different types of plant and sea creature.

The greatest cause of their destruction is climate change which brings warming seawater. If the temperature in coral areas rises 1 degree Celsius above the normal for more than one day, then those corals become 'bleached' and may die. Ten percent of the world's corals have already died and over 50 per cent of the coral reefs have been degraded. It is estimated that 60 per cent will be lost by 2030. Marine biodiversity will continue to be severely affected unless we tackle the causes of climate change on an international scale.Over-fishing has brought stocks in the seas and oceans to and beyond collapse. One crucial initiative offering hope for our ocean fisheries is the Marine Stewardship Council. If we all bought only fish bearing its logo, and we stopped ocean warming, the future of fisheries would be assured.

How the world tackles its failures to agree on post-Kyoto measures to curb climate change will finally show whether or not humanity has evolved enough to earn a continued presence on our truly remarkable Blue Planet. The fact we have come this far and still choosing disagreement gives a measure of how drastically mankind has strayed from the path that the natural order demands of us.

Fresh water habitats

Freshwater fish in rivers, streams and lakes do not fare much better: they are being decimated by habitat loss and pollution. Forty-one percent of all fish species live in fresh water and represent 12 per cent of all animal species. One fifth of all freshwater fish species have become extinct, threatened or endangered in recent years.

Wetlands are a very important habitat for fish and other wildlife. Since 1900 we have cleared 50 per cent of all wetlands, mainly for agriculture. One important factor has been the rapid increase in world population since 1900, putting pressure on land to produce more food. In the USA between 1780 and 1980, 24 hectares an hour of wetlands were lost and now only 54 per cent of the original wetlands remain. Asia has lost 60 per cent of its wetlands and Africa 30 per cent.

Forests
Spiritual Insights

Hinduism

In India trees were considered to be the incarnation of Lord Shiva and highly valued. The ancient Hindu practice of tree planting goes back 1,500 years, as every tree was considered to have its resident deity. Ancient Hindus were even aware that trees helped maintain purity. The Rig Veda explains that trees are a vital part of the ecosystem. The ancient Laws of Manu state that cutting down trees is an unholy act and should be punished (Manu 11.63-66). The Vedas also say that trees and plants are valued because God has imbued them with curative and beneficial properties (Rig Veda 9.12.7, Atharveda 20.76.1). Many tree species had particular deities associated with them: the Asvattha or Peepal tree was seen as an incarnation of Krishna. Almost all deities resided in the Tulsi (holy basil) tree and they kept Yama, the Lord of Death, away. Tulsi is planted in many domestic gardens. Seeds of the Rudraksa tree are considered sacred and used for making rosaries. Many trees or plants are associated with specific deities: the Tulsi with Lakshmi and Vishnu; the Bela tree with Shiva; the Amalaki tree with the Buddha; the Vati Tree with Brahma; the Neem tree with Ganahara; and the Tamal and Peepal trees with Krishna.

One of the world's first major environmental movements began in India. Called the 'Chipko' movement, a term meaning 'embrace', its energies were focused by Sunderlal Bahuguna, an Indian eco-campaigner. Village women in Tehri, Uttarkashi state and elsewhere on the sub-continent hugged trees to prevent forest contractors from cutting them down. This forced a 1980 Indian government to ban commercial felling of trees at 1,000 metres or more above sea level.

> *Trees are our friends. Protect them and ensure their proper growth -* Rig Veda 8.11.13
> *Trees remove pollution so don't fell them -* Rig Veda 6.48.17
> *Trees are alive, they have life like others because on cutting they feel sorrow -* Mahabharata
> *The rivers are the veins of the cosmic person, trees are the hairs of His Body -* Bhagavad Gita II.1.33-34

Islam

Muhammad always valued trees and encouraged wildlife areas.

> *Plant trees. Sow seeds in fertile fields. These are the acts of true philanthropy* - Muhammad

Sikhism

Sikhs saw trees as an expression of God.

> *Trees, plants and all that is inside and outside, is He himself* -Guru Granth Sahib, p.223

Because forests - temperate and tropical - are the natural habitat for so much of the Planet's rich diversity of fauna, man in pursuing agriculture has been assaulting these life forms across a broadening front. Since the advent of agriculture 10,000 years, ago half the world's original forest of 3 billion hectares has now been destroyed. That is, according to now less than reliable official data:

- **60 per cent of temperate forests.**
- **45 per cent of tropical wet forests.**
- **70 per cent of tropical dry forests.**

Between 1990 and 2006 the annual loss of forest cover was 50,000 km² per year, about one third of which was primary forest. It has been predicted that, at current rates of felling, by 2020 only 40 per cent of the world's original forests will remain.

In the tropics, mangrove swamp forests are vital to ocean fish species as they offer a protective hatchery where vast shoals of tiddlers can feed and grow. But 35 per cent of all mangrove swamp has been lost in the last 20 years, largely to expanding shrimp farms—on learning this, many consider shrimp fasting. Asia - especially India, Pakistan and Thailand - West Africa and Latin America have now lost 75 per cent of their mangrove forests. Given mangrove's vital role as a hatchery, it's perhaps surprising ocean fish populations have not been plummeting faster.

Temperate forests, in terms of biodiversity numbers, are not super-critical as tropical rainforests are. Unlike tropical forests, it is not rare for surviving temperate to be under management, increasingly with biodiversity as well as timber stocking in mind. Forests are generally restocked once felled - and less often now as monoculture. Deciduous trees support a greater range of species of wildlife than conifers, yet conifers predominate.

So we consumers can learn which timber products originate from sustainably managed woodlands, certification schemes have emerged. One pioneering movement, the Forest Stewardship Council, works nationally in over 70 countries and internationally in promoting the sourcing of timber from sustainable forests, temperate and tropical, by licensing the use of its logo only to companies in certified supply chains.

Loss of tropical rainforests

Tropical rainforests support 50 per cent of all known species on Earth. The largest single rainforest area is found in the Amazon basin, some 7 million km² (700 million ha or 2.6 million square miles), which represents 60 per cent of all rainforests. According to Greenpeace, 70 million ha (257,000 sq miles) of Amazon Rainforest had been destroyed up to 2009. At this current rate it could entirely disappear in 40-50 years.

- **An estimated 1 hectare of rainforest is cut every second, adding up to an area larger than New York City over a period of one day.**
- **Between 2000 and 2005 the net loss of rainforests was 7.3 million hectares - an area the size of Panama or Ireland *every 12 months*.**
- **In 2008, 12,000 km² (4,663 sq miles) of rainforest was lost in Brazil, an area the size of Connecticut.**
- **In 2008, 800,000 ha of rainforest was lost in the Congo Basin, an area the size of Massachusetts.**
- **By 2025 there will be no tropical forests left in Central America, apart from small areas in Guatemala and Costa Rica.**

Cutting down trees, converting forest land to cropland has been humankind's legacy to the Planet ever since he first switched from being a hunter to a farmer. So today's deforestation has been 10,000 years in the making, starting with temperate regions of Europe and later North and South America. In continuing the eradication of so much of today's remaining tropical rainforest, we are of course all implicated in loss of species on an unprecedented scale. A statistic that astounded me is that at the current rate of rainforest destruction between 4 and 8 per cent of all rainforest species are in danger of extinction within five years - by 2015. Some have claimed that there will be a disappearance of 20 per cent of rainforest species within 30 years.

But why is there so much destruction of the rainforests? Reasons are many, but three stand out: ballooning populations, hamburgers and the palm oil trade expanding into bio-fuels. Corrupt officials and pirate logging come close behind.

The hamburger is becoming the fast food order of choice for millions in the South with new disposable income. Meanwhile, one billion landless people eek out a subsistence with 'slash and burn' agriculture (explained below). Following behind the shifting agriculturalists comes agribusiness which completes the destruction by clearing vast swathes of charred forest remnants. With the ballooning population and the insatiable demand for hamburgers, agribusiness seems guaranteed a strong market and good price for its soy and maize as animal feed for the burger cattle. These farmers favour more profitable export markets over the home market. So for Brazil's hungry, even the destruction of rainforest to croplands is no guarantee of adequate or affordable food supplies at home.

Brazil has more recently adopted a more proactive policy of slowing rampant forest destruction in response to international pressure. Federal policy to deliberately open up the Amazon for agriculture was abandoned due to the massive increase in forest burning it precipitated and the international outcry it provoked. But fuelwood collection, logging, mining, industrial developments, dam construction and tourism development all play their part in the ongoing Amazon tragedy Brazil shares with Paraguay, Peru, Ecuador, Colombia, Venezuela and others.

Deforestation in Indonesia has been in part linked to its problem of extremes of population density. Its 'Transmigrasi' programme moved millions of landless people from densely populated regions to the sparsely populated outlying areas of the vast archipelago over several decades. With mixed results, the programme has necessarily involved the destruction of large swathes of rainforest. Oil palm estate expansion continues to take swathes of prime forest in Indonesia and Malaysia and pirate logging, especially by army units on Borneo, remains rife.

In Africa - and now recognised as probably the result of climate change - the drought ridden Sahel region has experienced much famine and in consequence, 1.4 million people have migrated south into countries such as the Ivory Coast contributing to an annual population growth of 4 per cent. There, they have cleared the already decimated forests to grow food and now only 10 per cent of the original forest remains.

Traditional agriculture practised in the rainforest is called slash and burn, or shifting cultivation. Originally, before roads and mechanised transport, when populations were a tiny fraction of today's, it might be two generations until a family returned to an earlier 'garden.' At this frequency, the practice was sustainable. But when as today it is practiced by perhaps near a *billion* of the landless across thousands of kilometres of the burning fringe of the shrinking forest it makes for wanton destruction. A recent study found that a quarter of the world's population (1.7 billion) depends for its existence on the degradation of land.

Worse, where the cleared land is not used to grow soy, if secondary forest does not return after the burning, then soil erosion will result. Tropical rainforest soils are often red or yellow earths, extremely powdery when dry; they are thin and, without leaf litter compost, are infertile. Torrential tropical rains wash unprotected, thin soils away. If the topsoil is eroded, sub-soil often supports only scrub. The inevitable result is loss of habitat and a biodiversity cull on a massive scale.

Little recognised is that richer nations are also major contributors to the destruction of rainforests. Many governments in South America and Africa are still very indebted to Western banks for loans taken out in the 1980s. These nations are forced to generate foreign currency income through exporting timber or clearing forest for cash crops, such as wood pulp chips, soy, oil palm or burger beef cattle.

Such cash crop dependent developing countries include Thailand, Malaysia, Indonesia, the Philippines, Ivory Coast and those in the Congo Basin. Palm oil, the latest earner, is set to increase fivefold by 2030 and power 4 per cent of road transport. As well as being the cheapest of all edible oils, palm oil is the bio-fuel feedstock of choice for growers and traders - but not for environmentalists. The expansion of oil palm estates has resulted in escalating clearances of rainforest. Recent research highlights the huge contribution to global GHG emissions from deforestation (globally, it is 20 per cent). So, bio-fuels made from palm actually *increase* net CO_2 emissions levels.

Indonesia already has 6 million hectares of oil palm plantations, but has plans for another 4 million by 2015 dedicated to biofuel production alone. The bio-fuel rush has already pushed Indonesia's oil palm clearances up rapidly. The massive increase in meat consumption in the developed and developing world has led to the ballooning of soy animal feed production in Amazonia, with a massive 210,000 km² in production by 2003, much of it in the Matto Grosso area.

If the forest is not destroyed by shifting agriculture or agribusiness, the next threat to the rainforest is logging. According to the UNFAO Forestry Department wood consumption was set to increase by 23 per cent between 1996 and 2010. Tropical hardwoods were much in demand, as 17 per cent of the world's population - in North America, Europe and Japan - consume 75 per cent of this type of timber. Now there is extra demand from the emerging economies of China and India. Destruction is in part driven by those pressures on debt-burdened governments to pay off old loans to Western banks. However, the rich, developed world is central to the very rainforest destruction process its Green campaigners work at curbing.

Incentives for licensed loggers to behave in a caring sustainable way by leaving less mature trees to grow on are few. Short leases and at best patchy supervision mean any care goes unrewarded. Even if selective felling of only the mature commercial species is practised, the extraction process can be highly destructive and wasteful unless supervised. Logging methods in legit operations are highly mechanized but waste can be excessive: 30 per cent of the trees in a given area might be extracted but another 20 per cent of the trees destroyed. Beyond that, research in Amazonia suggests that 25 per cent of logged timber is never recovered and left to rot anyway. The soil is also compacted by the use of heavy equipment, which can severely hamper grow back.

Next time you see a spanking new table in tropical hardwood, remember that for each plank the tree had to grow two other planks' worth of wood went to waste—in the forest or at the mill as 'slab,' planer shavings, or sawdust. The mill waste may seem exorbitant but is largely unavoidable even with great care. Pirate logging and logging waste are the greater thieves.

The East Malaysian states of Sarawak and Sabah on Borneo have since the 1950s been major suppliers of hardwood timber to Japan, China, Taiwan, Korea, USA and Western Europe. These areas have been close to 'logged out' since the 1980s so the loggers next turned to Papua New Guinea, to Indo-China, to less accessible parts of West

Africa, such as Gabon and Cameroon and particularly to Amazonia for new sources of hardwood timber.

Cattle, or burger beef ranching has been and still is destroying swathes of rainforest. The Brazilian government did, once, positively encourage this activity by providing grants to clear forest and set up cattle ranches. Rich countries have accelerated this process through the World Bank, which funded the Brazilian Government's 5,000 km (3,000-mile) Trans Amazonian highway, a long abandoned project to 'open up' the interior of the Amazon Basin. In consequence in the sixties and seventies 10 million hectares of forest were felled and planted with imported grasses. In one year alone, an area the size of Scotland was cleared to provide grazing. It is only now grudgingly acknowledged that cattle quickly destroy the fragile soil structure, leading to soil erosion, land degradation and infertility.

The fast food explosion and mushrooming of deforestation to create new grazing lands first hit in the sixties and seventies when Central America became an epicentre for burger beef rearing for the American market. This resulted in the destruction of two thirds of Central America's rainforests. It has been estimated that each hamburger made from imported beef has destroyed 5 m^2 of tropical rainforest. Fast food chains account for 25 per cent of all beef consumption in the USA, so that is a lot of forest. It was estimated that every kilogram of beef produced in Costa Rica meant the loss of 2.5 tonnes of soil!

So our brief world survey shows little less than a war of destruction waged against the species with which we share this Planet. If instead of giving highest priority to wealth creation our cultures gave priority to saving species, we might do better and live up to the World Charter for Nature, signed by UN member countries in 1982. It states that all species warrant respect regardless of their use to humanity. If we listened to the teachings of the spiritual traditions on Nature we might change our ways to benefit all the Earth's living creatures.

Today, more than ever before, life must be characterized by a sense of Universal responsibility, not only nation to nation and human to human, but also human to other forms of life - 14th Dalai Lama

Possible spiritual and physical responses to species loss

As we have seen from this chapter, humanity has made the situation dire for millions of the Earth's creatures, many of which are now standing on the edge of the abyss or already driven to extinction. Evolution is a natural process that incorporates extinction, but our activities have massively accelerated it. The clear message from all the spiritual traditions is that all life is sacred and all species, not just mankind, have the right to life. The unwritten ancient spiritual traditions of Shamanism and Paganism come down to us from people who lived close to Nature and depended on it for their survival. This gave rise to a reverence and respect for the natural world that as a culture we Westerners have chosen to discard.

A major part of the problem is that we have become artificially separated from Nature in urban environments. Reconnecting with Nature can help us regain our respect and understanding for all species. The spiritual traditions of Jainism, Islam, Christianity, Judaism, Sikhism and Hinduism, all see Nature as divine, a manifestation of God in all His glory. If through a rediscovery of our Green spirituality we adopted an attitude of mutual respect for all species we would be joining a growing band of all faiths and none determined to see a reduction in the wholesale destruction of our fellow creatures on Earth.

There is no doubt that the explosion in world population from 1 billion around 1920 to 6.8 billion today is the driver of destruction for natural habitats. One practical solution is for richer countries to provide more resources to help poorer countries address this problem by funding women's education and family planning clinics: more awareness, fewer babies. Public debate, long taboo, would help and that may have begun with an international conference in London in March 2009 which opened up debate to palatable strategies hitherto overlooked.

We've seen how tropical rainforests are a vital repository of the biodiversity of species. The remaining equatorial forests of Africa, Central and South America and Southeast Asia and the Pacific isles are still being plundered for timber or destroyed for cattle rearing and the growing of oil palm and other cash crops. We need to halt this destruction and provide resources to help maintain tropical rainforests for their biodiversity and as carbon sinks in the fight against climate change. Other main players behind the destruction of rainforests are large landowners who use agribusiness methods to profit from cash crops such as palm oil used in our soaps, toiletries, cosmetics, our margarine, biscuits, ice creams and oatcakes - and now for bio-diesel - and soy to feed burger beef cattle. Join campaigners by boycotting these products or by cutting down your consumption of meat; campaign against bio-fuels that ruin the Planet and raise the price of staple foods in the world's hungry regions (Rainforest Action Network http://ran.org).

The preservation of our fellow species starts with the individual. We can still counter further climate change if we reduce our carbon footprints and slow emissions. To minimise destruction of the rainforests we need to consider the meat in our diets and to look at our ecological footprints in terms of unsustainable resources we take from forests—furniture and plywood use. Collectively we need to make our voices heard so governments are persuaded to adopt sustainable procurement practices. One reliable source on avoiding threats to biodiversity can be found at www.greenfacts.org/en/biodiversity/index.htm#6

Biodiversity personal action ideas

With so much in the biosphere under threat, the question we face is: where do we start? The broad range of actions below indicates how direly our participation is required. A meta site worth checking is the World Index of Social and Environmental Responsibility at www.wiserearth.org

1. Campaign to save the rainforests: www.rainforestsite. com www.fsc.org http://savetherainforest.org www.ecologyfund.com www.ran.org www.worldlandtrust.org www.rainforestsos.org
2. Campaign to save mammals from extinction: www.wwf.org www.planetsave.com www.endangeredspecie.com www.audubon.org
3. Campaign to save bird life: www.keepersof thewild.org_ www.fatbirder.com www.beakspeak.com www.rspb.org.uk
4. Campaign to save reptiles: www.pbs.org www.wolfhollowwildlife.org www.earthspecies.com www.earthwatch.org
5. Campaign to save whales and dolphins: www.wdcs.org www.bluevoice.org www.savethewhales.org www.animalwelfare.com
6. Campaign to save the ancient temperate forests: www.fsc.org www.greenpeace.org www.treesforlife.org.uk www.sierraclub.org
7. Campaign to save the wetlands: www.surfbirds.com www.sierraclub.org www.wildlifetrusts.org

8. Try and provide a Nature reserve in your garden: www. wildlifetrusts.org www.hdra.org www.rhs.org

9. Boycott non-sustainable tropical hardwood products and campaign against their use: www.illegal-logging.info www.iswonline.com www.globalwitness.org

10. Preserve wetlands: use a peat-free compost: www. fertilefibre.com www.peateringout.com www. peatfreecompost.co.uk

11. Cut down on your personal carbon emissions and help stop climate change: www.actonco2.com (See websites in climate change chapter).

12. For healthy oceans, ensure all fish you buy bears the MSC logo of the Marine Stewardship Council. Buy only rod-caught tuna not net, to protect dolphins. www.msc.org/ www.mcsuk.org

13. Reduce your meat consumption: www.vegsoc.org

CHAPTER 18 : THE WASTE WE GENERATE

Consumerism—death by a thousand cuts for our Planet?

"Where is 'away?'" the man asked. "What do you mean," said the other. "I mean, when you said you'd throw your old fridge away." "Well, I meant 'out.'"

He just doesn't get it. He imagines there is an 'away' or and 'out' which has boundless space for all the old goods we all throw out every time we come home with a replacement - though we're taught to call them 'upgrades' or 'latest models.' Because of 'progress,' we in the West are *all* educated, advised and persuaded—we *choose*—to purchase the 'latest,' unceasingly, many of us.

But—and here is the shock - the waste we throw is the tip of the iceberg. Few of us are aware that for every truckload of finished goods that reaches the shops—and then us, the consumers—there are *twelve*, yes, *twelve truckloads* of wastes that have to be disposed of during manufacture. An OECD study established that world household rubbish was approximately 1.6 billion tonnes in 2005 (1kg per person), expected to rise to 3 billion tonnes by 2030.

The wastefulness of the consumer lifestyle is thrown into sharp relief when we realise that we are sending to landfill many of the non-renewable resources we are about to run out of! Recycling these would not just keep us from running out; it would save on all the mess and fouling of earth, air and water involved with mining, transport and processing of ores.

In developing countries people have on average much less *to* throw out: whereas in the US, the average citizen produces 720 kg of waste per year, the average citizen in urban India produces only 150 kg of waste. The US epitomises the "waste all" society, producing 33 per cent of total solid waste in the world, which works out at a staggering 2 kg of waste per person per day! Given the number of poor within the US, the most wasteful must be off the page.

Consumerism, that conveyor-belt stacking the waste mountain ever higher, is kept stimulated by the oracle with the greatest influence in human history, the advertising industry. Its message: "To be happy you have to appear successful, and to do that you must buy, buy, buy, and keep acquiring more and more."

I remember a sad tale told by a Western monk who spent time in Mathura, in India. He'd known the locals in the community from way back. Despite having little, the villagers like their forbears had been generally content with their lot - until they acquired televisions. Exposed to the poison of advertising they had swiftly fallen victim to the corrosive dissatisfaction of want for material things - things their income would never stretch to. But the trap—or the treadmill - those Indian villagers so clearly fell into is the same illusion we Westerners have been tricked by since around 1950. The Jones's have a lot to answer for.

We've all been caught out by the glitzy gismo that goes defective within a few months of the guarantee expiring; or the upgrade model with those 'must-have' features mysteriously absent when we made our initial investment. Expanding greatly in the 1920s, mass production radically reduced costs, but it had a downside: it risked saturating markets and quickly quelling the buying urge. So early marketeers invented 'planned obsolescence', with a 'new, enhanced' model to 'launch' each and every year. Because we may later be persuaded to buy once again, planned obsolescence enlarges the market. It is also an underhand way of persuading us to purchase goods we might not buy if we knew the full and final financial cost—of the two (or three) items. If we knew the full *environmental* costs of the wastes, a growing number of us would probably not part with money at all. These are the insidious little deceits, the half truths and assumptions—the Planet doesn't mind, doesn't matter, the Planet won't notice, my purchase can't possibly do serious damage—with which we are threatening our Planet, and thereby ourselves, with death by a thousand cuts.

Because each deceit has been packaged to seem insignificant, our culture has lost sight of the reality, which is that our ways—especially with waste - are dangerously destructive to our habitat. One of the most powerful antidotes to this sanctified insanity is the alternative spiritual value system represented by the teachings from the different spiritual traditions which challenges the materialist culture at its foundation. Let us reflect on what the spiritual traditions say about the creation of waste through the accumulation of material possessions.

Spiritual insights on creation of waste

Judaism

The Talmud specifically forbids people dumping refuse where it could interfere with the environment or crops. The *Bal Tashkhit Mitzvah* rule informs Jews that they must not waste, because all things are God's property and must be utilized in service of the creator. For instance, Jews were told not be wasteful by cutting down fruit-bearing trees if they laid siege to a town (Deut 20 19-20). Judaism has a tradition of frugal Green living in which excessive waste does not arise.

Islam

Muslims are instructed in the Qur'an to spend money wisely and not on wasteful extravagance. Following this is surely good for the environment: it avoids the creation of needless waste and all the associated disposal problems, not least of which would be the loss of land to landfill sites and the groundwater pollution risks associated with it. Islam's prohibition of wastefulness requires that instead of disposing of old goods as rubbish we reuse them and that we recycle materials and waste products in so far as is possible. Islam emphasises the need for cleanliness in the environment and the need to avoid polluting it with waste.

> But waste not by excess: for God loveth not the wasters – Qur'an 6:141
> Cleanliness is the basis of a clean environment - Kwarja Nalsan Sani Nizami, Sufi, Keeper of the Sufi Shrine at Nizamuddin Mosque, Delhi, India.

Hinduism

Hinduism has a long tradition of seeing undisturbed Nature as the abode of deities. To pollute it with waste would be considered an act of sacrilege. The Hindu way of life emphasises limiting the consumption of material things. Its focus is on the spiritual quest for higher consciousness. Such traditions, if adhered to, would result in Hindus producing very little material waste.

Teaching meditation means that they will not be mad for getting more comforts and thereby consuming more and producing more waste - Swami Shatrananda, Rishikesh, Uttarakhand, India
Products should be produced in such a way that they are enabled to be recycled easily - Swami Dharamanda, Head of the Shivananda Ashram, Rishiklesh
Hinduism teaches us to live in Nature and have a peaceful atmosphere and not to waste or degrade anything - Ketar Suhar, Lecturer, Mysore University, Mysore, Karnataka, India

Buddhism

Buddhism sees the accumulation of material wealth as another attachment and an obstacle to the attainment of enlightenment. Therefore a devout Buddhist will produce a minimum of material waste. Evidence suggests that the Buddha was Green in that he prevented waste by encouraging reuse and recycling. In Buddhist scriptures there is a description of Ananda's conversation with King Udena, where he describes how the worn out robes of monks were reused. Firstly the discarded robes were made into coverlets; when these became worn they were put to use as old rags and dusters; finally when they were too worn for that purpose they were mixed in with clay to fix floors and walls. For anyone who recognises the true value of resources, this way of managing affairs is only natural.

Jainism

Jainism has definite rules about the limits to material possessions. This ensures less waste is produced. The Jain monk is the epitome of someone who produces little waste through pursuing a spiritual life which has the main focus of becoming more enlightened. Monks may own only what they can carry.

Spiritual and religious life is renunciation and not acquiring - Satish Chand, Assistant Commissioner for Delhi, Delhi, India
People should practise self discipline as regards the consumption of things; therefore the tendency of consumerism will be given up - Acharya Shri Mahaprajna, Head Monk of the Terapanth sect, Gujarat, India.

Acharya Shri Mahaprajna

Jainism says we should limit our desires and the use of natural resources - Ramesh Chandra, Ex-Director, The Times of India newspaper, Delhi, India

Sikhism
The Sikh gurus modelled a life devoted to God rather than the pursuit of riches. The material waste they produced was minimal.

> *Live in moderation and contentment, preserving Nature* - Dr Haminder Kaur, Lecturer at Guru Nanak University, Amritsar, Punjab, India
> *When I have a feeling of sharing my resources with others I will not waste resources* - Dr. Surjeet Kaur Chalal, Lecturer at Pune University, Maharashtra, India, and writer on Sikhism and ecology

Taoism
The human ideal for Taoists is the sage. He lives frugally and simply. Any waste he produces is easily within the capacity of Nature to process.

> *The Tao helps others. So no one is lost. And uses things wisely so nothing is wasted* - Lao Tzu.

Shamanism
Native Americans provide a valuable example of all but eliminating waste. When they hunted and killed an animal, every part was utilized. At least prior to the disruptions caused by the Europeans, the Plains Indians hunted Bison at sustainable levels and herd numbers were maintained. This seems to have changed with the coming of the white

man, who hunted the Bison effectively to extinction within a few years. Additionally, for Native Americans, a Shaman was not expected to accumulate material wealth and therefore create waste. Their true wealth was seen as the range of experiences gained on Vision Quests.

Bahá'í
Today, many Bahá'ís in developed countries address the issue of waste by actively promoting local recycling along with other Green practices. The Bahá'ís, notable doers, are consistently highly supportive of the UN's practical programmes to create sustainable communities.

Christianity
Christ was not materialistic. He did not accumulate material possessions and therefore little waste would have been attributable to Him.

> I only feel angry when I see waste; when I see people throwing away things that we could use - Mother Teresa, Kolkata, India.

Household waste
It's a sobering fact that it is wealth that produces waste. The poor of this world who have no accumulated wealth produce the least waste, for instance the one billion people who have less than one dollar a day to spend. The waste these poorer people do produce is generally biodegradable in contrast to the mainly non-biodegradable waste richer people discard. Often less than 50 per cent of municipal waste in poorer countries is taken by regular local authority collection. On my travels in India, I remember the sight of illegally dumped waste on the roadside on the way out of Gaya in Bihar. The waste had formed high mounds to each side of the road. It must have stretched for a mile or more.

In industrialised countries in the past 20 years municipal waste generated per person has increased threefold to almost half a tonne - an average of 475 kg per person per year. Taking industrial, commercial and municipal waste together, the USA produces about 10 billion tonnes of solid waste a year. This is 33 per cent of the world total waste, coming from just 4.6 per cent of the world population. Now the developing countries are catching up, with an OECD survey estimating that their waste will increase by 200 per cent by 2020. Over the same period in developed industrialised countries there will be a predicted increase of between 70 per cent and 100 per cent. Clearly, 'one-planet living' is some way off.

A major concern regarding waste is that in the developing countries with high birth rates more people now aspire to the consumerist lifestyle of the developed countries. If there were 11.5 billion people on the Planet in 2100 and they all produced 1 tonne of waste per person per year, there would be enough waste produced to cover the island of Sri Lanka. If they continued to consume at the same rate, then in a mere 1,700 years the whole Planet would be covered in garbage!

- **Municipal waste being collected in America has nearly tripled since 1960, reaching 2.94 million tonnes in 2006. This is equivalent to 63,000 garbage trucks being filled each day. One third is generated through packaging. Meanwhile, according to EU statistics, the amount of municipal waste produced in Western Europe increased by 23 per cent between 1995 and 2003, to reach 522 kg (1,228 lb) per person per year in 2008.**
- **In England in 2005/06 a total of 28.7 million tonnes of municipal waste was collected, enough to fill the Albert Hall in London once every hour for the year.**

Until a year or two ago most of the mountains of municipal waste generated in developed countries ended in 'landfill', large excavations in the ground. Globally, two thirds of collected municipal waste is dumped to landfill, storing 1.2 billion tonnes of waste. Recycling rates are improving, but eighty per cent of all municipal waste in USA, Canada, UK and Australia *still* went to landfill sites. Unsurprisingly, perhaps, in many countries the supply of suitable land is running out. The US EPA says that 80 per cent of the landfill sites in operation in the US will be full within 20 years.

Yet dumping is also an act of criminal short sightedness: we are throwing away finite resources which will be needed by future generations. Landfill also uses up invaluable agricultural land and unless properly engineered, landfill waste degrades to render local groundwater supplies toxic. There are climate implications, too: on a global scale the methane produced from the rotting waste adds significantly to global warming GHGs. It has been predicted that when we start running out of finite resources landfill sites will be mined—indeed, as shown in the

2009 film *Slumdog Millionaire*, the urban destitute have been mining such sites for some decades already.

Until the issue of waste becomes mainstream and all humanity accepts the fundamental changes demanded by the Laws of Nature, waste dumping will remain the Achilles Heel of our species. Fortunately, part of this message has sounded clearly in town halls and ministries - where these are functioning. While consumerism reigns, theirs will always be an uphill battle, but they are at least trying and deserve our acknowledgement, support and our guidance, especially around incineration.

Incineration
'If you cannot bury it then you can always burn it.' We covered this unwise option in the chapter on air pollution. Incineration is tempting because you can reduce municipal waste by 70 per cent and produce electricity, though only one fifth as much as can be saved by recycling instead. Moreover, these gains come at a high cost in toxin-degraded quality of the air we breathe and our health.

In Europe there has been a drive by the EU to expand the use of incineration to minimise the amount of waste going to landfill. EU states intend to commission 50 new incinerators by 2015. This pressure has driven both central and local government into embracing incineration technology as a 'quick fix' without necessarily considering all of the impacts on health, the environment and the economy. In the UK 70 incinerators burn 7 to 10 per cent of all municipal waste and the UK government is expanding this to 25 per cent. In the USA 130 sites incinerate 16 per cent of all municipal waste. In Japan at least 40 per cent of all waste is incinerated. Why is this bad news?

Because the waste stream is usually unsorted, incinerators produce large quantities of gaseous emissions and solid and liquid residues that are often contaminated with toxic substances, such as heavy metals, dioxins, furans and other so-called persistent organic pollutants, or POPs. They persist because they are substances unrecognisable to the natural organisms on which we rely for processes of natural decay yet they end up being ingested.

There have been some claims that technological innovations in filtering largely remove dangerous toxic gases but this has yet to be substantiated by reliable research. Dioxins are particularly dangerous.

We now know that dioxin is a serious health hazard at levels as low as a few parts per *trillion* in mammalian body fat. Apart from serious birth defects in all mammals, dioxins have been shown to cause a wide range of health problems, including cancer, immune system damage and reproductive and developmental problems. Cancer is the biggest threat and even an early study of the problem showed that cancer amongst children living near municipal waste incinerators doubled between 1974 and 1987. Exposure of animals to dioxins has resulted in several types of cancer.

Dioxins also 'bio-accumulate' in the fatty tissues of living organisms and are passed on up the food chain, especially concentrating in fish, eggs, and dairy products (dioxin levels in fish are 100,000 times that of the surrounding environment). The safe dosage guideline for a dioxin is 1 picogram (a trillionth of a gram) per kilogram of body weight. In the UK the average exposure is already 1.3 picograms and according to the British Foods Standards Agency, one third of the UK population regularly consumes food with unsafe levels of dioxins in it. The average daily intake of the American people is already well above two federal guideline levels for 'safe' exposure. The US average daily intake is more than 200 times higher than the Environmental Protection Agency's cancer risk guideline.

Small wonder then that, as local people learn of the risks, plans to further expand incineration meet with increasingly vehement opposition. Yet, the options are few, short of persuading people to significantly reduce levels of consumption and waste, making this one of the most powerful arguments for us to reduce our levels of consumption overall.

Recycling

The fact is that we would not have to burn or bury waste if we recycled it, thus achieving enormous savings in energy and resources. This was one of my passions when I wrote and performed a 'Recycling Road show' for environmental charity Action 21 and took it round local primary schools. Recycling can save three to five times more energy than can be generated by the most efficient incinerators.

Below are the percentages of energy saved in manufacture by using recycled instead of raw materials.

**Energy savings using recycled
compared to virgin materials**

Glass	40 per cent
Newspaper	40 per cent
Plastics	70 per cent
Steel	74 per cent
Aluminium	95 per cent

Apart from newsprint, which draws on wood, a *potentially* renewable resource, all the other materials are derived from oil or ores, all non-renewable resources. As well as the impacts of mining, drilling and refining, recycling reduces the drain on these finite resources.

- **Every tonne of glass recycled saves 130 litres (34 US gallons) of oil.**
- **Each tonne of recycled paper can save 1,440 litres (380 US gallons) of oil, 4,000 kilowatt-hours of energy and 26,500 litres (7,000 US gallons) of water.**

Recycling also creates employment. Incinerating 10, 000 tonnes of waste creates one job; with landfill, 10,000 tonnes of waste creates six jobs; recycling 10,000 tonnes of waste creates 36 jobs. It has been estimated that recycling could create up to 50,000 new jobs in the UK.

Public acceptance of recycling has grown over the last 15 years throughout the industrialized world, driven by a variety of factors: concerns about increasing waste generation and dwindling landfill capacity; air pollution from incineration; and a general recognition of the need to protect the environment. Uptake rates in developed world economies vary dramatically. Germany is a leading nation with a recycling rate for municipal wastes of 60 per cent. Japan recycles between 43 per cent and 53 per cent of all waste. The US recycled 79 million tons of municipal waste in 2005 achieving a 32.1 per cent recycling rate, this having doubled in 15 years. However, nearly one half of the US population—either in tall buildings or in deepest countryside - does not even have access to kerbside recycling and probably never will.

Rates of recycling in the UK position it as one of the worst in

Europe. In total, 25.5 million tonnes of household waste was collected in England in 2005/06 - just less than 27 per cent of which was recycled. While UK residents landfill 75 per cent of municipal waste, Belgium, Sweden, Germany and Luxembourg all send less than 25 per cent of their rubbish to landfill. The Greeks have the worst record and landfill 90 per cent of their rubbish! But collecting refuse from islands too small to have engineered landfill is expensive and challenging. Britain's local authorities lost almost all their independence to power-hungry central government. Hopefully, the one-size-fits-all approach that has put it next to Greece on landfill will be revisited by the new coalition.

By 2020 Germany wants to have completely phased out landfill of municipal wastes and to have achieved a sustainable waste management system. The first of June 2005 was a milestone for waste management in Germany, when the land filling of unsorted waste was prohibited.

Paper recycling has seen progress: each tonne of recycled paper saves 17 trees and three cubic metres of landfill space. Despite the computer age and the arrival of the supposed paper-free office, Americans still throw away enough office and writing paper each year to build a wall twelve-feet high stretching from New York City to Los Angeles. On paper reuse, Australia leads the world, recycling 75 per cent of all newsprint.

Glass can be recycled indefinitely as part of a simple but highly effective process cutting energy use, air pollution, machinery wear as well as its raw material, sand. Glass's structure does not deteriorate when reprocessed. The UK has a current municipal recycling rate of 34 per cent for container glass which means people throw away five out of every six bottles and jars sold in the UK, resulting in over 6 billion items going to landfill every year. This is poor, considering that Switzerland and Finland recycle more than 90 per cent of their glass bottles waste, Germany and Sweden over 80 per cent and recycling figures of more than 50 per cent are the norm. The US has a poor glass recycling rate, just 24 per cent in 2007. Oregon State legislation requires glass bottles to be returnable and in 2009 this was extended to include mineral water bottles.

Steel recycling is long established in the world. The US has recently reached a rate of 75 per cent recycling steel and European nations achieve similar figures. Recycling aluminium drink cans saves up to 95 per cent of the huge amount of electrical energy needed to make aluminium from its raw ore, bauxite. The energy saved by recycling one aluminium drink can is enough to run a television for three hours! The average for total metal recycling in the USA in 2005 was only 37 per cent because only 55 per cent of aluminium cans were recycled, *down* from 67 per cent in 1992. The energy saved each year through recycling all aluminium cans could light the city of Washington DC (pop 600,000) for almost 4 years. In the UK only 32 per cent of aluminium cans are recycled per year, with people throwing away 12 billion cans, which leads to 160,000 tonnes of them ending up in landfill, yearly. The performances of these two countries are poor when the global average is 60 per cent and countries such as Norway, Switzerland and Iceland achieve 91 per cent recycling of drinks cans.

A common problem with recycling plastics is that they are often made up of more than one kind of polymer or there may be fibre added for strength. This makes recovery difficult and disposal expensive as plastic can take up to 500 years to decompose. A fundamental problem is that facilities to recycle all types of plastics hardly exist. For instance in the US, packaging makes up 42 per cent of total plastic consumption and very little of this is recycled. Such problems will remain unsolved until a systemic approach is adopted incorporating 'cradle to cradle'— C2C - design, referred to as biomimetic because of how it requires that materials mimic Nature in sourcing and biodegradability. This may be the approach industry will be required to follow from the 2010s on.

Plastic water bottles are recyclable, yet more than 60 million of them are thrown away *each day* in the US - six times more than in 1997. About 22 billion plastic bottles end up in US landfills or incinerators annually. The Earth Policy Institute estimates that making bottles to meet the US demand for bottled water requires more than 1.5 million barrels of oil annually, enough to fuel 100,000 cars for a year. Only about one in six plastic water bottles sold in the US in 2004 was recycled, a rate of about 17 per cent. Sweden has an 80 per cent recycling rates for clear plastic bottles, which is near to the rate achieved, by several European countries such as Germany and Switzerland. The UK's 7 per cent on plastics recycling is derisory.

The UK produces 3 million tonnes of plastic waste each year and approximately 85 per cent is land filled, 8 per cent incinerated; and, yes, only 7 per cent of plastic is recycled. The UK is saved from being at the bottom of the league by Greece where one-fifth of the entire waste produced is plastic and yet just 1 per cent of it is recycled. What is it about Brits and recycling? Is it not cool? Then who has been given the job of making it so?

278

Hazardous wastes

Hazardous materials recognized as extremely harmful to all life forms are essential to the manufacture of most commonplace household items: plastics, paints, batteries, metallic appliances, pharmaceutical products, petroleum products, TVs, phones, electronics and computers *ALL* involve hazardous chemicals directly or indirectly. And this is nothing new: the problem of environmental pollution from hazardous chemicals being used in or produced during manufacturing processes first arose along with the industrial revolution in the 1700s. Chemicals manufacture and metals refining and processing generate 90 per cent all hazardous waste. Many organic (as in carbon-based) chemicals are lethal. The production of these has skyrocketed over the last century to an estimated 1 billion tonnes in 2000.

In terms of waste disposal, the greatest crime against the environment, its creatures and us humans is the irresponsible disposal of hazardous waste. The industrial world, including the emerging economies of China and India, produces 90 per cent of all hazardous wastes.

This hazardous waste burden is the price the Planet pays for our material standard of living but we fall seriously short of bearing the full monetry cost of its responsible disposal. Worldwide, 400 million tonnes of hazardous waste is produced per year, of which 300 million is from the rich club OECD countries. In the USA each year more than 260 million tonnes of hazardous wastes are produced; this amounts to more than 1 tonne per head of population.

The hazardous wastes most dangerous to human health are the reactive wastes, which react chemically with each other or with air and water to create further hazardous substances. Examples are cyanides, acids, heavy metals, chemicals, solvents, propellants, paint thinners, PCBs, phenols, dioxins, furans and contaminated sludges. The dire health effects of exposure to many of these substances are numerous. We address them in Chapter 13 on water.

Such tragic short-sightedness over hazardous materials stems from an 'end of pipe' mentality: rather than radically revisioning a company's offering in such a way to eliminate production of toxic wastes, technology and resources are invested in dealing with the end-product wastes of yesterday's industrial processes. In Europe, 80 per cent of the investment in environmental protection is in dealing with hazardous waste *after* manufacture and only 20 per cent in the actual manufacturing process and product re-design. Surprisingly, there is also little effort by industry to reduce the amount of hazardous waste through recycling. In OECD countries only about 4-5 per cent of hazardous waste is being recycled. But there is potential to do 20 times more: for instance 80 per cent of waste solvents can be recycled.

There are a total of over 65,000 chemicals now in regular commercial use, yet—incredibly - the data on toxicology is only available on about 1 per cent of these chemicals, to which are added two or three new chemicals every *day* in the business-friendly 'try it out first, test it later,' minimally regulated regimes of free market economies found everywhere today.

A good example of a particularly hazardous toxic waste is PCBs or polychlorinated biphenyls. These oily, non-flammable liquids were used for decades, untested, in thousands of applications - as coolant and insulating fluids in large electrical transformers, in hydraulic oils, as a plasticizer in PVC, in paints, floor finishes, caulking and in surgical implants even. But manufacture was finally halted only after tests revealed its extreme toxicity. Once released into the environment, PCBs can spell disaster for all biota and humans alike: it is soluble in fatty tissue and accumulates at progressively higher levels up the food chain. When it enters the human body it can disrupt hormone function because it mimics the actions of some hormones. If a pregnant woman is exposed, she risks a baby with defects. The most serious effect of all is that PCBs initiate and promote cancers. Health generally can be affected because PCBs weaken the immune system.

A survey in the US has shown that *two thirds of hazardous wastes* produced by industry are disposed of in such a way that they will contaminate groundwater. The cost of cleaning up the toxic wastes is estimated to be in the region of $100 billion. One major culprit is the vast American military machine; the Pentagon is responsible for a third of all hazardous toxic wastes produced. It is often the case that the US military is not subject to the stringent environmental controls of the civilian industrial sector and often its waste sites are poorly managed. Former Soviet Union states have their problems, too. In the poorer republics like Uzbekistan, 2 billion tonnes of hazardous toxic waste are badly stored and are now leaking into groundwater. Ukraine's Ministry of Environmental Protection reports that about 4 *billion* tonnes of hazardous toxic wastes, containing high concentrations of mercury, cadmium, lead, copper, nickel, vanadium and other heavy metals, are stored in wholly inadequate conditions. In many places, especially in east

Ukraine, aquifers are already contaminated and dangerous to human health.

Some of the most toxic of wastes come from the manufacture of electronics: computers, peripherals, TVs, mobile phones and gadgets. Statistics show that one computer contains more than 700 kinds of chemical materials, over 50 per cent harmful to human health such as lead, cadmium and mercury. These are not only toxic but can leach into soil and contaminate groundwater.Yet, within 60 months or less, most electronics are 'binned' and the problem of safe e-scrap disposal begins.

Electronic waste is increasing at a rate of 3-5 per cent per year from its 2008 level of about 268 million tonnes. By 2012 it is projected to increase to 426 million tonnes per year. The University of Wuppertal in Germany estimates that the manufacture of one personal computer generates 1,500 kg of waste. Just to make one Intel 6 inch microchip, 3.2 kg (7 lb) of *hazardous* waste is generated. The European Environmental Agency calculates that the volume of e-scrap is now rising roughly three times faster than other forms of municipal waste, comprising nearly 5 per cent of the world total. Mobile phone users around the world more than doubled in one year to reach 4.6 billion in 2009.

By 2010 no fewer than three billion units of consumer electronics had become obsolete. Greenpeace estimate that worldwide, as much as 4,000 tonnes of toxic e-waste is discarded every *hour*, equivalent to the weight of 1,000 elephants. By buying a laptop to write this book I am contributing to the problem, as manufacturing a 2.3kg laptop is estimated to create 9 tonnes of waste. At present only 11 per cent of PCs are recycled. The EU has now legislated that electronic waste should be properly recycled or discarded in a safe way under the important Waste electronic and electronic equipment (WEEE) directive. In 2008, in the UK, 450,000 tonnes of e-waste was treated under the requirements of this new legislation. Safe disposal is now the responsibility of retailers.

Unsurprisingly, the US generates more e-waste than any other nation. A total of 220 million tons in old computers and other technological hardware are trashed in the United States each year. In 2008 that worked out at 112,800 computers discarded each *day*. In the US an estimated 50-80 per cent of e-waste from recycling is shipped for dismantling to China, India, Pakistan or other developing countries. Unusable equipment is also being donated or sold to developing nations as a way to avoid recycling costs. They end up in places like China's

Guangdong Province where, for a dollar or two a day, unprotected migrant workers pour acid over boards to extract precious metals and burn plastics, inhaling the carcinogenic smoke.

Developing nations are catching up: they were expected to have tripled their output of e-waste by 2010. In Beijing alone they were forecast to throw away 158,300 tonnes of e-waste in the same year.

Finally, our e-waste is not only poisoning people. Throwing away these finite resources commits our industries to mining, transporting and refining ores to replace them. In addition to well-known precious metals such as gold, palladium and silver, unique and indispensable metals and minerals have become increasingly important in electronics. Among them is Indium, a by-product of zinc mining used in more than 1 billion products per year, including flat-screen monitors and mobile phones. High demand for one mineral, Coltan, which yields metals vital to manufacture of electronic goods such as cell phones, is said to be a driver behind the decades long conflicts in DR Congo over rebel control of lucrative mining areas.

So we can now see even more clearly how the age-old spiritual teachings on waste remain valid for us today. By ignoring them we are creating problems with waste, many lethal to life in all forms, problems that future generations will not thank us for.

Spiritual and physical responses to problems of waste

Problem wastes are the product of a society that puts wealth above health. I'm not saying that we should become poor, but the spiritual teachings on the accumulation of wealth are illuminating. The clear message is that far from making us happier, possessing more and more obscures and detracts from the spiritual dimension of our lives and the profound contentment that can bring. With a careful look at our desires, we may reflect on whether the many things we feel we need to buy will actually make us any happier. The spiritual traditions tell us that the real source of happiness is found in the spiritual path. This change of attitude and raising of consciousness may help us in reducing our levels of consumption thus reducing the volume of wastes produced on our behalf.

The physical solution is to radically change the very foundation of the corporate world including its epicentre, the military-industrial complex. We also need new terms of trade requiring goods (and packaging) are made to stand up to wear and last longer and as per C2C, cradle-to-cradle, in materials suitable for instant recycling. We need our economic system to evolve into one that meets our basic physical needs, but no longer requires us to consume ever greater amounts of resources and produce vaster and vaster amounts of waste as has been the case. Reduce, re-use, re-cycle is the mantra for a greener lifestyle. So once we reach a high level of personal recycling, we should move on to examine the Reduce and the Re-use phases.

Personal waste action ideas

1. Recycle glass, save on landfill and energy: to manufacture glass from sand requires super-high temperatures. www.recycling-guided.com www.mylot.us www.nrc-recycle.org www.greendaily.com
2. Recycle aluminium cans, save on landfill and save 95 per cent of the energy used to make them in the first place. www.thinkcans.com www.recycle-more.co.uk
3. Recycle foil as it can be made into various metal alloys.
4. Recycle and reuse newspapers and cardboard to save landfill, save energy and save trees. www.newspaperbins.com www.gogreeninitiative.org www.make-stuff.com www.greenlivingideas.com
5. Recycle clothes and save water: (use clothing banks), they can be re-made into new clothes or used to make bags or cloths. One cotton shirt recycled will save many thousand litres of water. www.jekoo.com www.everyrule.com www.recyclenow.com www.thriftyfun.com www.tcritic.com
6. Recycle kitchen food waste to make compost rather than disposing it in landfill waste whence more dangerous methane emissions; also saves having to buy compost. www.mastercomposter.com www.vegweb.com www.wasteonline.org www.davesgarden.com www.americanprogress.org
7. Campaign locally to get more facilities to recycle more goods such as different types of plastics. www.recoup.org www.recycling-guided.com
8. Get advice on the Internet about how to Reduce consumption, Reuse and Recycle to cut down waste. Some UK sites are www.wasteonline.org.uk www.crn.org.uk and www.wastewatch.org.uk www.reusereducerecycle.

co.uk For USA: www.sustainablog.org www.epa.gov/epawaste/paternerships/wastewise

9. Buy goods made from recycled materials. www.naturalcollection.com www.recycledproducts.org.uk www.surprise.com, www.traid.org.uk www.recycledgoods.com www.recycle.net www.greenandmore.com

10. Take unwanted materials such as wool, card, paper, clothing and bric-a-brac to a Scrapstore where they can be used by local schools for art. www.reusereducerecycle.co.uk www.wastebook.org

11. Take unwanted items to the local charity shop or stall at the local refuse tip to find a second user.

12. Take car batteries to the local recycling centre. They can be rebuilt.

13. Use rechargeable batteries; when you can't, take spent dry-cell (and rechargeable) batteries to a recognised disposal point in your area.

14. Try to buy reconditioned goods such as furniture and to donate when you change yours. www.ebay.com www.ilovefreegle.org

15. If doing DIY take opportunities to find materials such as timber in local skips or reuse building materials. www.salvoweb.com www.building-guides.com

16. Have your own carrier in your bag or on your bike to cut out plastic bags and save on landfill.

17. Buy whole foods in bulk to cut down on any form of packaging. www.suma.co.uk www.wholefoodsmarket.com www.wholefoods.com

18. Grow your own food to cut down on food packaging and food miles. www.gardenorganic.org www.selfsufficientish.com www.inhabit.com www.verdant.net

19. Campaign to halt the high use of packaging by supermarkets: organise a community 'take it back' packaging event at your supermarket. Some even cooperate.

20. Share before buy: borrow power tools rather than buy them. Check for a local LETS exchange trading scheme, which are international or start a tool library. www.lets-linkup.com www.letslink.org

21. Give unwanted tools to the recycling centre or to Tools for Self-Reliance which gives them to people in the developing world. www.tfsr.org
22. Do not throw away your printer cartridges to add to landfill; donate them or have them refilled then reuse.
23. Use jam jars for homemade jam - from locally picked wild fruit is best.
24. Donate functioning computers to organisations that pass them on to developing world projects. www.donateape.org www.usedcomputer.com
25. Take pride in repairing items—or learning how - so that they can be kept in use rather than throwing out and buying new.
26. Use the local library to borrow DVDs and CDs rather than buy them and support it by using its book lending.
27. Before you buy *any* item new, think carefully if you really need it. If you do, ask, where could I get a well cared for used one?
28. Reduce junk mail by writing to companies to be taken off their lists or in the UK use a mail preference service www.mpsonline.org.uk

CHAPTER 19 : THE POVERTY WE CREATE

Introduction

When I came out of Delhi airport in India in 2002 to carry out my research for this book, I thought that I had landed on a different planet. I could not believe the abject poverty or the constant *hassle* from beggars on the street. I had to make a choice from the start about which people I was going to give money to. I decided I would give money only to people who were obviously physically handicapped or old. In Delhi, every time I stopped in a taxi at traffic lights, women clutching young babies begging for money bombarded me, but I soon found out that many of these women rented the babies for the day as a means of making an income. In rich countries we live in a bubble. We Westerners are divorced from the realities of poverty in the majority of the world. Yet as we shall be seeing, we are rich in part because our businesses and traders have been able to take advantage of a global trading arrangement that systematically disadvantages producers in the poorer countries. In this chapter we explore the causes of world poverty and possible solutions to it.

Spiritual insights on how to help people in poverty

Spiritual teachings of the different traditions are clear as to what we should do about poverty.

Christianity

Jesus pointed out that wealth - with the material goods and worldly pleasures it can bring—and the state of godliness or enlightenment pull us in opposing directions. To discover our true purpose in life—to have a good relationship with God—we first have to put aside our luxuries and the distractions of materiality. Jesus was a good example of someone whose happiness did not depend on his having material things, since he had complete faith that God would provide for him and his disciples all material needs. Jesus himself lived frugally; he spent his time amongst the poor and destitute. So Jesus by message and example highlighted how for those that could, offering help and support to the poor was a step closer to godliness. And it's not a big step from this to suggest—as Christianity has always implied - that wealth should be distributed more equitably. Yet until Socialism came along, little of lasting impact changed. The Labour party in the UK had some of its origins in Christian Socialism. Some Christians practise 'tithing,' giving 10 per cent of their income via the church to help the needy.

> *If you want to be perfect, go, sell your possessions and give to the poor, and you will have treasure in heaven. Then come, follow me* – Jesus, Matt 19:21
> *All the believers were together and had everything in common. Selling their possessions and goods, they gave to anyone as he had need* - Acts 2:44-45
> *Again I tell you, it is easier for a camel to go through the eye of a needle than for a rich man to enter the kingdom of God* – Jesus, Matthew 19:24
> *There will always be poor people in the land. Therefore I command you to be open handed toward your brothers and toward the poor and needy in your land* - Deut 15:11

Judaism

Judaism also is concerned with social justice and equality. Adam was the first amongst equals, so we all have the same root and have equal status in the eyes of God. As stated in Jewish law, it is the intention of God that wealth is shared. Under the Obligation of Tzedakah, Jews are required to give one-tenth of their income to the poor. Those dependent on public assistance or living on the edge of subsistence may give less; no person should give so much to make him a public burden. Tzedakah is the highest of all commandments, some say, and who fails to perform Tzedakah is equivalent to an idol-worshipper.

The religious Kibbutz provides a practical example of these benign principles. These small farming communities strive to be as self-sufficient as possible and to farm in a way to conserve the environment. They emphasise the sharing of effort and members share the proceeds of production.

And if you spend yourselves on behalf of the hungry and satisfy the needs of the oppressed, then your light will rise in the darkness - Isaiah: 58:10
If a man shuts his ears to the cry of the poor, he too will cry out and not be answered - Prov 21:13
He who oppresses the poor shows contempt for their Maker, but whoever is kind to the needy honours God - Prov 14:31

Islam

Muhammad lived a very simple and frugal life. He was always associating with poor people and gave any money he had away to them. *Zakat* is a tax of two and half percent of yearly income and Muhammad instructed that this be used to help the poor and needy. A Muslim can also give another voluntary contribution to help the poor called *Sadaqah*.

Help your neighbours - Muhammad
O ye who believe! Stand out firmly for justice, as witnesses to God, even as against yourselves, or your parents, or your kin and whether it be (against) rich or poor: for God can best protect both. Follow not the lusts, lest ye swerve and if ye distort (justice) or decline to do justice, verily God is well-acquainted with all that ye do – Qur'an 5:135
He is not a believer who eats his fill whilst his neighbour remains hungry by his side - Muhammad
Those who ill-treat others do not win Allah's favour - Muhammad
Poor is the man whose life shows no good deed - Muhammad
When you see a person who has been given more than you in money and beauty, then look to those who have been given less - Muhammad

Buddhism

The Buddha was keen on social justice. He said resources should be shared communally. The Buddha lived simply and frugally. In the monasteries and nunneries he set up, financial means are shared equally. He also emphasised that we must show compassion to all beings, implying that if someone is impoverished we should help them.

Give generously. Feel the power of generosity - The Buddha
Seek for the welfare of men but look not for recompense, not even to be born in heaven - Buddha
Meditate on pity so that you develop deep compassion for all beings in distress - Buddha

288

If you take care of each other, you will take care of all mankind
- Buddha
We can share the Earth and take care of it together rather than trying to possess it to destroy the beauty of life in the process - The 14th Dalai Lama
Being selfish, they only think about themselves and not others and this reflects their inner state -Tsering Tashi, Tibetan Monk at Nam Gyl Monastery, Dharamsala, India

Sikhism

All Sikhs are expected to work and not rely on charity; in fact they are expected to give 10 per cent of their income to community projects. This practice is called *Daswandth* and ensures that there is money available to help the less fortunate in society. Indeed, in Sikhism, *sewa* or service to others is emphasised constantly. Sikhism is Green because through teaching individuals and families the duties they have towards society it highlights the need for a more equitable society. All come as equals to the *Gurdwara* and sit on the floor with only the Guru Granth Sahib raised higher. All eat in the *Langar* or community kitchen together. In the sight of God all are equal. This engenders a marked sense of community, the antithesis of the self-centred society.

Riches cannot be gathered without sin - Guru Nanak
Under the Guru's instruction, regard all men as equal, since God's light is contained in every heart - Guru Nanak
There is no love of God without active service - Guru Granth Sahib
Only those who love can find God - Guru Granth Sahib
He alone, O Nanak, knows the way who earns with the sweat of his brow and then shares it with others - Mahalla I, p.1285
The Sikh basic principle of life is that we should be willing to serve the other - Dr. Surjeet Kaur Chalal, Lecturer at Pune University, India and writer on Sikhism and Ecology

Taoism

The Taoist concept of equality originates in the idea that the Great Tao gives birth to all human beings equally. Taoist scholars see all beings as equal and without difference in terms of their essentials. On the basis of the equal attributes of Tao, human beings share a common source. So notions of difference, discrimination and confrontation are unreasonable. Equality leads to concern for others and the generation of mutual love among people in a society. All people should share the wealth of the world. Guidance from the Celestial Masters in their scripture implores people to give assistance to the poor and oppressed.

Bahá'í
Bahá'ís have a Green view of social justice and equality and expect the better off to help the less fortunate. Bahá'u'lláh promoted the ideal of equality of wealth. Through laws that address extremes of wealth, Bahá'ís advocate an egalitarian approach. Baha'ís believe that all who work should contribute usefully to society. As they see it, you cannot contribute usefully *and* accumulate wealth at the expense of the poor. And if you are wealthy, it is your spiritual duty to help those in poverty. The poor, the elderly and the disabled should, they say, be provided for by a graduated income tax.

> *Be generous in prosperity* - Bahá'u'lláh
> *Equity is most fundamental amongst human virtues* - Bahá'u'lláh.
> *To serve mankind is to minister to the needs of the people* - Abdu'l-Baha

Hinduism

> *Action for one's own self binds; actions for the sake of others deliver from bondage* - Gandhi
> *Earth belongs to all, not to any individual* - Hindu Scriptures
> *Develop universal love gradually through selfless service* - Swami Shivananda

Poverty: its causes, our responses
Can Social Businesses tackle world poverty?
What would a visitor from Mars make of the extremes of inequality we have in the world today? What conclusions would s/he draw about the human race? Though deaths from famine do seem to have declined since the 1980s and 90s, many of us in the West realise it's still not a pretty picture. Instead we have growing numbers of climate change victims—of which Darfur is a sad but clear example—and increasing vulnerability to diseases which, as climate belts shift, are expanding their areas of impact, not to mention the ubiquitous spread of the deadly HIV/ Aids virus. Part of the many sided problem of poverty is that the better-off quarter of the human population know so little about the lives and

circumstances of the other three quarters. Because of this Westerners remain largely blind to the mechanisms and consumerist trends via which they contribute to global poverty often unwittingly: 'stretching the dollar in your pocket,' 'three for the price of two,' 'the £20 interview suit,' 'a complete wardrobe for under $100,' 'kitchen offer: £250 now, nothing to pay till 2011.' Price drives business. As competition forces prices unremittingly downward on our high streets, living standards are driven through the poverty floor in the countries supplying the fabric, the sweat labour, the timber pirated from fast-disappearing rainforest, giving another boost to climate change.

Poverty is still 'thriving' today: 2.8 billion people, or two in every five, are living on less than $2 a day. Poverty has many more agents working for it every day: majority world debt repayments—the much publicised debt cancellations by the G-8 in 2005 were but a pin-prick—unfair trade terms, exclusion from the money system to name but three.

The 18 countries given debt relief at the G8 Gleneagles meeting back in July 2005 represent only around 10 per cent of the global problem. Concessions on trade were derisory, with the US's massive exports of subsidy-assisted cotton still dominating that market worldwide. Much aid is still in the form of massive infrastructure projects which have been shown not to address poverty in any direct way, but to greatly benefit donor-country contractors instead.

Yet while the media give blanket coverage to the downside, the means of countering much of this is with us and has been shown to work: 'Social enterprises.' Millions of formerly poverty wracked families have been lifted to a new level where they can afford basic improvements to their homes and living conditions with perhaps a safe supply of water and even electric lighting and schooling for children for the first time. Many of these happy reversals, with stories that bring tears to the eyes, are down to a whole rash of 'social enterprises.' These are run by business people but they come from a new mould. For them, the results, the happy reversals, are in large part the reward. Not that they work for nothing. What's different is their reason for being in business. Freed of the corporate, shareholder-first creed, this new breed work to make profit for two reasons only: first, to repay the capital loaned by the businesses' founders or stakeholders; second to generate for the organisation sufficient additional surplus to fund its legitimate expansion to broaden the range and the number of beneficiaries. Such a business's 'output' might be the provision of care or of job training, literacy classes or a health clinic.

Few models better illustrate the new 'social business' than the one that has raised tens of millions of families out of poverty and debt through lending to people thought not to be trusted with money. With micro-credit 'circles,' villagers have helped one another keep their craft-based business on track, not just with astonishingly high repayment rates of over 97 per cent, but often then taking out still larger loans and further expanding their businesses - successfully. Most who take up the loans are working mothers. Micro-credit frees them from the bondage of loan sharks who kept them in dependency and poverty. The majority choose to see to their family's real needs first. Amazingly, some of these new entrepreneurs themselves have broader social aims, like the semi-literate lady in a favella in Brazil who one day took in a clutch of street children to stop gang fights and offered them a soda drink and a story. Today she is head teacher of a highly popular local school. One woman in Haiti sells beds second hand and on the proceeds has launched a social business providing affordable accommodation.

With high repayment rates unmatched in the West, micro-credit institutions have thrived and even up until May 2009 at least seemed to have maintained adequate inflows of capital despite the downturn. This has allowed steady expansion, especially over the past three years, in India, China and Indonesia in particular. So successful have they been that these majority world exemplars have served as models for the newest growth in micro-credit: tackling poverty in the rich countries themselves. With poverty levels in the UK as high as four out of ten families - for London, half that level nationally—it's more widespread than we may think. In France, where a micro-credit initiative began in the 1980s, there were in 2008 a reported 50,000 sole trader businesses up and running thanks to this form of 'bottom-up' social enterprise.

Population growth

When families are larger, children can go hungry; when families are smaller, there is more to go around and they are more likely to receive an education, even girls. When a girl who has received schooling grows up, she can see the misery of large families and she avoids that fate. There are more people on Earth now than there ever have been. Ninety per cent of population growth is in developing countries, whose people are poor and ill equipped to cope. In April 2010 the world population was 6.81 billion and growing at 80 million a year—an additional 1 *billion* every 12 years (for a rolling update see www.optimumpopulation. org/).

- **UN estimates for 2050 are: low, 7.5 billion; medium, 8.9 billion; and high, 9.1 billion.**
- **85 per cent of world population growth will occur by 2050.**

The greatest increases in population are recorded in the regions most prone to poverty. This is because poverty excludes education. Education is seen as the key to population balance and with it the elimination of poverty.

Sub-Saharan Africa already has the greatest increases in population at 3.2 per cent per year. Taking all of Africa, the population is projected to double to 2 billion over the four decades to 2050 and will then have 21 per cent of the world population. Within one decade, India will become the most populated country on Earth, overtaking China with a predicted population of 1.5 billion people by 2050.

Since the Industrial Revolution, people have been drawn to cities in search of employment and an easier way of life. Every year, another 66 million people move to urban areas so that by 2008 for the first time, urban dwellers outnumbered the world's rural population. In the least developed countries numbers of city dwellers will double in the next 30 years to 3.9 billion. Many who drift to cities do not find work. Because they are not supported by any kind of infrastructure in terms of housing, health and social services, one in four families in cities in the developing world live in poverty.

Few of us know about it, but a population time bomb is ticking away: nearly half the world's population is under 25 and they will soon reproduce. One obvious solution is the provision of education about birth control to help women control the size of their families. This is a case where the richer countries could provide resources to implement a worldwide birth control campaign, but this is not happening. The reason for this lies in cultural problems found in both poor and rich countries. The Pope has spoken out against any form of birth control apart from *coitus interruptus* and the rhythm method. As a result, millions of people in Catholic-controlled countries are denied access to this facility. In poorer rural areas of the world such as in India and Africa, large families are the cultural norm: a high infant mortality rate (down mostly to poverty) causes parents to imagine that they have to have additional children to ensure enough survive to work the land and look after them in their old age. In India, Hindu women are dominated by their husbands who are resistant to limiting numbers of children. This is encouraged by politicians of the Hindu far right. Muslims in India are also resistant to limiting numbers of children and in this they are encouraged by the Islamic fundamentalists. I heard of Muslim families in Delhi with up to 23 children - living in abject poverty.

What is clear is that when women have access to education, the standard of living—and the infant mortality rate - improves and, they have far fewer children. This is proven in the state of Kerala in India, which I visited. The first thing that struck me was that the urban landscape was not decaying due to population pressures as I had seen in Mumbai, Delhi and Kolkata. The Protestant union Church of South India has shaped the education system and this has resulted in literacy rates the equal of those in Europe. As women have become better educated they have limited their families. The population of Kerala state is declining.

Gap between rich and poor: spiritual causes
Greed and Materialism

There has always been a divide between rich and poor, but today's wealth gap is huger than ever. And this has been the cause of increasing acrimony and argument, both within Western societies and in the debate over social justice for the world. Some point to our capitalist system which they say was 'designed by the rich for them to get richer and richer, quicker and quicker—and it works.' Others see a system that celebrates a culture of greed, one by which much of the wealth of people in well off countries—and the elites within developing countries - is acquired at the expense of the poor. Certainly, the poor are excluded and the accumulation of wealth is driven by greed. It may help us to reflect upon spiritual teachings on greed.

Buddhism

Buddha taught people to 'walk the middle way' avoiding great wealth or degrading poverty. Buddha saw *Lobha* or greed as a defilement based on desire. He advised his monks to live simply and frugally, relying on what was essential for life. Buddha taught that it was delusion to seek happiness in the accumulation of material things

> *To live a pure unselfish life, one must count nothing as one's own in the midst of abundance* - Buddha
> *True happiness is not built on the sorrows of another* - Buddha

Hinduism

The Hindu ideal is the life of the *sannyasin* or holy man who has given up all desire for material things and wanders from place to place with few possessions. Hinduism calls on us to give up attachment to material things because it distracts us from the spiritual path.

> *The human being is greedy - after all, if there is no peace in their heart, they will be* - Swami Jivanmukhtananda, Rishikesh, India.

Christianity

Jesus was clear in his teachings that greed is an obstacle to coming closer to God. He taught that true wealth lay in heaven rather than on Earth.

> *It is more blessed to give than to receive* – Jesus, Acts 20:35
> *Watch out! Be on your guard against all kinds of greed; a man's life does not consist in the abundance of his possessions* – Jesus, Luke 12:15
> *The suffering of some can be blamed on the greed of others* - Mother Teresa

Jainism

Mahavira taught that attachments to the physical world are a barrier to spiritual progress. This is why Jain monks and nuns have so few possessions. The Jain laity follow the example of the monks and nuns. Also, the Jain vow of not stealing can prompt us to reflect on the world's limited resources and to recognise that we are effectively stealing the necessities of future generations. In Jainism using any resource beyond our needs or the misuse of any part of nature is considered a form of theft.

Sikhism

The Gurus laid emphasis on living a simple life with control and moderation without great attachment to material things. Sikh teachings are an antidote to materialism and selfish behaviour. As was said to me by my guide when I visited the Golden Temple at Amritsar, Sikhs should follow the rule of 'simple living, high thinking'. "The focus of life should be on God rather than the accumulation of material wealth."

> *They do well who have destroyed the five evils of lust, anger, greed, covetousness and pride; they shall be known as the inheritors of the kingdom of God* - Guru Granth Sahib

We should not be greedy all the time - and remember God - Dr. Indergit Kaur, Medical Doctor and Director of the Pulgalwara Charitable Society, Amritsar, India

Islam

Muhammad taught that attachment to material things interfered with concentrating on God.

> *Wretched are the slaves to wealth* - Muhammad
> *Allah has made it obligatory for them to pay the Zakat from their property and it is to be taken from the wealthy among them and given to the poor* - Book 23, Hadith 478
> *Blessed is the wealth of a Muslim from which he gives to the poor, the orphans and to needy travellers* – Muhammad, Book 24 Hadith 544
> *Happy is the man who is content with what he has* - Muhammad
> *There is no feast where only the rich are invited and not the poor* - Muhammad
> *If you cannot get things as much as you desire, then be content with what you have* - Ali ibn Abi Talib

Baháʼí

The accumulation of great wealth is seen by Baháʼís as a potential barrier to spiritual progress. Baháʼuʼlláh emphatically rejected the materialism of the West, when he said it brought "great evil upon men." To Baháʼís, there is advancement within material civilisation but only if taken in a truly balanced and harmonious way:

> *Material civilisation cannot advance without divine civilisation* - Baha' 'u' lla'h

Unequal share of resources

The expanding gap between the rich and the poor is the outcome of a complex mix of cultural, political and arithmetic factors. After seeking to understand this interplay, our challenge in the West is to find ways we can take some responsibility for the situation and its impacts.

- **1.2 billion of the world's poorest people are undernourished, underweight and often hungry. Meanwhile the 1.2 billion richest people are overweight, over-fed and in need of exercise. The poorest live on less than a dollar a day while** total global personal earnings are estimated at $24 trillion per annum.

- The number of people living in poverty with under a dollar a day has increased by 100 million in the last 10 years. The UN forecasts that another 100 million will be added by 2015.
- Today the poorest 20 per cent (1.36 billion people) only receive 1.1 per cent of the global income.
- 2.8 billion people, or two in every five, are living on less than $2 a day and this is considered the minimum for meeting basic needs.
- In 2004, average annual per capita income was $2,100 in the poorest countries compared to $30,000 in the richest countries.

Paradoxically India, with GDP annual growth rate of 8.1 per cent, was in 2006 home to more than 100,000 (dollar) millionaires, more than in many Western countries, but to millions in dire poverty as well. So the wealth gap is widening within developing countries as well as between these nations and developed economies.

Quite understandably increasing numbers of the not-so-poor in developing countries want to emulate the lifestyle of the wealthy. The harsh reality is the Planet does not have the raw materials to sustain this globally. But there is wide scope to pull people from the very depths of poverty. Of course, the American lifestyle, epitome of the consumerist dream, itself involves consuming at rates far beyond the sustainable capacity of the Earth. Yet, outside of the world faith communities, the many ills arising from the disparity in wealth between the rich and the poor continue to be overlooked, a sad reflection on the mores that go with the Western lifestyle now rapidly being adopted worldwide.

- The resources consumption of an average American citizen is 13 times more than a Brazilian, 35 times more than an Indian, 140 times more than a Bangladeshi and 250 times more than a citizen of Sub-Saharan Africa.
- Just 20 per cent of the world's people account for 86 per cent of private consumption.
- The richest 225 people in world had assets more than $1 trillion in 2007, which was approximately the combined annual income of almost half the world's population.

- It would take the resources of 30 planets to bring the world's poor to the level of consumption of the world's rich.
- The average income in the richest countries is 37 times greater than that in the poorest 20 countries.

Exploitation of the poor

Is ethical behaviour a hallmark of the human race as some claim it is? History suggests not. Economic exploitation may rate as less barbaric than military conquest but it is the modern equivalent. There is world wide a historical legacy of economic imperialism, of richer nations seizing the resources of poorer countries and using them to enrich themselves. The forefathers of today's Europeans included the Spanish conquistadors who plundered South America for gold, the Portuguese who colonised Brazil, the Spice Islands, Angola, Mozambique and Madagascar and Britain's merchants who indentured India and its swashbucklers who slaughtered tribespeople in pursuit of land, diamonds and gold in Africa and fed opium to the Chinese.

Dominance of the economic sort is nowhere more clearly illustrated today than by the advent of the trans-national corporation or TNC. Although these economic powerhouses operate across a vast array of countries of the globe, 90 per cent are headquartered in the USA, Europe or Japan. A corporation's raison d'etre and its *legal* primary obligation are to return maximum profit to shareholder investors. Because of their reach and resources TNCs are often in a position to outmanoeuvre the governments of the countries in which they operate. If one government acts against them they will move operations to another jurisdiction, flitting between continents to maximise profit. Information about environmental performance is often difficult to gain and since profit is always the first priority and compliance eats up profits, cases of flouting environmental regulations would fill many a book.

Corporations see opportunity in privatised utilities and natural resources such as water, gas, oil and in agriculture; they concentrate acquisitions in energy, communications, transport and water and sanitation sectors. Some have estimated that of the total land used to grow crops for export, TNCs own 80 per cent world wide. This is particularly significant in soy production in South America and palm oil in Malaysia and Indonesia, which have been shown not only to exploit poor workers but also to have destroyed massive areas of rainforest, the process now recognised as a greater cause of greenhouse gas emissions than all global transportation combined.

TNCs are also heavily involved in manufacturing in developing economies which their proponents claim bring benefits to the nationals of host countries who are employed. While there have been examples with positive outcomes, many less developed countries have fared less well over time. Countries desperate for foreign investment such as Sri Lanka, Vietnam, Mexico, Honduras, Haiti and Indonesia, invite corporations in only to find few real, long lasting benefits for their people. Often manufacturing takes place in free trade zones, where there are poor working conditions and with workers receiving no more than 1.3 per cent of the final price of goods and where governments have waived all revenues from trade tariffs. Wal-mart, Nike, Reebok, Apple and Adidas have been linked with practices such as these and said to be exploitative.

- **Of the world's 100 largest economies, 51 are transnational corporations.**
- **The combined sales of the top 200 corporations are greater than the sum total of the economies of 182 of the 191 countries in the world. This means there are only nine national economies larger than these 200 enterprises.**
- **The world's five largest companies have annual sales greater than the annual national turnovers of 46 countries.**

TNCs in reality do little to alleviate the poverty in their host countries. They do however contribute to the incomes of people in richer nations—shareholders, advisors, board members, consultants—and help them become even wealthier. As if this were not enough, TNCs often destabilise the economic infrastructure of local economies and destroy markets for local producers.

Poverty and trade

The persistence of poverty—indeed its spread—highlights the ineffectiveness of the systems in place to address it. That is perhaps why the World Trade Organisation (WTO), which sets and enforces the global rules of trade by which member countries have to abide, is the butt of such intense and long-lasting criticism: that the WTO is run by the rich for the rich and attaches little importance to the challenges facing developing countries. For example, rich countries have not fully opened their markets to products from poor countries. In 1999 this criticism came to a head when the WTO met in Seattle. The result was a mass anti-globalisation demonstration demanding more action on protecting the environment in the developing world and fairer trade. The Doha Round of world trade negotiations was launched in 2001 and has remained stalled for some years. One major unresolved issue is the subsidies that rich country governments in the EU and the US Federal government pay to their farmers. These subsidies are huge and completely counter to "free trade," yet they are still handed out. To avoid collapse, the WTO needs to reach a deal on this and other issues very soon.

At the root of the problem is a string of broken promises made by the EU and USA. When this round was launched, it was widely billed as the Doha Development Agenda, supposedly designed to deliver a trade deal that would genuinely help the world's poor. It would include ending farm export subsidies in the EU and US - against which developing country exporters cannot compete; also ceasing the periodic dumping on Third World markets of excess EU and US farm produce; and rolling back the damaging new agreements brought in by the last round of trade talks.

Yet the promised focus on a development agenda has proved completely hollow. The EU and US preserved their farm subsidies intact, while proposals to address the problems caused by previous agreements have been sidelined and forgotten. What is worse is that both the EU and US have tried to force developing countries to open up their agricultural, industrial and services markets to multinational corporations. It re-emphasises that in order to become members of the WTO club, they must first implement dubious economic reforms such as privatisation of water supply and other services. The result: local firms are driven out of business, hundreds of thousands of workers lose their jobs and millions *more* families are thrown into desperate poverty. Those who survive are forced into insecure or dangerous work at the margins of society.

Another factor generating poverty rather than prosperity for developing countries trading internationally is that governments are not in control, profit-driven corporations are. Their obligations to maximise profits leave no room for cares about the trading outcomes for poorer countries.

- **Cargill is a Canadian grain-trading giant controlling 60 per cent of the world trade in cereals. Cargill's 1990 turnover amounted to the same as Pakistan's GNP.**
- **Two thirds of the trade in the world is with the largest 500 TNCs.**
- **500 corporations control 70 per cent of all world trade, 80 per cent of foreign investment and contribute to 30 per cent of the global GNP.**
- **Trade between subsidiaries within the same parent corporation now accounts for one third of all world trade.**

With rich world TNCs having economic dominance and control of poor country natural resources, commodities, produce and trade, developing country businesses hardly get a look in on trade in world markets. For developing countries, 75 per cent of their export income comes from selling primary commodities, usually in the form of cash crops or minerals. Many countries depend almost entirely on a single product: Zambia produces copper, Uganda coffee, Ghana cocoa, Chad and Sudan cotton and the Caribbean islands bananas. If they can, corporations will fix prices and if—as happens a few times each decade - there are wild fluctuations on trade markets then the economies of these countries can be devastated overnight. Not only is the price of primary commodities dictated by developed country traders, it is not in their interest to sit and watch poorer countries gain a bigger stake in world trade. In one 20-year period the developing countries' share of world trade (not including oil) declined from a mere 15.2 per cent to 12.9 per cent.

First World countries create protective tariff barriers that deprive poorer countries of the opportunity to export manufactured goods made from local primary resources. For example, export of raw logs to a developed country often means the import duty is waived, but to export even sawn timber, a 5 per cent import duty is imposed which rises to 15 per cent for furniture exports. Corporations and richer countries still seek to fight off competition in the manufacturing sector - just where goods reach their highest value.

Richer countries also have an unfair advantage in the way they subsidise their agricultural products. For instance the EU Common Agricultural Policy gives unfair subsidy to arable and livestock products. Whole sectors of US agribusiness is built around subsidy, with a massive cohort of lobbyists paid handsomely to ensure no politician opposing the subsidy ever gets re-elected. They don't. It works. The US government recently subsidised cotton to the extent that the subsidy paid out was more than the value of the actual cotton. This action meant that Sudanese cotton farmers had to sell their cotton on world markets at a much lower price.

EU farmers and fisheries received in 2008 some €46.5 billion. The US total subsidy in 2004 was $8.022 billion: feed grain (35.4 per cent), cotton (17.7 per cent), wheat (14.6 per cent), rice (14.1 per cent)—last three: 46.4 per cent, total these four: 82 per cent of $8.022 billion.

Financial support to developing countries

The eight leading industrialized nations, USA, China, Germany, Japan, UK, France, Canada and Italy, have the power to determine the terms of world trade and how the debts owed by developing countries are treated. These debts, a number of them now accepted as of dubious origin, others as unjust, were incurred some as long as 30 years ago in what are now seen as a "mis-selling" situation. Developing nations were led to believe that the economic gains they would make in properly utilizing the loans would provide revenues more than sufficient to cover the interest due. For a much disputed set of reasons, however, it seldom worked out that way. Undoubtedly, with then young financial institutions often largely controlled by self-serving political elites in many or most developing countries, only fractions of the loaned funds were spent on the projects for which they were intended. So, serious shortfalls on returns were foreseeable. And the lenders, too, have their critics: these foreseeable difficulties could have been averted had they curtailed opportunities to misdirect funds. There was, also, unhealthy haste among lenders to 'get the business' for their nationals. This came in the form of contracts for massive infrastructure projects, both building them and supplying materials and equipment. These were massive projects, but while the gains TNC contractors made were massive and surefire, the gains to the economies of the developed nations in many instances were modest, in some cases too meager to pay the interest charges.

Some have argued that even if misdirected loan funds had never been an issue, the 'trickle down' model for the process of development based on massive projects has just never been shown to work. It's not difficult to see why. Benefits from massive projects accrue to the educated local elite and to the ex-patriot contractor management. Local labour gains little. So what happens might more accurately be described as 'within the bubble,' the bubble being a transplanted micro-economy that implodes as soon as the motorway or dam or airport project is completed.

Arguments over responsibility for outstanding debts and unpaid interest raged throughout the 1980s and 1990s. Eventually, there came a recognition that there was blame on both sides and that a resolution would benefit both sides. To traditionalists in the Western camp, such an idea would undermine all transactions and was unacceptable.

The supposed function of the World Bank is to lend money to poorer countries to help them develop. This institution, set up along with the UN in the post-WWII settlement, has 152 member countries, but with a 'one dollar one vote' principle control rests with the USA. It having put up 16 per cent of the capital, it can veto any action it does not like. About two thirds of the votes on the World Bank are represented by richer countries. G8 members control half the votes. Thus, poorer countries do not get a look in. This has severely distorted the Bank's priorities in favour of its majority members.

As a result, development priorities for poorer countries are overlooked, while aspirations on export of equipment, materials and expertise from wealthy nation members are met, often in full. What has happened in the past is that the bank has lent money to governments for very prestigious projects which have benefited few locals. An even worse scenario is where they have lent money which has contributed to further environmental destruction on a massive scale, such as in great dam projects or the building of the Trans Amazonian highway. The Trans Amazonian Highway project, since abandoned, predictably accelerated illegal logging and the consequent destruction of large swathes of the Amazon rainforest.

If a country gets into balance of payments difficulties then the International Monetary Fund, a World Bank subsidiary, intervenes. The IMF was intended to oversee currency values and provide short-term loans to countries with balance of payment difficulties. But now the IMF is using loans as a lever to force poor countries to adopt a raft of free-market measures, often to the detriment of them funding vital health and education projects. Sometimes there is rebellion against these reforms as in the case where the Bolivian Government stopped a US TNC taking over and took back control of water resources. More recently, Venezuela has started to renationalize its assets, sever connections with the IMF and tried to create an alternative financial institution to aid development throughout South America.

World debt
In the seventies and eighties Western commercial banks began lending money to poorer countries for 'development'. Some very large sums were loaned to fund ill-conceived projects which failed because of corruption or poor lender advice or, worse, paid to dictators sympathetic to American economic interests. This was the case in, for instance, Zaire (now the Democratic Republic of Congo) and Sierra Leone, where rich-world funds propped up corrupt and oppressive regimes. Most of these countries depended on the income from export of commodities to fulfill their debt commitments. The tragedy is that in the 1980s commodity prices crashed and interest rates climbed. The developing countries were not making enough money from exports to pay off their loans to foreign banks. By the mid-eighties the problem became the Third World debt crisis. It continues to the present day despite a Millennium promise from some countries to cancel these debts. Some of the very poorest countries have had their debts cancelled but for the majority it continues.

I was at the G8 protests in Edinburgh in 2005, trying to make trade justice a reality, for the poorer countries of the world to have their debts written off. Despite the media hype and the great triumph heralded by Bob Geldof, the pledges that richer countries have made to alleviate developing countries debt and improve trade, have not all been honoured. Now, many poor developing countries owe more in interest than they earn from exports.

- **The world's most impoverished countries are forced to pay over $100 million every day to the rich world in debt repayments, while poverty kills millions of their people.**
- **In 2006 the poorest 49 countries had debts totalling US $375 billion, whilst for the poorest 144 countries, it is over US $2.9 trillion.**
- **Debt repayments by some developing countries have reached nine times what they originally received from developed countries.**

The outcome of the debt crisis and economic dominance by corporations is that poverty in the world is perpetuated. In consequence, poorer countries cannot develop. They spend little on health, education, social services, industrial development or agriculture. Some have estimated that globally, 650,000 children die each year because of the debt crisis, which is not surprising in that it is estimated that 1.5 billion people have no access to any health services whatsoever.

- **In Africa they spend four times the amount in debt repayments as they do on education and health.**
- **In 2005/06 Kenya's budget for debt payments was as much as for water, health, agriculture, roads and transport combined.**
- **Annual expenditure on health per person per year in the USA is $2,765 whereas in Tanzania it is $4 and Ethiopia $2.**
- **UNICEF estimates that each day 4,000 young children less than five years of age die from disease and malnutrition.**

The debt crisis prevents governments from dealing with common potentially fatal diseases such as polio, TB, diphtheria, whooping cough, typhoid, tetanus, measles, plague, anthrax, rabies, cholera, influenza and rubella. WHO estimates that 3 million children are dying each year because of lack of vaccinations. Administering vaccinations and antibiotics to under-fives would cost $2.6 billion and save the lives of the majority of children.

The governments of poor countries can offer no social security for those unemployed, no guaranteed medical care and no right to education, food or shelter. These human rights are enshrined in UN charters and taken for granted in developed countries because they have the resources to fund them.

Aid to developing countries

So, if certain countries are as poor as this, why can rich countries not give them aid? Well, in 1968 UN member states agreed that 0.7 per cent of the GNP of each country should go towards foreign aid. Only Denmark, Sweden, Norway, Netherlands, Kuwait and Saudi Arabia have regularly met this commitment. Yet the USA, the richest country on Earth, being 2.5 times wealthier than after WWII, gives only 0.22 per cent of its GNP, which is less than any other industrialised country.

USA contribution in 1970 was 0.32 per cent of GNP, yet by 1990 it was down to 0.21 per cent, just one third of the agreed UN goal.

- **Development assistance decreased from $69 billion in 1992 to $53 billion in 2000.**
- **In the past decade the real value of aid to developing countries has declined by 8 per cent.**

Spiritual and physical responses to world poverty

In rich countries, we cannot totally redress the harm done to poorer peoples by our forefathers in the imperialistic era. What we can do is to reflect on spiritual insights into how to help those in poverty based on commonly held principles of social justice. Leaders from throughout the spiritual traditions have been living examples of helping the poor and downtrodden. Many spiritual leaders have in fact led their lives among the poor and destitute, setting examples for us all. What is clear is that the spiritual traditions have demonstrated the values of love, compassion and understanding involved in helping those in poverty. If we are to make inroads into global poverty, we who are alive today need to rediscover the same values and apply them. We do well to remember that it is poverty that, via the ballooning of population that it brings, underlies virtually ALL the other crises facing the World as we enter the second decade of our 21st century.

The Make Poverty History campaign attracted 100,000 to its Edinburgh march at the G8 in 2005. People wanted to write off the debts of poorer countries and end TNC dominance in international commodity trade. Governments have it in their power to control corporations and make sure there is a fair deal in trade for the poor. Governments are quite able to increase the percentage they give in aid and development with no strings attached to help poor countries find their way out of poverty, but they need to be told loud and clear to do so. People can campaign, too, for the UN to take action to relieve the suffering of the poor.

As of 2009, 24 highly indebted poor countries have had their debts written off. With the world recession some developed countries will be more reluctant to meet their commitments to help with debt relief, though at least the UK has done so. This still leaves 41 potentially eligible poor countries to receive debt relief in the future.

After debt is written off and aid increased, the international community needs to overhaul the whole trading system. Subsidies and import taxes operated by rich countries should be stopped to allow poorer countries to export primary and manufactured goods to them. Commodities prices on international markets should be set at fair levels ensuring real increases in income for poorer countries which would allow development.

Poorer countries have to play their part by addressing their increasing populations. Some of the best investment opportunities for richer countries are to help fund resources in areas like poverty reduction, birth control and the education of women. Poorer countries, particularly in Africa, need to prioritise the problem of corruption, where government officials frequently pocket aid given by richer countries or use it to fund lavish lifestyles and the fleets of sleek 'official' limousines thereby perpetuating poverty in the countries they pretend to serve.

In our own lives we can make a difference. One way that we can relieve the poverty of the poor is by buying their products at a fair price and this is where the Fair Trade goods campaign comes in. I have supported the Fairtrade campaigns locally in Leamington, UK, writing and performing a song to promote Fairtrade shops in Leamington Spa. We can also avoid buying goods that are produced exploiting workers with low pay, unhealthy conditions and long hours. We can donate more of our income to projects helping those in poverty in developing countries, for instance by giving regularly to OXFAM or another development NGO. And we can speak up for fair trade everywhere.

Poverty action ideas

1. Join a campaign organisation that is fighting for justice for those in poverty. www.waronwant.org www.makepovertyhistory.org www.one.org www.millenniumcampaign.org www.peopleandplanet.org www.wdm.org.uk

2. Join your local United Nations Association group to pressurise the UN to fight poverty in the world. www.un.org www.unsystem.org www.undp.org

3. Campaign to help lift children out of poverty. www.unicef.org www.care.org www.globalfundforchildren.org www.christian-aid.org www.savethechildren.org

4. Join a campaign for fair trade for poor nations. www.maketradefair.com www.globalexchange.org www.

fairtrade.org www.wdm.org.uk www.mainefairtrade.org
www.sierraclub.org www.oxfam.ca

5. Buy products where the producers get a fair return.
www.fairtradefederation.com www.fairtrade.org
www.leagueofartisans.org www.getethical.com www.
ethicalwares.com

6. If you are a student or an active retiree, think about taking
a gap year to help people in poverty. www.gapyear.com
www.unitedplanet.org www.realgap.com

7. Sponsor organisations which are trying to help poor
countries deal with population increases. www.
overpopulation.org www.globalpovertychallenge.com
www.optimumpopulation.org

8. Donate unwanted possessions to shops that raise funds to
address poverty in the developing world. www.oxfam.org
www.christian-aid.org

9. If you have a skill or enthusiasm give up a year and
volunteer to help in a poor country. www.vso.org www.
ifrevolunteers.org www.jubileeventures.org www.
thisisthelife.com

10. Campaign to have the debt by poorer countries cancelled
www.jubileedebtcampaign.org www.usccb.org www.
millenniumcampaign.org www.makepovertyhistory.org

PART 3

EVOLVING FROM DYSFUNCTIONAL TO FUNCTIONAL

CHAPTER 20 : YOU ARE THE EMERGENCY SERVICES

Dreams and visions of Utopia

Having dreams and visions is natural especially when you are young. In an age of pathological conformity it is a blessing to have a dream, a vision of a positive future. This book is the result of a vision I had in 1971. I was 21. It arose in response to a report on environmental problems of global proportions. Experts for the Club of Rome stated we were already in 1971 living beyond our means in terms of using up resources, behaving unsustainably and destroying eco systems. The report had a profound effect on me.

My vision was of a society that fulfilled humankind's physical, cultural and spiritual needs yet which did not damage our environment. The basis of this society was consciously planned, dynamic communities of an optimum size that could be supported largely by the resources found in their locales. As all activities of the community would be ecologically benign, the ecological footprint of each member of the community would be sustainable.

I envisioned that all community members would jointly own the means of production and share equally in its fruits. All members of the community would spend time each week working on the land and thus maintain their connection with nature. The people would treat the Earth with respect by maintaining a non-exploitative economy producing goods that were needed using renewable energy and local resources and practising organic agriculture.

The community would democratically elect representatives who would help run the community for the maximum happiness of the majority. This happiness would be created in the individual and thus the whole community by each person pursuing their own spiritual path supported by an enlightened educational system and a variety of spiritual centres. This happiness would be further enhanced by encouraging cultural pursuits of all kinds with full participation of community members. So in my utopian society everyone's physical, emotional, intellectual, social and spiritual needs were met.

Though it remains the vision of an idealistic 21-year-old, untainted by experience of my personal limitations and those of mankind, to me this vision seems today, 40 years later, more relevant than ever as a signpost, at least. We have all slipped from these ideals, and understandably. But contained within them is, I believe, the essence of what we need to be striving to reinstate: respect for life, for humans, for Nature, for the essence in each one of us, for a spirituality that is Green.

A turning point in history

Those of us alive today are witnessing arguably the single most challenging epoch in the entire 50,000 year timeframe of mankind: it's clear from our reviews of the comprehensive nexus of global crises arising all around us - on land, in sea, air and climate and on energy, food and water supplies, on population and social justice - that much of what we know of Earth today will be changed within less than two generations.

And, from our unique end-of-era vantage point—viewed as a 250 year run since the onset of industrialisation, as the 5,000 year era since agriculture caught on or as the 50,000 year epoch since the emergence of homo sapiens—we can see more clearly now than even 12 months ago the divergence point, that the moment of choice is now at hand: we - or some growing number of us - can see where 'business as usual' is taking us and we're clear we don't want to go there. We must now realise that we are all in this together and we need to choose to take decisive action individually, collectively, regionally, nationally and internationally. And it won't happen without a concerted push.

So we know we want an alternative path. The question is how do we create a consensus on what that alternative path should look like? Then we would need to successfully make the case for taking it. It's clear not everyone wants to join us, or not at least while Nature keeps showing restraint on climate and disease.

Do not be concerned if the route seems daunting. It may matter less than we imagine. Why? Because ultimately what counts is not the ideas of our outdated models of thinking in politics, economics or the media; what counts is the individual. Increasingly the influence of the individual, often aggregated via NGOs and web campaigns such as

Avaaz, is being felt right up at national government and cabinet and Administration level as with the passing of the UK Climate Bill. Totally against the government's original intention, the amended Climate Act 2008 calls for an 80 per cent cut in GHG emissions (in place of 60% in the Bill) by 2050 (not 2060) and it has emissions from Aviation and Shipping included (not excluded as in the bill).

Make no mistake, the number of people already taking active and co-ordinated steps to green our civilisation was even in 2006 estimated in the millions. Green organisations are active in virtually every aspect of the biosphere and in every nation on Earth. The list of their specialisms runs to over 350 (see www.wiserearth.org).

Intentional communities - model for the future?

Pre-eminent among green action-takers are the members of intentional communities around the world of whom there are as many as a quarter of a million living in thousands of settlements often defined principally by their minimal eco-impacts. In their commitment to their low-impact choices, these individuals are visionaries. The lifestyles they enjoy, with greatly increased reliance on local resources and local skills and talent, serve as inspiring examples for how our children might choose to live if they commit their lives to saving themselves from the destructive effects of the consumerist lifestyles we still pursue today.

Through their experiments in living, these pioneers teach us that people in ways as diverse as ever can lead fulfilling lives and enjoy committed relationships with each other and with the Earth.

Further, as anyone who has spent time in an intentional community will tell you, they teach us that to engage in authentic relationship we must first engage in a personal journey in search of our own authentic self. And it may—or may not - be here that one or other of the Spiritual Traditions that we have visited has a part to play. A look at the activities of individuals associated with one intentional community illustrates this.

- Working for a monthly allowance as an in-house volunteer in close-knit teams providing the community's basic daily needs in tasty meals, home-care, home grown produce, uplifting grounds, inspiring spaces for community events and for daily quiet-time or meditation, programmes for memorable community events and a programme of public event offerings which may generate significant parts of community revenues; or

- Working as one engaged with an affiliated unit doing business within the local and national economies and who 'subscribes' to or helps provide community services on offer.

These are illustrations of the work component of communal living only. Individual members, either alone or together in groups small or large pursue a vast array of interests, some such as dance and music often more visible than others such as study or writing or one of the many craft activities often catered for.

Necessity is the Mother of Invention but perhaps of Adoption, too: for knowing that business as usual is the short cut to annihilation we will find ourselves *choosing* to adopt one of these lifestyles and the reordered value systems they embody. And so the Future Pathway Question may be seen as a challenge to our creativity, our imagination and our powers of visioning: how *would* we like to live our lives and to bring up our children? How *would* we like to enable exchange between ourselves so that we continue to enjoy some of the conveniences and comforts to which we became so accustomed?

It is just these questions that have exercised the minds, hearts and spirits of most of the 250,000 and upwards of members of intentional communities that have been functioning around the globe for much of the past 15 to 50 years and longer. So we've gathered here the results of a brief survey of their lifestyle choices, values and successes. I believe they have earned our gratitude.

We need to replace the all-out consumerism being spread virally via TV to the last of the world's rural poor. We need to find a sustainable alternative, one in which rural people, who are much closer to it than urban dwellers, can thrive not starve. The new model we need for all is based on living sustainability. And if we are to avoid the spread of endless conflicts such as suffered by the Darfuris, the Palestinians and the Afghanis, we must have social and economic justice as well as environmental justice. So if humanity is to make these evolutionary leaps, we will need a society based on principles of a social justice that encompasses our surroundings, a healthy biosphere and humans operating in balance with Nature.

Ideals such as these may sound heady and unrealisable but thanks to the many intentional communities around the world we have amassed many decades of experience in living out just such goals. Intentional communities appeal to me because they attempt to address some of the most fundamental, unresolved problems associated with our present system: they take seriously the responsible use of resources; they ensure the resources are shared; and by setting levels of reward that match commitment they address all the vexed issues around the widening disparities of wealth.

Some of these communities would recognise themselves in the following definition of an eco-village: "a human scale, full-featured settlement which integrates human activities harmlessly into the natural environment, supports healthy human development and can be continued into the indefinite future." This is a concept that has passed the test of time for over four decades or more. In 1994 the Global Eco-village Network (the definition is theirs) was formed by Robert and Diane Gilman who researched intentional communities.

An eco-village is a community of 50 to 2,000 people united by a common goal, usually based on shared ecological, social and/or spiritual values. They share a vision of living in small communities that are both fun to live in and at the same time are closely connected to Nature and Spirit and exemplify the need to live more lightly on the Earth. The variations however are endless.

We cannot here do justice to the delicately woven webs of personal connection, collaboration and inspiration created by individuals. Each of these intentional communities has its own wavelength, life-force, its own ethos and ways of maintaining and renewing its vitality. We cite them as examples for inspiration, what our western society now needs more than anything.

At close on 2,000 souls, Auroville's network of some 90 communities has described itself as the world's first 'Ecoville'–though it is very much a part of the Global Eco-village Network. An example of a planned ecological community, it was founded in south India in 1968 by Mirra Alfassa also known as the Mother. She was inspired by her guru, Sri Aurobindo to found a "universal township" with the guiding principles that it was to be a spiritual community focussing on divine progress and human unity using educational, environmental, cultural and spiritual research to achieve these ends. Auroville's community today come from 35 countries. It boasts more than 100 small handicraft businesses as well as technical centres researching energy systems and eco-building and housing. The land its members steward, some 1,200 ha (3,000 acres) was formerly eroded and barren. They have planted nearly 2 million trees. Having visited Auroville myself, I can vouch that it is a well ordered and peaceful place.

Models for a sustainable green economy

The Twin Oaks Community in the USA is an income-sharing community of 100 people living on 180 ha (450 acres) of farmland and forest in Virginia. Community lifestyle reflects values of egalitarianism, income sharing, eco-living and non-violence. The Twin Oaks community, founded in 1967, collectively owns everything. Members work on the land and in community businesses up to 44 hours a week and in return the community provides all basic needs such as housing, food and clothing.

The Farm in Tennessee in the USA, 405 ha (1,000 acres), was one of the earliest eco-villages, founded in 1971 by social innovators from San Francisco. Now with 300 members, it exemplifies good use of local resources and prowess in skills development. This community specialised in growing soy beans and consequently developed expertise in the production of tofu and soy milk for sale. Farm members developed expertise in other areas. The Book Publishing Company and an Eco-village Training Centre are both commercial successes.

Auroville's Industrial Zone for Green industries focuses on creating a self-supporting township. It provides individuals with special skills and the opportunity to develop human scale services and industries: guest houses, building construction units, information technology, small and medium scale businesses producing items such as handmade paper, incense and other arts and crafts. Over 5,000 people, mostly from nearby localities, are employed in Auroville's many enterprises.

The Findhorn eco-village in northern Scotland was founded in 1962 on a 12 ha (30 acre) site and by the 1980s had grown to some 300 members. Though now the Foundation has fewer than 100 in-house members, a loose but committed mainly local community of an estimated 500 regulars engage in its projects and businesses and contribute in other ways. Beyond a very special ethos and energy field, Findhorn Foundation's skills and expertise are essentially practical, organisational, inspirational and educational in a wide range of areas including cultivation, sustainable living and spirituality. Its wide ranging programme of courses regularly attracts up to 9,000 participants a year.

A successful publishing company specialises in alternative lifestyles and sustainability. An on site wind energy business that sells surplus electricity to the National Grid is also exemplary. One study found that Findhorn had the lowest-ever ecological footprint of any community in the industrialised world.

Damanhur, in Italy, is an eco-village focussed on culture. It was founded in 1975 when a group of people came together around the figure of philosopher and healer Oberto Airaudi to plan the creation of a new society where everyday life could be the practical application of spiritual values. There are now 800 members who are organized as a federation of separate communities, with their own currency, constitution, schools, flag, calendar and daily newspaper. Damanhur demonstrates economic diversity as only an eco-village can. Their farms produce wines and cheeses, crafts people produce glass, pottery, jewellery and hand woven shawls and therapists have developed a line of natural healthcare products.

Svanholm Eco-village near Copenhagen, in Denmark was founded in 1978 with the purchase of over 405 ha (1,000 acres) of land and it now has 130 residents. They specialise in growing organic produce particularly carrots, potatoes and onions which are sold in Denmark. In all, Svanholm produces over 50 per cent of its own food.

Back in 1966, in Latin America, a group of scientists, artists, agronomists and engineers set up the Gaviotas Community in the Llanos area of Colombia lead by Paulo Lugari. This community set about creating a new local resource in planting 1.6 million Caribbean pine. By harvesting the resin then refining it in a process they pioneered, this innovative community now produce a bio-liquid, eco-friendly turpentine. The pollution-free factory to refine the resin won Gaviotas the 1997 United Nations World Zero Emissions Award. Gaviotas's technologists broadened its economy further by developing innovative designs for solar cells, water pumps and a particular "sunflower" type of wind turbine which they have since successfully installed in locations throughout South America.

Also in Colombia, the Sasardi Eco-village deliberately set up their community in 1985 in the middle of a rainforested region in order to promote and protect its bio-diversity. Sasardi uses the local natural resources to generate income in a sustainable way by producing jewellery, carved animal figures and wooden kitchen accessories using wood and seeds. Bags and baskets out of natural palm fibres and oil essences and wild fruits from the forest plants are further examples of generating wealth from the forest with zero negative impacts.

Models of sustainable culture

Damanhur has a unique spiritual and religious group whose beliefs are derived from several ancient traditions both Christian and Pagan. Damanhur is renowned throughout the world for the Temples of Humankind, an underground work of art, completely realised by hand. The Halls of Water, Earth, Spheres, Mirrors, Metals, the Blue Temple and the Labyrinth are all used for cultural and spiritual activities. All members of the community participate in courses aimed at personal and spiritual development and study in different schools of meditation, social theory and realisation, 'The Game of Life' and individual inner refinement.

Auroville's commitment to art, music, dance and culture has remained undiluted, recognising that honouring beauty and the inner being nourishes the imagination and brings joy of a profound sort. This 'cluster of eco-villages' has more than 25 experimental schools, a large healing centre and impressive programmes in martial arts, Indian studies and linguistics, including Sanskrit. Its iconic central dome is dedicated to contemplation and inner work. And Auroville now has its own television and radio stations that broadcast to the community and can be accessed via the web.

Models of democracy

In many of the communities I have looked at, things are decided by consensus. Achieving consensus often involves serial meetings, a sometimes lengthy process. At Zegg, an intentional community in Germany, they have developed a novel form of community meeting called the Forum, a ritualized and creative space that deepens communication.

The Zegg Forum offers a stage upon which an individual can express directly to all present their thoughts, feelings or anything that moves them. This supports a healthy transparency when it comes to the issues of love, power and decision structures. It helps to maintain a clear distinction between factual discussion and emotional processes. The forum has proved a significant building block in the development of self-knowledge and trust within this community.

Treating water with respect

If there is one lesson to be taken from all the world's sad tales of scarcity of water fit to drink, it is that we must treat it as a precious resource. The attitudes adopted by Jains and Hindus - who see water as a living being which must never be wasted or polluted - is helpful here. The teachings of Islam on the need to share water beyond just self-interest show people how they can avoid conflict over water supplies.

There are many examples of communities overcoming or averting the problems with water we discussed in Part 2. One way of keeping sewage from polluting the local water sources is by using a dry composting toilet. The basic idea is to separate liquid and solid wastes and leave the solids to decompose naturally to a rich compost. A very different, wet technique involves creating beds of reed that by encouraging microbe activity aid the decomposition of toxic organic compounds. This technology was pioneered at an eco-village in Denmark by Jorgen Logstrup. The Torup Eco-village was founded in 1988 with 13 ha (32acres) of land and now has 150 plus residents.

At Findhorn they have developed the "Living Machine" water treatment system. Sewage is passed through a series of tanks containing bacteria which break it down naturally to where conditions become favourable for raising aquatic plants and fish. The water is thoroughly purified and can then be recycled.

Back at Auroville, the department for water resource management has run the water harvest project since 1996. This organisation has even had success in preventing seawater intrusion into agricultural land, one of the most destructive aspects of sea level rise associated with global climate change. Aroville's team has also pioneered small-scale sewage treatment plants some of which not only produce fertilizer and biogas but drinkable water. Success in bringing soil erosion in the monsoon season under control by skilful surveying, landscaping, their massive plantings and water harvesting serves as a beacon of excellent practice.

Crystal Waters, in Australia, has developed what they call a biolytic water filter system. Equipped only with a water pump, this system in conjunction with worms kept busy digesting organic waste, treats all human and kitchen waste to produce naturally clean water. This community, established in 1988 on 260 ha (640 acres), now has 230 members. In 1995 it won a UN award for demonstrating sustainable living.

Taking care of the food chain

Our review of food production pointed to a world facing rampant desertification and at risk of impending famine. Yet the 2009 harvest broke records—as it needed to—and *still* 1 billion people went hungry. In a world of plenty it is disgusting that people die of malnutrition. As industrialised farming pushes the surviving subsistence growers off their lands, the market economy is undermining what self sufficiency remains in rural areas of the developing world. That trend will need reversing. Eco-villages are playing the role of laboratories testing new approaches to the age-old challenge of growing more food than the growers themselves require. In doing so, many are re-discovering the deep respect - reverence, even - for soil and the miraculous ways it brings forth nourishment that we lost to agribusiness.

Twin Oaks produces approximately 75 per cent of all its own food. For meat and dairy food the community is about 95 per cent self sufficient. They also grow organic vegetables, reducing their impacts on the Earth (including the energy for transportation and refrigeration) and providing healthier food for themselves. Their organic methods release nothing toxic into the environment.

Since 1975 organic farming and self-sufficiency in food have been priorities for Damanhur, where they produce 50 per cent of all their own food. It has pigs and cattle and fish farms; it produces vegetables, fruit, milk, cheese, oil, cereals and bakery products, wine and honey.

Permaculture Design is an approach to living with a system of growing based on co-operation with nature and caring for the Earth and its people. There is maximum food production consistent with minimum disruption of natural systems. Crystal Waters was founded on these principles. It is now a centre for teaching Permaculture, which was originally developed in Australia.

Auroville adopted a Permaculture approach to its massive land restoration project. Over a 20 year period, land that had been severely scarred by gully erosion now has established forests that produce food and sustainable firewood for local communities.

Clearing the air, slowing the climate changes

Air and our atmosphere are vital parts of the global commons. Restoring their purity and minimizing air pollution of all forms are crucial to our shared future. Eco-villages strive to raise energy efficiency and energy independence ever higher as they move their entire communities to low-carbon living.

Examples of communities using environmentally friendly and progressive building methods to create energy-saving buildings and using self build techniques include Findhorn, Sieben Linden, Twin Oaks, the Farm and Torup. The serious energy savings come when you build with materials that have low embedded energy. This rules out most metals, cement concrete and wall linings from gypsum plaster.

Big energy companies forget to remind us that the cheapest energy of all is the energy you avoid using—through its conservation. Flemming Abrahamsen and Kolja Hejgaard in Denmark and David Eisenberg of the Development Center for Appropriate Technology in Tucson, Arizona in the US have all developed building techniques that enhance energy efficiency while using low-energy, natural building materials. And Findhorn runs highly practical courses on eco-building every year.

The Centre for Alternative Technology in Wales in the UK and the Folkecenter for Renewable Energy in Denmark have been instrumental in developing and promoting alternative energy of every kind. CAT's 'Zero-Carbon Britain' report caused stirs within the UK energy industry and in the corridors of Whitehall, where new nuclear had been facing setbacks over safety.

Eco-villages have pioneered the use of sustainable, non polluting energy production. Damanhur, in the forefront of adopting new technologies, especially solar, generates 30% of its electricity via photo-voltaic and micro-hydro with plans to add another 500 kW. Meanwhile 90 per cent of all its heating comes from carbon neutral wood from sustainable sources.

At Kibbutz Samar in Israel the abundant desert sunlight is harnessed to produce electricity via pV. Formed in 1976, Samar is now home to 100 families. The world's first solar *hybrid* power plant was set up here in June 2009. Besides solar energy, the power station can run on alternative fuels including bio-gas, bio-diesel and natural gas. This pioneering station, on which 70 households depend, keeps producing electricity even at night or when it is cloudy.

As well as wind energy developed from its early days, Findhorn had by 2006 expanded this to 750 kW capacity with any surplus generating revenues. Findhorn also uses solar thermal heating extensively on buildings. Gaviotas's special sunflower type of wind generator has taken off and is used throughout South America. And it has its success generating electricity using bio-fuel made from refined pine resin.

So while Big Energy fought off the changes vital to our survival, eco-villages have clocked up decades' worth of low-carbon living experience. At Sieben Linden a University of Kassel study found that CO_2 emissions per capita were 28 per cent of the German average. At eco-village Ithica in US one survey found that one of its neighbourhoods used 40% less energy than similar homes in the region. And in a survey of carbon footprints, the average UK eco-village per capita footprint is under half the national average and is falling.

Preserving bio-diversity for all

At Auroville over two million forest trees, nut and fruit trees, hedges and shrubs have been planted to restore - and now increase - biodiversity. The Gaviotas village is noted for the planting of over 1.5 million trees in its area and excitingly creatures such as deer, anteaters, capybaras and eagles are now returning. The Farm has created a Swan Conservation Trust and thereby protected 400 ha (1,000 acres) of wildlife habitat. At the Mbham Faoune Eco-village in Senegal they have started to reverse the destruction of mangrove swamp forest by re-planting. By restoring biodiversity Mbham is helping the fishing industry by restoring vital breeding grounds and nurseries for fish of all kinds.

Trees for Life, founded in 1989 at Findhorn by Alan Watson Featherstone, has the vision of re-establishing a vast, 155,400 ha (600 square mile) area of the ancient biome of the primeval Caledonian Forest. In 20 years, its mainly volunteer work parties had planted 800,000 trees and restored 4,500 ha (11,250 acres) of forest land now protected from over-grazing by deer. Wild boar re-introductions have begun. Beaver are next.

The Manitou foundation which helped establish so many spiritual communities in Colorado has created the Earth Restoration Corps. It trains young people in conservation and operates many projects both in Colorado and the Amazon.

Sasardi Eco-village works with the Darien Foundation to maintain the bio-diversity of the Sasardi Natural Reserve in Colombia. They are guiding locals on preserving their area's unique bio-diversity, particularly the Leatherback Sea Turtle and on tree planting.

There are, mercifully, thousands more examples of biodiversity restoration all over the world. Can anyone say the world lacks models and examples of protection and restoration of bio-diversity? With 2010 the UN Year of Biodiversity, perhaps we need full recognition of the importance of Nature's richness and to celebrate it wholeheartedly.

Cutting out waste—at source

Unremarkably, recycling rates are close to 100 per cent in most eco-village settlements, though of course volumes are exceptionally low. Most members avoid purchasing everyday items in packaging that give rise to waste, thus modelling a much needed trend. Some eco-villages, such as Monksogaard in Denmark were planned around their recycling needs.

There is also a healthy tradition in reusing materials for building. This is very prevalent in the eco-house buildings at Findhorn, Twin oaks, Torup, Sieben Linden and Lebensgarten.

The Global Eco-village Network brings an international dimension to the movement. Regular educational and cultural exchanges and an annual conference allow communities to exchange ideas and developments and share resources. The co-operative spirit within communities is reflected in GEN personnel exchanges. It has blossomed in the new Gaia University, the first online source for quality learning in sustainability. These people want us all to have a world that works—by creating harmoniously *with* Nature, not working against her.

Models for combating world poverty

Eco-villages provide an excellent model of the fair sharing of resources so nobody descends into poverty nor reaps outlandish rewards. Typically, community members agree levels of allowance for different levels of commitment. This eliminates not only the issues of both poverty and extreme wealth but also addresses the need to live in ecologically benign ways. True wealth for community members is found in pursuing a life rich in personal fulfilment including service to the community, spirituality and cultural engagement. With shared goals like these, common ownership of the means of production and the equipment needed to generate the revenue that allows the community to function properly is only natural.

The Farm eco-village provides a good example of helping the poor. Its members formed an organization called Plenty International to help poor people affected by natural disasters. In 1976, after a devastating earthquake, a hundred volunteers travelled to Guatemala to help build a soy dairy and health clinics.

Individual solutions
The change we need and how we bring it about

The UN's Copenhagen COP15 failure provided a harsh reality check: mostly it's only the victims of climate change and their sympathisers who are prepared to look climate change head on and take measures. It is those most entrenched in high carbon activities that have most power in the world as we find it today—industrialists, traders, bankers and financiers, four-home jet-setters, long-haul commuters, four-car home owners and the like. Some might say we should focus our education efforts on them. Others say they will never be persuaded and that it is the operating rules of the world we need to change: redistributing not just some of the wealth but the power that goes with it.

Perhaps this is the tack emerging from Bolivian president Evo Morales's initiatives to bring ecocide into the code of international law. Victims of environmental damage would then have some prospect of remedy and perpetrators would have reason to properly consider their actions. It appears we may be entering a new phase where those humans on the receiving end of ecocide's impacts for the first time gain influence over the behaviour of the exploiters.

One challenge is that we are all, in some measure, exploiters either directly through what we ourselves do in travel and in our purchases or indirectly by what we demand or expect as consumers. So blaming others may not be the best way forward.

In the west, we need to own up to those of our purchases and our habits that put work into the hands of those exploiters—in meat and its rainforest component (soy feed), in 'cheap' (illegally caught) fish, in gadgets and their rare metal components, in new-fired bricks and high-temperature cement, mortar and metals, in pirated rainforest garden furniture, in ex-orang utang habitat palm oil buiscuits, in unnecessary high-emission flights to overseas holiday destinations. What we can hope is that our future choices will reflect what we learn about the impacts of our past choices. Certainly, it is truly an inspiration to find every day new offerings in ways we can fulfil our needs and make our choices without adding to the escalating global crises.

Meanwhile, down-home local campaigners continue the struggle to persuade neighbours and anyone they can find in their communities to engage in de-carbonising their lifestyles. However, there is now a recognition of a deep inbuilt resistance in most of us to making changes more radical than a few items from 'the 50 things you can do' list. Apparently, we're most of us resistant to undertaking anything unless and until our friends and neighbours are undertaking them, too. This is social resistance. Unless and until we understand it, we campaigners will only push people away. To our aid comes depth psychology, an area now being explored and avowed by fast growing numbers of people, many of them engaged in an innovative phenomenon which has 'gone viral' around the world, the Transition Towns movement, which is seen as a beacon of hope.

Here, then, we examine examples from the six major global environmental issues and world poverty from the point of view of a typical, unengaged individual in the west.

The individual and water use

Our taps and our loos have no day-glow orange warning signs "Using this appliance may endanger untold numbers of life forms in your watershed area." But perhaps they should. Why? Because in industrialised countries our per capita domestic water consumption has been rising for decades - along with the number of bathrooms per home. Without day-glow reminders, we tend to assume we can use as much water as we like and that there are no consequences to the environment. But in increasing numbers of catchment areas we are creating water 'stress' and destroying wildlife habitats. My town's water supplies may become stressed. Increased uptake from local rivers and streams leaves their banks and beds dried out. This may kill off water life, insect life, plant life and bird life and thus biodiversity throughout the region where I live.

With the great convenience of running water comes unconsciousness of our impacts. Many life-forms will perish if we continue to demand more water year-on-year as we in the west have been doing these last 100 years or more. Wherever we exceed Nature's capacity to provide we wreak havoc with Nature's delicate web. We know about drought only in dry years. For birds life can be as hard between drought years. Insect populations may take several seasons to recover, if they ever do.

The individual, climate change and energy usage

Despite years of declared intentions under the Kyoto Protocol, world emissions of GH gases continue to rise - as have our levels of energy use. Like many governments, individuals too readily reason that climate change is somebody else's problem and that they can do little to alleviate it alone. Thinking like this keeps alive the fantasy that we can continue our energy-dependent lifestyles. This keeps us blind to our own carbon footprint and to its increasing average size. The consequences of this mind-set and the rising temperatures it brings include threats to glaciers and to the freshwater supply of half the world's population, the extinction of up to half of animal and plant species and the inundation of swamp and low-lying coastal areas. Rising sea levels risk displacing millions, putting ports, their road links and nuclear stations under water not to mention many metropolitan areas like Kolkata, Mumbai and Shanghai, New Orleans, even Manhattan and London.

Most people when they become 'carbon numerate' quickly learn what makes the largest cuts in their carbon footprint—reducing flying, insulating their home, more 'fresh air' transport, fewer fossil fuel forays. If we take meaningful action now, we may just be able to maintain a reasonable living standard into the future without endangering millions.

Our hidden trails of waste

Electronic goods may be one of the easiest areas in which to cut down our personal waste trail, though reductions in any of our personal consumption rates are desirable. Just suppose, like many, I have a taste for gadgets. I feel I have to own all the latest gizmos I can use. Faced with a new model, I succumb. What assumptions might I have made? I may have assumed that all the waste - much of it highly toxic - generated during the manufacture of all the hundreds of components is responsibly disposed of - unfortunately, the majority is not; that the waste created by my discarded unit will be recovered and will not lead to toxic poisoning of water or lifeforms - unfortunately, the majority is unrecovered; that the Earth's supplies of all the metals and other resources used in making my gizmo are adequate for the foreseeable future and do not cause serious land degradation and air pollution in their extraction - unfortunately many of the resources are illegally mined in areas controlled by rebels who rely for arms on revenue coming ultimately from us gizmo enthusiasts.

What results and consequences have followed? I will have contributed to some very depressing statistics. The manufacture of electronic goods like computers, mobile phones and gadgets produces some of the most toxic types of waste on Earth. One computer contains more than 700 kinds of chemical materials, over half are harmful to humans. The manufacture of one personal computer generates 1,500 kg—1.5 *tonnes* or 3,300 pounds - of waste including heavy metals such as lead, cadmium and mercury that are toxic and can leach into soil and contaminate ground water. No fewer than three *billion* consumer electronic units are expected to become 'obsolete'—thrown out to you and me - by 2011.

What is the learning I am ignoring in making decisions like these? The importance I attach to owning these gizmos suggests I want to maintain an 'image.' I may believe my wellbeing and happiness depend on it. True self-worth is invaluable, but it's only too easy to enjoy or feel a need for admiration from peers as a substitute when the authentic self-worth is in short supply. Owning gadgets cannot make me truly happy in the way I am persuaded to believe they will. Fundamentally, they are just tools to help us but if I develop a need to own every new model it is not me who posses them but they that possess me. I am trapped. Without self-awareness, I will not break free. So cutting back—or learning how to - is in fact my opportunity!

Taking to heart our need for clean air

People assume that they can fly on foreign holidays without any consequences to others. They reason as long as they can afford it, it is acceptable behaviour. In reality when we choose air over surface travel we generate four or more times as much CO_2, the main climate warming greenhouse gas. But few are aware that each aircraft taking off, landing and flying overhead emits a recipe of toxic compounds in massive amounts that are felt by humans and all life forms living around the airport. One 747 airliner arriving and departing from JFK airport in New York City produces as much smog as a car driven over 5,600 miles and as much polluting nitrogen oxides as a car driven nearly 26,500 miles—all within a 12 miles radius. Unbelievably, one takes off every 90 seconds!

The consequences for local people are increases in asthma, breathing disorders and associated diseases, an increased risk of cancer and raised premature death rates. Then there are the climate change consequences: aviation is presently said to account for a modest 4-9 per cent of emissions globally. This though is nowhere near the true measure. Aviation's impact on climate is worse than this because at altitudes of 30,000 feet (9,100 metres) the emissions mix has been shown to have a warming effect equal to around three times what it would be on the ground, yet we seldom see this factored in.

So what can we do about it? "Don't anyone try telling me I have to remain at home for ever," we can hear some declare, defensively. We can, however, think creatively about ways to do similar things but differently. My partner and I, aware of climate change, travelled to Portugal by train and coach when we went on holiday recently. By flying we would have created 325kg of CO_2 each but by travelling by train we created just 31kg of CO_2 each. Not content with this saving, my band, the Eco Worriers, successfully campaigned against the expansion of nearby Coventry airport and even appeared on the local television news putting to music the reasons for our protest in a song. Best of all, the third runway at Heathrow has been cancelled!

Turning our 2,000 food miles into food metres

Say I go into the supermarket and buy some pears. It's early summer in the UK, when there are no local pears available. The pears I buy have come—by air, unknown to me - from Argentina, some 6,900 miles (11,000 km) away. With the pears, I 'buy' their carbon footprint, but no one is counting, no one seems to care. But perhaps we should.

Except for local organically grown foods, everything we eat has a large hidden fossil fuel emissions footprint—fertilisers, agrichemicals, tractor power and transport accounted for almost 70% of cost inputs at 2007 prices. Because these pears have flown almost a quarter of the way around the world, they come with a high 'food miles' count. This denotes the carbon emissions associated with the distance foods travel from production until it reaches us, the consumer. *Average* food miles for UK groceries is an unbelievable 1,500 to 2,500 miles (2,400 – 4,000 km). That figure shocked me.

If the pear is not organic it could have residual pesticide contamination which in some cases can cause hormonal abnormalities or even cancer. In one survey in the UK it was found that 70 per cent of all pear samples contained pesticide pollution.

With awareness, however, the shopper may learn there are alternatives to the high food-mile option. Farmers markets are one expanding response. One increasingly accessible option is buying from a local Community Supported Agriculture or CSA scheme. When market gardeners grow to order, their production tuned to match exactly what's needed, they minimise waste and reduce costs impressively. To work well, CSA takes good communication between a local community and a group of growers working as a team; but it's hard to beat as a model for how we could source our fresh foods. The CSA scheme of which I am a member, Canalside Community Foods, grows only organically, so that takes care of the pesticide pollution and cuts the food miles to food metres.

A threat to a family of Orang Utangs? Me?

A person buys a new front door for their house. The door they choose, on looks and price, is in hardwood - an uncertified tropical hardwood. They assume that if it's a secure door, if they can afford it and it improves the look of the house, it makes no difference what material the door is made in.

In making this choice, however, these buyers have joined the massive tie-in via commerce, marketing and corrupt officials between Western tastes and the destruction of the world's rainforests, including the last remaining habitat of primates such as the Orang Utang. If the destruction continues at its present rate, in just 30 years there will be virtually no tropical rainforests left. Yet in part because of the low price for uncertified tropical timber products, the official rate of tropical forest destruction is actually predicted to *accelerate* even further.

As if that were not enough, there is more. That door in uncertified tropical hardwood also comes with a size 14 carbon footprint that results in further acceleration of global climate change. There is now consensus that recorded deforestation contributes around 20% of total global greenhouse gas emissions, more than the world's entire fleets of cars, mopeds, taxis, trucks, buses, trains, ships and airliners combined. Scientists say one days' deforestation is equivalent to the carbon footprint of eight million people flying transatlantic! That put deforestation in a totally new light for me.

There are alternatives to buying a door or garden furniture in uncertified tropical hardwood. You could buy a door made out of a certified hardwood—most likely from a sustainably managed *temperate* forest. This could be certified as from a sustainable source by the Forest Stewardship Council or FSC which now operates in 50 countries.

There are risks of extinctions closer to home as well. We can all help wildlife where we live by doing a few simple things. I have always left an area in our garden in a wild state. And in 2004 I had the good fortune to get funding to create in the grounds of the school where I currently work a 1 hectare (2.5 acre) nature reserve with a wildlife pond. This good-sized reserve is deliberately planted with native tree species that will provide a food source for insects and birds. The wildlife pond helps the survival of native amphibians such as frogs and newts, which have been decimated in the countryside by widespread pesticides use.

Ending poverty by empowerment, not handouts

Like most people beyond 30, I have a pension 'nest egg' I contribute to regularly. But to be honest, I'm hazy on the ethics of the companies my pension invests in. Most will be in the very profit-maximising companies I have criticised elsewhere. So, like millions of others, as a pensioner I would be living off the proceeds of ventures that exploit people or the Planet. Think outsourced manufacture reliant on dirty processes banned in a TNC's home jurisdiction; think companies using sweat labour, often under-age. The maxim 'only invest to maximize your return' leaves the knock-ons to my grandchildren out of the equation. Have you checked if your nest egg is in the clear? A clean investment—a truly 'ethical' one - is still a rarity requiring painstaking research. But help is now available in the form of full service financial advisors specialising in ethical investments. And a new web service by EIRIS, Ethical Investment Research Services gives in-depth coverage of around 3,000 companies globally, covering over 100 different environment, social and governance issues (www.yourethicalmoney.org).

Having cleaned up our investments, we can all help redress poverty by supporting international aid organisations like Oxfam or Practical Action.

Global problems, global solutions
Need for global governance

Today's world could be likened to a chariot to which has been harnessed close on 200 horses, the nation states. The pulling power is tremendous, yet for our chariot there is no agreement on who is the driver, nor on how to select or direct one. Paralysis on righting the wrongs of social injustice is perhaps our greatest ongoing failure.

National self-interest precludes any hoped for consensus. The world's least represented underclass, shut out as ever, sees the IED and the suicide waistcoat as the only way to make known their dissent and determination. The signatories to the Copenhagen 'Accord,' including a new alignment of the nations of the rich North with China, India and Brazil—by setting their ambitions at keeping temperature rises to within 2°C - have chosen to ignore *today's* impacts of climate change in the poor nations. Their demand at Copenhagen was for a 1.5°C upper limit. Now, after Cochabamba, it is for a 1°C upper limit. So the need for consensus on climate has 'gone critical' on the priority lists of an expanding grouping of regimes of the poor South led by President Evo Morales of Bolivia.

Still North America acts blind to the global South's crisis of which it remains in denial. Just when they're being challenged to see two or more generations ahead the North's leaders appear conveniently struck by the myopia of indulgent self-interest. Meanwhile, desperation builds in countries whose rural poor are in the front line facing climate change's devastating impacts. Such myopia can only increase the risk of a showdown.

We can't yet see how the schism will play out nor even what tactics Morales's camp will see as most effective. But who, we should ask, apart from the fossil fuel camp and its followers would lose out if Morales's camp got its way?

The Cochabamba resolutions include calls on developed countries to:

- Limit increases in global average surface temperature to 1° C
- Bear the costs and ensure technology transfer necessary to compensate developing countries for their lost development opportunities due to a compromised atmosphere;
- Take responsibility for climate change migrants, through the conclusion of an international agreement.

The Conference's final declaration:

- Urges the approval of a second commitment period under the Kyoto Protocol in which developed countries commit to reduce domestic emissions by at least 50% against 1990 levels without resorting to market-based mechanisms.
- Calls for the recognition and integration of the UN Declaration on the Rights of Indigenous Peoples in the climate change negotiations.
- Rejects a definition of forests that includes plantations and condemns market-based mechanisms such as 'reducing

emissions from deforestation and forest degradation' in developing countries (REDD).

Seen from the global South's perspective, the lines are clear: "those people who came with their new-fangled economics and tried stealing our national resources to give them to their ill-begotten corporations that we then forced out, it is the same people who are now fouling up our Earth's entire atmosphere so that WE, the poor, have to pay the penalty in wrecked livelihoods from droughted winters and deluged summers."

This alignment of no-budge states—whose views on economic policy match the intransigence of the North on emissions cuts - is not entirely new. Consensus on a different model, a new paradigm for our world governance has been growing among the 'wronged' states, states which find ready support among anti-globalisation groups and dissenters throughout the global North and South. They seek ways to bring the driving of the chariot under some sort of influence benign to people and Planet, one that would no longer allow its wheels to trample the world's weakest and most vulnerable.

Trampled every bit as much as people is Planet Earth, its teeming life, the biosphere, no mention of which appears in *any* economics books before the 2006 Stern Report on the economics of climate change. Recognition of this omission came into focus around the concept of the *Global Commons*, 'that which no person or state may control, but upon which life depends.' Such initiatives are part of a world-wide popular response to the Planetary emergency involving as many as one million non-profits as estimated in 2006 by Paul Hawken in *Blessed Unrest*, his inspiring book about the global Green movements. His Natural Capital Institute had by 2007 listed nonprofits in 243 countries and territories under 42 main heads covering perhaps 300 areas, specialisms and issues (see www.wiserearth.org).

However, there will never be a shortage of 'climate culprits' out there at whom we can all take swipes. Our problem is worse. It's our very own consumer culture that is the greatest culprit. We westerners all have a part in the damage it wreaks every day. Take green beans airfreighted from east Africa, suffering its direst drought for a decade. And who orders the blood minerals hand-excavated by children in eastern Congo for Chinese middlemen? We do, for our throw-away mobile phones, MP3 players and 'free' laptops. We average one new handset a year when most are designed for a five-year life. We are not reminded of that when we get the new phone 'free' with a contract. Why not? Would capitalism work if it were obliged to go ethical? One wonders. We will have to change that: the later we leave it, the more drastically. Start now: buy ethically, or do we chuck the whole thing in?

Positive developments and achievements – Have humans a capacity to advance consciousness?

Positive examples can be a powerful aid when we are committing to something we've not tried before. So, if we humans are struggling to find self belief around de-carbonising our lives, what sorts of examples can we cite of accomplishments by our race beyond the eco-village success stories?

Only a generation or two back in the West, countless people used to die premature, sometime horrible deaths due to industrial diseases such as those caused by coal dust, smoke, asbestos, lead and solvents. The life-threatening activities were first to go, then the substances endangering health. Standards are far from uniform. There remain plenty of countries where there is no ban on using the surplus production of dangerous substances and this continues, but small-scale. However, in the West at least, employees are now largely well protected. One up for human compassion.

In the 1950s and 60s we had polar exploration proceeding apace in the Antarctic. It could have lead to creation of a massive conflict zone between the Superpowers. Instead, it resulted in the Antarctic Treaty. It confines activities on the continent of Antarctica to scientific ones. It has so far precluded any territorial claims.

In the 1980s we had the debacle over the ozone 'hole' caused by fluorine-chlorine based aerosols and refrigerants, which endangered life across our Planet. We got the Montreal Treaty; the 'hole' will cease expanding soonish and will eventually heal. One up for human foresight and co-operation.

In the 1990s we saw the emergence of a movement for corporate social responsibility. While it is not difficult to dismiss much CSR talk as window-dressing, there are elements, around transparency, disclosure, environmental impact auditing and workers rights that have begun setting a new agenda for business. Thanks in large measure to the effectiveness of responsible consumerism, failure to sign up to this agenda brings risks for a company's acceptance among investors and thus its all-important share price and company worth. It may be slow, but it is working. One up for — common sense and activism?

Where to from here?

There is no escaping it: to avert climate catastrophe we need great changes; the time remaining is fast shrinking—ideal for stimulating transformation, in fact. In the UK it may even have begun with the new coalition. First, came its pledge to create a new Green investment bank to catalyse funding for Green infrastructure. Then came its signing up wholesale to the 'Age of Stupid' team's '10:10' pledge to cut departmental emissions by 10 per cent over the coming year.

Here we have *10:10*, an unstoppably vigorous citizen's movement recruiting a government willingly into its carbon cutting campaign. To keep it coming, it's crucial we hold out a positive vision of a society that sees the benefits in the transformations we so urgently need. The challenge to enrol more individuals, more organizations is there waiting for us to take it. It is, indeed, down to each one of us. As Joanna Macy told a group in London recently: "Don't CALL the emergency services. You ARE the emergency services."

So, what does our response look like? Here's a list of priorities, hints and suggestions, one we aim to update periodically on www.greenspirituality.org.

1. Act on whatever you feel passionately about. Do it in your own way. If you don't already know, listen out: it may be a social justice issue, a public health issue or creatures or plants or a green space you see needing rescue. Invite awareness in. Take walks in Nature. Allow her in with her chaos and her order.
2. If it works for you, join with others in what you do or get others to join you. Be ready to be of service—to Nature, to others or to community. Avoid reinventing the wheel; find out if others acting already can put your energies to use. Whole communities acting together become unstoppable. Acceptance, satisfaction, good company and friendship have a value far beyond anything money can buy.
3. Remember while we need to be doing what we do now less destructively, we also need new values, new attitudes, new aspirations, new visions so that our children and theirs will

recognise a new 'forwards' and will not be seduced any more by what takes us 'backward' to more destruction. We will not get there in one leap. It will take time for us to reinvent ourselves as aware guardians of our biosphere rather than its disconnected destroyers.

4. Look at ways you can 'leverage' your impact, your effectiveness: ask others to do as you do, to send messages, to network, to engage with local power brokers to amplify and reinforce your initiative; be inventive, use web 2.0 to link with like-minded others, to spread your message.

5. Look for allies in every quarter, even or especially among your cause's 'enemies;' try your local government representatives and officials; ask at your library. Buy one company share then attend the shareholders annual meeting and raise your concerns. Bring others along with you. Do not be bullied.

6. Think globally, act locally, even if it's "Think globally, *drink* locally" - your local monthly GreenDrinks (www. greendrinks.org) may be the most fun of networking. Venues and pubs need our support as hubs for community life.

7. Remember, most individuals at some level do have an awareness of their membership role vis-à-vis Nature, they're just not up-to-date. When we avoid confrontation and address that part in them, we can often be surprised at the response that comes.

To reinvent ourselves as aware guardians of our biosphere rather than its disconnected destroyers is the challenge for each one of us now. May fortune smile on all your endeavours!

Websites that explain, encourage and enable Intentional communities
www.gen.ecovillage.org
www.ici.org
www.auroville.org
www.twinoaks.org
www.findhorn.org
www.damanhur.org
www.thefarmcommunity.com
www.kibbutz.org

www.opengreenmap.org
www.friendsofgaviotas.org
www.siebenlinden.de
www.zegg.org
www.lebensgarten.de
www.bridgestocommunity.org
www.thefec.org www.nomadsunited.com
www.esseniaecovillage.com

Growing food locally
www.greenedge.org
www.soilassociation.org
www.makingfoodwork.co.uk
www.localharvest.org
www.csacenter.org
www.greeneconomypost.com

Green movements, campaigns and initiatives
www.ageofstupid.net
www.transitiontowns.org
www.350.org
www.wiserearth.org
www.guardian.co.uk/environment/10-10
http://www.liv.ac.uk/researchintelligence/issue34/oil.htm

Climate science facts
www.realclimate.org
http://www.eo.ucar.edu/basics/index.html
www.scepticalscience.com

Climate campaigns
www.1010global.org
www.climatecamp.org.uk
www.climatecamp.org.au
www.climateconvergence.org
www.indymedia.ie
www.climatenetwork.org
www.usclimatenetwork.org

www.climateactionproject.com
www.climatestrategies.us
www.zerocarboncaravan.net
www.chooseclimate.org
www.climate-concernuk.org

Ethical investments, green spirituality and education
www.yourethicalmoney.org
www.ethicalinvestment.org.uk/
http://www.uksif.org/
www.barchestergreen.co.uk
www.joannamacy.net
http://www.gaiauniversity.org

Forest protection
www.treeshaverightstoo.com
www.rainforestSOS.org
www.ecologicalsolutions.com

Green socialising
www.greendrinks.org

APPENDIX

Author's questions to spiritual leaders in India.

1. What do you understand by the word Environment? Can you give some examples of what you mean?
2. What do you understand by the words spiritual or religious ways of living? Can you please give examples?
3. What are the environmental problems that affect where you live?
4. What are the causes of these local environmental problems?
5. Who is responsible for these problems? What are the global environmental problems which affect you?
6. What are the causes of these global environmental problems?
7. Who do you think is responsible for these global environmental problems?
8. What solutions do you see to the problems that we have just talked about?
9. Is caring for the environment part of the teachings of your religion? Can you please give examples from your scriptures or sacred writings?
10. Do you think that following the teachings of your religion is a solution to global environmental problems? In other words how do you think your spirituality offers a solution to global environmental problems?

For **Bibliography**, see www.greenspirituality.org (to save trees)

Areas: 1 km² = 100 hectares = 0.37 square miles

ABOUT THE AUTHOR

Green Spirituality author Chris Philpott is fascinated with Nature and feels concerned for the Planet our home which humankind seems intent on destroying. Why are we so self destructive, asks Chris. To get answers, he set off to Africa and on to India to talk with some of its wisest to gain from their wisdom on how we can address these crucial issues facing us humans today.

The germ for the project came to Chris in 1972 when he learned about the then famous Club of Rome report *Limits to Growth*, the first to highlight the impacts of a consumer society and to warn of the impossibility of unlimited growth within a finite system.

Chris's involvement as educator activist in the green movement goes back 28 years. Chris is a regular campaigning organiser and participant in local and national issues as wide ranging as climate change and recycling as well as an initiator in biodiversity projects with children, local grow-your-own, local exchange trading or LETS, the local Transition Town as well as meditation, inter-faith and green spirituality groups. He has contributed time to Agenda 21 and the Green Party locally and nationally.

He has given talks on Green Spirituality at UK Green Party national conferences, the Big Green Gathering, the Climate Camps, the Campaign against Climate Change Forums and the Birmingham Inter-faith group. He is available for workshops on green spirituality.

Other hats Chris wears include workshop leader, public speaker, musician-performer and classic clown with which he entertains .youngsters. His band, *The Eco Worriers*, entertains with Eco-music and lyrics.

His research for *Green* Spirituality took Chris to a UN conference in Johannesburg and on to India where he spent time with 130 spiritual leaders from Hindu, Jain, Sikh, Muslim, Christian and Buddhist traditions whose wise words are woven throughout the book.

Lightning Source UK Ltd.
Milton Keynes UK

173584UK00002B/1/P